THE TET OFFENSIVE

THE TET OFFENSIVE

Edited by
Marc Jason Gilbert and William Head

Westport, Connecticut
London

Library of Congress Cataloging-in-Publication Data

The Tet offensive / edited by Marc Jason Gilbert and William Head.
    p. cm.
   Includes bibliographical references and index.
    ISBN 0–275–95480–3 (alk. paper).—ISBN 0–275–95481–1 (pbk. :
alk. paper)
    1. Tet Offensive, 1968. 2. Vietnamese Conflict, 1968—United
States. I. Gilbert, Marc Jason. II. Head, William P.
DS557.8.T4T47   1996
959.704'3373—dc20   95–49604

British Library Cataloguing in Publication Data is available.

Library of Congress Catalog Card Number: 95–49604
ISBN: 0–275–95480–3
    0–275–95481–1 (pbk.)

First published in 1996

Praeger Publishers, 88 Post Road West, Westport, CT 06881
An imprint of Greenwood Publishing Group, Inc.

Printed in the United States of America

∞™

The paper used in this book complies with the
Permanent Paper Standard issued by the National
Information Standards Organization (Z39.48–1984).

10 9 8 7 6 5 4 3 2 1

Can you feel it, Bill, Come around again? Yeah, you must. It stays with me. I'm just getting there . . . hustled off the plane and into a truck, whispered orders, unsighted M-16s, helmets and flak jacks hurriedly pulled over wrinkled dress uniforms bearing only the National Defense Ribbons we were about to earn, out to the perimeter flightline at Bien Hoa, where Air Policemen and Viet Cong are blowing holes in each other for their country, for freedom, for peace . . . I still feel it, unfolding across the years. I'll turn that corner again tomorrow morning in Bien Hoa, hoping the VC really have pulled out, my heart pounding in my throat, my mouth lined with sandpaper . . . around that corner, in neat lines along the street, there are beautiful trees in full bloom and American soldiers, dead for days, in full bloat. And I knew right there and then that the war, which we were winning when I left the States, yesterday, was as lost as I was.

From "Tet Plus Twenty-Four, for Bill Ehrhart," in *Lost in America* (1994) by David Connolly.

Contents

Photographs follow Chapter 6

Abbreviations and Acronyms

AA	Antiaircraft
AAA	Antiaircraft artillery
AAR	After Action Report
AF	Air Force
AFB	Air Force Base
AFM	Air Force Manual
AID	Agency for International Development
ALC	Air Logistics Center
ARVN	Army of the Republic of Vietnam (South)
ASEAN	Association of Southeast Asian Nations
ATO	Air Tasking Order
AVF	All Volunteer Force
BDA	Battle Damage Assessment
CDEC	Combined Documents Exploitation Center
CIA	Central Intelligence Agency
CINCPAC	Commander in Chief, Pacific Command
CINCPACAF	Commander in Chief, Pacific Air Forces
COMUSMACV	Commander, United States Military Assistance Command, Vietnam
CORDS	Civil Operations and Revolutionary Development Support
COSVN	Central Office for South Vietnam
CTZ	Central Zone
D.C.	District of Columbia (Washington)

DIA	Defense Intelligence Agency
DOD	Department of Defense
DMZ	Demilitarized Zone (17th Parallel)
DRV (DRVN)	Democratic Republic of Vietnam (North Vietnam)
EOTR	End of Tour Report
FANK	Forces Armec Nationale
FWMAF	Free World Military Assistance Force
GPO	Government Printing Office
GVN	Government of Vietnam
H&I	Harassment and Interdiction
I Corps	U.S. Army First Corps' South Vietnamese Area of Operations
II Corps	U.S. Army Second Corps' South Vietnamese Area of Operations
ICP	Indochinese Communist Party
INR	Intelligence Research Bureau
JCS	Joint Chiefs of Staff
KIA	Killed in Action
LOE	Letter of evaluation
LOG	Logistics
MAAG	Military Assistance Advisory Group
MAC	Military Airlift Command (U.S.)
MACV	Military Assistance Command, Vietnam
MAF	Marine Amphibious Force
MLR	Main Line of Resistance
MP	Military Police
NASA	National Aeronautical and Space Administration
NCO	Noncommissioned officer
NLF	National Liberation Front
NVA	North Vietnamese Army (same as PAVN)
NVN	North Vietnam
OB	Order of Battle
OER	Officers' Effectiveness Report
OPlan	Operation Plan
OSS	Office of Strategic Services
PACAF	Pacific Air Forces (U.S.)
PAVN	People's Army of Vietnam (North) (same as NVA)
POL	Petroleum, oil, lubricants
PRVN	People's Republic of Vietnam (North Vietnam)
R&D	Research and development
RF/PF	Regional Forces/Popular Forces (ARVN)

R&R	Rest and relaxation
RTAFB	Royal Thai Air Force Base
RVN	Republic of Vietnam (South Vietnam)
SAC	Strategic Air Command (U.S.)
SAM	Surface-to-air missile
SAR	Search and rescue
SIOP	Single Integrated Operational Plan
SKS	Samozaryadnyi Karabin Simonova, Russian 7.62 Boevey 1943 carbine supplied to Vietminh and VC, 1945 to 1964
SOW	Special Operations Wing
SRV	Socialist Republic of Vietnam
STRICOM	Strike Command (U.S.)
SVN	South Vietnam
TAC	Tactical Air Command (U.S.)
TDY	Temporary duty
TFW	Tactical Fighter Wing (U.S.)
The "Trail"	The Ho Chi Minh Trail
UN	United Nations
UPT	Undergraduate Pilot Training
U.S.	United States
USA	United States Army
USAF	United States Air Force
USAID	United States Agency for International Development
USARV	United States Army, Vietnam
USIA	United States Information Agency
USIS	United States Information Service
USMC	United States Marine Corps
USN	United States Navy
VC	Viet Cong
Vietminh	Short name for 1940s/1950s Vietnamese Independence Faction (Viet Nam Doc Lap Dong Minh Hoi—League for the Independence of Vietnam formed 1941)
VNAF	Vietnamese Air Force (South)
VNCC	Vietnamese Commander in Chief
VWP	Vietnamese Workers' Party
War Zone A	A VC redoubt north of Saigon
War Zone B	A VC redoubt northeast of Saigon
War Zone C	A VC redoubt northwest of Saigon, roughly encompassing northwest Tay Ninh Province

War Zone D   A VC redoubt north-northwest of Saigon centered on the in-
                  tersection of the borders of Bing Long, Phuoc Long, and
                  Bin Buong Provinces
WIA   Wounded in Action
WIEU   Weekly Intelligence Estimate Update

Preface

Marc Jason Gilbert and William Head

At 3:00 a.m. on January 31, 1968, Viet Cong sappers entered the U.S. Embassy compound in Saigon. Thus, began a two and one-half month struggle commonly known as the Tet Offensive. On March 31, 1968, President Lyndon Baines Johnson, who, in 1964, had won one of the greatest landslide presidential election victories in U.S. history, declared he would not seek reelection and that he would offer America's enemies in Vietnam a negotiated peace. It was the beginning of the end for U.S. involvement in the Second Indochina war.

Why did Tet become such a watershed?

This book explores this question not with a view to providing a final answer, but to act as a beginning from which serious scholars and students of the Second Indochina War can attempt to explain the phenomenon called the Tet Offensive. To be sure, in spite of all the disagreement over the meaning of Tet, one consensus has evolved over the years: it was the climactic event of America's involvement in the Indochina wars. For that matter, if one event can be said to have been the single defining moment for the entire Vietnamese struggle for national unity and independence, Tet is that event. But why? The following articles begin the search for that answer.

In composing such a work, the editors must have the support of many people. In this case, we wish to express our appreciation to all the authors for their patience during the editorial process, and to David Palmer for his yeoman service as Production Editor. We would also like to express our gratitude to Professor Harry Basehart of Salisbury State University, Maryland, who began the process of collecting the papers which make up much of this anthology, and to Randee Head for her assistance in preparing the index. Most of all, we wish to dedicate this work to those who experienced the Tet Offensive first hand, that it may serve as a memorial both to those who perished in its flames and to those of its veterans in whose eyes the fires of Tet still burn.

Introduction

Marc Jason Gilbert and William Head

The Tet Offensive caused one of the deepest and most lasting of the many rents that the Vietnam or Second Indochina War made in the fabric of American life: hence the reputation of that campaign as the Vietnam War's Vietnam. Americans have since come to regard it either as defining the moment when the United States seized defeat out of the jaws of victory, or as the wake-up call that finally alerted America to the unwinnable nature of the Vietnam conflict. Such struggles within a body politic usually possess the redeeming virtue of inexorably leading to the broad synthesis that awaits even the most heated of historical debates. Yet, such are the political stakes and personal passions that swirl around this aspect of America's defeat in Vietnam that the integration of the competing interpretations of the Tet Offensive has proven elusive.

To most former allied military officers, some scholars of American history, and much of the American public, the Tet Offensive launched in January–February 1968 was a "last gasp," a failed all-or-nothing bid to win the Vietnam War on the ground, which, though stymied in the field, succeeded, largely by accident, in persuading America to throw away the fruits of a major allied victory and start down the road to defeat and humiliation. As they also believe that the high casualties incurred by the Vietnamese foe during the offensive increased the potential of the allied pacification program and Vietnamization, many adherents of this approach to the Tet Offensive translate its results into a stab-in-the-back thesis: while American forces defeated the enemy on the battlefield and stood on the brink of success in the war for the loyalties of the Vietnamese people, they were betrayed on the home front by a meddling news media and their own weak-willed leaders.[1] To these students of the American war in Vietnam, the only success enjoyed by the enemy was achieved on the American home front; as a military campaign, it not only ended in a tactical victory for the United States, but struck a blow against the Viet Cong from which they never recovered.

Few Vietnamese historians, American historians of modern Vietnam, or Vietnam-era American policy analysts would agree with this assessment of the nature and impact of the Tet Offensive. They argue that the Tet Offensive was a three-phase application of military pressure that governed operations conducted as late as November of 1968 and was not a failed, desperate gamble that had to win the war at one stroke, but a successful, multifaceted effort to drive the Americans to the negotiating table. They also contend that the number of enemy casualties and the post-Tet potential of the pacification and Vietnamization efforts were grossly overestimated by the United States at the time and since. They further maintain that the offensive, while more costly to Hanoi and the Viet Cong than anticipated and falling far short of many of its projected intermediate goals, succeeded in its primary aim of demoralizing not the American people, but their leaders, and in securing a bombing halt followed by the commencement of negotiations for a settlement in Hanoi's favor. These scholars conclude that, despite the defeat meted out to the enemy in the field during Tet, the blood shed by the enemy was not shed in vain. As planned, the Tet campaign forced America's war leaders to reexamine their strategy and recognize that the war would continue to be a protracted one. The most important result of this post-Tet self-analysis was that it revealed that the means the American military establishment itself defined as necessary to continue the war or bring it to a rapid conclusion were simply too costly to warrant their adoption. Whereas their opponents invoke the postwar testimony of many American generals who speak of an abandonment of a war that was being won after Tet, these analysts point to the lack of a theory of victory among these selfsame generals during the war and the self-interest and duplicity among Pentagon officials, some of whom, in the aftermath of Tet, judged the offensive to have been a major blow to the American and allied Vietnamese cause. In their view, if Tet is to be represented as a mortal blow, it should be viewed as a thrust through the heart of America's war-making machine, not as a domestic stab in the back.[2]

So disparate was the debate over the nature and meaning of Tet Mau Than that for many years it appeared that consensus would be reached only on two issues. Whatever their background, ideology, or academic discipline, students of the Tet Offensive were in agreement that it was both the climactic event of America's involvement in the wars in Indochina and the single defining moment for the entire Vietnamese struggle for national unity and independence.

In recent years, however, largely as a result of improved access to Vietnamese and American documentation on the war, scholars are revisiting former areas of disagreement with fewer preconceptions and a more critical eye. They also have sought to open new paths of investigation. For example, proponents of the "Tet as a tactical victory" thesis no longer accept as authoritative what appear to have been the inflated battlefield "body counts" of Viet Cong during Tet and now look more critically at the phases of the campaign that occupied and bloodied American forces for the rest of 1968. For their part, proponents of the "Tet as a strategic victory" thesis are more aware of the magnitude of Hanoi's vulnerability in 1967–1968, its miscalculations in planning the offensive, and the political and military costs of its operations both during and immediately after the campaign. Further, the champions of both interpretations are now seeking to more acutely assess the Tet Offensive within the context of Vietnamese and American domestic politics and within its international setting. A desire for consensus rather than confrontation seems to infuse these first tentative steps toward synthesis and closure. The chapters that follow reflect this new spirit of inquiry. They fall into two categories: those that deal with political and strategic issues, and those that address the combat and intelligence components of the conflict.

The volume opens with a chapter by Larry Berman based on current research at the Lyndon B. Johnson Presidential Library. He examines the maze of personal relations and the fog of arrogance that led the president and his advisors to assume full responsibility for fighting the war in Vietnam and describes how this confusing web of power malfunctioned just prior to and during the Tet Offensive. He demonstrates how the Johnson administration's public relations success before Tet to explain how this helped turn Tet into a U.S. foreign policy failure.

Berman examines the various aspects of Johnson's public relations program and the president's intimidating personal style of leadership, which strained his administration's Vietnam policy to the breaking point. In looking at the inner workings of the White House, he discusses the president's view of the nature and course of the war. He decries Johnson's misguided view of limited war, discusses the president's typically American concerns regarding the spread of communism in Asia, and also focuses on President Johnson's growing concerns over the potential expansion of the Indochina conflict into a wider war directly involving the Soviet Union and the People's Republic of China. He examines how the president's preoccupation with limiting the conflict forced him to place debilitating restrictions on allied forces by micromanaging the strategic planning and tactical execution of the war.

One of the most important aspects of Berman's work is his description of the advisory factions within the administration. He examines the nuances of decision making within the White House and explains how the war supporters came to dominate policy, prior to 1968. He also explains how this policy eventually came to antagonize most senior military leaders, who in most cases knew less about Southeast Asia and its history than Johnson did.

Berman observes that from the outset Johnson and most American leaders wrongly determined that a victory over North Vietnamese forces would win the war in the South since they believed that Ho Chi Minh completely controlled the activities of the National Liberation Front and their military forces, the Viet Cong. This misconception caused Johnson to craft a policy of limited war designed to intimidate the enemy into a negotiated peace by slowing and incrementally raising the quotient of pain, always with the imminent threat of more suffering should the North fail to seek peace on U.S. terms.

Finally, Berman demonstrates that the need to show progress in this debilitating and increasingly micromanaged war led to a public relations campaign which, by the second half of 1967, promised the American people that "victory" (whatever that meant) was just around the corner. In fact, the administration did a better job of selling the idea than it did of realizing the reality. The North Vietnamese Politburo, desperate to halt U.S. bombing in the North, initiated the spectacular Tet Offensive, using southern guerrillas and irregular forces as well as regular NVA (North Vietnamese Army) forces, which smashed U.S. public illusions of imminent victory.

Even though Berman believes that Communist leaders based the Tet Offensive and the siege of the Khe Sanh marine base on misconceptions of their own strength and on a probably mistaken belief among some of the leadership in Hanoi that they could attain victory on the ground in one decisive action, he notes that the effect it had on the Johnson White House, the U.S. Congress, and U.S. public sensibilities was devastating. From a purely tactical military standpoint the Tet attacks were not successful. Communist leaders failed to gain two of their many parallel objectives: inflicting a signal defeat on American forces and creating a mass southern uprising. Worst of all, they suffered grievous losses which took two years to replace. It is clear, however, that the most important of the enemy's tactical objectives was the breaking of the morale of what Tran Van Tra called the "war party" in Washington; and this breakdown, from the panic that Tet caused in the Pentagon to the demoralization of the "Wise Men" who advised Johnson, was fully achieved. Berman shows how the timing of the attacks could not have been better for the achievement of this objective.

The patience of the American people with the government's failure to achieve progress in the war was wearing thin at a critical juncture: the beginning of a presidential election year. Tet simply added evidence to a growing public perception that the sacrifices they had been asked to make in Vietnam were for dubious purposes and, worse, for a war that the United States was unable or unwilling to win. An increasing number of Americans came to believe that the war was sapping U.S. strength, had little to do with U.S. interests, was diverting the country from greater missions and goals, and should be fought by the Vietnamese, not by Americans, whatever the consequences.

Berman closes his chapter with the observation that even President Johnson came to many of these same conclusions. His deep concerns over public discontent and his fears that his domestic agenda would fall apart under the pressure of the war led to his decision to halt the bombing and seek a negotiated settlement. He announced he would not run for reelection and, as can be seen in hindsight, initiated a process that would de-escalate U.S. involvement and five years later lead to total U.S. withdrawal. This despite the fact that many in Vietnam believed that Tet had been a great allied victory. In the changed climate after Tet, William C. Westmoreland's possibly ill-considered and certainly mistimed request for 205,000 more troops to finish a job he started almost four years earlier led, at least in part, to the general's reassignment as army chief of staff and eventually to Secretary of Defense Clark Clifford's redirection of U.S. policy in Southeast Asia. Berman examines this entire process and concludes that Walter Cronkite's declaration on national television that the war was stalemated "mirrored public opinion," and led first the president's inner circle and then the president himself "to the same conclusions."

John Garver follows in Chapter 3 with a detailed examination of the relationship between the PRC (People's Republic of China) and the Communist leadership in both North and South Vietnam. His exploration of the "China card" has unveiled important evidence which proves that the People's Republic of China seriously meant to support the North Vietnamese if the United States invaded that country, a course of action favored but never formally endorsed by some American military leaders. He uses newly uncovered documents to demonstrate how significant a role China played in the Vietnam War and how mercurial its relationship with Vietnam really was. He thus brings much-needed definition to a key aspect of the war which most authors and scholars, especially in the West, have glossed over or ignored all together.

Garver's main focus is on the PRC's dilemma in the late 1960s posed by its foreign policy commitments to the North Vietnamese. Stung by border incidents with their erstwhile Communist cousins in the U.S.S.R., fearful of a full-scale war with this powerful northern neighbor, and with the country destabilized by the internal nuances of the Cultural Revolution, Chinese leaders wanted to draw closer to the United States, a step they believed might be necessary for their survival, but which also meant pulling back from the Democratic Republic of Vietnam at the very moment it seemed to need China the most.

Garver declares that the PRC's decision to disengage from Vietnam was made to prevent what it believed was the possibility of superpower "collusion," that is, an alliance between the Soviet Union and the United States.

To this end, Chinese leaders believed that a continuation of major commitments to the North, especially as the war entered a more intense and conventional stage, might thwart their efforts to ameliorate relations with Washington and thereby to impede what they believed were anti-Chinese plans on the part of Soviet leaders. However, Garver correctly notes that total disengagement by Chinese leaders would not only have damaged their image within the socialist world, but also risked total world isolation. Thus, their best alternative was a partial disengagement which would diminish the possibility that the PRC would have to face the growing Soviet military threat on its northern border and at the same time be engaged in a military confrontation with the United States on its southern border. The irony of this policy was, as Garver notes, that "China's withdrawal of its forces from North Vietnam in 1968–1970 was a counterpart of the U.S. withdrawal from South Vietnam during 1969–1973. Both helped open the door to Sino-American rapprochement," and bring an end to the Second Indochina War.

In Chapter 4, "The NLF and the Tet Offensive," Robert Brigham progresses naturally from Garver's contribution by investigating many of the same issues from the point of view of the leaders of the NLF (National Liberation Front) and explains why the Chinese tried to discourage the Tet campaign and sought the continuation of pre-Tet policies. Brigham examines the NLF's ideological foundation and most especially its foreign policy with regard to Hanoi, Beijing, Moscow, and Washington. In this analysis he demonstrates that the NLF was much more than a puppet of Hanoi. However, he also notes that the influence of Ho Chi Minh and other northern leaders was significant.

Brigham describes the relationship of the NLF with the Communist Party and government in North Vietnam as a murky one. Douglas Pike, in his books on the Viet Cong and the People's Army of Vietnam (PAVN) has tried to make it clear that the NLF was not a strictly Communist organization. At least at first, it was a coalition of leftist and nationalist parties and groups opposed to the regime of the Catholic president of South Vietnam, Ngo Dinh Diem. Moreover, as Pike reminds us, the NLF was not, at least until the late 1960s, subordinate to the North Vietnamese. Indeed, the entrance of large numbers of U.S. combat troops into the conflict, the death and displacement of non-Communist NLF leaders in the early 1960s, and the devastation of Tet led the NLF to become more Communist in its makeup and more subordinate in its relationship with Hanoi.

Also important in this mix were the attitudes of various Communist leaders and factions toward the reunification of their country. Ho Chi Minh had always focused the Politburo's ultimate sights on a unified and socialist Vietnam. However, some of the Politburo's members and many in the NLF did not regard the immediate achievement of this objective as a primary or non-negotiable goal. Traditional Vietnamese regionalism and the inevitable growth of an indigenous NLF agenda during its long struggle in the south inevitably acted to complicate this matter. Brigham addresses these factional issues and closely examines the fluctuating goodwill and material support of Hanoi as well as China and the Soviet Union for the NLF. As Garver notes in Chapter 3, by 1967 these associations took on a different tenor as China and the Soviet Union fell out with each other and the PRC tried to draw closer to the United States. Even so, China consistently believed that the NLF's political underground propaganda and guerrilla military tactics provided the best opportunity for success. It did not hurt that this strategy also fit in well with the traditional Maoist dogma regarding people's revolution.

However, as Brigham notes, both the NLF and Hanoi, despite their differences, had much in common, and, despite pre-Tet rancor over initiating a Tet-style campaign, by the time Tet began the NLF was as close to Hanoi as it had ever been. In fact, Brigham concludes that by January 1968 NLF leaders had not only agreed to the offensive, but embraced it. They, like their counterparts in Hanoi, had backed away from the Chinese and felt as independent as they had since the late 1950s. They saw the relationship with Hanoi as symbiotic and dedicated themselves to planning and carrying out what they had convinced themselves would be a great and successful effort to push the foreigners out of Vietnam.

The next three chapters discuss the Tet Offensive from a variety of Vietnamese perspectives. In Chapter 5 Cecil Currey examines the internal disagreements in the North between Senior General Vo Nguyen Giap, rival ideologues, and comrades. Using unique sources and interviews, he defines how Giap perceived the gestation and purpose of the Tet Offensive. Currey's scholarship complements that of Garver and Brigham. The three together indicate that there was no clear agreement on revolutionary policies, strategy, or tactics in the revolutionary camp in Vietnam or among supporters of the revolution in China and Russia. As a result, the Tet Offensive possessed the flaws of a campaign made by a committee in disarray, if not in actual discord.

Currey examines Giap's military career and the political travails he experienced during the period leading up to and during Tet. He discusses General Giap's rivalries with members of the Politburo such as Le Duan and Le Duc Tho. He also delves into the tenuous support for Giap from his old comrade Ho Chi Minh and explains Giap's reluctance to plan and carry out the Tet Offensive and Khe Sanh campaign. He follows by explaining why, despite his misgivings, Giap did undertake Tet and why he later declared that it had been a military catastrophe. Currey notes that General Westmoreland, soon after the fighting subsided, decried the home front derision of allied efforts during Tet by declaring that the enemy had "suffered a catastrophic defeat in battle [in order] to salvage a 'psychological victory' for themselves." Currey believes that, insofar as the results on the ground were concerned, "Giap would have agreed with this conclusion. . . . [because] he knew as well as anyone the extent of communist losses." Yet, as Currey concludes, the sacrifice ultimately did prove worthwhile, for President Johnson halted the bombing, offered truce talks (accepted on April 3), replaced Westmoreland with General Creighton Abrams, and decided not to run for reelection. The result, by the early 1970s, was a willingness in the upper echelons of the Nixon administration and among senior military leaders to declare that the previous policies had been a failure and to move toward "Vietnamization," a negotiated settlement, and an end to America's role in the conflict in Southeast Asia. With this in mind Currey concludes, "On these points, Giap and his fellows could all take pride in the accomplishments of Tet. There was now a political victory to be gained from the Tet Offensive, and although the military road ahead was still long and hard, it had to be pursued vigorously for whatever advantage it might give."

Chapter 6, by Ngo Vinh Long, is a watershed work about the effects Tet had not only on the NLF, but on all Communist forces fighting below the seventeenth parallel. It is based on exhaustive primary research and is noteworthy for its plethora of interviews with southern guerrilla participants in Tet. As such, it may well become the definitive work on this topic in many ways. Unlike American revisionists, who have argued since 1968 that the NLF was destroyed as a fighting force after Tet, Long convincingly maintains that such a claim flies in the face of both the actual damage done to and recuperative powers of the Viet Cong. He provides good evidence that while southern guerrilla leaders initially resisted the campaign, they finally accepted the idea of a general offensive/general uprising and did their best to carry out the plan. In the end, argues Long, even though few tactical objectives were realized and significant numbers of Viet Cong forces were killed, the southern guerrillas remained a viable force after 1968.

Long maintains that Tet might have been even more successful had NLF troops returned to their rural bases after the first or second phase of the campaign instead of attempting a third attack. Losing the element of surprise and needing to keep large numbers of troops massed near urban centers made the NLF forces particularly susceptible to ARVN (Army of the Republic of Vietnam) counterattacks and U.S. air attacks. Accordingly, it was during this phase, 1969–1970, that the greatest VC (Viet Cong) losses were experienced, the difficult phase of regrouping was endured, and their opponent's pacification campaign was able to make significant gains. In spite of these difficulties the widespread popular support enjoyed by the Viet Cong and the determined efforts on the part of the local and rural cadres enabled the NLF and VC to slowly recover, and by 1971 they were stronger than ever. As a result, they were able to play a significant role in the final phase of the Second Indochina War. Long holds that the story of

Tet and its aftermath thus demonstrates that "popular support in the South allowed the NLF to rise from the ashes of defeat like the phoenix in spite of American efforts to destroy it" and that to argue that the "NLF was defeated after the spring of 1968 never to recover again," as many American scholars have, "ignores or distorts the facts."

Long concludes that though the Tet Offensive did not overthrow the Saigon government, it was successful "in accomplishing its main objective of forcing the United States to de-escalate the war in North Vietnam and to begin negotiations that would eventually lead to a peace agreement based on NLF terms in January 1973." It certainly was a "devastating blow to the Saigon regime" in that it spawned a widespread urban peace movement and vastly increased the desire for peace among all southerners, which weakened the regime's authority and imperiled continued U.S. support.

A different perspective of Tet is provided in Chapter 7 by Ambassador Bui Diem, whose role as ambassador of the Republic of Vietnam to the United States gave him a unique view of the inner workings of both the Washington and Saigon governments during Tet. Diem not only provides the reader with a view of how the Johnson administration—especially the president—viewed and reacted to Tet, but also shares his impressions of how the leaders and citizens in Saigon and throughout South Vietnam reacted to the Tet debacle.

The very fact that Ambassador Diem was in Washington and that he met with President Johnson privately during these days provides the reader with a unique insight into the president's inner thoughts during and just after Tet. We see how Tet affected Johnson and why Ambassador Diem believes that during these meetings with the president he sensed that Tet had spelled the beginning of the end for direct U.S. military involvement in the Vietnam conflict, as Ngo Vinh Long and others suggest. However, unlike Ngo Vinh Long, Bui Diem concludes that Tet was not a Communist success and that with more resolve on the part of the United States it might have led to a complete allied victory. He notes that upon his return to Saigon its citizens and leaders alike were in a very positive mood and seemed to feel that they had taken the best the vaunted VC could dish out and had beaten them back. In Diem's opinion, General Westmoreland may well have been right when he declared that with 205,000 more U.S. troops that U.S. and ARVN forces could have "finished off" the enemy. Ambassador Diem writes as a participant, rather than a scholar, and his account differs somewhat from American evaluations of the long-term effects of the Tet Offensive in Saigon. The latter noted that while many members of Saigon's social elite were encouraged by the successful defense of the city, they attributed their salvation to the presence of U.S. troops. They seemed convinced that a post-Tet draw-down of American forces in keeping with a policy of Vietnamization would lead inevitably to the end of the Republic of Vietnam. Ambassador Diem acknowledges this, but argues that the im-

mediate post-Tet mood among Saigon's political leadership was as up-beat
as the mood among Washington's war leaders was sour.

The first half of the book closes with Anthony Edmonds' analysis of the
impact of the Tet Offensive on Muncie, Indiana, the fabled town that some
sociologists have regarded as the typical American community. Employing
Muncie as a case study of the impact of Tet on American public opinion,
Edmonds attempts to determine if the reactions in Muncie were typical of
those throughout the United States in 1968.

Like several of his fellow contributors to this volume and unlike so
many authors from the extreme left and right, Edmonds believes the Vietnamese Communists, despite subsequent statements to the contrary,
never intended Tet to be primarily a public relations ploy to destroy U.S.
public morale. That the public may have been affected was, in his opinion,
more a case of happenstance than planning. According to his analysis, the
antiwar movement in Indiana and probably throughout the United States
was only indirectly affected by Tet. He argues that public fatigue over
America's expensive, protracted Vietnam commitment and leadership failures, together with public perception of leadership weakness and lies, had
more to do with the country's willingness to withdraw U.S. support of the
South after Tet than did the offensive itself. Edmonds asserts that "it
would be ludicrous to argue that there was a Muncie consensus on the Tet
Offensive. . . . While some cried doom, gloom, and stalemate, others saw a
chance to apply maximum force for maximum results." Based on this Edmonds concludes, "The conventional wisdom that there was a national *cri
de coeur,* a sense of pessimism over the obvious psychological victory of
the enemy during Tet may well be true. But this modest local study does
not prove the case."

Thus the first half of this anthology focuses on the background, the components, and the whys and wherefores of Tet. Chapter 2, by Larry Berman,
is a view of American policy makers, while Chapter 8, by Anthony Edmonds, is about the concerns of the American citizenry in a single case
study. The intervening chapters relate to non-American views and aspects
of the road to Tet. Most of these deal with Vietnamese views of Tet—
northern and southern, Communist and non-Communist. Several provide
the reader with an unique insight into the internal conflicts and struggles
within the Communist world during the 1960s. They discuss the varying
concepts, national interests, and ideological beliefs held by various leaders
in the U.S.S.R., China, North Vietnam, and the NLF. For example, they
discuss in detail the varying views of what "people's war" means and how
to carry it out. They discuss the tensions created by quarrels over whether
there should be a unified Vietnam, whether to seek a negotiated settlement,
and whether to seek a protracted guerrilla/political solution in the South
or to initiate a general offensive/general uprising, or Tet Offensive.

The second half of this work begins with a pair of studies that focuses upon combat, U.S. intelligence, and debate over how much warning U.S. and allied personnel in South Vietnam had prior to Tet. It begins with John Prados' evaluation of the performance of U.S. intelligence analysis at Tet. Prados' expertise in the area of American intelligence analysis has long been recognized. In Chapter 9 he provides the reader with a detailed view of who knew how much about what and when they knew it. Unlike some scholars who have suggested that the enemy's element of surprise during Tet was effective due to the general intelligence failure of the allied intelligence community, Prados suggests that while many mistakes were made and senior officials took too little precaution, there was enough intelligence data to have provided a warning before Tet. He goes on to describe how U.S. forces used such intelligence data to support the American counterattack. But he asserts that too much intelligence that should have been gathered was not, and much of what was gathered was misused or not used at all.

Prados determines that Hanoi's leaders realized that there was a probability that the Tet campaign would be discovered in advance. Surely, says Prados, they understood that an operation of such magnitude would provide the allies with some indicators. Prados therefore believes that northern leaders "structured a second plausible interpretation to face their adversaries with the conundrum of choice." To be sure, writes Prados, General Westmoreland also took a chance since "he focused upon a certain facet of the evidence which supported his strategic preferences and resisted expanding his interpretation to encompass all the evidence." Prados concludes, "Even at the last moment, MACV [Military Assistance Command, Vietnam] continued to take chances, assuming risks entailed in conducting business as usual in Saigon. Having taken these chances, MACV was caught out and disaster followed. That Hanoi also made mistakes and incurred tremendous losses in the battles of Tet should not be allowed to obscure the intelligence failure that occurred."

The next essay, by Larry Cable, provides fresh insight into U.S. intelligence matters and how the knowledge or lack of knowledge of enemy activities and plans in late 1967 and early 1968 effected U.S. strategic planning and ultimately operational execution. Cable is a veteran of three tours of duty in Vietnam and has both scholarly and practical experience in most facets of American military and intelligence gathering operations in Indochina. He bases his analysis on over 400 original documents from the files of the Central Intelligence Agency which have only been declassified over the past four years. He challenges the widely accepted notion that U.S. intelligence organizations and strategies failed to adequately warn U.S. forces in Vietnam of the impending Tet attacks by VC and PAVN forces. Effectively employing once classified CIA files, Cable bids the reader to reexamine what he believes are popular myths and misinterpretations of "intelligence failure." His conclusions reach beyond those of John Prados in his equally thorough chapter. Cable posits that it was flawed overall U.S. policies and not "intelligence failure" that led to Tet because it forced intelligence analysts to fit their interpretations of data into preconceived U.S. strategic dogma. Cable concludes that Tet cannot be understood except as part of the greater strategic blunders by U.S. political and military leaders and thus not as a failure of U.S. intelligence officials and operatives to properly collect, analyze and disseminate data. Cable's chapter will raise many new questions and enlarge the already expansive debate over Tet and its meaning, not the least because of the unique spin he places on the long-standing allegation that Hanoi willingly sacrificed the NLF during Tet to serve its own political agenda. Cable lends more weight to this view than scholars such as Garver and Brigham, but the issue he seems to be addressing is not merely whether this was in fact the case, but that U.S. leaders rejected whole classes of intelligence sources indicating that Hanoi was being driven by the American bombing of the north to take a more predatory approach to its southern ally. This rejection, Cable concludes, is, in itself, powerful evidence that American strategic thinking in Vietnam, not flaws in intelligence gathering, prevented the effective evaluation of the enemy's strategic intentions.

One could argue that U.S. surprise and Communist determination during Tet was, and to many historians still is, a microcosm of America's overall lack of understanding of Southeast Asia throughout the war. Thus, the surprise at Tet wasn't due to intelligence failure as much as it was due to essential ignorance about the enemy and his resolve, a flaw Doug Pike has dubbed "vincible ignorance." Robert Nourse's observations (Chapter 10) of the Tet Offensive reflect on how the units he was with during the operation were caught off guard not by the attacks, which they knew would come, but by the ferocity and resolve of their enemy. Nourse seems to pass no specific historical judgment on Tet or its aftermath. Instead, he strives to provide the reader with a sense of what it was like to be an American combat soldier caught in this crucible of death and destruction. From this perspective, intelligence was not a geopolitical strategic consideration, as seen by Prados, but a tool to be used to stay alive.

No study of the Tet Offensive would be complete without an analysis of the NVA siege of the marine base at Khe Sanh. Peter Brush, who was present during the January–April 1968 siege, provides the reader (Chapter 11) with an overview of U.S. Marine preparations for, and operations during, the three-month battle that, as Larry Berman has indicated, became President Johnson's obsession. While much of Chapter 11 is dedicated to recounting events from late January to early April 1968, Brush also tries to examine many of the nagging questions still surrounding Khe Sanh and provides the reader with suggested answers to these questions. One significant issue Brush raises is whether Khe Sanh was a diversion for Tet operations, as General Vo Nguyen Giap contends. Brush is relatively convinced that it was.

A second question Brush addresses is whether or not Khe Sanh was a Communist effort at a second Dien Bien Phu, as General William C. Westmoreland believed it was. Brush indicates that the temptation certainly was there and certainly may have been a secondary goal. He reasons that since the victor of Dien Bien Phu, General Giap, whose reputation had been made at the siege, had drawn up the strategic and tactical plans for Khe Sanh, it is safe to say that the general had to have been influenced, at least in part, by the 1954 victory.

Brush also raises the question long debated by scholars, analysts, and participants: where was Giap during the siege? He believes that he was at the front in the Communist caves near Laos at least part of the time. Lastly, Brush also ponders a question that most marines at Khe Sanh have asked since 1968: why the NVA never attempted to cut off the marines' vulnerable water supply, which was so vital to their survival. Brush has no absolute answer for this question. However, he does believe that such action, or rather, inaction, may have been intentional and only strengthens the argument that Khe Sanh was primarily a diversion.

One other point of import that Brush focuses on is a Communist monument to the siege located on the site of the marine base. It has a text that "explicitly refers to the fighting at Khe Sanh as another Dien Bien Phu." Thus, says Brush, "The Communists appear to regard the battle of Khe Sanh as the victory that enabled them to win the war in Indochina, or at least prefer to have it remembered that way." Brush shares Edmonds' view that if Khe Sanh and Tet were psychological victories for the Communists, the psychological effects were "largely unintentional and represented an unexpectedly positive consequence of the fighting."

No anthology on Tet would be complete without an essay on the air war. Mark Jacobsen approaches this dimension of Tet through a study (Chapter 12) of President Johnson's decision to curtail the American air offensive over the North after Tet. Employing recent primary research, he examines air operations leading up to Tet and Khe Sanh, focusing on the 1965–1968 aspects of American targeting policies commonly known as Operation Rolling Thunder. Jacobsen examines how President Johnson and his advisors influenced the relative effectiveness of the air campaign in North Vietnam. He subsequently attempts to explain how Tet altered the thinking of the president and his senior military leaders and how the tension resulting from this alteration led the president to curtail the bombing and thus give the enemy essentially what it wished to obtain from the offensive. President Johnson wanted to limit liberal opposition to the war and also maintain support from military leaders. Ultimately, writes Jacobsen, he ended Rolling Thunder "because doing so offered the best chances of defusing an explosive political situation at home, one that General Westmoreland's request for 200,000 more troops threatened to detonate." He goes on to declare that "Johnson had never thought of the air war as part of a strategic offensive directed against the nation with whom the United States was at war; rather, Rolling Thunder remained a tool of coercive diplomacy." At the same time, Jacobsen believes that shifting the focus of the air war to the South was neither an "afterthought nor a trick played upon a war-weary population." Instead, he argues that it was designed to address the "military peril that Westmoreland feared," a move that could be carried out with "negligible political costs." This move also obviated the need to ask Congress to call up reserves during an election year, and besides, says Jacobsen, Johnson was confident that he could restart Rolling Thunder if needed. As Jacobsen notes, this was a pipe dream.

The reality was that curtailing Rolling Thunder was "a step from which there was no return." To be sure, says Jacobsen, this was not the first time Johnson had misjudged the Communists, the U.S. public, and the Congress, Johnson being primarily a political tactician, thinking only "one or at most two moves ahead." Thus, as Jacobsen concludes, the president

did not expect peace to result, only that Khe Sanh would now not fall and the ARVN would survive to fight another day. Because of the failure of its Tet Offensive, the North Vietnamese accepted the bid to negotiate while they regrouped and reorganized their rearward areas. Their need to regroup coincided, of course, with the Johnson administration's desperate need to do the same.

The volume closes with Robert Buzzanco's exploration (Chapter 13) of some of the myths surrounding Tet addressed by several of the preceding chapters. It thus functions well not only as a conclusion to the second half of this anthology, but also as a general conclusion. The author opens his analysis by asking if Walter Cronkite's famous TV remarks about U.S. performance during Tet were representative of the real cause of allied failure after Tet and the eventual U.S. withdrawal from Southeast Asia. He also looks at the opinion of General Earle Wheeler of the Joint Chiefs of Staff and asks why Wheeler appears to come to rather different conclusions from Cronkite's. He examines revisionist views of the "media as the villain" theory they have advocated and debunks their simplistic claims that the American news media provided the enemy with victory after Tet. He also brings into question whether accusations of shortsighted executive policies and restrictions on U.S. forces can be held solely responsible for American defeat in Vietnam.

Ultimately, says Buzzanco, what Tet and the overall American defeat in Vietnam really did was to create ghosts to haunt American foreign policy and public sensibilities for the succeeding decades. President George Bush proclaimed after the 1991 Gulf War that "by God, we've kicked the 'Vietnam syndrome' once and for all," a remark that reflected the views of

Vietnam War revisionists who believed that America had lost in Vietnam "because its warriors had been undermined at home." To Buzzanco, Bush's words do not constitute good history; they merely demonstrate that "control over the historical memory of Vietnam had become a foreign policy strategy as well, for, as George Orwell had warned, those who define the past can control the present and thus the future." To Buzzanco, "The legacy of Vietnam is so much more complex than the revisionists would have Americans believe."

One of the most popular of all Asian parables concerns the three blind men who, when led to touch a specific portion of an elephant's anatomy, described the whole animal in relation only to that which they knew: the man who grasped the trunk thought the beast was a type of snake, the man who grasped the tail thought it was a kind of rat, and the man who grasped the leg thought his arms encompassed a tree trunk. Unfortunately, many of the most knowledgeable teachers and most devoted students of the Vietnam War regard the Tet Offensive much as the blind men regarded the elephant of the ancient parable. So central is their interpretation of Tet to their vision of the entire war that they are unable to consider that the Tet Offensive may possess at least some of the characteristics of their competing visions or, perhaps, be another kind of animal altogether. Some scholars are so concerned with this development that they urge us to regard Tet not as a beacon illuminating the war, but as merely a dimly seen and elusive point of light.[3] The problem, however, is not a want or excess of light, but an intellectual malaise that acts as a blinder limiting our range of vision. The authors' contributions to this volume are among the very first analyses to seek to dispel the wishful thinking, analytical dogmas, and political agendas that have obscured past efforts to master this key turning point in Vietnamese and American history. They reveal that, when conducted without such blinders, the debate surrounding the Tet Offensive can illuminate and improve our understanding of historical patterns and political and military policies that have shaped much of the recent past and may well help shape the future.

NOTES

1. See Peter Breastrup, ed., *Vietnam as History* (Washington, D.C.: University Press of America, 1984); Philip B. Davidson, *Vietnam at War, the History: 1946–1975* (New York: Oxford, 1984); Guenter Lewy, *America in Vietnam* (New York: Oxford, 1978); Bruce Palmer, *The Twenty-Five Year War* (New York: Simon & Schuster, 1985); Harry G. Summers, *On Strategy: A Critical Analysis of the Vietnam War* (Novato, Calif.: Presidio Press, 1982); and General William Westmoreland, *A Soldier Reports* (New York: Doubleday, 1976).

2. See Eric Bergerud, *The Dynamics of Defeat: The Vietnam War in Hau Nghia Province* (Boulder, Colo.: Westview Press, 1991); David W.P. Elliot "Hanoi's Strat-

egy in the Second Indochina War," in Jayne S. Werner and Luu Doan Huynh, *The Vietnam War: Vietnamese and American Perspectives* (Armonk, N.Y.: M.E. Sharpe, 1993) pp. 66–94. Victoria Pohle, *The Viet Cong in Saigon: Tactics and Objectives during the Tet Offensive* (Santa Monica, Calif.: Rand Memorandum RM-5799-ISA ARPA, January 1969); and William Turley, *The Second Indochina War: A Short Political and Military History, 1954–1975* (Boulder, Colo.: Westview Press, 1986). As an indication that the difference between these "schools" is less than the premise of this exercise might suggest, both Douglas Kinnard's *The War Managers* (Hanover, N.H.: University Press of New England, 1977), pp. 78–80, and Bruce Palmer's *The Twenty-Five-Year War* (New York: Simon & Schuster, 1985), pp. 74–81, note that the post-Tet behavior of General Wheeler led to Clark Clifford's decision to begin the winding down of the war.

3. Richard Falk, *Appropriating Tet* (Princeton, N.J.: World Order Studies Program, Occasional Paper No. 17, Center for International Studies, Woodrow Wilson School for Public and International Affairs, Princeton University Press, 1988) p. 39.

2

The Tet Offensive

Larry Berman

> I just don't understand it. Am I that far off? Am I wrong? Has something happened to me? My wife said, I think so. But she said you don't know what year you are living in. This is '68.
>
> *Remarks by President Lyndon Johnson to a congressional delegation in the White House, January 30, 1968.*

On January 11, 1968, U.S. intelligence detected a buildup of forces in the Laotian panhandle west of the demilitarized zone, threatening the marine base at Khe Sanh in western Quang Tri Province of South Vietnam. Khe Sanh was located eight miles east of Laos and eighteen miles south of the DMZ (Demilitarized Zone). The base occupied a strategically important location for the purposes of hindering enemy infiltration down the Ho Chi Minh Trail as well as providing a staging post for possible operations into Laos.

The enemy force buildup of two additional North Vietnamese divisions was incontrovertible, but Hanoi's motives were wildly disputed. Prisoner reports and captured documents revealed that a massive winter-spring offensive was being planned. Truck traffic down the Ho Chi Minh Trail had reached massive proportions and major North Vietnamese troop reinforcements were in the border areas. Was Hanoi merely setting the stage for negotiations or was the offensive intended to topple the government of South Vietnam? What was the enemy up to? General William Westmoreland believed a maximum military effort was under way, possibly to improve chances of achieving an end to the war through negotiations which would lead to a coalition government involving the NLF. Hanoi's major offensive also might have been aimed at achieving one major psychological victory in the United States prior to the start of the presidential campaign.

The enemy was finally coming to Westmoreland for battle. This would not be search and destroy in the jungle. Years of waiting for the enemy were almost over, and even though U.S. forces were significantly outnumbered, Westmoreland cabled Wheeler on January 12 that a withdrawal from Khe Sanh was unthinkable. "I consider this area critical to us from a tactical standpoint as a launch base for Special Operations Group teams and as flank security for the strong point obstacle system; it is even more critical from a psychological viewpoint. To relinquish this area would be a major propaganda victory for the enemy. Its loss would seriously affect Vietnamese and US morale. In short, withdrawal would be a tremendous step backwards."

With 15,000–20,000 North Vietnamese reinforcements circling Khe Sanh, Westmoreland hit the lure by ordering the 6,000 marine troops to defend the garrison. General Westmoreland also set in motion plans for implementing Operation Niagara (evoking an image of cascading bombs and shells), which became the most intense and successful application of aerial firepower yet seen in the war.

During the predawn hours of January 21, 1968, Khe Sanh came under constant rocket and mortar fire. The battle was on and it appeared to President Johnson and his principal advisors that the North Vietnamese envisioned Khe Sanh as a potential Dien Bien Phu. During a January 23 White House meeting with members of the Democratic leadership, the president reported that "intelligence reports show a great similarity between what is happening at Khe Sanh and what happened at Dien Bien Phu." Johnson became preoccupied with the Khe Sanh–Dien Bien Phu analogy. He had a sand-table model of Khe Sanh plateau constructed in the bunkerlike Situation Room of the White House. He feared that Khe Sanh would be his "Dinbinphoo," as LBJ was prone to pronounce it.

The Khe Sanh–Dien Bien Phu analogy was fraught with historical misapplication. The actual siege of Dien Bien Phu had lasted fifty-six days. The French forces included Montagnards, North Africans, Vietnamese, and Foreign Legionnaires. The total force was about 13,000 and casualties amounted to 1,100 killed, 1,600 missing, and 4,400 wounded. The Viet Minh totaled 49,500 combat troops plus 55,000 support troops. At Khe Sanh, U.S. forces numbered 6,000 Americans versus an enemy strength of about 20,000. The enemy's advantage was less than four to one rather than eight to one as it was at Dien Bien Phu (including support troops). Moreover, usable supplies parachuted into Dien Bien Phu averaged about 100 tons per day; General Westmoreland had a capability of 600 tons per day. The French possessed 75 combat aircraft and 100 supply and reconnaissance aircraft. By comparison, the United States had more than 2,000 aircraft and 3,300 helicopters.

Uncertainty about the military situation at Khe Sanh led LBJ to question the Joint Chiefs. At a meeting on January 29 the president requested that each member submit "his views concerning the validity of the strategy now pursued in South Vietnam by the Free World Forces." The declassified meeting notes show that LBJ asked the Chiefs "if they were completely in agreement that everything has been done to assure that General Westmoreland can take care of the expected enemy offensive against Khesanh." General Wheeler and the Joint Chiefs "agreed that everything which had been asked for had been granted and that they were confident that General Westmoreland and the troops were prepared to cope with any contingency."

It was during this period that Johnson, finding it difficult to sleep, would walk the halls of the White House or call down to the Situation Room for a report on Khe Sanh. Secretary of State Dean Rusk recalled that "we couldn't break him of the habit, even for health reasons, of getting up at 4:30 or 5:00 every morning to go down to the operations room and check on the casualties from Vietnam, each one of which took a little piece out of him."[1]

An NSC (National Security Council) staff assistant, Major Robert Ginsburgh, frequently found himself on night watch at the Situation Room in the basement of the White House. The Situation Room was actually two rooms—one windowless room with a long table for private meetings, the other an active hub of communications with AP, UPI, and Reuters teletypes. Four clocks were mounted on the wall—Washington, Greenwich mean time, Saigon, and the official presidential time which followed LBJ. The room also contained three television sets, burn gags, and other forms of technology befitting a White House communications center—especially a telephone. Ginsburgh recalled that during the battle for Khe Sanh, "I had the night-time watch. And so, every two hours I was either in touch with the President on the phone, that is, he would call me or I would have sent him a message, a little memo to try and preclude his calling. He wanted to know, 'how is it going, what is happening?' "[2]

Johnson wanted to know how things were going because he was running out of trust for those who had brought him to this point. Johnson later denied pressuring the Chiefs, but the declassified record contradicts his position. Meeting on February 2 with White House correspondents, the president discussed the JCS assurances about Khe Sanh. "I asked the JCS to give me a letter saying that they were ready for the offensive at Khesanh." Yet, when reporters wrote that Johnson had obtained these letters from the Chiefs, the president vehemently denied the claim.

The president then asked his assistant Tom Johnson to review all meeting notes to see whether there was any proof to the charge. Tom Johnson soon wrote the president,

I have reviewed all of the notes of meetings held during the past two weeks. In addition, I have searched my memory thoroughly. . . . At no time do my notes show, or my memory recall, an incident when the President said: "I do not want any Damn Dien Bien Phu." The President said we wanted to make sure we had done everything here and the JCS had done everything to make certain there is not another Dien Bien Phu. The word "damn" was not used in any meeting I attended in this context. Never did the President say he had "made each Chief sign a paper stating that he believed Khe Sanh could be defended.

LBJ could thus claim that he had neither said "damn" nor "each"; but he had made the Dien Bien Phu analogy as well as requiring "the chiefs" to sign a paper.[3]

During a particularly contentious morning meeting on January 30 with the Democratic congressional leadership, Senator Byrd remarked, "I am very concerned about the buildup at Khesanh. I have been told that we have 5,000 troops there compared with 40,000 enemy troops. Are we prepared for this attack?" The president responded,

This has been a matter of great concern to me. I met with the Joint Chiefs yesterday. I went around the table and got their answer to these questions. In addition, I have it in writing that they are prepared. I asked, "Have we done all we should do?" They said yes. I asked, "Are we convinced our forces are adequate?" They said yes. I asked should we withdraw from Korea. They said no, that Khesanh is important to us militarily and psychologically. . . .

General Wheeler sought to provide clarification for Byrd's queries:

On the matter of your question, Senator Byrd, about 5,000 U.S. troops versus 40,000 enemy troops. Khesanh is in very rugged areas. There are 5,900 U.S. troops in the Khesanh Garrison. There are support troops including 26th Marines and a battalion of the ARVN. . . . There are 39,968 friendly forces versus 38,590 enemy forces. Roughly, there are 40,000 allied troops to match the 40,000 enemy. We think we are ready to take on any contingency. In addition, there are 40 B-52 sorties and 500 tactical air sorties in the area Niagara each day hitting the enemy. . . . General Westmoreland is confident he can hold the position. To abandon it would be to step backward. The Joint Chiefs agree with General Westmoreland. The Joint Chiefs believe that he can hold and that he should hold. General Westmoreland considers it an opportunity to inflict heavy casualties on North Vietnam. We have 6,000 men there, and 34,000 available. It is 40,000 versus 40,000.

A week later during a White House meeting of the principals the president again asked Wheeler, "Are you as confident today as you were yesterday that we can handle the situation at Khesanh?" General Wheeler answered, "I do not think the enemy is capable of doing what they have set out to do. General Westmoreland has strengthened his position. He has contingency plans and can meet any contingency. There is nothing he has asked for that he has not been given. Khesanh is important to us militarily and psychologically. It is the anchor of our defensive situation along the DMZ." Johnson again asked General Wheeler, "Are you sure that you have everything that is needed to take care of the situation in Khesanh?" Wheeler responded, "Yes, we are. General Westmoreland has been given everything he has requested."

TET: MOVE FORWARD TO ACHIEVE FINAL VICTORY

During the early morning hours of January 31 approximately 80,000 North Vietnamese regulars and guerrillas attacked over 100 cities throughout South Vietnam. Tet involved enemy attacks on thirty-five of forty-four province capitals, thirty-six district towns, and many villages and hamlets. Over 80,000 enemy troops were involved in attacks directed against population centers. For weeks prior to the offensive, enemy forces had been infiltrating into Saigon in civilian clothes in preparation for a well-planned campaign of terror. The goal was to achieve a popular uprising against the GVN (government of Vietnam) and to show the American public that the very notion of security was null and void.

Communist forces were given the general order "Move Forward to Achieve Final Victory." Combat orders urged the assaulters to do everything possible to completely liberate the people of South Vietnam. The orders found on captured guerrillas described the Tet strategy as one which would launch "the greatest battle ever fought throughout the history of our country." The infiltrators were exhorted to

move forward aggressively to carry out decisive and repeated attacks in order to annihilate as many American, Satellite and Puppet troops as possible in conjunction with political struggles and military proselyting activities. . . . Display to the utmost your revolutionary heroism by surmounting all hardships and difficulties and making sacrifices as to be able to fight continually and aggressively. Be prepared to smash all enemy counter attacks and maintain your revolutionary standpoint under all circumstances. Be resolute in achieving continuous victories and secure the final victory at all costs.

While the attack itself did not surprise the principals, its timing during the Tet holiday truce phasedown did. In Washington, Walt Rostow was called away from a foreign affairs advisors' luncheon to receive news of the offensive. Rostow quickly returned to report, "We have just been informed we are being heavily mortared in Saigon. The Presidential Palace, our BOQ's, the Embassy and the city itself have been hit." General Wheeler did not seem very alarmed:

It was the same type of thing before. You will remember that during the inaugu-
ration the MACV headquarters was hit. In a city like Saigon people can infiltrate
easily. They carry in rounds of ammunition and mortars. They fire and run. It is
impossible to stop this in its entirety. This is about as tough to stop as it is to
protect against an individual mugging in Washington, D.C. We have got to pacify
all of this area and get rid of the Viet Cong infrastructure. They are making a major
effort to mount a series of these actions to make a big splurge at Tet.[4]

But General Westmoreland quickly cabled Admiral Sharp that the enemy
attacks constituted more than a D.C. mugging. The enemy

appears to be employing desperation tactics, using NVA troops to terrorize populated areas. He attempted to achieve surprise by attacking during the truce period.
The reaction of Vietnamese, US and Free World Forces to the situation has been
generally good. Since the enemy has exposed himself, he has suffered many casualties. As of now, they add up to almost 700. When the dust settles, there will
probably be more. All my subordinate commanders report the situation well in
hand.

Military assessments indicated that the VC suffered a major defeat at
Tet. Over half of their committed force was thought to be lost and perhaps
a quarter of their whole regular force. Moreover, the Communists failed
to achieve what MACV assumed to be the major goal of the attacks on
urban centers: the diversion of U.S. forces from Khe Sanh or elsewhere.
Nevertheless, the psychological impact of Tet was demoralizing. The enemy
demonstrated a capability to enter and attack cities and towns and do vast
damage. Bunker cabled Johnson on February 8 that

Hanoi may well have reasoned that in the event that the Tet attacks did not bring
the outright victory they hoped for, they could still hope for political and psychological gains of such dimensions that they could come to the negotiating table with
a greatly strengthened hand. They may have very well estimated that the impact of
the Tet attacks would at the very least greatly discourage the United States and
cause other countries to put more pressure on us to negotiate on Hanoi's terms.

The impact on the American public would indeed be great. A front-page
photograph in the February 1 *New York Times* showed three military policemen, rifles in hand, seeking protection behind a wall outside the
consular section of the U.S. Embassy in Saigon. The bodies of two American soldiers slain by guerrillas who had raided the compound lay nearby.
All nineteen guerrillas had been killed, but not until they had blasted their
way into the Embassy and held part of the grounds for six hours. Four
M.P.'s, a marine guard, and a South Vietnamese employee were killed in
the attack. President Thieu declared a state of martial law. Yet during a

news conference from the Cabinet Room, President Johnson likened Tet to the Detroit riots, asserting "a few bandits can do that in any city."

Meeting with key congressional leaders on January 31, LBJ reviewed the events preceding Tet as well as Khe Sanh:

The Joint Chiefs, and all the Joint Chiefs, met with me the day before yesterday and assured me that they had reviewed the plans and they thought they were adequate. I told them I thought I almost had to have them sign up in blood because if my poll goes where it has gone, with all the victories, I imagine what it would do if we had a good major defeat. So General Westmoreland and the Joint Chiefs of Staff are sure that we are not anticipating some major activity there that we have not heard about.

General Wheeler then explained to the congressional leaders that Hanoi's military purpose was to draw forces away from the Khe Sanh area. The second objective seemed to be more political, to demonstrate to the South Vietnamese people and the world that the Communists still possessed considerable strength in the country and thereby to shake the confidence of the Vietnamese people in the ability of the government to provide them security, even where they were within areas held by government and U.S. troops:

A significant thing about this attack is that in many areas, particularly in Saigon, and at Bien Hoa, the attackers were dressed in one of three types of clothing: Civilian clothes, military, ARVN military police uniforms, or national police uniforms. Apparently, they gave no attention at all to whether or not they killed civilians. This is a sort of an unusual action for them because they have posed as the protectors of the civilian populace. Apparently this is the effort to reestablish by terror a degree of control over the population.

The meeting of congressional leaders was followed by a cabinet meeting which Johnson opened by acknowledging, "There is a lot of stress and plenty of overtime for us all." The president then engaged in a series of free-flowing remarks in which he came close to blaming the pope for Tet:

I think I admired President Kennedy most during the Bay of Pigs when he said "no one is to blame but me." I know that wasn't true. . . . We went into Rome at night and we could have been faced with two million Red demonstrators. The Pope appealed to me. We had no differences, no quarrels. He said "I want to do something, anything for peace—can't you give us one extra day of the holiday truce?" General Westmoreland told me how many American lives it would cost, but we did give the Pope his extra day. Now it's hard not to regret the number of boys who were killed. It is now so much worse after the Tet truce. Westmoreland cancelled the Tet truce because the house was on fire. So you look at Pueblo, Khe Sanh, Saigon and you see them all as part of the Communist effort to defeat us out there. We can dodge it by being weak-kneed if we want to. I said at San Antonio that we have gone as far as we could—farther, I might add, than the military wanted. We made it clear how much we want to talk and not bomb, just so long as there is some prompt and productive response. But if you sneak in the night and hit us, we can't stop bombing. Now we have their answer with this new offensive. It just should satisfy every dove who loves peace as much as any mother does.

The President then read excerpts from a memorandum received from Ambassador Bunker, drawing particular attention to a passage recalling Thomas Paine's remark, "[These are the] times that try men's souls. . . . What we attain too cheaply, we esteem too lightly."

Attending the annual presidential prayer breakfast at the Shoreham Hotel, the president sounded weary and burdened by events: "The nights are very long. The winds are very chill. Our spirits grow weary and restive as the springtime of man seems farther and farther away. I can, and I do, tell you that in these long nights your President prays." Indeed, as these personal pressures grew, LBJ sought private solace in late-night prayer at St. Dominic's Church, in southwest Washington. Accompanied only by the Secret Service, the president and his "little monks" would read scriptures and psalms, and sing hymns.[5]

On February 1 Wheeler cabled Sharp and Westmoreland that if there was any validity to the Khe Sanh–Dien Bien Phu comparison, perhaps they should consider "whether tactical nuclear weapons should be used if the situation in Khe Sanh should become that desperate." While Wheeler considered that eventuality unlikely, he requested a list of susceptible targets in the area "which lend themselves to nuclear strikes," and asked "whether some contingency nuclear planning would be in order, and what you would consider to be some of the more significant pros and cons of using tac nukes in such a contingency."

Westmoreland soon responded that "the use of tactical nuclear weapons should not be required in the present situation." However, should the situation change, "I visualize that either tactical nuclear weapons or chemical agents would be active candidates for employment." Adding even more fuel to the credibility-gap fire, Johnson vehemently denied that nuclear weapons had ever been considered. During an emotional February 16 news conference, LBJ stated that it was "against the national interest to carry on discussions about the employment of nuclear weapons with respect to Khesanh."

The long-promised light at the end of the tunnel was about to be turned off. Satirist Art Buchwald likened administration optimism to another type of historical revision: " 'We have the enemy on the run,' says General Custer at Big Horn. 'It's a desperation move on the part of Sitting Bull and his last death rattle.' " Senator George Aiken wryly remarked, "If this is a failure, I hope the Viet Cong never have a major success." Yet Rostow again wrote Johnson that the degree of Communist terrorism during the

Tet period would actually strengthen the South Vietnamese resolve to get even with these terrorists. "There is a chance that South Viet Nam will emerge in the weeks and months ahead with stronger political institutions and a greater sense of nationhood and common destiny than before."

MORE TROOPS

General Wheeler understood the severity of Westmoreland's military position. His forces were stretched to their maximum extent and effectiveness. On February 3 Wheeler cabled Westmoreland that "the President asks me if there is any reinforcement or help that we can give you." Receiving no answer, Wheeler tried again on February 8: "Query: Do you need reinforcements? Our capabilities are limited. . . . However, if you consider reinforcements imperative, you should not be bound by earlier agreements. . . . United States government is not prepared to accept defeat in Vietnam. In summary, if you need more troops, ask for them."

Westmoreland now cabled Wheeler that there was cause for alarm:

From a realistic point of view we must accept the fact that the enemy has dealt the GVN a severe blow. He has brought the war to the towns and the cities and has inflicted damage and casualties on the population. Homes have been destroyed, distribution of the necessities of life has been interrupted. Damage has been inflicted to the LOG's and the economy had been decimated. Martial law has been invoked, with stringent curfews in the cities. The people have felt directly the impact of the war.

While U.S. forces had repelled the Communist onslaught and inflicted major losses on the enemy manpower pool, Tet revealed the enemy's courage and great skill in planning and coordination. The enemy had infiltrated previously secure population centers and exploited the GVN claim of security from attack. There was no general uprising and the enemy did not hold a single city, although enemy units waged a fierce three-week battle at the ancient city of Hue, where they occupied the citadel—a nineteenth-century fortress which shielded the nation's historic imperial palace. Hue, a city of 100,000, was also the traditional center of religious and intellectual life in Vietnam. After weeks of fighting, U.S. and ARVN forces secured Hue, but not before some of the worst carnage of the war had been unleashed on its civilian inhabitants.

Westmoreland cabled Wheeler that enemy activity at Hue and elsewhere had helped Hanoi to score "a psychological blow, possibly greater in Washington than in South Vietnam, since there are tentative signs that the populace is turning against the Viet Cong as a result of these attacks." The enemy had also succeeded in temporarily disrupting the South Vietnamese economy, and Westmoreland believed the enemy would continue to strain the will of the people by maintaining pressure on the populated areas with his forces already committed. The general also expected another major offensive in the Saigon area, commencing in mid-February.

Meeting with the Democratic congressional leadership at breakfast on February 6, 1968, the president once again faced tough questions from Senator Byrd: "I am concerned about: 1. that we had poor intelligence; 2. that we were not prepared for these attacks; 3. we underestimated the morale and vitality of the Viet Cong; 4. we over-estimated the support of the South Vietnamese government and its people." Johnson shot back at Byrd: "I don't agree with any of that. We knew that they planned a general uprising around Tet. Our intelligence showed there was a winter-spring offensive planned. We did not know the precise places that were going to be hit. General Abrams said the Vietnamese are doing their best. There was no military victory for the Communists. Just look at the casualties and the killed in action."

The discussion then moved to a more general level of political discussion:

Senator Byrd: I have never caused you any trouble in this matter on the Hill. But I do have very serious concerns about Vietnam. I think this is the place to raise these questions, here in the family.

Congressman Boggs: What about Bob Byrd's charge that we are under-estimating the strength of the VC? I personally do not agree with that.

The president: I have never under-estimated the Viet Cong. They are not push-overs. I do not think we have bad intelligence or have under-estimated the Viet Cong morale.

Senator Byrd: Something is wrong over there.

The president: The intelligence wasn't bad.

Senator Byrd: That does not mean the Viet Cong did not succeed in their efforts. Their objective was to show that they could attack all over the country and they did.

The president: That was not their objective at all.

Senator Byrd: You have been saying the situation with the Viet Cong was one of diminishing morale. When I say you, I mean the Administration.

The president: I personally never said anything of the sort. I am not aware that anyone else has been saying that. What do you think the American people would have done if we had sent in troops and had lost 21,000 of them as the enemy has?

Senator Long: If we had planned to have an up-rising in Cuba and you had caused 21,000 men to be lost as the Viet Cong did, I am sure you would have been impeached.

The president: I am of the opinion that criticism is not worth much. I look at all these speeches that are in the *[Congressional] Record*. I look at all the people who are going around the country saying our policy is wrong. Where do they get us? Nowhere. The popular thing now is to stress the mis-management to Vietnam. I think there has been very little. I wish Mike (Senator Mansfield) would make a speech on Ho Chi Minh. Nothing is as dirty as to violate a truce during the holidays. But nobody says anything bad about Ho. They call me a murderer. But Ho has a great image.

Senator Byrd: I don't want the President to think that I oppose you. I am just raising these matters.

The president: I don't agree with what you say.

Senator Long: I am happy you raised the point, Bob.

The president: Everybody should say and do what they want to. But we have put our very best men that we have out there. I believe that our military and diplomatic men in the field know more than many of our Congressmen and Senators back here. Anybody can kick a barn down. It takes a good carpenter to build one. I just wish all of you would expose the Viet Cong and Ho. We have got some very crucial decisions coming up. Personally, I think they suffered a severe defeat. But we knew there would be a general uprising, and they did not win any victory. It seems to be an American trait to ask why. I just hope that we don't divert our energies and our talents by criticizing unnecessarily. We've got all we can of this "What's wrong with our country?" Fulbright, Young and Gruening haven't helped one bit.

Senator Byrd: I do not want to argue with the President. But I am going to stick by my convictions. [During a meeting the next day the president left the room to take a call from Senator Byrd. "The President returned to say that the Senator had called to apologize for his criticism at the morning leadership meeting."]

The Tuesday luncheon following Tet revealed frustration among the participants. For the departing secretary of defense, Robert McNamara, the Tet offensive demonstrated that Hanoi had

more power than we credit them with. I do not think it was a "last-gasp" action. I do think that it represents a maximum effort in the sense that they poured on all of their assets and my guess is that we will inflict a very heavy loss both in terms of personnel and material and this will set them back some but that after they absorb the losses they will remain a substantial force. I do not anticipate that we will hit them so hard that they will be knocked out for an extended period or forced to drop way back in level of effort against us. I do think that it is such a well-coordinated, such an obviously advanced planned operation, that it probably relates to negotiations in some way. I would expect that were they successful here they would then move forward more forcibly on the negotiation front and they are thinking they have a stronger position from which to bargain.

Johnson wanted to know what should be done militarily to sock it to the enemy. McNamara argued that the Joint Chiefs possessed no answer:

I have talked to the Chiefs about some kind of a reciprocal action—retaliation for their attack on our Embassy or in retaliation for their attack across the country. There just isn't anything the Chiefs have come up with that is worth trying. They talk about an area-bombing attack over Hanoi but the weather is terrible. You can't get in there with pinpoint targeting. The only way you could bomb it at all at the present time is area bombing and I would not recommend that to you under any circumstances. They have just not been able to think of retaliation that means anything. My own feeling is that we ought to be able to depend upon our ability to inflict very heavy casualties on them as our proper response and as the message we give to our people.

But the Chiefs did have an answer. In a meeting with the president they proposed removing the restrictions around Hanoi and Haiphong, reducing the circles to three miles around Hanoi and one and one-half miles around Haiphong. Secretary of State Rusk feared that the proposed action "opens up the possibility of large civilian casualties and leads to extensive devastation of the area. From what we have seen in other areas this leads to almost total devastation. What to hit is up to the pilot." Wheeler responded, "We do not advocate attacking the population centers. We never have before, and we don't ask for that now. I admit there will be more civilian destruction, but we will be going after trucks and water craft. They are secure now, but represent genuine military targets."

Secretary McNamara challenged Wheeler's logic: "Any attack of this type is very expensive both in the number of U.S. aircraft lost and in civilian destruction. I do not recommend this. The military effect is small and our night time attack capability is small. Civilian casualties will be high. In my judgment, the price is high and the gain is low. The military commanders will dispute all the points I have made except air craft loss."

Wheeler now placed his cards on the table in a direct rebuttal of Secretary McNamara:

I do not think the effects on the civilian population will be that high. As you know, they have an excellent warning system and most of them go to shelters and tunnels. From that standpoint, civilian loss could be lower than it is in other areas. We have had nothing like this civilian destruction that took place in World War II and Korea. But the targets which are there are military targets of military value. Frankly, this (civilian casualties which might result) does not bother me when I compare it with the organized death and butchery by the North Vietnamese and the Viet Cong during the last two weeks in South Vietnam. All of this relates to the matter of pressure.

Choices had to be made. The president told the Chiefs, "I believe somebody in government should say something. I do not share the view that many people have that we took a great defeat. Our version is not being put to the American people properly. . . . What are we going to do now on these bombing targets?" It was left to the incoming secretary of defense, Clark Clifford, to recommend accepting the Chiefs' proposal. Clifford believed that the Tet offensive constituted Hanoi's answer to the San Antonio Formula[6]: "I am inclined to resume the bombing in North Vietnam and go ahead with the suggested three mile and one and a-half mile limits. As long as the enemy had demonstrated that they are not going to respond positively we should go ahead with this."

When Rusk and McNamara warned about the need to distinguish restricted from authorized targets, Wheeler showed his discontent: "I am fed up to the teeth with the activities of the North Vietnamese and the Viet Cong. We apply rigid restrictions to ourselves and try to operate in a humanitarian manner with concern for civilians at all times. They apply a double standard. Look at what they did in South Vietnam last week. In addition, they place their munitions inside of populated areas because they think they are safe there."

The effects of Tet were discussed at a February 7 National Security Council meeting. Dialogue among the principals revealed the continuing uncertainty concerning enemy capabilities and U.S. military strategy:

Secretary Rusk: What about the possibility of the MIGs attacking a carrier?

General Wheeler: No, I do not think this is likely. The carriers do have air caps and are distant from the MIG bases.

The president: Go in and get those MIGs at Phuc Yen.

General Wheeler: We will as soon as the weather permits.

Secretary McNamara: The MIGs would have negligible military effects but they would have spectacular psychological impact. We do get the feeling that something big is ahead. We do not exactly know what it is, but our commanders are on alert.

The president: I want all of you to make whatever preparations are necessary. Let's know where we can get more people if we need to move additional ones in.

General Wheeler: I have a preliminary list on my desk. I am not satisfied with it.

Secretary McNamara: This would include Army, Navy, Air Force and Marine units.

The president: What about the allies?

General Wheeler: The Australians are incapable of providing more troops. The problems in Korea are such that it will be hard to get the South Koreans to even send the light division they had promised. The Thai troops are in training and to move them in now would be more detrimental than helpful.

The president: So it would be only Americans? Well, I want you to know exactly where you could get them, where they are located now and what we need to do. Get whatever emergency actions ready that will be necessary.

Secretary McNamara: All we would recommend at this time are the three items we had discussed earlier. There may be some increase in draft calls but this would have no immediate effect.

The president: Do we have adequate hospitals and medical personnel?

General Wheeler: We have ample space, ample supplies, and enough doctors for the present.

Secretary McNamara: There are 6,400 military beds. Of that, 2900 are occupied by U.S. troops and 1100 by Vietnamese civilians. So we have an additional capacity of about 2400.

The president: Look at this situation carefully. If we have another week like this one, you may need more.

Secretary Rusk: How do you interpret their use of tanks?

General Wheeler: They had to bring them all the way from Hanoi. This shows that this plan has been in staging since September. It represents a real logistic feat. They want to create maximum disruption.

Director Marks: Could they do anything at Cam Ranh Bay?

General Wheeler: They could. On this last attack, we caught frogmen in there. They could put rockets in the hills and fire on to the base.

The president: How many of the 25,000 killed were North Vietnamese Regulars?

General Wheeler: Approximately 18,000 were of a mixed variety of South Vietnamese enemy. Approximately 6,000 to 7,000 were North Vietnamese.

The president: How do things look at Khesanh? Would you expect to have to move out of Lang [Vie]?

General Wheeler: It was not planned that we would hold some of these outposts. We may have to move back that company on Hill 861.

The president: Bob, are you worried?

Secretary McNamara: I am not worried about a true military defeat.

General Wheeler: Mr. President, this is not a situation to take lightly. This is of great military concern to us. I do think that Khesanh is an important position which can and should be defended. It is important to us tactically and it is very important to us psychologically. But the fighting will be very heavy, and the losses may be high. General Westmoreland will set up the forward field headquarters as quickly as possible. He told me this morning that he has his cables and his communications gear in. He is sending a list of his needs, including light aircraft. We are responding to this request.

The president: Let's get everybody involved on this as quickly as possible. Everything he wants, let's get it to him.

STALEMATE IN VIETNAM

The shocking depiction of enemy strategy for Tet led Rostow to the conclusion that "it is time for a war leader speech instead of a peace-seeker speech." The speech offered a way to "slay the credibility-gap dragon with one blow or rather with one speech." Writing to the president on February 8, Rostow made the following observations and recommendations:

It is, I think, also the time to say plainly that hard fighting and heavy casualties lie ahead. They do, and the way to minimize their impact on American public opinion is to acknowledge them in advance and set the national tone by a call for steadiness and resolution. Finally, sooner or later, we are going to have to take on the peace issue squarely. There is a widespread assumption in the country, even among those who support our policy, that peace requires only that the right button can be found to push—the right gimmick discovered. This is, of course, naive. But it furnishes the basis for what will probably be a growing issue as the year proceeds. The serious opposition will not call for a pull-out from Vietnam. They will, instead, promise to do it better. They will say you cannot find the right button—and they will imply they can. We can defuse this issue by saying plainly that there can be no peace because the enemy still wants war. And those who talk of peace only cause the enemy to redouble his attacks on our men in Vietnam.

President Johnson would need all the help he could muster. On February 7 Major General W. E. DePuy provided General Wheeler with an assessment entitled "The Meaning of the Communist Offensive in Vietnam." In an effort to achieve a popular uprising against the government, the enemy had sent his VC main, local, and guerrilla forces against the GVN at every level simultaneously. DePuy offered a chilling analysis of the enemy manpower situation: "It seems that he is pushing all his chips into the middle of the table. Ours are there also. It is not credible to think in terms of a peak of effort followed by subsidence and a return to the status quo ante. Vietnam will never be the same again."

The Senate Foreign Relations Committee had just published Senator Joseph Clark's report based on a recent study mission to South Vietnam. *Stalemate in Vietnam* constituted a singularly powerful indictment of U.S. policy. The report concluded that "the war in Vietnam is at a stalemate which neither side can convert into a military victory without leaving the country—and perhaps the world—in ruins." America's national unity was threatened by the divisiveness of convictions on the war, creating a condition whereby "the political fabric of our society is at the tearing point." Senator Clark believed that Vietnam had become "a cancer" which threatened to destroy our country. "Never, never again," concluded the senator, "should we commit a ground army on the mainland of Asia."

The president had clearly been shaken by recent events, and during a White House meeting of the principals he told his advisors, "Well, it looks as if all of you have counseled, advised, consulted and then—as usual—placed the monkey on my back again." Johnson believed he could lose Vietnam:

I do not like what I am smelling from those cables from Vietnam and my discussions with outside advisers. We know the enemy is likely to hit the cities again. They will likely have another big attack and there undoubtedly will be surprises. I want you to lay out for me what we should do in the minimum time to meet a crisis request from Vietnam if one comes. Let's assume we have to have more troops. I think we should now tell the allies that we could lose Southeast Asia without their help.

The president's meeting on February 8 with the Joint Chiefs revealed perceptions of a deteriorating military situation. Westmoreland needed an immediate deployment of 45,000 men to meet a similar increase in enemy strength. But if the enemy had been losing men, why did Westmoreland need the increment? Had the enemy suffered erosion over the last few months? Was Hanoi planning for a psychological victory prior to negotiations? Did the enemy have sufficient strength to renew the attacks? What strength did the ARVN possess to resist these attacks?

The president first asked Wheeler, "What is the ARVN strength?" General Wheeler responded, "Approximately 360,000 men now. Total forces about 600,000." The discussion then turned to the enemy's strength. Since it appeared that few North Vietnamese regular forces had been utilized for the Tet attack, how many guerrillas and irregulars (recently moved from OB) were still available as reserves or replacements? Secretary Rusk explained to Johnson that "I have been asking for several days if there was a new order of battle. This is the first time that I have heard of this."

LBJ instructed the Chiefs to "work up all the options and let's review them together. I want you to hope for the best and plan for the worst. Let's consider the extensions, call ups, and use of specialists. Dean, should we have more than the Tonkin Gulf resolution in going into this? Should we ask for a declaration of war?" The secretary answered, "Congressional action on individual items would avoid the problems inherent in a generalized declaration. I do not recommend a declaration of war. I will see what items we might ask the Congress to look at." President Johnson persisted, "What would be the impact internationally of a declaration of war?" Rusk responded that "it might be a direct challenge to Moscow and Peking in a way we have never challenged them before. There would be very severe international effects."

At this point in the meeting, Clark Clifford, soon to be confirmed as the new secretary of defense, interjected with a series of questions concerning what he saw as historical and institutional schizophrenia:

There is a very strong contradiction in what we are saying and doing. On one hand, we are saying that we have known of this build up. We now know the North Vietnamese and Viet Cong launched this type of effort in the cities. We have publicly told the American people that the communist offensive was (a) not a victory, (b) produced no uprising among the Vietnamese in support of the enemy, and (c) cost the enemy between 20,000 and 25,000 of his combat troops. Now our reaction to all of that is to say that the situation is more dangerous today than it was before all of this. We are saying that we need more troops, that we need more ammunition and that we need to call up the reserves. I think we should give some very serious thought to how we explain saying on one hand the enemy did not take a victory and yet we are in need of many more troops and possibly an emergency call up.

The president, clearly shaken by Clifford's remarks, offered the following observation: "The only explanation I can see is that the enemy has changed its tactics. They are putting all of their stack in now. We have to be prepared for all that we might face. Our front structure is based on estimates of their front structure. Our intelligence shows that they have changed and added about 15,000 men. In response to that, we must do likewise. That is the only explanation I see."

The meeting ended with Secretary Rusk pointing out the contradiction in U.S. strategy. "In the past, we have said the problem really was finding the enemy. Now the enemy has come to us. I am sure many will ask why aren't we doing better under these circumstances, now that we know where they are."

Johnson's own frustrations were evident during his next meeting with the Joint Chiefs. In this instance LBJ appears close to the caricature of an embattled and unyielding president:

The president: All last week I asked two questions. The first was "Did Westmoreland have what he needed?" (You answered yes.) The second question was, "Can Westmoreland take care of the situation with what he has there now?" The answer was yes. Tell me what has happened to change the situation between then and now?

General Wheeler: I have a chart which was completed today based on a very complete intelligence analysis. It relates to all of South Vietnam, Laos and the area around the DMZ. It shows the following: Since December the North Vietnamese infantry has increased from 78 battalions to 105 battalions. Estimating there are 600 men per battalion that is approximately 15,000 men. This represents a substantial change in the combat ratios of U.S. troops to enemy troops. This ratio was 1.7 to 1 in December. It is 1.4 to 1 today. In the DMZ and I Corps area, there is a 1 to 1 ratio. There are 79 enemy battalions in the 1st Corps area (60 North Vietnamese and 19 Viet Cong). In the same area there are 82 Free World battalions (42 U.S.; 4 Free World; and 36 ARVN). This is about 1 to 1.

The president: What you are saying is this. Since last week we have information we did not know about earlier. This is the addition of 15,000 North Vietnamese in the northern part of the country. Because of that, do we need 15 U.S. battalions?

General Wheeler: General Westmoreland told me what he was going to put in tonight's telegram. This is the first time he has addressed the matter of additional troops.

Paul Nitze: I was not aware of this new intelligence.

General Wheeler: The last report was that there was approximately 15,000 enemy near and around Khesanh. As of today, our estimates range between 16,000 and 25,000. Their infantry has been built up.

During a February 10 meeting of foreign policy advisors, Secretary Rusk was still puzzled about enemy strength: "I can't find out where they say those 15,000 extra enemy troops came from. They say that these battalions came in between December and January." The president responded that "the Chiefs see a basic change in the strategy of the war. They say the enemy has escalated from guerrilla tactics to more conventional warfare." Clark Clifford added another perspective: "All we have heard is about the preparation the North Vietnamese have made for the attack at Khesanh. I have a feeling that the North Vietnamese are going to do something different. I believe our people were surprised by the 24 attacks on the cities last week. God knows the South Vietnamese were surprised with half of their men on holiday. There may be a feint and a surprise coming up for us."

ORDER OF BATTLE

Westmoreland cabled Wheeler and Sharp concerning the high number of enemy casualties during Tet. How, for example, could the enemy have absorbed such a high number in light of their manpower shortages? The high enemy casualty figures had caused a great deal of consternation for MACV.

The enemy committed virtually every VC unit in the country regardless of combat effectiveness and regardless of normal area of operations. They were committed with do-or-die orders, forbidden to retreat, and with no withdrawal or rallying plans. The enemy attacks might be described as a country-wide series of "Loc Ninhs." The very high casualties are not strange in this light. We cannot, of course, provide a very precise breakdown of casualties by type of enemy force.

Westmoreland then tried to deflect any insinuation that irregulars might have been involved. "I do not doubt that some of the enemy's casualties were guerrillas, porters, and such, but the percentage will probably be small. Thus, the enemy obviously banked heavily on surprise in its Tet offensive. This may account for minimal participation by guerrillas."

On February 11, 1968, Rostow forwarded the most recent order of battle estimates to President Johnson. MACV's figures for the period December–January reflected "no significant change" in the confirmed strength of main force and local force combat units. Rostow explained to LBJ that changes had occurred in the listing of noncombat elements such as combat support and administrative support, which involved "a bookkeeping character which do not really reflect changes in the enemy's combat potential."

Once again, MACV's statistics proved the United States was winning the war. CIA analyst Sam Adams wrote his colleague George Carver, the CIA's primary in-house expert on Vietnam, requesting a transfer from SAVA (Special Assistant for Vietnamese Affairs):

I do not feel that SAVA has been sufficiently diligent in bringing to the attention of the intelligence community the numerical and organizational strength of our adversaries in Vietnam. . . . I feel we (the CIA in general and SAVA in particular) have basically misinformed policy makers of the strength of the enemy. The pressures on the CIA and on SAVA, I realize, have been enormous. Many of the pressures—but not all—have originated from MACV, whose Order of Battle is a monument of deceit. The Agency's and the office's failing concerning Viet Cong manpower, I feel, has been its acquiescence to MACV half-truths, distortions, and sometimes outright falsehoods. We have occasionally protested, but neither long enough, nor loud enough."

Carver shared Adams' viewpoint and he now recommended reopening the OB debate in order to realistically reassess the enemy's overall capabilities. Excluding from the numerical military order of battle all Communist components other than main and local force, and administrative service and guerrillas, strictly defined, had been an error. CIA analysts strongly suspected that many of the Communist forces in Tet were drawn from secret self-defense components, perhaps the assault youth, and other elements written out of the order of battle because they had no military significance.

A CIA Directorate of Intelligence memorandum of February 21 which analyzed the Communist units participating in attacks during the Tet offensive concluded that if MACV's latest estimates were correct, the enemy would have committed over 50 percent of their regular force to battle. "If the reported losses of 32,500 killed in action and 5,500 detained applied solely to the VC/NVA regular forces, the commands would have lost more than 65% of the forces committed to the Tet offensive. This would have been a devastating blow. However, there are a number of pieces of evidence which suggest that such an interpretation would overstate the Communist manpower drain." What were these factors? The VC/NVA forces participating at Tet were augmented by large numbers of guerrillas operating in independent units or integrated into local force units. Moreover, prior to Tet the VC had actively recruited additional laborers and civilians, who almost certainly constituted the higher proportion of casualties during the offensive.

WHEELER'S PLOY FOR MORE TROOPS AND MOBILIZATION

Wheeler had twice asked Westmoreland if, in the wake of Tet, he needed more troops. On February 12, 1968, Westmoreland cabled Sharp and

Wheeler with his assessment of the military situation and force requirements in Vietnam. Westmoreland emphasized that the enemy "had launched a major campaign signaling a change of strategy of protracted war to one of quick military/political victory during the American election year." The enemy had failed to secure the border areas or to initiate a public uprising.

Westmoreland now argued that since the enemy had changed his strategy,

We are now in a new ball game where we face a determined, highly disciplined enemy, fully mobilized to achieve a quick victory. He is in the process of throwing in all his "military chips to go for broke." We cannot permit this. . . . I have approximately 500,000 US troops and 60,981 free world military assistance troops. Further contributions from the Thais and Koreans are months away. I have been promised 525,000 troops, which according to present programs will not materialize until 1969. I need these 525,000 troops now. It should be noted that this ceiling assumed the substantial replacement of military by civilians, which now appears impractical. I need reinforcements in terms of combat elements. . . . Time is of the essence. . . . I must stress equally that we face a situation of great opportunity as well as heightened risk. However, time is of the essence here, too. I do not see how the enemy can long sustain the heavy losses which his new strategy is enabling us to inflict on him. Therefore, adequate reinforcements should permit me not only to contain his I Corps offensive but also to capitalize on his losses by seizing the initiative in other areas. Exploiting this opportunity could materially shorten the war.

In addition to the previously authorized 525,000, Westmoreland requested an additional six battalions (10,500) for resuming offensive operations against a weakened enemy. Wheeler wrote to President Johnson that Westmoreland "does not know how sacrosanct that (525,000) figure is." Moreover, "He does not anticipate 'defeat,' but he desperately needs the troop elements requested in order to capitalize on opportunities available to him. . . . If requested troops are not made available, he would have to undertake an unacceptably risky course of drawing additional forces from elsewhere in South Vietnam."

The Joint Chiefs rejected Westmoreland's request for the 10,500 (a request which their chairman had pressed on Westmoreland) on grounds that U.S. military manpower requirements were at their limit; any further authorizations without a mobilization of reserves might erase even minimal levels of readiness for other military contingencies. Wheeler's ploy had been to use the Tet crisis as justification for reconstituting the strategic reserve. The 10,500 was a minor issue compared to mobilization. Wheeler had tried to force Johnson's hand into accepting a reserve call-up. Having encouraged Westmoreland to make the request, Wheeler then rejected it on grounds that U.S. forces were already pushed to their limits. Wheeler's plan backfired; the commander in chief rejected the JCS recommendation and directed the deployment of the 10,500 troops to South Vietnam.

President Johnson was very worried about the political costs of mobilization. Would the new units be used as reinforcements in Vietnam, for contingencies outside Vietnam, or to reassure NATO allies that the United States would meet its military commitments? Johnson worried about the size of the call-up and whether it could be diminished by reducing overseas garrisons in Europe or Korea. What were the budgetary implications of these actions?

Before making any decisions, the president ordered Wheeler to Vietnam for an on-the-spot report of Westmoreland's manpower needs, but the general's visit was delayed one week because the Senate Foreign Relations Committee was holding hearings on the 1964 Tonkin Gulf incident and Wheeler was needed in Washington. President Johnson's political standing was now plummeting. A Gallup poll conducted in early February showed that only 41 percent of the nation's adults approved of the president's handling of his job.

EXPLAINING THE UNACCEPTABLE

It now appeared unavoidable that Johnson would have to mobilize the reserves. The enemy had shaken U.S. and world opinion with its offensive, and the government of South Vietnam was tottering on the brink of insolvency. Rostow tried to nudge Johnson toward a positive decision: "Only you can make the political assessment of what it would cost to call up the reserves; but that would be the most impressive demonstration to Hanoi and its friends." Rostow believed that the issue needed to be handled carefully, particularly with respect to explaining mobilization in terms of past statements of progress: "We are sending men to assure Westy the reserves he needs; we are calling up reserves to make sure no one gets the idea that we can't handle our other world commitments."

Doubts about military strategy were emerging from all quarters. In a message communicated directly to the president, former president Eisenhower expressed personal support for a reserve call-up. The fact that Westmoreland was only asking for 10,500 suggested to Eisenhower that MACV did not have enough troops to fight the kind of campaign necessary to win the war and that U.S. forces were so scattered and committed that "we cannot hit the enemy when he concentrates, for example, around Khe Sanh." Eisenhower asked, "Has Westmoreland really been given the forces he is asking for; if he has asked for 525,000 men why didn't we send them sooner, and are we going to have enough in the area to provide a 'corps of maneuver'?" Eisenhower continued, "He said that moving a relatively small force of this size sounds as though we have been on a shoestring, suggests weakness on our part to the enemy, and gives the critics of what we are doing in Vietnam a target."

Ambassador Taylor also possessed grave doubts on the military situation in South Vietnam and he endorsed the Joint Chiefs' proposal on grounds that the possibilities of an unpleasant surprise in Korea or elsewhere in the Far East were sufficiently acute "that it is an act of prudence to move additional ground forces to the area as rapidly as possible." Taylor believed a call-up of reserves was justified by the military requirement and that, in addition, it would have some political-psychological value in demonstrating to the world, including Hanoi, that the United States meant business. "It would also serve as a reminder to our people at home that, while we are not technically at war, we are in a situation of similar emergency which places on our citizens duties and responsibilities analogous to those in a state of declared war."

General Westmoreland's decision to hold Khe Sanh now came under careful scrutiny. The occupation of Khe Sanh had been premised on establishing a forward operating base against infiltration routes in eastern Laos. But, there had been little effect on infiltration from Laos. Moreover, General Westmoreland did not argue strongly for the defense of Khe Sanh because of its present value in relation to impeding infiltration routes or in the defense of major areas of the northern provinces. Instead, his cables stressed rather the difficulty of getting out of Khe Sanh and the adverse psychological effects of a withdrawal upon South Vietnam and upon the American people. What was the military importance of maintaining Khe Sanh? Why not withdraw and redeploy the troops? Maxwell Taylor wrote LBJ that "whatever the past value of the position, it is a positive liability now. We are allowing the enemy to arrange at his leisure a set-piece attack on ground and in weather favorable to him and under conditions which will allow us little opportunity to punish him except by our air power."

Taylor urged LBJ to have the Joint Chiefs instruct Westmoreland to pull out. Rostow then weighed in with the opinion "that Khe Sanh probably can be held but that it will be at a heavy price in terms of casualties and in terms of other ground troops necessary to support and reinforce it. I have real doubt that we can afford such a defense in view of the limited reserves which General Westmoreland is likely to have in the time frame during which these events may take place."

It was evident that Westmoreland needed direction from Washington and Rostow explained to LBJ that "I would feel greatly relieved if the Joint Chiefs of Staff would see fit to send General Westmoreland guidance which would provide Westmoreland with a way out of Khe Sanh." For example, the Chiefs might suggest that "it is less clear that its present value now justifies the cost of an all-out defense." Perhaps Westmoreland could be persuaded to reassess the feasibility or desirability of withdrawing from Khe Sanh.

The president decided to stand by his field commander's judgment. Moreover, he instructed Clark Clifford to draft a statement of unequivocal support to General Westmoreland—but support which left Westmoreland a way out of a no-win situation:

The President wants General Westmoreland to know that he has freedom of action to conduct his military operations as he thinks wise from a military point of view without being inhibited by political or psychological factors originating in the United States. To the extent that such factors in South Vietnam itself are an important part of the struggle, General Westmoreland should take those into account in close consultation with Ambassador Bunker and President Thieu.

Specifically with regard to Khe Sanh, the President does not wish to inhibit General Westmoreland's judgment as to when, where and under what circumstances he wishes to fight his battles. When the President became convinced that General Westmoreland intended to defend Khe Sanh, the president threw himself into the task of insuring that General Westmoreland had the means to do so successfully. He further sought the judgment of the Joint Chiefs of Staff both as to the desirability and capability of defending Khe Sanh. This interest on the part of the President should not be interpreted, however, as a directive from the Commander in Chief to defend Khe Sanh under all circumstances if, in General Westmoreland's judgment, it is better to have his battle somewhere else. The purpose of this message is not to export to General Westmoreland the responsibility for events which are inherent in the responsibilities of the Commander in Chief. The President just wants General Westmoreland to know the General has his fullest confidence and does not want his hands tied by the build up of irrelevant factors on the home front in a way that would cause General Westmoreland to make military judgments which are contrary to his best thinking. If General Westmoreland wishes to defend Khe Sanh he will be supported; if he wishes to avoid a major engagement in a fixed position which does not utilize the peculiar mobility of U.S. forces, he will also be supported.

The time for reassessment was fast approaching. With the Senate Foreign Relations Committee's inquiry on Tonkin done, Wheeler flew from Washington to Vietnam. In anticipation of the visit, Maxwell Taylor wrote the president, "Reflecting on the possible objectives of General Wheeler's visit, I would hope that he would obtain answers to some of the fundamental questions which are troubling us, derived from detailed private discussions with General Westmoreland and his staff." Taylor wanted Westmoreland to answer questions on his operational plans, force requirements, and force availabilities. In particular,

"What enemy units have been identified in the attacks on the cities? What uncommitted units are available for a second cycle? What grounds are there for the allegation of an "intelligence failure" at the time of the first wave of attacks on the cities? How does General Westmoreland feel about the functioning of his own and the Vietnamese intelligence services in connection with this situation? What has been the nature of our psychological warfare activities directed at North Vietnam and the VC since January 30? These are all hard questions for which there are probably no final answers at this time but whatever Bus can bring back will be most helpful."

On February 24, Rostow wrote LBJ that the enemy was preparing to make a total effort "with all their capital soon. They will then try to lock us into a negotiation at their peak position before we can counter-attack." Rostow and Taylor both agreed "with Napoleon that Providence is on the other side with the last reserves. Therefore, right now we should be moving out to Westy all the ready forces we have and calling up reserves for: A Vietnam counter-attack; Korean contingency; General purposes, for our world posture." Rostow believed

we face the decisive battle of the war. They will try to dissipate Westy's reserves by simultaneous attacks at a number of places and take Khe Sanh if possible. I am uncertain about timing; but they are so obsessed with memories of 1954 I suspect they will hit soon, get a maximum position, and then force a negotiation, perhaps via the San Antonio formula before the weather opens up for us in I Corps and at Hanoi-Haiphong. The Geneva Conference of 1954 opened on April 26. Dien Bien Phu fell on May 7/8.

While in Vietnam General Wheeler concluded that the last three years had adversely impacted the U.S. worldwide military posture. Something had to be done and Wheeler took responsibility by cabling LBJ at his ranch with the tentative conclusions from his trip to Vietnam. The cable must have ruined Johnson's day. Had Westmoreland not redeployed some of his troops from border areas to urban centers in mid-January, severe setbacks would have occurred. "I will have on my return examples of how narrow the margin was between victory and defeat in certain key areas," Wheeler reported. "The enemy has suffered very substantially, but he still has size-able uncommitted reserves. He displays a tenacity which we have not seen before in this war."

Wheeler also believed that "Westy's forces are stretched too thin. . . . I believe that we must reinforce him promptly and substantially." Wheeler's conclusion left Johnson on uncertain ground:

In summary, the military situation continues to be fluid; the enemy is determined and tenacious; troop morale, both U.S. and ARVN, is good; Westy's forces are stretched thin in view of the enemy threat and the courses of action open to the enemy. I do not have any apprehension that we will be run out of the country by military action, but I do believe that to achieve victory we must expand our effort substantially and promptly.

On February 27, 1968, General Wheeler sent LBJ his "Military Solution and Requirements in SVN." The report was based on three days of conferences with Westmoreland and the senior American commander in each of the four corps areas. (Clifford described Johnson "as worried as I have ever seen him," after hearing Wheeler's report.) As Major Andrew Krepinevich later observed, "Wheeler's report reflected the bankruptcy of the Army's strategy. Although in the Tet Offensive the Army had destroyed enemy forces in far greater numbers than in any other period in the war, it had had a negligible impact on the United States' prospects for victory. Hanoi had demonstrated its ability to accept extraordinary losses, without reaching its breaking point. Instead, the enemy had both the capability and the will to continue the struggle indefinitely."[7]

Wheeler now asked for troops. Specifically, MACV needed 205,000 troops in order to regain the strategic initiative. According to Wheeler,

The enemy has undoubtedly been hurt, but he seems determined to pursue his offensive—apparently he has the capability to do so. . . . It is the consensus of responsible commanders that 1968 will be the pivotal year. The war may go on beyond 1968 but it is unlikely that the situation will return to the pre-Tet condition. The forces committed and the tactics ionvolved are such that the advantage will probably swing one way or the other, during the current year. . . . In many areas the pacification program has been brought to a halt. The VC are prowling the countryside, and it is now a question of which side moves fastest to gain control. The outcome is not at all clear. I visualize much heavy fighting ahead.

Casualties would be high. Equipment losses would continue at a high level. ARVN would prove to be shaky under sustained pressure. "If the enemy synchronizes his expected major attacks with increased pressure throughout the country, General Westmoreland's margin will be paper thin. He does not have a theatre reserve. We can expect some cliff-hangers, and with bad luck on weather or some local RVNAF [Republic of Vietnam Armed Forces] failures he may suffer some reverses. For these reasons he is asking for additional forces as soon as possible during this calendar year."

During a February 27 White House meeting attended by Rusk, McNamara, Clifford, Katzenbach, Bundy, Rostow, Califano, and McPherson, debate focused on Westmoreland's still secret request for the 205,000. Clark Clifford, who would shortly be sworn in as secretary of defense, suggested that instead of proceeding incrementally,

Another possibility that should be considered—and I am not pushing it—is announcement that we intend to put in 500,000 to million men. Secretary McNamara responded, "That has virtue of clarity. Obviously we would have decided to put in enough men to accomplish the job. That and status quo both have the virtue of clarity. I do not understand what the strategy is to putting in 205,000 men. It is neither enough to do the job, nor an indication that our role must change." The discussion then focused on what really had happened at Tet:

Bundy: We must also prepare for the worst. SVN is very weak. Our position may be truly untenable. Contingency planning should proceed toward possibility that we will withdraw with best possible face and defend rest of Asia. We can say truthfully that Asia is stronger because of what we have done in past few years.

Katzenbach took call from Habib in Hawaii. Reports Habib is "less optimistic" about political situation in Saigon than he was when he went out. Reports that there is various disagreement in American circles in Saigon over 205,000 request. Bunker has doubts about this.

Rusk: If we have to call up reserves, we should take some of our troops out of Europe. Europeans will have to put some more in for their defense.

McNamara: Agree, if we call 400,000.

State of Military Situation:

Rusk, Rostow think enemy took beating in Tet offensive. Rostow says captured documents show enemy was disappointed, may be unable to mount heavy coordinated attack on cities. Rusk reminds that enemy took 40,000 casualties. No US units out of operation. Rostow says if we can re-enforce Westy now, he should be able to handle situation until good weather comes to I Corps and NVN.

McNamara: What then? Let's not delude ourselves into thinking he cannot maintain pressure after good weather comes.

(Rostow apparently had air attacks in mind. McN: We are dropping ordnance at a higher rate than in last year of WWII in Europe. It has not stopped him.)

Bundy: SVN forces uncertain, but almost certainly not as strong as were before.

Clifford: Look at situation from point of view of American public and Vietnamese. Despite optimistic reports, our people (and world opinion) believe we have suffered a major setback. Problem is, how do we gain support for major program, defense and economic, if we have told people things are going well? How do we avoid creating feeling that we are pounding troops down rathole? What is our purpose? What is achievable? Before any decision is made, we must re-evaluate our entire posture in SVN. Unfortunately, Pres. has been at ranch with hawks.

McNamara: Agreed. Decision must not be hasty. Will take a week at least to work out defense and economic measures, if we go big. Wheeler, Habib will meet with Secretaries Wednesday morning at breakfast with President. Decision should certainly not be announced that night.

General Impression: Prevailing uncertainty. Radically different proposals were offered and debated, more rejected out of hand. We are at a point of crisis. McNamara expressed grave doubts over military, economic, political, diplomatic and moral consequences of a large force buildup in SVN. Q is whether these profound doubts will be presented to President.

The doubts would be presented to the president but in a circuitous fashion. During a February 28, 1968, cabinet meeting President Johnson warned cabinet members that

the big problem is the impression we make with the public. . . . We have to be careful about statements like Westmoreland's when he came back and said that he saw "light at the end of the tunnel." Now we have the shock of this Tet Offensive. Ho Chi Minh never got elected to anything. . . . He is like Hitler in many ways. . . . But we, the President and the Cabinet, are called murderers and they never say anything about Mr. Ho. The signs are all over here. They all say "Stop the War," but you never see any of them over there. Then he launches the Tet attack, breaks the truce and escalates by firing on 44 cities, all at the time that we are offering bombing pause. It is like the country lawyer who made the greatest speech of his life but they electrocuted the client. We are like that now.

February ended with Johnson fighting back. In his first visit to Dallas since President Kennedy's assassination, he announced that the war had reached a critical turning point and said, "I do not believe we will ever buckle." Flying from his ranch near Austin to attend a convention of the National Rural Electric Cooperative Association, the president spoke about the war: "There will be blood, sweat and tears shed. The weak will drop from the lines, their feet sore and their voices loud. Persevere in Vietnam we will and we must. There, too, today, we stand at a turning point."

Johnson would need all the help he could get because he was about to lose Middle America. CBS news anchor Walter Cronkite had told a national television audience that the war was stalemated: "We have been too often disappointed by the optimism of the American leaders, both in Vietnam and Washington, to have faith any longer in the silver linings they find in the darkest clouds. . . . For it seems now more certain than ever that the bloody experience of Vietnam is to end in a stalemate. Today, that we are mired in stalemate seems the only realistic, yet unsatisfactory, conclusion."

A television anchorman had declared the war over. After watching the broadcast Johnson concluded, "Cronkite was it."[8] But Johnson was wrong. Cronkite mirrored public opinion, he was not ahead of it. The weeks ahead would lead the president's inner circle of advisors and then Lyndon Johnson to the same conclusions. The initial impetus would be pressure to meet General Westmoreland's troop request. Should the nation's reserves be mobilized? The president appointed his new secretary of defense, Clark Clifford, to head a task force to evaluate General Westmoreland's request. The president's initial instructions to Clifford were "give me the lesser of evils."

NOTES

The documents used in this essay are part of the National Security Council history, "The March 31st Speech," at the LBJ Library. The project traces the events between the 1968 Tet attacks and the president's speech on March 31 in which he announced the partial cessation of the bombing and his decision not to seek reelection.

1. Quoted in Kenneth Thompson, ed., *The Johnson Presidency* (Lanham, Md.: University Press of America, 1987), pp. 89–90, 258.

2. Robert Ginsburgh, deposition for CBS-Westmoreland trial in author's possession.

3. See Tom Johnson's meeting notes.

4. See Tom Johnson's meeting notes.

5. See Doris Kearns, *Lyndon Johnson and the American Dream* (New York: Harper and Row, 1976), pp. 360–361.

6. It was a peace proposal by the U.S. sent secretly (in late 1967) to Hanoi by Harvard Professor Henry Kissinger backing away from hardline mutual de-escalation of the war. The U.S. would end the bombing if a productive discussion would begin immediately.

7. Sam Adams to George Carver, February 1968 (CBS-Westmoreland trial document in author's possession).

8. Larry Berman, *Lyndon Johnson's War: The Road to Stalemate in Vietnam* (New York: W.W. Norton, 1991), p. 175; Daniel Hallin, *The Uncensored War: The Media and Vietnam* (New York: Oxford University Press, 1986) pp. 169–170.

3

The Tet Offensive and Sino–Vietnamese Relations

John Garver

This chapter seeks to answer the questions: Did the Vietnamese Worker's Party (VWP) decision to launch the Tet Offensive lead to a deterioration of Sino-Vietnamese relations? Did the leaders of the Chinese Communist Party (CCP) object to the Tet Offensive? If so, why?

There is strong evidence of new strains in Sino–North Vietnamese relations beginning in 1968. According to Hanoi, during 1968 when planning the 1969 aid program, China reduced the amount of aid by 20 percent compared with 1968. The next year, aid was again cut by 30 percent. Beijing threatened to cut off aid altogether, again according to Hanoi.[1] Beijing denounced the charge that it threatened to suspend aid entirely as "sheer fabrication," but did not dispute the changes in annual levels of assistance cited by Hanoi.[2] This and other evidence suggests that Chinese aid did in fact decrease at this juncture. Chinese media attention to the North Vietnamese and Viet Cong (VC) struggle also declined drastically during 1968 and 1969.[3]

Most important of all, the withdrawal of Chinese armed forces from North Vietnam began in the spring of 1968. Between October 1965 and March 1968 China sent 320,000 soldiers to North Vietnam to run railways and to build and man coastal defense fortifications and antiaircraft artillery positions. Chinese forces also repaired North Vietnam's transportation infrastructure after American bombing. Chinese forces in North Vietnam reached a peak of 170,000.[4] This Chinese assistance was vital to North Vietnam's effort to keep open the logistic supply lines to South Vietnam. The withdrawal of those forces from North Vietnam began in the spring of 1968 and was complete by July 1970.[5]

What were the policy objectives underlying these shifts in Chinese policy?

Were they related to Chinese displeasure with the launching of the Tet Offensive? If so, why were Chinese leaders unhappy with Tet? Were other factors involved in Chinese displeasure with the VWP at this juncture which were perhaps more important that Tet? If so, how did those issues relate to the Tet Offensive?

THE TET OFFENSIVE VERSUS PEOPLE'S WAR

As is well known, the Tet Offensive involved a combination of the National Liberation Front's (NLF) long anticipated general uprising, a largely urban phenomenon, and a general offensive in the countryside launched in successive waves. It was also accompanied by an assault in force by two crack divisions of North Vietnam's People's Army of Vietnam (PAVN) on the U.S. Marine base at Khe Sanh. The offensive of early 1968 was thus a comprehensive and powerful, three-pronged general assault. It brought to bear virtually the entire combat force of the NLF as well as the main combat divisions of PAVN. It was the first major offensive by PAVN forces since North Vietnamese units assaulted the 1st Air Cavalry Division in the Ia Drang valley in November 1965.

The decision to launch the offensives of early 1968 were made by the VWP sometime in the spring or early summer of 1967. Final approval for the plan was apparently given at the VWP's Fourteenth Plenum in late 1967. The strategic objective of the 1968 offensives was to break the stalemate that had existed on the battlefield for the previous several years by bringing about a great leap in the revolution. If preparatory work was done well and conditions were right, the VWP hoped, the Saigon regime might disintegrate. If the government did not collapse as a result of the general uprising in the cities, the urban uprising was to be followed by a further series of military offensives during succeeding months to wear down the enemy and open the way for either victory or a negotiated settlement.[6] Were the U.S. base at Khe Sanh overrun, this addition of a "Dien Bien Phu" to the concoction would increase the prospects for a U.S. withdrawal. Even if Khe Sanh held, the intense fighting there would draw away enemy strength, further shifting the correlation of forces in favor of the NLF-PAVN forces on other urban and rural battlefields.

VWP and NLF directives issued just prior to the offensive conveyed an optimistic estimate about the chances of impending complete victory. Although this optimism can be partially discounted as exhortation designed to encourage troops about to enter battle, in the sober estimate of William Duiker it does seem that the VWP leaders were persuaded that the situation in Saigon and other southern cities was "highly revolutionary" and that the progressive social classes were "increasing their sympathy for the revolution."[7] The presence of a half million U.S. troops in South Vietnam and the expansion of government of Vietnam (GVN) control in the countryside only disguised the deep political weakness of the Saigon government, in the VWP view. Urban unrest was pervasive, and created the necessary subjective and objective conditions for an urban revolt that, combined with an offensive in the countryside, could set off a chain reaction that would topple the Thieu regime.

The Tet Offensive deviated substantially from Mao Zedong's doctrine of protracted people's war in several important ways. Before exploring those discrepancies, however, we must look briefly at Mao's doctrine of people's war. According to that doctrine, there were three distinct stages to people's war. The first stage was strategic defensive by the revolutionary forces and strategic offensive by the counterrevolutionary forces. The second stage was strategic stalemate. The third stage was strategic offensive by the revolutionary forces and strategic defensive by the counterrevolutionary forces. During the first and second stages, the revolutionary forces would abandon the cities to superior enemy forces and wage extensive guerrilla warfare in the countryside against the increasingly dispersed and static enemy forces. During the long second stage of strategic stalemate, guerrilla warfare would gradually be supplemented by mobile warfare. The revolutionary forces would expand their control over the countryside, while the enemy would attempt to safeguard the cities, and the lines of communications the revolutionaries had already seized. The second stage of the war would be particularly long and difficult, according to Mao, but during that stage the balance between the revolutionary and imperialist forces would gradually shift. Political mobilization of the rural masses was paramount in bringing about this shift. This was the prime strategic objective of the revolutionary forces during the first and second stages. Village organizations of all sorts, under party leadership, were to be created to provide soldiers and support the front. As larger and larger guerrilla armies were created they would be hardened by battle against dispersed enemy outposts or by supporting mobile operations against larger enemy forces. Enemy strength would be progressively sapped by this continual attrition and by psychological exhaustion arising from such factors as homesickness and antiwar sentiments. Finally, a crossover point would be reached when the strength of the revolutionary forces exceeded that of the enemy. The war would then enter its third stage of strategic offensive by the revolutionary forces. Mobile war supplemented by positional and guerrilla war would become the dominant tactical form in the third stage. At this point the revolutionary forces would launch a general offensive and capture the large cities and drive the imperialists from the country.[8]

The strategy of Tet thus differed from Mao Zedong's people's war in at least four ways. First, it shifted the focus of revolutionary military struggle from the countryside to the cities well before the third stage. Second, it involved a large-scale strategic offensive by the revolutionary forces before a crossover point had been reached. Third, it prematurely committed the revolutionary forces to positional war. And forth, it exposed the revolutionary infrastructure to an enemy who still enjoyed clear military superiority. In doing this it jeopardized the party's mass base, the single most important condition for revolutionary victory.

Tet departed from the primarily rural-based strategy of people's war. It was an attempt to combine that rural strategy with urban insurrection à la the Bolshevik seizure of power in October 1917. An NLF document of April 1961 explained the weakness of a purely rural strategy:

Due to the non-uniform development of the Revolution in the rural areas, the balance of power between us and the enemy varies from area to area. Consequently farmers do not rise up everywhere at the same moment. Even in those areas where there is a partial uprising and enemy control is broken, this [control] is ended only at the hamlet and village levels. The enemy's higher administrative apparatus remains, and he still has strong armed units and he is still safe in the urban areas. . . . But in the struggle we have many strong points and advantages. . . . The movement toward the General Uprising under the leadership of the Party will grow more fierce and widespread until it finally takes place.[9]

The Tet Offensive also involved a general offensive by the revolutionary forces well prior to the crossover point demarking the second and third stages of people's war. Although the aggressive VC tactics pursued against U.S. forces in 1966 and 1967 inflicted heavy casualties on the enemy, those tactics were also very costly to the North Vietnamese Army (NVA) and VC. Many veteran soldiers and officers were lost. Moreover, the U.S. and South Vietnamese forces had grown steadily in size. The United States had also built a large and elaborate support base in South Vietnam which contributed substantially to its mobility and sustained firepower. The Tet Offensive was an attempt to overcome these difficulties and break the strategic stalemate that had developed on the battlefields of South Vietnam by bringing about a national uprising, thereby gaining a decisive advantage for the revolutionary forces. To achieve this NLF units repeatedly assaulted heavily fortified enemy positions.

Perhaps the most devastating cost of the general uprising of Tet, however, was the exposure of the NLF's clandestine infrastructure. The public activity of previously clandestine cadre greatly facilitated the task of the Phoenix Program then coming on stream.

In its exposé of Chinese-Vietnamese relations released after the 1979 war, Hanoi charged that Beijing urged Vietnam to follow a strategy of "prolonged ambush." The Chinese leaders "refused to help the Vietnamese people build their regular army and only agreed to give Vietnam light weapons and logistical supplies," Hanoi charged. After Beijing failed to prevent the "simultaneous uprising of the South Vietnamese people" [i.e., the resumption of armed struggle in 1959–1960], they said that South Vietnam should conduct only guerrilla warfare, fighting small battles using small units like platoons and companies.[10] The polemic continued:

With the Vietnamese people, the Chinese rulers kept insisting: protracted war, guerrilla warfare, small battles. They help[ed] the Vietnamese people mainly with light weapons, ammunition and logistic supplies. They did not want an early end of the Vietnam war, because they wanted not only to weaken the Vietnamese revolutionary forces, but also to avail the longer the better, of the publicity obtained by "aiding Vietnam" to hold high the banner of "thorough revolution," to muster forces in Asia, Africa and Latin America and to intensify their anti-Soviet campaign.[11]

Again China denied Vietnamese charges. According to Beijing's rebuttal to Hanoi's 1979 white paper, in 1968 Mao recommended to Ho Chi Minh the organization of large formations and the launching of annihilation warfare in South Vietnam. Ho reportedly accepted Mao's recommendations and communicated them to his comrades in Hanoi.[12]

Unfortunately, there is still very little direct evidence regarding the content of CCP-VWP discussions in 1967 about the proposed 1968 offensives. We still do not know what CCP leaders told their VWP comrades during 1967, when critical decisions were being made about the wisdom of a general uprising and a head-on attack on a major marine base. There is, however, some indirect evidence that Chinese leaders objected to those moves. The VWP leader Hoang Van Hoan, who defected to China in 1979, discussed his reservations about Tet in his memoir. Hoan charged VWP Secretary-General Le Duan with seeking a short-term military victory. Le, Hoang charged, "spread among the masses his views that were opposed to President Ho's [teachings that] the struggle may be protracted and arduous." Le Duan taught instead that "we must try to win a decisive victory in a short period of time so as to resolve the issue."[13] Hoan lauded the strength of the Tet Offensive, but went on to note that

The relative strength of ourselves and the enemy being what it was at the time, the enemy would not take his defeat lying down. . . . The U.S. forces and their puppet troops launched violent counter-attacks on places occupied by our army. Our army had to withdraw, suffering heavy loses of men and weapons. Having been reassured that the Liberation Army would not be able to capture all of South Vietnam, the enemy went on with his mopping-up operations, while letting it be known that he wanted to engage in peace negotiations with the Liberation Army in an attempt to put the latter off guard and weaken its will to fight.[14]

It seems unlikely that China's veteran leaders would have opposed the Tet Offensive merely because the strategies implicit in those moves deviated from Mao's teachings. While some of the ideologues influential during the Cultural Revolution may have been inclined toward such a course, the

seasoned leaders of the CCP and the People's Liberation Army (PLA)—
Mao Zedong, Zhou Enlai, and Foreign Minister Chen Yi—would very
probably *not* have taken such a parochial view. One of the central precepts
of Mao's thinking was that each nation must find its own road to revolution. While Mao believed that the CCP's own experience could serve as a
useful reference for parties in other "neocolonial" countries, he also understood that the circumstances of each country were different. Mao had
also been cautioned by his own earlier experience with Comintern efforts
to dictate political-military strategy to the CCP. Finally, Mao and Zhou
were very much aware of traditional Vietnamese suspicions of China, and
on occasion bent over backward to assuage such fears.

More probable grounds for top-level Chinese objections to Tet were (1)
recourse to such a flawed strategy endangered the goals for which the NLF,
the VWP, and China had all jointly struggled—driving the United States
out of South Vietnam, and (2) a shift to larger-unit, more conventional war
was a major shift away from the strategy of carefully camouflaged pseudoinsurgency of the mid-1960s, and as such, threatened to create new tensions in China's relations with the United States.

Regarding the first point, the CCP's own Hundred Regiments Offensive
of 1940 may well have been the relevant "historical lesson" through which
Mao Zedong judged the Tet Offensive. In many ways the Hundred Regiments Offensive was comparable to Tet. Like Tet, it threw almost the entire
armed strength of the CCP in north China into mobile and positional war
against the Japanese and Japanese-puppet forces. The Hundred Regiments
Offensive lasted from July until the end of December 1940 and involved
400,000 CCP-led troops in 115 regiments attacking Japanese-held transportation and communications lines across north China. The campaign inflicted heavy casualties on Japanese and Japanese-puppet forces, but also
meant very heavy losses for Communist armies. Communist-led military
forces fell by a third as a result of the offensive. Moreover, this demonstration of Communist strength was followed by an intense Japanese pacification campaign which cut by half the population in areas controlled by
the CCP. Mao had had grave doubts about the wisdom of the Hundred
Regiments Offensive. It deviated from his doctrine of protracted war and
was launched without his authorization. After 1949 evaluation of the Hundred Regiments Offensive was a controversial issue. Some writers upheld
the contributions of the offensive to the eventual defeat of Japan. Others
stressed the fact that it was not approved by Mao and inflicted heavy costs
on the CCP.[15] We can only guess at Mao Zedong's own view of the similarity between 1940 and 1968. Leaders often draw on their own earlier
experience to judge new and foreign events. Quite possibly he believed that
the Tet Offensive was a costly mistake along the lines of the Hundred
Regiments Offensive.

Mao may have believed that by prematurely shifting to positional and urban warfare, and by endangering the revolution's vital mass base, the VWP had unwittingly made it more likely that they would be compelled to accept an eventual compromise settlement leaving Saigon in control of some part of South Vietnam, with a continuing U.S. presence there. This apprehension, if in fact it existed in Mao's mind, was linked to the question of negotiations, and we shall return to it in our subsequent discussion of peace talks.

If Chinese leaders opposed a major intensification of Hanoi's war effort in 1968, their major objection may not have concerned the urban uprising and the general offensive in the rural areas, but the assault on the U.S. Marine base at Khe Sanh. This was conventional and positional warfare par excellence. It also discarded the hitherto carefully maintained camouflage of pseudoinsurgency at Khe Sanh; and by drastically intensifying the level of conflict throughout the country, the combined offensives of Tet threatened to create new friction between China and the United States. This may well have been the overriding Chinese concern. We must remember that Chinese leaders were very fearful of war with the United States. They were determined not to be cowed by these fears, and insisted on supporting Hanoi and the NLF even though this risked war with the United States. But simultaneously, they maneuvered to avoid such a war. One aspect of Beijing's strategy of risk minimization was keeping wars of national liberation at a subconventional level.

Beijing's desire and efforts to avoid war with the United States in the 1960s must be seen against the backdrop of deteriorating Sino-Soviet relations. A major aspect of the CCP-CPSU (Communist Party of the Soviet Union) debate during the late 1950s and early 1960s was about whether the imperialist countries would attack the socialist countries for supporting wars of national liberation in developing countries. Khrushchev argued that the danger of this was great and, therefore, that the socialist countries should be very cautious in supporting foreign wars of national liberation. This was especially true in the age of thermonuclear weapons and massive retaliation, Khrushchev argued. Mao, on the other hand, maintained that there was not a great danger of imperialist attack on the socialist countries over the latter's support for foreign revolutionary movements—at least so long as the socialist camp was firm and united. The Soviet nuclear umbrella over the socialist camp and the absolute military supremacy of the socialist camp would probably prevent imperialist attacks, Mao argued.

The final collapse of the Sino-Soviet alliance in 1963 eliminated the critical premise upon which Chinese deterrent strategy rested. No longer would the united strength of the socialist camp help deter U.S. attack against China because of Chinese support for the VWP's drive to take over South Vietnam. Beijing now faced the choice of shifting to a more conciliatory, less confrontational policy, or of persisting in its militant approach to the United States and world revolution. Some people within the CCP argued in favor of reducing tension with the United States and reducing support for foreign revolutionary movements. Mao rejected such an approach and directed that China would continue, and even increase, its support for the VWP and the NLF. This was a high-risk policy. Mao recognized the risks, and ordered measures to reduce or manage them. The most important measure was a massive, top secret program to prepare China for war by relocating industry to China's interior. Another measure was to try to keep the fighting in Vietnam from escalating to the full-scale conventional level.

Reliance on a low- to mid-intensity war conducted by subdivisional units had the advantage for China of minimizing links between that war and China. The logistic needs of NLF and NVA forces in South Vietnam were less, and the logistic lines running to and through China were, therefore, less strategically significant. Low- and mid-intensity war also obfuscated the political links to China. The war in the South was, Beijing could and did argue, essentially a revolt of the South Vietnamese people against the United States and its local lackeys. Any help received from North Vietnam or China was, Beijing could argue, of secondary importance. If, on the other hand, the war became a high-intensity, large-unit war, supply depots and lines in China would necessarily play a more important role. It would also become obvious that tanks and heavy artillery were not the weapons of a popular revolt, but the tools of highly trained soldiers supported by the arsenals of China or the Soviet Union. High-intensity, large-unit war was therefore more likely to tempt the United States to take moves which would confront China with the choice of continuing support for Hanoi and risking deeper conflict with the United States, or partial abandonment of Hanoi for the sake of avoiding increased conflict with the U.S.

THE QUESTION OF NEGOTIATIONS WITH THE UNITED STATES

Another issue in dispute between Beijing and Hanoi in early 1968 was at least as important as differences over military strategy—the question of opening negotiations with the United States. The beginning of talks resulted most immediately from Lyndon Johnson's change of heart on the war and his subsequent acceptance of Hanoi's conditions for beginning talks (complete suspension of the bombing of North Vietnam). But the initiation of negotiations was also linked to the dual offensives, Tet and Khe Sanh. Although they could not imagine the exact circumstances, VWP planners clearly hoped that those offensives would create favorable conditions for talks. Beijing disagreed, and argued that since the military situation still favored the United States, so too would the outcome of negotiations. According to Hanoi, during aid talks in August 1969 the Chinese side said, "[Do] you want to continue fighting or to make peace? China must know the answer when considering the question of aid."[16]

The dispute over negotiations with the United States was also tied to the question of relative Soviet and Chinese leverage with Hanoi. International diplomacy was Moscow's forte, while Beijing, isolated as it then was, had little to offer Hanoi in this regard. To the extent that Hanoi relied on international diplomacy to achieve its ends, it would look to Moscow rather than to Beijing. Thus, Moscow repeatedly floated various peace talks schemes.

From 1964 to 1968 Hanoi rejected Soviet proposals for negotiations. It also kept in close touch with Beijing over this issue. According to Hoang Van Hoan, since August 1964 the VWP leadership had discussed the pros and cons of opening talks with the United States. Secretary-General Le Duan generally favored such a course. According to Hoang Van Hoan, in 1964 Le Duan "began to seek Soviet mediation for peace talks with the United States to resolve the South Vietnam issue."[17] Ho Chi Minh was open to the tactical benefits to be derived from such a course, but believed that "in any case, these matters should be discussed carefully with the Chinese comrades." Ho, Hoan said, "attached great importance to the exchange of views with the Chinese comrades." Le Duan cited the Chinese principle of "fighting while talking" to try to convince Ho, but without success. Hoan interpreted the 1968 decision to accept Johnson's offer without securing Ho's prior approval as a virtual coup by Le Duan's pro-Soviet group: "Le Duan deliberately over-stepped his authority, making President Ho a figurehead, avoiding discussion with the Chinese comrades, and taking it on his own to give a reply to Johnson in the hope of making it a fait accompli for President Ho."[18] Le Duan "promptly accepted" the U.S. proposal and dispatched "in a hurry . . . a big delegation for negotiations with the United States in Paris," according to Hoan. He had done this "because he had made an incorrect analysis of the situation and had been impetuous in his action."[19]

Related to the question of initiation of peace talks by Le Duan's pro-Soviet group was the question of China's role in that decision-making process. According to Hoang Van Hoan, the decision to begin negotiations with the United States was made without consulting Beijing. According to Hoan's memoir,

When Premier Zhou Enlai heard the news (about Le Duan's 3 April statement announcing that Hanoi would send a delegation to negotiate with the United States), he went to President Ho, who was recuperating in Beijing, to talk with him about that matter. It turned out that President Ho was totally unaware of Le Duan's statement. Before making decisions on a matter of such importance Le Duan should have gone to Beijing to report to President Ho and exchange views with the Chinese comrades.[20]

The fact that Hanoi made a decision directly affecting North Vietnam's relations with the Soviet Union and the United States without consulting

China deeply troubled Chinese leaders. By 1968 China had invested considerable wealth and prestige, and had taken very considerable national risks in support of Hanoi's national liberation struggle. This, Mao felt, entitled China's opinion to consideration.

According to Chinese polemics in 1968, Beijing believed that Hanoi's agreement to talk with Washington was a tactical mistake. Johnson's purpose in beginning peace talks was "to gain a breathing space on the Vietnam battlefield so as to further expand the war."[21] They believed that the Johnson administration was reeling from serious defeats on the battlefields of South Vietnam and from economic and political crises at home and abroad. It fully intended to further escalate the war, but needed time to regroup its forces. Johnson also hoped to use "peace talks" to manipulate the upcoming presidential elections. "[As] anyone with a discerning eye can see . . . this disgusting performance by Johnson is nothing but the clumsy trick of a bourgeois politician." "Peace talks [the term was always put in quotation marks by Chinese propaganda]," the article said, were "essentially a smoke screen for covering up expansion of the war." The article continued,

Whatever changes [U.S. imperialism] may make, it will never depart from its fundamental purpose, namely to partition Vietnam permanently and occupy south Vietnam for ever. Therefore, the Vietnam question can be solved only by completely defeating the U.S. aggressor on the battlefield and driving it out of south Vietnam.[22]

Hoang Van Hoan also feared that the decision to open negotiations with the United States would lead to a compromise settlement. He explained in his memoir:

At a time when the war was at a stalemate, that is, when our side had not yet gained the upper hand and our opponent had not yet been landed in an utterly passive position, our negotiations with the United States would only result in dividing Vietnam into two parts, the North and the South. Although such a result would have been favorable to us—let's say our side would get Quang Tri and Thua Thien provinces, and even the entire Fifth Joint Defense Zone, and the U.S. side would have only Nam Key under its control—Vietnam would still remain divided, [which] would be tantamount to our recognition of American rule over Nam Ky.[23]

Hoang Van Hoan's objections to opening talks in 1968 were apparently shared by Chinese leaders. According to Hanoi's 1979 exposé, during Sino-Vietnamese discussions during April 1968 of the upcoming negotiations, the Chinese side maintained that "the time has not come and a favorable position has not been secured for Vietnam's entering into negotiations with the United States. We have been making concessions too hastily."[24] The following October, Beijing purportedly told Hanoi that negotiations with the United States were a "mistake." In deciding to hold negotiations with the United States, Vietnam had taken "Soviet advice." Vietnam had to make a choice: "If Vietnam wants to defeat the United States, it should cut off relations with the Soviet Union; if Vietnam wants to reach a compromise with the United States, using Chinese aid for the fight against the Americans with a view to negotiating with them, Chinese aid would then lose all its significance."[25] According to the same source, a week after the preceding comments were made, Chinese Foreign Minister Chen Yi told a Vietnamese representative,

Your agreement to hold four-party negotiations will help Johnson and Humphrey to win the elections, leave the South Vietnamese people under the domination of the U.S. imperialists, and their puppet, South Vietnam, will not be liberated and its people may suffer still greater losses. So is there anything for our two Parties and states to talk about?[26]

Finally, the peace talks question was linked to Soviet-American relations. Moscow, like Beijing, was concerned that its support of Hanoi's cause would lead to a further deterioration of relations with the United States. Like Beijing, Moscow sought to avoid such a consequence, even while persisting in its support for Hanoi. Soviet efforts to manage this contradiction focused, at this juncture, on the initiation of U.S.–North Vietnamese peace talks.

Apprehension about the impact of the Vietnam peace talks on Soviet-U.S. relations may have been Mao and Zhou's most basic concern. They believed that Moscow and Washington were engaging in steadily deeper "collusion" against China, and feared that Soviet-American cooperation in "solving" the Vietnam War might move those powers dangerously further along this path. In its 1965 polemic explaining its rejection of "united action" with Moscow in support of Hanoi, for example, Beijing explained that Moscow was bent on "collusion" with U.S. imperialism for world domination, and that, under such circumstances, to "unite" with Moscow would only lead to Soviet sabotage and betrayal of the world revolution:

Some people ask, why is it that the Marxist-Leninists and the revolutionary people cannot take united action with the new leaders of the CPSU, yet can unite with personages from the upper strata in the nationalist countries, and strive for united action with them in the anti-imperialist struggle, and can even exploit the contradictions among the imperialist countries in the struggle against the United States? The reason is that in the contemporary world opposition to or alliance with U.S. imperialism constitutes the hallmark for deciding whether or not a political force can be included in the united front against the United States. . . . The crux of the matter is that, so far from opposing U.S. imperialism, the new leaders of the CPSU are allying themselves and collaborating with it to dominate the world. . . . The new leaders of the CPSU are . . . pulling the Vietnam question into the orbit of Soviet-U.S. collaboration. . . . The U.S. imperialists appreciate the trick being played by the leaders of the CPSU. They know full well that it is to their advantage for the new leaders of the CPSU to get involved in the Viet Nam question. . . . The U.S. authorities have made it clear that Soviet involvement in the Viet Nam question is preferable to Soviet non-involvement.[27]

Support for a negotiated settlement of the Vietnam conflict, and diplomatic efforts in that direction, were a primary body of evidence pointed to by Beijing as proof of Soviet betrayal of revolutionary, anti-U.S. struggles. When Premier Alexei Kosygin visited Beijing in February 1965 during a stopover on his way to Hanoi, he exchanged views with Chinese leaders about the Vietnam situation, stressing "the need to help the United States 'find a way out of Vietnam.' "[28]

According to Beijing's 1965 polemic, "This view was firmly rebutted by the Chinese leaders. We expressed the hope that the new leaders of the CPSU would support the struggle of the Vietnamese people and not make a deal with the United States on the question of Vietnam." Although Kosygin agreed with Chinese views during the February 1965 stopover in Beijing, Soviet diplomacy soon took another direction, according to Beijing's account. After Kosygin's return to Moscow, the Soviet government officially proposed to Vietnam and China convocation of a new international conference on Indochina without prior conditions. This fit with the U.S. call for "unconditional negotiations" which had already been rejected by Hanoi. After Johnson's fraud of "unconditional discussions" met with a "stern rebuff" from the North Vietnamese government,

The new leaders of the Soviet Union then began publicly to insinuate that negotiations could be held if only the United States stopped its bombing of North Vietnam. They engaged in vigorous activities in the international field with a view to putting this project into effect. In communications to certain fraternal Parties, they said explicitly that they favored negotiations with the United States on condition it stopped bombing North Vietnam. . . . In a nutshell, their purpose is to help the United States to bring about "peace talks" by deception, "peace talks" which could go on indefinitely and also allow the United States to keep its hands on South Vietnam indefinitely.[29]

Chinese leaders believed that the United States and the Soviet Union were entering into steadily deeper collusion against China and other revolutionary Asian peoples. Bringing about a "peaceful," "political" settlement of the Vietnam War was a major focus of this deepening superpower collusion. Moscow was "the principal 'peace talks' broker for U.S. imperialism and the latter's leading "accomplice" in arranging the U.S.–North Vietnamese peace talks," declared a Chinese polemic issued just before Johnson's speech maintained.

As soon as Johnson had broached the idea of "peace talks" in September 1967, "The Brezhnev-Kosygin clique went a step further in making more deals with U.S. imperialism on international issues. . . . It did its best to create a favorable atmosphere for U.S.-Soviet 'co-operation' on the Vietnam question, and encouraged Washington to go ahead more boldly with its war blackmail and 'peace talks' schemes in Vietnam." Moscow used its influence in various quarters, including "pressuring" and "cajoling" Hanoi, to open the way to a "political solution" in Vietnam. Washington and Moscow were also conniving to use the United Nations as a forum for their "plots" against the Vietnamese revolution. During the last quarter of 1967, "U.S. imperialism and Soviet revisionism worked in close collaboration, and on many occasions tried to get the United Nations and its Security Council to intervene in the Vietnam question." Moscow had let it be known that it "would not oppose the discussion of the Vietnam question in the Security Council."[30]

What made the peace talks especially dangerous, in Beijing's eyes, was that they pointed in the direction of greater Soviet and American cooperation in solving Asian problems. The possibility of continued division of Vietnam, or of southern Vietnam, was undesirable from Beijing's point of view, but it was, after all, something that impinged most directly on Vietnamese interests. If the leadership of the Vietnamese revolution, the VWP, decided on policies which risked leading to such a solution, that was perhaps unfortunate, but it was an outcome that only indirectly effected vital Chinese interests. The question of Soviet-American cooperation in Asia, to deal with mutually recognized Asian problems, was different. Such "superpower collusion," as Beijing would start calling it in 1971, threatened a whole range of vital Chinese interests, from deterring superpower attack to winning China's seat in the United Nations.

China was then in a state of international diplomatic isolation. It probably had little intelligence about the content of Soviet-American discussions of Vietnam, and could imagine the worst. It had even fewer diplomatic contacts and assets which it might use to block schemes it deemed antithetical to its interests. Most importantly, it saw Moscow and America inching toward an understanding about how to deal with revolutionary Asian countries. Mao Zedong and Zhou Enlai undoubtedly worried that the China problem might be the next item on the agenda of Soviet-American "collusion" in Asia.

EXPLAINING CHINA'S DISTANCING OF ITSELF FROM VIETNAM

Most broadly, what China sought in Indochina was to expel Western influence from that region and restore the special relation between that region and China that existed prior to the French intrusion in the 1880s. French imperialism tore Vietnam away from its special relation with China in 1885. Then the American imperialists stepped into France's shoes. China fought from 1949 to 1973 to drive the Western powers out of Indochina. China's leaders hoped that once those powers were gone a traditional benevolent, protective relationship would be established between China and the Indochinese countries. Mao and Zhou thought not in terms of the traditional pre-1885 tributary relationship that had existed between China and Vietnam, but in terms of "proletarian internationalism," that is, of close fraternal solidarity between two socialist allies. But in spite of the more modern forms, China's leaders still sought close and friendly relations between China and Vietnam, with Vietnam's leaders grateful for China's past support and protection, and desirous of similar support and protection in the future, and with the European and American powers driven far from the scene. Both Hanoi's shift to large-scale military offensives and its initiation of peace talks with the United States seemed to threaten these long-term objectives.

The expulsion of the United States from South Vietnam would also serve other Chinese goals. In terms of national security, Mao Zedong and Zhou Enlai wanted to ease the U.S. military threat to China by pushing U.S. forces further away from its southern borders. A U.S. defeat in Vietnam would also weaken the structure of containment in Asia, possibly allowing China to break out of the diplomatic and political isolation imposed on it by Washington since 1950. In ideological terms, Vietnam was the test case of wars of national liberation, support for which by the socialist camp was debated so intensely by the CCP and the CPSU in the early and mid-1960s. Victory in Vietnam's war of national liberation would demonstrate the "correctness" of the CCP's position. Defeat or a merely partial victory for Vietnam's war of national liberation would demonstrate the "incorrectness" of China's view (though not necessarily the correctness of the Soviet view). The question of "correctness" of ideological line was, in turn, linked to the relative stature and role of Beijing and Moscow in the international revolutionary movement. In pursuit of these important objectives, China's leaders had expended great wealth and energy. Now they saw them endangered by the initiation of negotiations between Hanoi and Washington.

These considerations fit together with another set of concerns which, to some degree, contradicted (at least in a logical sense) the desire to see the United States leave Indochina. The second set of Chinese concerns had to do with a fear of Soviet-American "collusion" over the Vietnam question. From 1963 to 1969 Mao Zedong was convinced that the United States and the U.S.S.R. were working together to jointly rule the world. The two superpowers were increasingly pursuing parallel policies vis-à-vis China. But Mao also realized that superpower "collusion" against China could go a lot further. This was his strategic nightmare. If the two superpowers worked together to find a mutually acceptable solution to the Vietnam question—which is what the Soviet-sponsored initiation of the Vietnam talks seemed to imply—they were more likely to work together to tackle other tough Asian problems. It was not until 1969 and 1971 that Moscow solicited American approval of a preemptive strike against Chinese nuclear facilities, and not until 1972 that Brezhnev hinted at a swap of suspension of Soviet aid to Hanoi for American approval of Soviet preemption of China's nuclear program, but Mao was probably already imagining such possible superpower partnerships. China, in its isolated international situation, would have little diplomatic leverage to block any resultant projects which might be directed against it.[31]

Partial disengagement from Vietnam also increased China's ability to cope with this deepening superpower "collusion." In Chinese vernacular, this was known as "grasping the contradictions" between the superpowers. Continuing heavy Chinese engagement as the Vietnam War entered a new, more conventional stage would make it difficult for Beijing to improve relations with Washington in order to thwart Moscow's anti-Chinese schemes. Continued deep Chinese involvement might also facilitate Soviet schemes to maneuver the United States into support of various anti-China projects. Partial disengagement, on the other hand, would lessen the likelihood that China would have to face the mounting threat from the north while simultaneously involved in a military confrontation with the United States to the south. Partial disengagement would also clear the way for Chinese efforts to maneuver the United States into opposition to Moscow's anti-China schemes. In a way, China's withdrawal of its forces from North Vietnam in 1968–1970 was a counterpart of the U.S. withdrawal from South Vietnam during 1969–1973. Both helped open the door to Sino-American rapprochement.

Mao Zedong and Zhou Enlai decided to partially disengage China from Vietnam in 1968 because they believed that China was loosing control over events there in an international situation that was increasingly threatening for China. The VWP's decisions to launch large offensives in early 1968 went against Chinese advice and raised the war to a new level of intensity and transparency. Likewise, the opening of negotiations with the United States went against Beijing's advice and was made without prior consultation with Beijing. Under such circumstances, continued deep involvement in Vietnam meant assuming substantially higher risks in a situation over which China had less control. Such a course would not have been prudent.

NOTES

1. Ministry of Foreign Affairs, Socialist Republic of Vietnam, *The Truth about Vietnam-China Relations over the Last Thirty Years,* 1979, p. 37 [hereafter *The Truth about Vietnam-China Relations*].

2. "Jishi gongchuang you shi chouxing" [Not Only an Affidavit, but Also Evil Behavior], *Renmin Ribao* [People's Daily], November 15, 1979, p. 1 [hereafter "Not Only an Affidavit"].

3. "Peking Reports Vietnam, 1965–1969," *China News Analysis,* no. 780, October 31, 1969, pp. 1–7.

4. "Not Only an Affidavit," p. 1.

5. Ibid. Also, "Yuenan kangfa, kangmei duocheng shiqi de zhongyue guanxi" [Sino-Vietnamese Relations during the Period of Vietnam's Anti-French, Anti-American Struggles], *Renmin Ribao,* November 21, 1979, pp. 1, 4.

6. William J. Duiker, *The Communist Road to Power in Vietnam* (Boulder, Colo. Westview Press, 1981), pp. 263–264.

7. Ibid., p. 264.

8. Mao Zedong, "On Protracted War," in *Selected Works of Mao Tse-tung,* Vol. 2 (Beijing: Foreign Language Press, 1967), pp. 136–141.

9. Douglas Pike, *Viet Cong: The Organization and Techniques of the National Liberation Front of South Vietnam* (Cambridge, Mass.: MIT Press, 1968), p. 77.

10. *The Truth about Vietnam-China Relations,* p. 28.

11. Ibid., p. 33.

12. "Not Only an Affidavit," p. 1.

13. Hoang Van Hoan, *A Drop in the Ocean* (Beijing: Foreign Languages Press, 1988), p. 331 [hereafter *A Drop in the Ocean*].

14. Ibid., p. 332.

15. Suo Shihui, "Bai tuan dazhan ying shongfen kending" [The Hundred Regiments Offensive Should be Substantially Upheld], in Zhu Chenya, ed., *Zhonggong dangshi yanjiu lunwenxuan* [Selection of Research Essays on CCP History] (Changsha: Hunan Renmin Chubanshe, 1984), pp. 147–148. For the opposing view see Peng Dehuai, *Peng Dehuai zishu* [Peng DeHuai Remembers] (Beijing: Renmin Chubanshe, 1981), pp. 226–236.

16. *The Truth about Vietnam-China Relations,* p. 37.

17. Hoang Van Hoan, *A Drop in the Ocean,* p. 331.

18. Ibid., p. 333.

19. Ibid., p. 336.

20. Ibid., p. 332.

21. "U.S. Imperialist Chieftain Johnson Tries New Fraud—'Partially Stopping Bombing' to Induce 'Peace Talks,' " *Peking Review,* April 12, 1968, pp. 14–15 [hereafter "U.S. Imperialist Chieftain Johnson"]. Also see "Murderous Intent Revealed Before the Scheme Is Fully Unfolded," *Peking Review,* April 19, 1968, p. 12.

22. "U.S. Imperialist Chieftain Johnson," p. 15.

23. Hoang Van Hoan, *A Drop in the Ocean,* p. 331. The particular geographic division of South Vietnam alluded to by Hoan can be found in his book mentioned above.

24. *The Truth about Vietnam-China Relations,* p. 36.

25. Ibid., p. 37.

26. Ibid.

27. *Refutation of the New Leaders of the CPSU on "United Action"* (Beijing: Foreign Languages Press, 1965), pp. 9, 14.

28. Ibid., p. 17.

29. Ibid., p. 18.

SINO-VIETNAMESE RELATIONS

30. "Soviet Revisionists Stop at Nothing to Salvage U.S. Imperialist Aggression against Vietnam," *Peking Review,* March 22, 1968, pp. 11–13.

31. For an analysis of these issues see John W. Garver, *Foreign Relations of the People's Republic of China* (Englewood Cliffs, N.J.: Prentice-Hall, 1993), pp. 63–65, 74–83, 310–311.

4

The NLF and the Tet Offensive

Robert Brigham

For over two decades, historians have debated the outcome and significance of the Tet Offensive.[1] Most conclude that the Communists incurred heavy losses and that Tet represented a "military defeat for the enemy."[2] Others argue that Tet was a costly victory for the United States and the Saigon government because the Communists came away with an "overwhelming psychological and hence political victory."[3] Political and diplomatic historians have studied the impact of the Communist attacks on decision making in Washington.[4] Vietnamese writers such as Tran Van Tra believe that Tet changed the character and nature of the southern revolution forever.[5] In all these studies, the Tet Offensive is the catalyst for events that follow.

This study examines the Tet Offensive as the end product of long-standing internal divisions within the Lao Dong, Vietnam's Communist party. After years of bitter disputes over war tactics and negotiating strategy, northern and southern Communists temporarily put their differences aside for the revolution's "great leap forward."[6] Although divisions within the party would resurface shortly after Tet, the offensive can be seen as the culmination of months of skillful negotiations between the Lao Dong's Political Bureau and the southern Communists who comprised the National Front for the Liberation of South Vietnam (NLF). Northern party leaders convinced southern Communists that the Political Bureau would be more attentive to southern needs and that the South would play a significant role in the new strategy line planned for 1968. As a result, the intraparty conflict was resolved on the eve of the Tet Offensive and relations between northern and southern Communists were at their best.

Differences within the Lao Dong had surfaced as early as Vietnam's 1954 partition at the seventeenth parallel, but grew especially intense with U.S.

military intervention in the three years preceding the Tet Offensive. In February 1965, the Johnson administration approved the strategic bombing of the North to save the Saigon regime. NLF attacks against U.S. Army installations at Pleiku and Qui Nhon convinced the president that something had to be done to stop the infiltration of men and supplies. It was impossible, Johnson concluded, to build a stable and democratic government in Saigon while Hanoi and its Communist supporters waged a war of aggression. Accordingly, Johnson ordered retaliatory attacks on northern targets that paved the way for Operation Rolling Thunder, the sustained bombing policy that many of his advisors had long advocated.[7] The expanded air war also changed the scope of U.S. military requirements on the ground. In late February, General William Westmoreland, the commanding officer of the U.S. Military Assistance Command–Vietnam (MACV), requested two marine battalions to protect the air base at Danang from NLF reprisal attacks. Johnson approved Westmoreland's request and on March 8, 1965, the first American troops arrived in Vietnam. American intervention caused considerable consternation in Hanoi, the capital city of the Democratic Republic of Vietnam (DRV). Since the 1954 partition, the party had adopted twin revolutionary goals: developing socialism in the North and carrying out the national liberation war in the South.[8] Increased American bombings of northern targets threatened socialist construction, and as a result, several northern Lao Dong leaders called for negotiations to limit the war and save nascent industries.[9] Southern Communists, on the other hand, argued that negotiations with the United States while Americans were still on the southern battlefield was tantamount to surrender.[10] Instead, they favored a decisive battlefield victory that would force the United States to commit to a withdrawal before negotiations got under way.

In late May 1965, the Johnson administration launched its first official bombing pause to explore with Hanoi the meaning of its four-point peace plan announced by DRV Premier Pham Van Dong in April and see if the Communists had any interest in negotiations.[11] Over the next several months, representatives from Hanoi and Washington met secretly to discuss various proposals to limit the war.[12] When word of the secret talks reached NLF officials, they complained bitterly to Hanoi.[13] On August 4, the Front's Central Committee issued a statement assuring the Johnson administration "that ending the bombing of the north did not change conditions in the south."[14]

For the next several months, "hawks" and "doves" within the Lao Dong argued over negotiations. Three powerful southerners, Le Duan, the party's secretary-general, Deputy Premier Pham Hung, and Nguyen Chi Thanh, director of COSVN (Central Office of South Vietnam—the party's southern office), led the call for an immediate end to the secret Paris talks in favor of a decisive military victory in the South.[15] In a *Nhan Dan* essay, General

Van Tien Dung, second in command only to General Vo Nguyen Giap, added his voice to those who condemned negotiations.[16] Political Bureau member Le Duc Tho complained about a small number of cadres who had developed erroneous thoughts and views "by calling for negotiations to limit the war."[17] Tho wrote that those favoring discussions with the United States "fail to realize clearly the deceptive peace negotiation plot of the enemy."[18] Still, those favoring negotiations had the majority in the party's Political Bureau, and a number of Central Committee members, led by Truong Chinh, argued that an aggressive and offensive war in the South would deplete northern resources and add to the prospects of further American bombing raids north of the seventeenth parallel.[19]

Deteriorating relations between the Soviet Union and the People's Republic of China exacerbated the tension within the Lao Dong. A split between China and the Soviet Union had developed in 1958 when Beijing accused Moscow of dangerous revisionism. Soviet Premier Nikita Khrushchev had denounced Stalin and called on the United States to hold a summit meeting with Moscow "to come to terms on major East-West issues."[20] Khrushchev was particularly interested in reducing the dangers involved in nuclear armaments. China, on the other hand, had seen the Soviets' nuclear superiority as an advantage for all Communist nations and used the strength of the united socialist bloc in 1959 to launch incursions into Tibet and India. Khrushchev, recently returned from the United States and a meeting with President Dwight Eisenhower, condemned Beijing's aggressive actions, stating that socialist countries should not test the stability of the capitalists countries by force.[21]

In 1960, at a meeting of Warsaw Pact countries in Moscow, the Soviets pushed through a declaration that announced that "the world has now entered on a period of negotiations about the settlement of the main international issues in dispute with the aim of establishing a lasting peace, while advocates of cold war are sustaining a defeat."[22] Beijing countered, however, claiming that the world was divided into two camps—socialist and capitalist—and that there could be no collaboration and ultimately no compromise. Once the war in Vietnam heated up, China charged that the Soviet Union had abandoned wars for national liberation.[23] By 1966, the diplomatic break was complete.

Moscow's newfound pragmatism led it to play a role in negotiations to limit the war in Vietnam. According to recently released Soviet documents and interviews with Vietnamese policy makers, Moscow presided over many of the secret initiatives from beginning to end.[24] The Soviets desired a negotiated settlement to the war to solve their diplomatic dilemma. If they acted too strongly in Vietnam, they faced a Cubanlike showdown with the United States. If, on the other hand, they moderated their Vietnam policy, they risked loss of prestige among the radical Communists. Soviet strategy in Vietnam therefore hinged on the twin goals of decreasing tension with the United States and limiting China's influence in the region.

Hanoi's move toward Moscow was subtle. For years, the Lao Dong had skillfully managed to avoid taking sides in the Sino-Soviet dispute and had successfully played one against the other to secure increased aid.[25] By the summer of 1966, however, the Political Bureau in Hanoi became convinced that it needed the Soviets' more sophisticated antiaircraft weapons to properly defend the North. Several Lao Dong leaders, including Truong Chinh and Vo Nguyen Giap, also argued that the offensive strategy in the South was going badly.[26] These factors, combined with Beijing's less than cooperative attitude toward Soviet arms shipments passing through China, convinced many powerful Lao Dong officials to accept Moscow's policy line.

In the past, the Lao Dong had boasted, "We use Moscow's technology and Peking's strategy."[27] By the fall of 1966, however, Hanoi had downplayed the significance of Mao's doctrine of people's war. In an essay written for *Hoc Tap,* the party's theoretical journal, Brigadier General Hoang Minh Thao explained that "the people's war outlook of our party is a new, creative development of the Marxist-Leninist ideas of revolutionary violence and revolutionary war."[28] In September, *Hoc Tap* editorialized that the Vietnamese struggle was unique in the history of liberation movements and was based on their past experiences with foreign invaders.[29] Le Duan, a southerner whose position was never static, argued in December that the Vietnamese revolution could never be led by the peasant class, a position quite different from that advocated in Communist China.[30] The Lao Dong also attacked China's Cultural Revolution by chiding national leaders, such as Mao, who had become deified "to the detriment of close Party relations with the masses."[31]

As Hanoi moved closer to Moscow and its pronegotiations strategy, the NLF began a slow but steady course toward China. In 1966, southern Communists learned of several secret contacts between northern leaders and the West and feared that the "doves" were gaining influence within the party. Indeed, American attacks on petroleum, oil, and lubrication supplies (POL) in the Hanoi-Haiphong area in March 1966, as well as raids against transportation lines connecting the two cities with the Chinese border, had prompted a renewed interest in negotiations among a significant number of Lao Dong officials.[32] From March until June, DRV Premier Pham Van Dong met secretly with the Canadian Chester A. Ronning to discuss a mutual de-escalation and a bombing pause.[33] Although the talks settled little, NLF leaders worried that the discussions with Ronning threatened the southern revolution. Within NLF circles renegade officials began to talk of a separate policy line for the first time.[34] According to several southern sources, there was a small but powerful group of NLF military and political leaders who believed that the Front could develop an independent battlefield policy with China's aid.[35] These officials argued that

Hanoi's more moderate, pro-Soviet stance endangered the future of the southern movement and that negotiations might leave Vietnam divided once more. They promoted a pro-Beijing stance with its reliance on a total battlefield victory to counteract northern actions.

Support for this position intensified when southern officials learned of yet another secret contact between northern leaders and the United States. In June 1966, Ho Chi Minh and Pham Van Dong met with Januscz Lewandowski, Poland's representative to the International Control Commission, to express the DRV's willingness to accept a political compromise.[36] The Front learned of the contact through its representatives who lived in Hanoi permanently and who had regular contact with the Lao Dong's Central Committee.[37] Apparently, Dong informed Lewandowski that the Lao Dong no longer demanded that the NLF be the sole representative of the peoples of South Vietnam, and said that the Front needed only to "take part" in the negotiations. The only precondition for negotiations, according to Dong, was a suspension of the bombing. Dong also stated that Hanoi would not require the immediate reunification of Vietnam nor would it insist that the South become a socialist state. He concluded by stating that the Lao Dong expected an American withdrawal to take some time to arrange.[38]

Although these talks eventually ended with no meaningful outcome, secret discussions between the United States and Hanoi intensified the intraparty rivalry between northern and southern Communists. As a result, the NLF prepared to launch its first "independent" foreign policy line based on the recommendation of a handful of disgruntled southerners. Beginning in July 1966, the NLF reinvented its ideological roots and manipulated its public image to enter Beijing's radical Communist camp. The Front sent several delegates to China, all to publicly reject Soviet-style revisionism in favor of a military victory through the strategy of people's war.[39] The Front's move toward China reflected its fear that Hanoi would negotiate an unacceptable peace to limit the war to the South. The NLF's diplomatic overture was the first attempt by southerners to express an independent policy line.

It would also be its last. Unlike earlier conflicts within the Lao Dong, Hanoi handled the NLF's pro-China policy course and the debate within the party with considerable finesse. Several Lao Dong officials convinced the Front that its association with China threatened a new revolutionary strategy in Vietnam, one that most southerners could support. Through careful political negotiations, Hanoi reasserted its control over the southern revolution and persuaded many NLF officials that the struggle had taken a positive course. As in the deliberations within the Lao Dong that had preceded the creation of the Front, party officials understood that without a commitment to revolutionary violence in the South, Hanoi risked losing control of the southern cadres. In early October 1967, the Lao Dong met with several high-ranking NLF officials and convinced them that the war had entered a new phase that required southerners to "hold firm their bronze fortress."[40] Party leaders explained that the new revolutionary path recognized distinctions in local conditions and followed more closely the needs of southerners. One NLF official later commented that "Hanoi finally understood that our problems were different than theirs . . . that we had to increase armed violence in order to bring down the Saigon regime."[41]

The Lao Dong campaign to reassert its control over the southern revolution begin in earnest in October 1967 when General Vo Nguyen Giap met with the new leaders of COSVN to explain a shift in strategy.[42] Since Nguyen Chi Thanh's death in June, Giap had assumed greater control over military events in the South. His ascendancy to supreme military power meant that he would direct the party's new policy line. The Lao Dong had adopted a bold plan to force the United States to the bargaining table through a combination of protracted war of attrition and morale-shattering attacks on southern urban centers. The centerpiece of this strategy was a projected three-phase offensive in South Vietnam. The Lao Dong's Central Committee reasoned that widespread attacks against southern urban centers would compel the United States to pull back most of its firepower to defend southern cities and thereby de-escalate the war against the North by necessity.[43] The offensive would show the Americans that they had two alternatives: to step up the war substantially, which would be difficult in an election year, or go to the negotiating table. In either case, the Lao Dong was committed to a protracted war until the United States withdrew from Vietnam under terms favorable to it.

Giap met repeatedly with the new leadership of COSVN in the fall of 1967 to explain the new policy line and convince the southerners that Hanoi was committed to the southern battlefield. Giap explained that the Tet strategy was sympathetic to southern needs and conditions. The Lao Dong's Political Bureau was sensitive, and the new strategy used the military struggle to achieve political and diplomatic objectives. Giap had an ally in Pham Hung, the new COSVN director. Both stressed the importance of Hanoi's shift and urged southerners to support the new strategy.

Even though some NLF members privately criticized Hanoi's continued reliance on a protracted war strategy instead of a decisive military victory, by early November the Front had been convinced of the efficacy of the Lao Dong's long-term strategy of *vua danh, vua dam* (fighting while negotiating)[44] As one NLF member later commented, "The Party's new strategy gave the south what we wanted, the right to determine the political future of the south as equal participants."[45] Tuyet Thi Vanh reasoned that a successful offensive would force the United States into negotiations, and that at this point the Front would be recognized by all sides as a political entity with a significant role to play in the settlement. Furthermore, she argued convincingly, the majority of military commanders in the South during the entire war were southerners, and southerners would provide the bulk of the forces for the planned offensive. In Vanh's and most southerners' minds, these factors would undoubtedly give the NLF greater influence within the party over affairs in South Vietnam.[46] The Lao Dong's protracted war strategy was therefore acceptable.

Once it had agreed to the correctness of the party's plan, and had rejected its close relationship with the Communist China, the Front played an integral part in setting the diplomatic stage for the offensives. On November 17, 1967, it announced cease-fires for three days each at Christmas and the Western New Year. These short truces would be followed by a seven-day respite at the Vietnamese New Year. Although the Front had always called a holiday truce, this year's was special because it represented, for the first time in several years, a practical and theoretical compact between northerners and southerners. This newfound harmony was underscored several weeks later when DRV Foreign Minister Nguyen Duy Trinh announced the first major negotiating change for Vietnam by declaring that "when the bombing is stopped unconditionally, talks will begin."[47] In the past, such a comment would have been followed by an NLF diplomatic initiative to assert the Front's "independence" and a public statement by a diplomat claiming that an end to the bombing in the North changed nothing in the South. The fact that NLF diplomats announced for the first time that "the Front supports negotiations with the United States once the bombing is stopped unconditionally" illustrates the unusual party concord.[48] It also represents the first volley of the Tet Offensive.

The relationship between the NLF and Hanoi on the eve of the Tet Offensive therefore appears to have been close and warm. After several years of diplomatic conflict, the Front had accepted the party's overall international strategy and had agreed to become an integral part of the general offensives. No one knows what might have happened had the Front continued its flirtations with China. What is clear is that northern Communists, especially "doves," understood that southerners could not be taken for granted and that the revolution needed their full cooperation and participation. The Tet Offensive opened a new revolutionary phase, but it also brought northern and southern Communists back together after years of estrangement.

NOTES

I would like to thank George C. Herring for his constant support and comments on this chapter.

1. George C. Herring, *America's Longest War: The United States and Vietnam, 1950–1975*, 2d edition (New York: Alfred A. Knopf, 1986) [hereafter *America's Longest War*]; William S. Turley, *The Second Indochina War: A Short Political*

and Military History, 1954–1975 (Boulder, Colo.: Westview Press, 1986); Gabriel Kolko, *Anatomy of a War: Vietnam, the United States, and the Modern Historical Experience* (New York: Pantheon, 1985); Marilyn B. Young, *The Vietnam Wars, 1945–1990* (New York: HarperCollins, 1991).

2. Don Oberdorfer, *Tet!* (Garden City, N.Y.: Doubleday, 1973), p. 34.

3. Bernard Brodie, "The Tet Offensive," in Noble Frankland and Christopher Dowling, eds., *Decisive Battles of the Twentieth Century* (London: Oxford University Press, 1976), p. 321.

4. Herbert Schandler, *The Unmaking of the President: Lyndon Johnson and Vietnam* (Princeton, N.J.: Princeton University Press, 1977); Larry Berman, *Lyndon Johnson's War* (New York: Norton, 1989); George C. Herring, *LBJ and Vietnam: A Different Kind of War* (Austin: University of Texas Press, 1994).

5. Tran Van Tra, *Ket Thuc Cuoc Chien Tranh 30 Nam* [History of the Bulwark B2-Theatre: Concluding the 30-Years War], Volume 5 (Ho Chi Minh City: Van Nghe, 1982).

6. *Vietnam Courier,* October 9, 1967.

7. Chester Cooper Oral History Interview, Lyndon Baines Johnson Presidential Library, Austin, Texas, 10.

8. Le Duan, *On Some Present International Problems,* 2d edition (Hanoi: Foreign Languages Publishing House, 1964).

9. *Nhan Dan,* August 5, 1965; January 17, 1966; February 3, 1966.

10. Liberation Radio, August 4, 1965, 1400 GMT.

11. George C. Herring, *The Secret Diplomacy of the Vietnam War: The Negotiating Volumes of the Pentagon Papers* (Austin: University of Texas Press, 1983), p. 110 [hereafter *Negotiating Volumes*].

12. *Chu Tich Ho Chi Minh Voi Cong Tac Ngoai Giao* [President Ho Chi Minh and the Diplomatic Works] (Hanoi: Nha Xuat Ban Su That, 1990), pp. 199–212.

13. Author interview with Tran Van Do, former NLF official whose name has been changed at his request, July 2, 1992, Hanoi, Vietnam.

14. Liberation Radio, August 4, 1965, 1400 GMT.

15. Le Duan, *Thu Vao Nam* [Letters to the South] (Hanoi: Nha Xuat Ban Su That, 1986), pp. 97–162; *Nhan Dan,* August 6, 1965.

16. Ibid.

17. *Hoc Tap,* February 1965.

18. Ibid.

19. *Hoc Tao,* February 1966; *Nhan Dan,* January 17, 1966; *New York Times,* February 13, 1966.

20. David Floyd, *Mao against Khrushchev: A Short History of the Sino-Soviet Conflict* (New York: Praeger, 1963), p. 68.

21. Ibid., p. 75.

22. As reported in *Nhan Dan,* December 2, 1960.

23. Donald Zagoria, *Vietnam Triangle: Moscow, Peking, Hanoi* (New York: Pegasus, 1967), p. 58.

24. Author interview with Ilya Giaduc, Soviet foreign policy expert, Woodrow Wilson International Center for Scholars, June 16, 1993, Washington, D.C.; author interview with Tran Van Do (name has been changed), former NLF official, July 12, 1989, Ho Chi Minh City, Vietnam.

25. Herring, *America's Longest War,* p. 148.

26. Thomas Latimer, "Hanoi's Leaders and Their South Vietnam Policies, 1954–1968," Ph.D. dissertation, Georgetown University, 1972.

27. Author interview with Tran Huu Dinh, historian, July 8, 1992, Hanoi, Vietnam.

28. *Hoc Tap,* December 1966.

29. *Hoc Tap,* September 1966.

30. *Hoc Tap,* May 1967. This article was actually written in December and broadcast over Radio Hanoi that same month.

31. *Hoc Tap,* May 1967; Melvin Gurtov, *Hanoi on War and Peace* (Santa Monica, Calif.: The Rand Corporation, 1967), p. 23.

32. *The Pentagon Papers: The Defense Department History of the United States. Decisionmaking on Vietnam,* Senator Gravel edition, Volume 4 (Boston: Beacon Press 1971), pp. 74–77; Wallace Thies, *When Governments Collide: Coercion and Diplomacy in the Vietnam Conflict, 1964–1968* (Berkeley: University of California Press, 1980), pp. 336, 341; Janos Radvanyi, *Delusions and Reality: Gambits, Hoaxes, and Diplomatic One-Upmanship in Viet Nam* (South Bend, Ind.: Gateway Editions, 1978), pp. 192–201; David Kraslow and Stuart Loory, *The Secret Search for Peace in Vietnam* (New York: Random House, 1968), pp. 3–88; Andrew Baggs, "Bombing, Bargaining, and Limited War: North Viet Nam, 1965–1968," Ph.D. dissertation, University of North Carolina, 1972.

33. Luu Van Loi and Nguyen Anh Vu, *Tieo Xuc Bi Mat Viet Nam-Hoa Ku Truoc Hoi Nghi Pa-ri* [Secret Negotiations between Vietnam and the United States before the Paris Meetings] (Hanoi: Vien Quan He Quoc Te, 1990), pp. 147–148 [hereafter *Tieo Xuc Bi Mat Viet Nam*]; Herring, *Negotiating Volumes,* p. 186.

34. Author interview with Tuyet Thi Vanh, former NLF official whose named has been changed at her request, July 12, 1989, Ho Chi Minh City, Vietnam [hereafter Tuyet Interview].

35. Douglas Pike Collection, NLF Documents, Document Number 002160, Indochina Archive, University of California at Berkeley; Radio Peking, July 14, 1966, 1600 GMT.

36. Luu Van Loi and Nguyen Anh Vu, *Tieo Xuc Bi Mat Viet Nam,* pp. 161–163; Herring, *Negotiating Volumes,* p. 237.

37. Tuyet Interview.

38. Herring, *Negotiating Volumes,* pp. 238–239.

39. "South Vietnam People's Delegation Welcomed in Kwangchow," Douglas Pike Collection, NLF Documents, Document Number 002722, Indochina Archive, University of California at Berkeley.

40. Author interview with Tranh Quynh Cu, historian and former NLF political writer, July 1, 1992, Hanoi, Vietnam.

41. Author interview with Le Van Tru, former NLF official, June 29, 1992, Hanoi, Vietnam.

42. Nguyen Chi Thanh, the former COSVN director, died unexpectedly in June 1967 shortly before the NLF's Third National Congress.

43. *Mau Than Saigon* [The Tet Offensive in Saigon] (Ho Chi Minh City: Nha Xuat Ban Van Nghe, 1988).

44. Phan Hien, "Vua Danh, Vua Dam Trong Chong My, Cuu Nuoc" [Fighting and Negotiating While Resisting the U.S. for National Salvation of the Fatherland] *Tao Chi Lich Su Quan Su* 25 (January 1988), pp. 74–82.

45. Tuyet Interview.
46. Ibid.
47. Lu Van Loi and Nguyen Anh Vu, *Tieo Xuc Bi Mat Viet Nam,* p. 265.
48. Liberation Radio, January 2, 1968, 1400 GMT.

5

Giap and Tet Mau Than 1968: The Year of the Monkey

Cecil Currey

Senior General Vo Nguyen Giap has long been credited as the major architect and proponent of Tet 1968, the most famous attack during the long years of America's involvement in the Vietnam conflict. Some still maintain this view. Giap's most recent biographer, Peter MacDonald, describes Giap as determined to "take the battle into the South in unprecedented force. To this end in October 1967 the Politburo in Hanoi had agreed in principle to his winter/spring campaign, part of which involved a widespread attack in the South at the time of the Tet festivities that on January 30, 1968 would inaugurate the Year of the Monkey."[1]

The irony, misunderstood by MacDonald and so many others, was that, for as long as possible, Giap stood in systematic opposition to this offensive, repeatedly clashed with his opponents over this issue, and only reluctantly carried out orders to plan an attack. Giap's objections to what came to be known as the Tet Offensive and his struggles with colleagues over its form and content were rooted in disagreements within the northern Politburo between Giap and his powerful rivals that date back to the founding of the Viet Minh. Although Western writers tend to view Giap and his associates as monolithic in their views, willing myrmidons to the whims of Ho Chi Minh, leading members of the northern Politburo argued long, often, and sometimes bitterly over the course of action they should follow. They did so over Tet with great ferocity and fateful results.

Janos Radvanyi, a Hungarian diplomat, visited Hanoi in April 1959. During his stay he met with Giap, who told him how thoroughly the battle at Dien Bien Phu in 1954 had exhausted the North. It was "the last desperate exertion of the Viet Minh army" and the country itself. The military was on the verge of complete disintegration. "The supply of rice was running out. Apathy had spread among the populace to such an extent that it was difficult to draft new fighters. Years of jungle warfare had sent morale in the fighting units to the depths."[2]

Faced with such a reality, Giap quickly concluded that all northern gains would be imperiled if Hanoi moved South to commence military actions against Ngo Dinh Diem's government and army. As early as March 1957, Giap proclaimed that the North should hold fast; it should not advance into the South. It was first necessary, it must be the party's priority, to complete northern agrarian reforms, to achieve economic recovery. All other activities within the Democratic Republic of Vietnam (DRV) should support those goals. "We must at the same time," said Giap, "struggle for the reunification of the country." That, however, should grow out of political action and not take the form of armed intervention.

Destruction of the Diemist regime, Giap argued, must be done by the people of the South. They must "rally and unite" to "demand" improvement of their living conditions, to "demand" their rights to a livelihood, to "demand" democratic freedoms, to "struggle" against government policies intent on reducing them to poverty, to "patiently struggle" against Diem's "fascist dictatorial policy." All these demands and patient struggles would be firmer for being based "on the ever-strengthened North." Giap then stated his case as plainly as he could. "The North will be transformed into a base for the struggle for the unification of the country." As the North grew stronger it would be able "to create favorable conditions so [the two halves of Vietnam] may draw closer to each other and advance toward reunification of the country." Out of such action would come "resumption of normal economic and cultural relations between the two zones."[3]

While this might be Giap's view, it certainly was not the position maintained by certain of his enemies. Two of his most powerful rivals had no qualms about pursuing a more aggressive southern policy. These men were Le Duan and Nguyen Chi Thanh. Le Duan was number two man on the Politburo in rank and influence, just behind Ho. He was utterly dedicated to the overthrow of the southern government in the quickest possible way. Born in Annam in 1908, son of a railway clerk, he joined Ho's Revolutionary Youth League in 1928 and in 1930 was a founding member of the Indochinese Communist Party (ICP). He was familiar with hardship and privation. Arrested by the French in 1931 for seditious activities, he was sentenced to five years' imprisonment. Rearrested in 1940, Le Duan spent the war years on the prison island of Poulo Condore (Con Son).

Following World War II, Le Duan served for a time in Ho's Hanoi government and was then sent south to foster a revolutionary spirit among the population there. Opposed to the Geneva Accords because of his dedication to Vietnamese unification, he went along with them only on Ho's urging, but his fervor earned him the nickname "Flame of the South." During 1954–1956 he consistently advocated the use of armed force to overcome the southern government. Recalled to Hanoi in 1957, he became a member of the Politburo and de facto secretary-general of the Communist Party, a position that was formalized in 1960. As Ho's health declined, Le Duan's influence grew proportionately. His views began to predominate and he tipped the balance in favor of greater action in the South.[4]

Beginning as early as 1945, Le Duan seldom missed an opportunity to denigrate General Giap and to publicly criticize, even in Ho's presence, Giap's leadership of the army. Le Duan attacked him viciously as "fearful like a rabbit," and "trembling in battle." Giap was not a real leader, Le Duan insisted, for "in fact, [he] does not lead at all."[5]

One such enemy might be enough, but Giap had another who was equally dedicated to ruining his reputation and to installing a "south first" policy. This was Senior General Nguyen Chi Thanh, alias "Nam Vinh," born to poor peasants in Annam in 1914 or 1915. He devoted himself to revolutionary activities by the mid-1930s and joined the ICP in 1937. He headed party activities in Thua Thien Province until 1938, when the French arrested him. He spent most of World War II in prison. In 1945 he was named to the party's Central Committee. He joined the People's Liberation Army, rose to ever higher rank through the sponsorship of Truong Chinh, but served in a political rather than a military capacity. By 1950 he was in charge of the army's General Political Directorate (GPD), which supervised ideological aspects of military training. In this position he was not subordinate to Giap but rather to the party's Central Committee. From this office he held forth on his notion that Communist theory should have primacy over professional military training. In 1959, two years after being named to the Politburo, he became a general of the army with rank equal to that held by Vo Nguyen Giap, who now could no longer silence him by an order. It was Truong Chinh who sponsored Thanh's promotion, wanting someone with high rank to serve as a check on Giap's activities. Chinh consistently maintained that Thanh was a more competent general than Giap. Whispers to that effect spread throughout the North.[6]

Not only did Nguyen Chi Thanh denigrate Giap with impunity, he also slandered Dang Bich Ha, Giap's wife, who had gone to study history in the U.S.S.R. in the early 1960s. Thanh speculated that during her time there she had been too greatly influenced by Soviet views. Thanh gained new ammunition during the summer of 1963, when Giap and Ha thoughtlessly used a government helicopter to fly to a resort area at beautiful Ha Long Bay north of Haiphong. Security guards ordered other bathers from the beach so Giap and Ha could relax and swim privately. News of this incident traveled quickly to Hanoi and aroused a great deal of resentment among those hardly able to afford a bicycle and who would never travel anywhere.[7]

At one point that summer of 1963, General Thanh went to Giap's villa to lecture him on his failings. In an aside to Ha, Thanh intoned that "Giap still has the attitudes of a bourgeois because of you. He does not have the virtues of a revolutionary cadre." Such allegations from a political general must have enraged the hero of Dien Bien Phu.[8]

Disputations between Thanh and Giap were not resolved until March 15, 1961, when Thanh was relieved of his GPD duties and transferred to the Directorate of Agricultural Collectivization. There he remained until 1964, when the Politburo selected him to head Central Office of South Vietnam (COSVN), giving him charge of military operations in the South. He promoted and followed a policy of large-unit warfare against growing numbers of U.S. forces there. In July 1967 he died, depending on the source, during a U.S. bombing raid, or from a heart attack, or of pneumonia, while formulating some of the initial plans for the Tet Offensive.[9]

And what of Truong Chinh, Giap's quodam friend? Named Dang Xuan Khu, he early adopted the name Truong Chinh ("Long March") out of admiration for Mao Zedong's revolutionary zeal. He became a leading advocate for adopting the same strategies in the Vietnamese struggle. As younger men, dedicated to throwing off the French yoke under the banner of communism, Truong Chinh and Giap worked well together. They even cooperated in a coauthored book, *The Peasant Question, 1937–1938,* in which they argued that a Communist revolution could be both peasant- and proletarian-based.[10] They remained close throughout the war; it was Truong Chinh who told Giap of the death of his beloved first wife, Nguyen Thi Quang Thai, at the hands of French tortures at Hao Lo Prison in Hanoi.

In 1941 Truong Chinh became secretary-general of the ICP and thereafter was one of its leading figures. Giap's meteoric rise in the Communist hierarchy finally broke this friendship. From late 1945 to early 1946, Truong Chinh watched with jealousy that grew into enmity as Giap served as de facto acting president of the Democratic Republic of Vietnam while Ho Chi Minh was at Fontainebleau attempting to negotiate with the French. Officially, Giap held the dual posts of minister of the interior and undersecretary of state for national defense. In actuality he ran the country. Then, shortly after Ho returned from France he promoted Giap to the rank of general. Truong Chinh claimed that Giap was insufficiently competent to command an army and succeeded in placing General Nguyen Son as Giap's chief of staff. Son was the only Vietnamese Communist officer with professional military training, having earlier attended the Moscow Military Academy. He had also commanded a Chinese Communist regiment during Mao's Long March.[11]

Truong Chinh and his supporters circulated a rumor throughout the North that Giap was not a very competent general.[12] He also managed to place the army under the control of political commissars of the GPD. This office, exercising authority at all levels of the military, remained under Truong Chinh's sole and direct control, although he placed one of his most reliable men, General Van Tien Dung, at the head of the GPD. Truong Chinh was not pleased when Dung and Giap, due to their close contact under battlefield conditions, gradually became friends and allies.[13]

Disagreements between Truong Chinh and Giap deepened in 1950, when the former ordered the execution of Giap's chief of logistical services, Tran Chi Chu. Then, intoxicated by success following his victory at Cao Bang/ Lang Son, Giap made a series of mistakes. He launched his elite divisions three times into open combat and human wave attacks against the mobile groups of French General Jean de Lattre de Tassigny at Vinh Yen, the Day River, and Hoa Binh. Each time they were crushed.[14]

Truong Chinh wasted little time in accusing Giap of being "responsible for useless massacres, which had no other purpose than to promote personal interests." This pressure forced Giap to submit a written self-critique, to eliminate those of his closest assistants deemed by Truong Chinh to be incompetent, and to reorganize the command of the army. In this restructuring of the military, Truong Chinh strengthened the position of his political commissar and placed Chinese military advisors at all echelons. The influence of Chinese advisors and of Truong Chinh himself increased accordingly as the pro-Chinese clan within the Vietnamese Politburo became ever more powerful. It took victory at Dien Bien Phu to restore to Giap all his lost ground and prestige.[15]

Then came payback time for Giap. Appointed by Ho to head the Communist-imposed land reform program, Truong Chinh saw all his plans go awry due to poor planning, impossible demands, and peasant resistance. The situation became so intolerable that Giap was forced to station some of his best divisions in certain Annamese provinces to control outraged peasants. Ho finally dropped Truong Chinh from his position as head of the program, and selected Giap as the one to publicly announce official displeasure over land reform excesses and to condemn Truong Chinh. Giap did so with relish.

Although Giap and Truong Chinh were now personal enemies of long standing, they were united in their considered political view that the problems of the South were secondary to the needs of the North. Their policy held sway for the first few years after the Geneva Conference of 1954. Minister of defense and commander in chief of the military, Giap was a man whose views were carefully considered even when his colleagues differed with them. Although focusing on the North's own problems, Giap still found ways to move men and supplies into the South. At his orders, Group 559 (organized in May 1959) moved men and material overland down the still primitive Ho Chi Minh Trail. Group 759 (organized in July 1959) found ways to infiltrate the South by sea. Group 959 (organized in September 1959) took supplies to Pathet Lao forces.

This was not enough. Within the government of the North, the chorus of southern voices grew louder and the mood of the Politburo shifted from the Giap/Truong Chinh view to that espoused by Le Duan, Nguyen Chi Thanh, and their supporters. Their argument that the North needed to be actively involved in the South finally received official Politburo support.[16]

In January 1959, even while Giap organized his groups, members of the Central Committee began discussions as to the wisdom of armed insurrection in the South against the government of Ngo Dinh Diem. They concluded that it was time to do so. that decision was gravely enacted into policy at the Central Committee's Fifteenth Plenum in May of that year. The Third Party Congress that followed on September 5, 1960, showed the strength of the "south first" movement. The northern government gave public notice of its support for the southern insurgency. Truong Chinh, despite his earlier failure as head of the land reform program, his subsequent public apologies, his public condemnation by Vo Nguyen Giap, now lost his job as party secretary-general but retained his number three ranking in the Politburo.

Giap fared less well. Ho relieved him of his total control over all military operations, even in the South, and, as mentioned earlier, assigned Senior General Nguyen Chi Thanh to command the southern sector. This was followed by Giap's demotion from fourth to sixth rank in the Politburo hierarchy. Giap and Truong Chinh were clearly stymied; their opponents would now have the upper hand in deciding how the war in the South would be fought.[17] Shortly thereafter in the southern zone, Hanoi formed and sponsored the newly proclaimed People's Revolutionary Party and its National Front for the Liberation of South Vietnam (NFLSVN).

Official policy did not mean that their private views had changed. On December 22, 1959, long after the Politburo had made its decision, Giap still resisted. He delivered an address on the occasion of the fifteenth anniversary of his People's Army. His words were later published in his first major book, *People's War, People's Army*.[18] Therein Giap continued to insist that the North was only the "liberated half of the country" and the Democratic Republic of Vietnam was no more than "a firm base for the *peaceful* reunification of the country."[19] The area south of the seventeenth parallel was "still under the yoke of American imperialists and the Ngo Dinh Diem clique, their lackeys."[20]

Some have analyzed the politics of the Politburo by dividing its members into those who favored the Soviet Union and their opponents, who favored China. This is misleading, for it does not allow for the long-standing alliance of the two bitter enemies, Giap and Truong Chinh, for Giap certainly preferred the revolutionary stance of the Soviets, while Truong Chinh was a devotee of China. Both nations were called upon by those fighting the internal struggle in Vietnam over whether to favor a "south first" policy. Giap, for example, made no secret of his pro-U.S.S.R./anti-Chinese attitudes. Having been stuck with Chinese advisors to his army, it is no wonder he felt as he did.

The Chinese, more militant, pressed Hanoi to provide stronger action against the southern republic. Those, like Giap, who favored the opposite policy, looked with grave suspicion upon this advice proffered by their giant northern neighbor. A thousand years of conflict was not easily forgotten. A later Hanoi official summed up those doubts when he recalled that "China used Viet Nam like a chess pawn."[21]

Soviet Premier Nikita Khrushchev had increasingly advocated peaceful coexistence with the West. Many in the Vietnamese Politburo looked upon such a position as doctrinal treason. Giap's Russophile views clearly put him out of harmony with Le Duan, Nguyen Chi Thanh, and their powerful colleagues. Finally, however, Vietnamese northern leaders had to decide for themselves what course of action to follow. Was active interference in the South appropriate? Should Giap be ordered to mass his armies and order them to march across the seventeenth parallel? Or should the North wait for people in the South to launch a general uprising, giving them only aid and encouragement to do so? Who was responsible for the unfinished business in the South? Northerners had fought their own fight. Should not southerners do the same? Or was it the responsibility of those in the North to go now to their aid?[22]

Nguyen Chi Thanh was convinced this last position was the answer. He set forth a strident call for intervention in the South:

A powerful north Viet Nam . . . does not mean . . . the revolutionary movement in the south will automatically succeed. The powerful north Viet Nam and the revolutionary movement of the south Vietnamese people are mutually complementary and must be closely co-ordinated; the building of the north itself cannot replace the resolution of the inherent social contradictions of south Viet Nam. . . . We have correctly handled the relations between north and south Viet Nam. This a Marxist-Leninist strategic concept which is in conformity with the latest experience . . . in our own country. . . . The United States should have used algebra in gauging the situation . . . instead it used simple arithmetic. . . . We have every reason to believe that victory will be ours![23]

Then came an event in Saigon that gave new hope to the "south first" group. In October 1963 a cabal of generals in the southern Army of the Republic of Vietnam (ARVN), led by Duong Van Minh, launched a coup against the existing government. It ended with the murder of southern president Ngo Dinh Diem and his brother Ngo Dinh Nhu and was the prelude to years of political instability below the seventeenth parallel.[24]

Excitement over this news filled the minds of Ho and members of his Politburo. Some, like Le Duan and Nguyen Chi Thanh, were particularly ecstatic; events in the South seemed to prove the correctness of their political view. The South was going to self-destruct before the United States could intervene in sufficient strength to save it. Such southern chaos could only work to the advantage of the North and Hanoi needed to exploit this new opportunity. Even Giap was caught up in this enthusiasm. By 1964 he was contemplating plans for an assault on Saigon. He had three Viet Cong divisions, all within fifty miles of that capital city of the Republic of Vietnam. Aided by northern troops, those Viet Cong units could mount an attack that would end the war with a northern victory. The United States and its southern puppet, Giap said, were "no longer discussing . . . whether they will lose or win, but when their defeat will come."[25]

Giap's optimism was premature and a little later that year he came to his senses. He lamented that Americans "will never retreat of their own accord unless the [Vietnamese] people use all forms of revolutionary struggle to combat them."[26] For him, however, "all forms" did not yet include armed intervention.

Smarting from his opponents' charges that he favored a pro-U.S.S.R. policy of coexistence, Giap wrote an article in 1964 accusing the U.S.S.R. of not knowing how to assure victory in underdeveloped countries; he charged that it was a partisan of capitulation, a nation endlessly credulous toward imperialists.[27] He publicly admitted the possibility of a quick conclusion to efforts to unite the country. He could do little else and still retain his position within the hierarchy.

Privately his views were unchanged. He and Truong Chinh agreed that, despite the division of their nation, the North's first responsibility was to solidify itself as the bastion of communism and to build the infrastructure of its own economy. Giap plainly desired to see the two halves of the nation unified. Preferably southerners would do this by themselves, overthrowing their government in a general insurrection, through sabotage and subversion coupled with a later great patriotic uprising. The North need only lend its separated brothers appropriate encouragement and assistance to enable them to throw off the bonds of the rotten, corrupt, and illegitimate regime that ruled over them. In this way, Giap said, they would sweep away all the "spies, bandits, and hirelings of the U.S. imperialists into the dustbin of history."[28]

Giap believed there was no other practical choice. China was in no position to back up northern posturing or military adventures into the South. Even Truong Chinh knew this. It was still recovering from its 1949 revolution and from the effects of its conflict with the United States in Korea, where it suffered about a million casualties, killed, wounded, or missing. Nor was the U.S.S.R. about to offer unqualified backing to Ho's government for armed intervention in the South. It wanted no part of a conflict that might escalate into World War III. Although it would provide some level of aid, the U.S.S.R. made it plain as early as 1957 that it sought regional stability in Indochina and even proposed admitting both Vietnams into the United Nations as separate entities.

Nor should the North initiate actions that might bring about a greater

American presence in Vietnam. A U.S. declaration of war and consequent invasion of the North would bring about intolerable pressures. The North must continue as a secure rear base. Perhaps reluctantly, but nevertheless plainly, Giap held to his position, concluding that the South would have to strive on its own for the foreseeable future.

His opponents did not agree. In early 1965 they argued that the complete collapse of the southern government was imminent. A groundswell of international opinion would overwhelm the conscience of America when this happened, they argued, forcing the United States to end its operations there. This viewpoint prevailed. As a result, in the spring of 1965, Hanoi made two fateful decisions, both of which were opposed by Vo Nguyen Giap. The first was to pass up an opportunity for direct negotiations with the United States, occasioned by a private Soviet initiative to the West to reconvene the Geneva Conference. The second was to reinforce the Le Duan/Nguyen Chi Thanh "south first" policy, to encourage the long-delayed southern insurrection by sending northern regular units there and using them in continuing offensive operations. General Giap entered his official protest to this declaration of Phase III (full scale open conventional combat) operations.[29]

In March 1965, President Lyndon Johnson introduced American ground combat troops into Vietnam when two marine battalions landed at Danang. The rapid buildup thereafter deprived General Giap of a victory already within his grasp. He became ever more aware of the disruptive effect of American firepower and mobility as unit after unit moved from other U.S. bases to new locations inside the Republic of Vietnam. Giap had no way of knowing whether this new enemy would refrain from attacking the North across the seventeenth parallel and he had no desire to provoke such a move. "We need," he said in an article for *Hoc Tap*, "to make every preparation to defeat the United States aggressors in case they expand the war to the whole of our country."[30] As a consequence of his fears, he ordered the formation of hamlet and village self-defense forces throughout every northern province.[31]

Giap's soldiers had their first significant contact with U.S. troops at Plei Me (October 19–27, 1965).[32] Then came the battles of the Ia Drang (November 14–20, 1965) as Giap's men fought with elements of the American 1st Air Cavalry Division (Air Mobile).[33] Long convinced of the folly of the Le Duan/Nguyen Chi Thanh strategy, Giap was now faced with firsthand evidence that his forces could not maintain face-to-face battles with American forces. It was time to draw back. Phase III operations must be postponed. What was needed was further protracted war, to grind down the enemy. He had long insisted on this view; now it was indelibly proven to him. It was difficult for him to understand how Le Duan and Thanh could be so blind to reality. Victory in this unequal contest with America, he said in January 1966, would not come from battlefield achievements but because U.S. superiority was "limited" while its weaknesses were "basic." Such limitations would best be exploited through Phase I operations of protracted guerrilla warfare.[34]

Senior General Vo Nguyen Giap allowed his irritation toward his rivals to show plainly. On April 27 or 28, 1966, he spoke at a meeting of the National Assembly, arguing again that conventional warfare against the United States was futile. The North, he insisted, must not become deeply involved in combat operations but must continue to remain as the bastion of a free Vietnam. Covert aid to the South and continued moral support must suffice. His remarks did not please his more powerful rivals, and his speech was omitted entirely from printed accounts of talks given to the Assembly.

Thanh counterattacked swiftly. He insisted that those who held Giap's views were "old-fashioned" and had "a method of viewing things that is detached from reality." For supporters of the "north first" view to continue in their stubborn opposition was to repeat "what belongs to history" and to ignore "the face of a new reality." Wrongheaded disbelievers who opposed helping the South, Thanh said, looked for answers "in books, and [by] mechanically copying one's past experiences . . . in accordance with a dogmatic tendency." That, he concluded darkly, was "adventurism."[35]

Once again Thanh's view prevailed. Silenced by his rival's charges, Giap seethed, and, save for a single public appearance on May 10, he disappeared from view until December 22, 1966. He was not without support. One Hanoi official who agreed with him shuddered at thoughts of the future: "If we keep fighting five more years all that will be left of Viet Nam will be a desert." Even allies were skeptical of the "south first" policy. A delegation from Cuba and North Korea secretly visited the war theater and, in their briefing, warned of the dangers in allowing combat actions to continue between northern forces and American troops. Yet Nguyen Chi Thanh and Le Duan continued to prepare for southern intervention.[36]

Ho Chi Minh convened the Thirteenth Plenum of the Central Committee in April 1967. Giap hoped delegates to that meeting would support his "north first" policy, but they did not. The Committee passed Resolution 13, calling for a "spontaneous uprising [in the South] in order to win a decisive victory in the shortest possible time." Such "spontaneity" could occur, of course, only with the greatest possible northern support. There would be an immediate and total drive for victory.

Giap's hopes for a reversal of this policy must have soared in July 1967, when his deadly rival, Senior General Nguyen Chi Thanh, suddenly died. Now no one remained who held equal rank to him, and his voice might again be heard, at least within military councils. Perhaps it was. It made no difference, however, in supreme political circles. No matter what kind of face Giap might put on recent developments, and despite his vehement objections, leaders of the Democratic Republic of Vietnam decreed that planning for the "uprising" would continue. They were about to abandon all vestiges of "peaceful coexistence."

As late as October 1967, Giap still opposed the launching of a Tet attack and continued to push for his own victory strategy of protracted warfare. He wrote a fifty-four-page statement that appeared both in *Nhan Dan* (People's Daily) and *Quan Doi Nhan Dan* (People's Army Daily), calling for the North to remain as a secure rear base area for the great revolutionary struggle. In a move that showed some independence, he publicly continued his pro-U.S.S.R. stance. On October 21, he wrote an article for the Soviet *Red Star,* extolling the Russian October Revolution as the beginning "of a new era in mankind's history." Thanks, he said, to the Russians, "The Vietnamese people are successfully advancing on the glorious path of the October Revolution."[37]

Yet disagree as Giap might with the Politburo's decision and try as he would to reverse it, he was still forced to bow to the inevitable. His advice ignored, already painted by the late Nguyen Chi Thanh as one guilty of "adventurism," Giap swallowed his objections. He had been ordered to plan an offensive and so he would do so. Slowly the outlines emerged and then fell into place for the coming great battle, known in the North as *tong cong kich/tong khoi nghia* (TCK/TKN) or general offensive/general uprising, finally launched officially on January 31, 1968.[38]

Tet was a tactical disaster. Despite Giap's brilliant logistics movement of men and supplies into the South, despite attacks on thirty-six of the forty-four provincial capitals and five of six major cities, despite northern control of Hue for some weeks, despite penetration even of the U.S. Embassy grounds in Saigon and the necessity for American ambassador Ellsworth Bunker to flee for safety to the home of Major General Edward Lansdale, despite screaming rockets blasting aircraft at Tan Son Nhut and other locations, despite all this, TCK/TKN failed. The people of the South did not rise against the government there. Instead, they huddled within such protection as they could find while rampaging armies fought across their lands, around their homes, and in their cities.

Communist battlefield losses in the general offensive were significant, but not as great as initially estimated by Military Assistance Command, Vietnam (MACV) in the first flush of its victory and facing the necessity to explain to the Pentagon and to the American people how the attacks could have happened at all. U.S. military public affairs officers quickly claimed that 100,000 enemy soldiers had been killed in the fighting. There is a rule of thumb used by generals of many nations to calculate enemy combat casualties that has grown out of assessing one's own losses: for every dead soldier, an additional three have suffered wounds. If MACV's statistics are to be accepted, that means U.S. soldiers and ARVN troops not only inflicted 100,000 deaths on the enemy, but Viet Cong and North Vietnamese soldiers suffered another 300,000 wounded as well. Since only 260,000 were initially available for use in the uprising, such figures were then and remain today highly suspect.

Viet Cong and North Vietnamese forces may have together suffered 40,000 battlefield deaths, compared to 1,100 for the United States and 2,300 for ARVN. This was still a heavy burden for Communist forces to bear. After Tet the North's army carried the brunt of the contest with America. "We have been guilty of many errors and shortcomings," said northern leaders.[39] Many had "lost confidence," had become "doubtful of victory, pessimistic," and "display[ed] shirking attitudes."[40]

One such may have been Ho Chi Minh himself. Vietnamese historian Thai Van Kiem writes that the northern leader "silently regretted not having listened to Vo Nguyen Giap and letting himself be swayed in error by a young, inexperienced militant who wanted to gain Uncle Ho's favor by a lucky poker play. Following this burning debacle, Ho's health declined day by day. He never got over this defeat. Unable even to sleep, he died the next year, in 1969."[41]

Tran Van Tra, a senior Communist general in the South who was certainly not a favorite of Vo Nguyen Giap, wrote later that "we did not correctly evaluate the specific balance of forces between ourselves and the enemy, did not fully realize that the enemy still had considerable capabilities and that our capabilities were limited." Northern objectives, he said, "were beyond our actual strength," and were supported "in part on an illusion based on our subjective desires." In the end "we were not only unable to retain the gains we had made but had to overcome a myriad of difficulties in 1969 and 1970 so that the revolution could stand firm in the storm."[42] Tra, in this quoted passage, admitted that Le Duan's "subjective" wishes were beyond the Communists' political and military capacities. It was, he wrote, "completely unrealistic for us to set the goal of the General Offensive–General Uprising in terms of 'taking complete power into the hands of the people' [for] our attacks could not be decisive"[43]

In their end, the execution and outcome of Mau Than Tet 1968 demonstrated that Giap, from a military standpoint, had been correct in his opposition to the move. So Giap was right to oppose it, but for him to be correct did not mean that the offensive had to fail completely in all its aspects. And it did not. Political ramifications of those battles, broadcast and analyzed over and again within the United States, also allowed Politburo spin doctors to put their own slant on the recent battles. As Communist general Tran Do confessed, "In all honestly, we didn't achieve our main objective, which was to spur uprisings throughout the south. . . . As for making an impact in the United States, it had not been our intention— but it turned out to be a fortunate result."[44]

General William Westmoreland, commander, MACV, tried to put the best possible face on the situation after the fighting quieted when he lamented that American reactions at home to the Tet attacks allowed Vietnamese Communists, who had just suffered a catastrophic defeat in battle, to salvage a "psychological victory" for themselves.[45] General Tra called such words "naive" and "blind xeno[phobia]."[46] Giap would have agreed with this conclusion. He knew as well as anyone the extent of Communist losses. He had argued against TCK/TKN, foreseen its dangers, and proclaimed it folly. He had risked his own career by his stubborn opposition to the plan.

Yet all the sacrifice finally accomplished certain major goals for the Communists. On March 31, President Lyndon Johnson ordered a partial (and temporary) halt to the bombing of the North and declared, "I shall not seek, and I will not accept, the nomination of my party for another term as your president." He further offered truce talks, accepted by Hanoi on April 3. Johnson replaced Westmoreland with General Creighton Abrams, who quickly fell in line, following the fall election of Richard Nixon as the new president, with the new policies of Vietnamization and de-escalation of the war. In America's highest military and political echelons there were now those ready to admit that the earlier U.S. approach to the conflict in Vietnam had failed. They were ready to recommend that the United States seek a negotiated settlement and end the contest in Southeast Asia.

On these points, Giap and his fellows could all take pride in the accomplishments of Tet. There was now a political victory to be gained from the Tet Offensive, and although the military road ahead was still long and hard, it had to be pursued vigorously for whatever advantage it might give.

NOTES

1. See Peter Macdonald, *Giap: The Victor in Vietnam* (New York: W. W. Norton, 1993), p. 262. I have elsewhere described this work as "without redeeming historical, literary or biographical merit, riddled with errors, lacking understanding, and misleading in its text." See my review essays of this book in *Conflict Quarterly*, Vol. 13, No. 3 (Summer 1993), pp. 64–75; *Vietnam Generation* (Spring–Winter 1993 [The Big Book]), pp. 409–410.

2. Janos Radvanyi, *Delusion and Reality* (South Bend, Ind.: Gateway Editions, 1978), p. 6.

3. Carlyle A. Thayer, *War by Other Means: National Liberation and Revolution in Viet-Nam, 1954–1960* (Sydney, Australia: Allen & Unwin, 1989), pp. 156–157.

4. Ibid., p. 196; Robert F. Rogers, "Policy Differences within the Hanoi Leadership," *Studies in Comparative Communism*, Vol. 9, Nos. 1–2 (Spring–Summer 1976), pp. 108–128 *passim*.

5. These charges by Le Duan were set forth in a review essay of MacDonald's *Giap* by Lam Le Trinh, "Vo Nguyen Giap: Victory without Triumph," in *Vietnam's People* (Huntington Beach, Calif., 1993). He quotes from Bui Tin's two-volume memoir, *Hoa Xuyen Tuyet* [Snowdrop] (n.p., Calif.: Nhan Quyen Editeur, 1991); *Mat That* [The Real Face] (Irvine, Calif.: Saigon Press, 1993).

6. "Biographical Sketch of Vo Nguyen Giap," DD Form 1396 (September 1, 1962), Report No. 6 832 0761 69, Defense Intelligence Agency [hereafter DIA Report]. This document was obtained under the Freedom of Information Act; the final two digits in the report number indicate that it was written in 1969. Internal evidence suggests it was based, in large part, on material provided by French intelligence [hereafter DIA Report].

7. Phillip B. Davidson, *Vietnam at War: The History, 1946–1975* (New York: Oxford University Press, 1991), pp. 305–306.

8. Ibid., p. 306.

9. DIA Report. Vietnamese historian Thai Van Kiem writes that Giap argued earnestly against Thanh's new position but Ho was unpersuaded. He adds that Thanh's later death "profoundly affected" Ho. According to Kiem, Thanh was wounded by a South Vietnamese artillery shell fragment and bled to death on the famous Street Without Joy in Quang Tri Province while being transported to a hospital. See Letter, Thai Van Kiem to Cecil B. Currey, Paris, April 22, 1994 (translated from the French) [hereafter Kiem Letter].

10. See Van Dinh [Giap] and Qua Ninh [Truong Chinh], *The Peasant Question, 1939–1938* (Hanoi, 1938), translated and with an introduction by Christine Pelzer White (Ithaca, N.Y.: Cornell University Southeast Asia Program, 1974).

11. DIA Report.

12. Ibid.

13. Ibid.

14. Ibid.

15. Ibid.

16. Interview, Cecil B. Currey with Dong Nghiem Bai, director, North American Department, Foreign Ministry, Socialist Republic of Vietnam, Hanoi, March 10, 1988.

17. See Kiem Letter. Cf. Davidson, *Vietnam at War,* pp. 289–290; Stanley Karnow, *Vietnam: A History* (New York: Viking Press, 1983), pp. 238–239 [hereafter *Vietnam*]; John S. Bowman, ed., *The Vietnam War: An Almanac* (New York: World Almanac Publications, 1985), pp. 48–50; William J. Duiker, *Historical Dictionary of Vietnam* (Metuchen, N.J.: Scarecrow Press, 1989), pp. 111–112.

18. Vo Nguyen Giap, *People's War, People's Army* (Hanoi: Foreign Languages Publishing House, 1961).

19. From U.S. edition of book in note 18 (New York: Frederick A. Praeger, 1962), pp. 40, 58.

20. Ibid., pp. 58–59. Cf. speech by Vo Nguyen Giap published in *Addresses: Third National Congress of the Viet-Nam Worker's Party,* Vol. 3 (Hanoi: Foreign Languages Publishing House, 1960), pp. 43–65 [hereafter *Addresses*].

21. Interview, Cecil B. Currey with Pham Binh, director, Institute of International Relations, Socialist Republic of Vietnam, Hanoi, March 10, 1988.

22. In the past many have believed that divisions within the Politburo centered around pro-U.S.S.R. and pro-China factions. Authors who suggest that this is an oversimplification include R. B. Smith, *An International History of the Vietnam War: The Kennedy Strategy* (New York: St. Martin's Press, 1985); and Thayer, *War by Other Means,* pp. 195–196. To quote Thayer, "Disputes in the Central

Committee were based more on relative priorities to be assigned to the consolidation of the north and the national democratic revolution in the south than on the question of pro-Soviet or pro-Chinese orientation."

23. Nguyen Chi Thanh, *Who Will Win in South Viet Nam?* (Beijing: Foreign Languages Press, 1963), pp. 4, 9, 11.

24. Cecil B. Currey, *Edward Lansdale: The Unquiet American* (New York: Houghton Mifflin, 1988), pp. 218–223, 283–286; Interview, Cecil B. Currey with Lucien Conein, Tyson's Corner, Virginia, March 16, 1991.

25. Press Release, Vietnam News Agency, Hanoi, International Service in Vietnamese, May 9, 1964, Foreign Broadcast Information Service.

26. Press Release, New China News Agency, Beijing, International Service in English, June 1, 1964, Foreign Broadcast Information Service.

27. Article, in French, dispatched to *L'Aurore* in Paris by Vietnam News Agency, Saigon, June 3, 1964, Foreign Broadcast Information Service.

28. Giap *Addresses,* Vol. 1, pp. 43–65.

29. Sherman Kent, chairman, Board of National Estimates, Central Intelligence Agency. Memorandum: "The View from Hanoi," for the director, Central Intelligence, November 30, 1966. This document was obtained through a Freedom of Information Act request and was declassified September 13, 1989.

30. Seymour Topping, "Hanoi Prepares People for War," *New York Times,* July 29, 1965, pp. 1, 9.

31. Robert Taber, *The War of the Flea: A Study of Guerrilla Warfare, Theory and Practice* (New York: Citadel Press, 1965), p. 11.

32. Lieutenant General Vinh Loc (ARVN), *Why Plei Me?* (Pleiku, Republic of Vietnam: Echoes Press, 1966), *passim.*

33. Lieutenant General Harold G. Moore, U.S. Army (Ret.) and Joseph L. Galloway, *We Were Soldiers Once Brave and Young: Ia Drang—The Battle That Changed the War in Vietnam* (New York: Random House, 1992), *passim.*

34. Printed in *Nhan Dan,* January 16–18, 1966, and in *Hoc Tap,* January 31, 1966. Published February 4, 1966, by Foreign Broadcast Information Service.

35. Nguyen Chi Thanh, "Ideological Tasks of the Army and People in the South," *Hoc Tap,* July 1966.

36. *Newsweek,* March 11, 1968, p. 30.

37. *Red Star,* October 21, 1967. Also published in *Nhan Dan* and *Quan Doi Nhan Dan.* Reported November 3, 1967, by Foreign Broadcast Information Service.

38. Don Oberdorfer, *Tet! The Turning Point* (New York: Doubleday, 1971); Robert Pisor, *The End of the Line: The Siege of Khe Sanh* (New York: W. W. Norton, 1982).

39. Karnow, *Vietnam,* p. 544.

40. Ibid.

41. Kiem Letter.

42. Karnow, *Vietnam,* p. 544.

43. Tran Van Tra, "Tet: The 1968 General Offensive and General Uprising," in Jayne S. Werner and Luu Doan Huynh, *The Vietnam War: Vietnamese and American Perspectives* (London: M. E. Sharpe, 1993), pp. 52–53 [hereafter *The Vietnam War*].

44. Karnow, *Vietnam*, p. 545.

45. Ibid. Scholars now contest this view by Westmoreland. For the best refutation see Werner and Huynh, *The Vietnam War, passim*.

46. Tra, "Tet," in Werner and Huynh, *The Vietnam War*, p. 57.

6

The Tet Offensive and Its Aftermath

Ngo Vinh Long

INTRODUCTION: BACKGROUND AND MOTIVATION

By 1967 the American "war of attrition" and its "pacification program" had failed in Vietnam, allowing the National Liberation Front (NLF) to control most of the countryside in South Vietnam. Confronted by the deteriorating situation in the South, the United States intensified its air campaign against North Vietnam to unprecedented levels. Throughout 1967, the United States hoped that the bombing would persuade the North to end NLF attacks in exchange for a bombing halt. It was under these circumstances, in October, that the Central Committee of the Democratic Republic of Vietnam (DRV) decided to carry out a series of widespread offensive operations against urban centers in South Vietnam. The NLF leaders wanted to remind U.S. leaders that their main enemy was in the South and not in the North. They also hoped that these operations would convince the United States to end the bombing of the North and begin negotiations.

The attacks began during the Vietnamese New Year in 1968, and thus were labeled the "Tet Offensive" in the West. The offensive was composed of three phases, lasting until October of that year. During the first phase, which lasted from the end of January to the beginning of March, the NLF strike force achieved dramatic gains while receiving relatively light casualties. In my opinion, at this point the attacks should have been broken off, with military forces retreating into the countryside to consolidate their gains in newly liberated areas. Instead, Politburo members decided to mount the second and third phases of the offensive. As a result, the revolutionary units were left too long in forward positions around the urban areas, where they were subjected to horrendous air and artillery strikes. In addition, after the third phase was mounted, American and Army of the Republic of Vietnam (ARVN) troops "leapfrogged" over the revolutionary forces who were still massed around the urban areas to attack them from the rear as well as to take over liberated areas. Caught on the outskirts of these urban areas, the revolutionary units not only suffered heavy casualties in 1968, but also were unable to return to the countryside in time to provide the necessary protection to NLF political cadres and sympathetic rural supporters confronted by the Phoenix program, an accelerated pacification program, and so on.

Worse still, the Vietnamese leadership in Hanoi made one of the biggest errors in the war by ordering the remnants of the revolutionary units in the South to retreat to the border areas of Cambodia and Laos to regroup. This was tantamount to surrendering populated areas of the South to the U.S. and ARVN forces without a fight. When NLF units decided to return to the villages to help rebuild the revolutionary infrastructure, they paid a high price for their absence. In addition, northern units sent south in 1969 and 1970 could not operate effectively and suffered large casualties due to the fact that they did not have the necessary grassroots tactical input or fifth-column support which had existed before 1968.

In the views of most southern revolutionary fighters, 1969 and 1970 were the two most difficult years in the entire war. Initiative was reclaimed only after the southern revolutionaries rebuilt connections between villagers and soldiers in 1971 and 1972. This rebuilding process was done mainly through the tactic of *bam tru* or "clinging to the post (remaining close to the people)". This took place even as U.S. and ARVN troops invaded Cambodia and Laos in 1970 and 1971. In fact, these invasions and the simultaneous increase in NLF urban operations actually served to divert allied troops from the rural areas of South Vietnam and provided the Communist forces with a sufficient respite to recover from its Tet losses. This is a new point of view—one which I first presented in 1988. It is based on the most current research from both the American and Vietnamese official records, and it runs counter to previous works. These focus only on selected U.S. records to draw conclusions about Tet which in total are not borne out by my more in-depth research.

THE CURRENT MISCONCEPTIONS ABOUT TET

With this in mind, I have written this chapter as part of my ongoing effort to combat what I perceive to be an increasing effort—in official and mainstream academic works on the war in both the United States and Vietnam since the end of the war—to claim that the North Vietnamese Army (NVA) played the decisive role in the liberation of the South not only during the final days but also for years before, starting with Tet. Officials in the DRV have even resorted to restricting debate on the conduct of the war so that the official party line would remain unchallenged. An example of this occurred in 1982, just after the publication of General Tran Van Tra's memoirs, when Communist Party officials arbitrarily banned the book even though it contained only a mild and indirect criticism of the official conduct of the war. Perhaps most surprising was the fact that Tra had been the commander of the B-2 NLF region (Saigon III and IV Corps), and deputy supreme commander of all the revolutionary forces in the South.[1]

THE NEW COMMUNIST VIEW OF TET

The best example of the turmoil in postwar Vietnam was the exclusion of southern political leaders and military commanders from the Defence Ministry's "Scientific Conference for an Overall Assessment of the Spring Offensive of 1968," held in Ho Chi Minh City, March 1–8, 1986, and hosted by General Hoang Van Thao, a northerner. Historically this was an insidious exclusion since the majority of the division, brigade, and regimental commanders during Tet were southerners. More than anyone they knew how the offensive unfolded and how party directives were implemented during the period from 1968 to 1972.[2]

Of particular note, Tran Bach Dang, the planner of the attack on Saigon, and Communist Party leader in the Saigon-Giandinh-Cholon area during Tet, was not invited. When he was finally allowed to publish an article on Tet in February 1988, he pointed out that a number of powerful party leaders had prevented even a cursory analysis of the Tet policy-making process. According to Dang, almost all historical writings in Vietnam, including local party histories in the South, had to follow politically correct guidelines (*lap truong*) in order to be published. As a result, these articles did not reflect the reality of what occurred during Tet.[3]

The fact that Dang's article was published in an official journal indicated that by early 1988 there was at least some official recognition that suppression of the debate over the Vietnamese revolution was counterproductive. Indeed, at the previously mentioned November 1988 conference held in Hanoi, (see unnumbered note at the end of this chapter) I spoke directly to this issue by introducing information gathered from interviews with NLF military personnel and political cadres from key provinces in the South.[4]

I realized that my analysis was quite different from the official views in Vietnam at the time of the conference and might be seen as controversial. Still, I hoped that the Vietnamese might use this as an opportunity to break with the practices of the past, at least in order to promote political accommodation and integration in Vietnam. Present during my presentation were Generals Cao Pha and Hoang Phuong—associate director and director of the Military History Institute in Hanoi. General Pha followed my paper with a presentation on the Tet Offensive and General Phuong concluded with the Nixon years. Together their papers paralleled my own.[5]

Both men repeatedly commented on the quality of my work and depth of my research, and except for disagreement on minor details, strongly seconded my conclusions. To the surprise of the Americans present General Pha even endorsed General Tra's earlier view of Tet in both his 1982 book and an article published in the February and April 1988 issues of the *Journal of Military History* (Vietnamese).[6]

Tra's essay was spirited, but measured. It is an account which I believe cannot be fully understood without a close examination of the literature in Vietnam and a thorough understanding of the underlying political currents and political struggles during the 1980s. General Tra accused some prominent party leaders of having come close to agreeing with reactionary American Tet analysts in their effort to deny southern revolutionaries their achievements during the Tet Offensive. Tra declared that, by 1967, the Politburo had already decided that it was impossible to have a complete victory while the American and ARVN forces were nearly five times larger than the total forces of the revolutionaries.

In October 1967, Resolution 14 or the Quang Trung Resolution—after Emperor Quang Trung, who defeated the Chinese in Tet 1789—was passed by the Central Committee. It envisioned the future of the war as follows:

1) the "highest victory" of forcing the U.S. to enter into negotiations to end the war; 2) partial success which would nevertheless allow the U.S. and Saigon forces to retake important areas and continue the war; and 3) complete failure which would encourage the U.S. to bring in more American troops and to extend the war to North Vietnam, Laos, and Kampuchea.[7]

However, the Politburo also ordered continuous attacks until the first objective was achieved. According to Tra the first phase of the offensive did bring about the intended success, since it forced the United States to limit bombing in the northern panhandle area and open preliminary talks. Tra, however, argues that this was only a ploy by the Johnson administration to control U.S. public opinion in preparation of a reescalation of the bombing throughout Vietnam. Realizing this, Politburo leaders ordered the second and third phases of the offensive to commence. Tra believed this was a mistake because of the subsequent carnage inflicted on the NLF in 1969–1970 and the delay in serious peace negotiations until 1972. Conversely, Tra also argues that it took the second phase of the offensive to force the United States to join the Paris peace talks. He also points out that it was not until November 1968, two months into the third phase, that President Lyndon B. Johnson finally ordered the complete cessation of the bombing of the North and announced the beginning of a four-party peace conference.

Tra went on to say,

This was only easily understandable in wars such as a gigantic war like this last one in Vietnam. Results on the battlefields were the key and deciding elements for political and diplomatic developments. . . . There was never such a thing as snatching political victory from the jaws of military defeat or gaining diplomatic success without blood having been spilled and bones scattered on the battlefield. . . . because of the "extraordinary efforts during the three phases of the Offensive by the revolutionary fighters and their supporters in the South, a decisive victory and a strategic turning was achieved.[8]

In his aforementioned paper General Phuong noted the intensity of the American and ARVN counterattacks on all fronts during the Nixon era, declaring that 1969 and 1970 were the worst years for the revolution in the South. However, he also argued that because Nixon expanded the war into Cambodia and Laos he subjected allied forces to some of their worst defeats of the war. He implied that the success of the regular northern forces (People's Army of Vietnam/PAVN) in Cambodia and Laos were principally responsible for Communist gains in the South, and ultimately in Paris. The general also agreed with me that NLF forces recovered primarily through their use of the *bam tru* policy, which also facilitated the return of large numbers of PAVN forces. Moreover, he supported my contention that the escalating urban opposition to the Saigon regime in the South also contributed to the recovery of the NLF and brought about subsequent military and political successes.[9]

These views have been supported by articles and books published in Vietnam during the last five years. An example of this is the lead article in the *Journal of Military History* in which Tran Vu discusses the magnitude of and the reasons for the Communist military success in 1971. He analyzes several Communist victories in South Vietnam and points out that the ARVN suffered 232,000 casualties. Vu insists that this proves that through increased NLF activities in the South

our main force units were again able to return one by one to the battlefronts and to reinforce the base areas along the western corridor of the central provinces, in the Highlands, in the eastern provinces of the South, and in the Mekong Delta. The enemy's resolute effort to push our main force units beyond the borders [of the South] therefore had failed miserably by this time.[10]

He goes on to say that these guerrilla activities against the pacification and Phoenix programs helped double the population in the liberated areas to nearly 3 million and expand the contested areas to 7,240 villages with over 11 million inhabitants. This not only provided revolutionaries with a contiguous area throughout the South from which to operate but also helped solve their logistics and supply problems. Vu credits the large opposition movements of women, students, workers, and intellectuals in the United States and in southern urban areas for isolating the Saigon regime

and for causing doubts about the Vietnamization program among officials
in Saigon and the United States. All these factors led to further defeats for
the allies in 1972 which, along with timely diplomatic initiatives by Hanoi
and the NLF, finally forced the Nixon administration to agree to sign the
Paris peace accords.[11]

In recent years the Vietnamese have participated in freer discussions of
the war. Moreover, there has been significant reassessment of official positions regarding the war. Although there is still a lot of disagreement in
Vietnamese literature on the relations between the Hanoi regime and the
NLF, this is something Vietnamese historians and analysts seem determined
to unravel in the future.

THE RIGHT-WING VIEW, STILL IN VOGUE IN THE UNITED STATES

What remains a concern to me is that in the United States, with only a
few exceptions, right-wing interpretations of Tet and its aftermath seem to
have gained acceptance even among authors who are considered liberals
by their peers.[12] Two recent examples illustrate this point. In a book he
dedicated to "the young Americans who fought in the Vietnam War . . .
and those who opposed it," George Donnelson Moss reiterates the three
main arguments of the American right on Tet. First, Moss asserts that Tet
was a desperate act by the NLF and PAVN undertaken because the war
had been going badly. He says that by the spring of 1967,

many Vietcong units and some NVA units fighting in South Vietnam had been
decimated. Others had been driven out of South Vietnam or forced to take refuge
in sparsely populated . . . central highlands. The NLF infrastructure controlled
fewer villages and less territory in South Vietnam than it had at the time when the
Twelfth Plenum had decided to fight attrition with attrition.[13]

Second, Moss argues that the first phase of Tet not only represented a
major military defeat for the NLF, but also destroyed the NLF as a political
organization in the South. He estimates that during the first three months
of 1968, Viet Cong and PAVN losses totaled nearly 58,000. Thus, he declares that the VC, who had undertaken the majority of the attacks, "were
largely destroyed as an effective military menace to the South Vietnamese."
He also argues that in a large number of the southern provinces "the Vietcong political infrastructure, . . . painstakingly erected over the years,"
was destroyed during Tet. Specifically, Moss maintains that

The VC cadres had come out into the open to organize and to lead the uprisings
that were expected to follow the assaults on the towns and cities. The expected
uprisings never materialized, and the VC cadres were eliminated. Nowhere in South

Vietnam did risings occur. Nowhere in South Vietnam were the Vietcong welcomed by the Vietnamese people, nor did any defections from GVN [government of Vietnam] political or military ranks occur. In fact, the ARVN forces fought well despite being caught by surprise. After Tet there was no chance that the Saigon regime would be overthrown by a revolution from within South Vietnam. After the spring of 1968, the Vietnam war became, for the most part, a conventional war between the main forces units.[14]

Finally, Moss reiterates the ultimate right-wing myth that while Tet was a military defeat for the NLF it was a psychological victory. The American military leadership both in Saigon and the United States viewed Tet as a great tactical victory. Moss goes on to say that General William C. Westmoreland, commander of MACV,

was eager to mount a major counteroffensive and . . . win the war. But Tet-68 proved to be the great paradox. . . . Tet brought Americans defeat encased within victory. . . . The scope, scale, and intensity of the Vietcong Tet offensive shocked most Americans. Nightly, television news beamed the sights and sounds . . . of battles in Saigon and Hue into American living rooms. . . . Initial wire stories, later corrected, exaggerated the Communist successes, contributing to a widely shared sense that Tet had been an allied disaster.[15]

The remainder of his book basically agrees with the right wing that by allowing the enemy to snatch victory from the jaws of defeat during Tet the United States not only made it possible for the eventual North Vietnamese conquest of the South but also for the rise of the so-called Vietnam syndrome.

Another variation on this theme is contained in James J. Wirtz' book *The Tet Offensive: Intelligence Failure in War,* published in 1991. The entire book is an elaboration of the author's key points made in the introduction:

Dire consequences usually follow a disastrous defeat. Ironically, the allies defeated the communists decisively during Tet. From the communist perspective, the offensive was a gamble, even a desperate gamble, taken to offset the overwhelming resources, mobility, firepower, technological sophistication, and professionalism of their opponent. The North Vietnamese and Vietcong hoped that the attacks would foster a revolt of the southern population against the government, thereby adding tens of thousands of combatants to the communist side. When the offensive failed to spark this insurrection, communist commanders lacked the resources needed to attain ambitious objectives, and the allies defeated their widely scattered forces piecemeal. . . .

If the communists failed to win the Tet offensive, what then accounts for its effect on American perceptions of the war in Vietnam? Ultimately, the shock it produced was the catalyst that led to the reevaluation of U.S. policy. The Tet attacks failed on the battlefield, but U.S. forces did not anticipate fully the scope, intensity, targets, and timing of the offensive. The allies suffered a failure of intelligence during Tet, a failure that set the stage for changes in U.S. strategy.[16]

He concludes that "over the longer term, Tet marked the beginning of what Ronald Reagan called the 'Vietnam Syndrome': a period of public disillusionment with military intervention, defense spending, and an active anticommunist approach to foreign affairs."[17]

The facts indicate to me that this is an entirely specious argument. Indeed, the "Vietnam syndrome" fallacy has been exposed by a long list of U.S. interventions in Third World countries since Tet and by the incredible increases in U.S. defense spending under Presidents Carter, Reagan, and Bush. To be sure, this fallacy allowed President Bush to rush headlong into the Gulf War and to announce later that the United States had "kicked the Vietnam Syndrome for good" and had "buried it in the desert sand of Saudi Arabia."[18]

There is also no need to waste any words on an effort to discredit the argument that Tet was a decisive military defeat for the NLF/NVA and that the United States could have won the war had it not been for the psychological shock created by the military intelligence failure, exaggerated media reports, and so on. By implying that the war was lost in the United States and not in Vietnam, American writers have knowingly or unknowingly prolonged postwar recriminations within the United States. Worst still, in their treatment of Tet and its aftermath they have ignored or distorted the facts by suggesting that PAVN forces did most of the fighting in the South after the spring of 1968. They would have us believe that southerners never again played any significant role. As we shall see, this a deeply flawed argument.

DESPERATE GAMBLE? AN ANALYSIS OF WHAT REALLY HAPPENED DURING TET AND AFTER

Is there any factual basis for the claim that by the spring of 1967 the NLF had largely been expelled from southern population centers to jungle hideouts along border areas? Was this really the reason Communist leaders decided to launch the desperate Tet Offensive gamble? A look at some 1967 Western news reports indicates that the revolutionaries were winning politically and militarily throughout South Vietnam.

The Associated Press reported on February 4, 1967, that during the previous month the NLF had enjoyed a series of military successes and therefore the number of American casualties was three times higher than during the same period the year before.[19]

Le Figaro reported on February 15 that by the end of 1966 ARVN forces had suffered several disastrous defeats, that the number of desertions had consequently reached a monthly figure of 500 per regiment, and that Pentagon generals were obliged to admit that the pacification program had become a complete failure.[20]

A Reuters dispatch on March 11, 1967, quoted Major John Wilson, the senior U.S. advisor in Long An Province, as saying,

For every hectare we pacify, we have devoted to this province more men, more dollars and other means than any other province in South Vietnam. Yet, the results of these efforts are meager. . . . In reality, we can control only a very small area, according to the required norms. I would say that we control only four percent in the daytime and only one percent during the night.[21]

The March 20, 1967, issue of *U.S. News and World Report* cited a report from the Senate Armed Services Committee saying that "at the end of the dry season, the Viet Cong still controlled 80% of South Vietnamese territory."[22] In fact, NLF forces moved into many towns and cities at will. The May 24 *New York Times* reported that

enemy forces overran Quang Tri city, the province capital, freed 250 guerrillas from jail and successfully attacked two regimental headquarters of the South Vietnamese First Infantry Division. . . . A few days later, in a series of events that were not fully reported at that time, they moved virtually unmolested into Hue, while the army and national police fled.[23]

On August 7, the *New York Times,* citing official U.S. statistics, stated that out of 12,537 hamlets in the South, Saigon controlled 168. On the other hand, those totally controlled by the NLF numbered 3,978. The rest of the hamlets were listed as "contested" or partially controlled by both sides.[24] In the *Pentagon Papers,* the 1967 official U.S. "Hamlet Evaluation System" (HES) report admitted that "recent reports state that to a large extent, the VC now control the countryside."[25]

Confronted by this deteriorating situation in the southern countryside, the Johnson administration, according to the *Pentagon Papers,* escalated the air war in the North during 1967. They hoped that the North would persuade the NLF to call off southern attacks in exchange for a bombing halt. This was what LBJ called his "peace offensive." It was later dubbed the "San Antonio Formula," since he presented it in a speech in San Antonio, Texas, on September 29, 1967. When DRV officials resisted such tactics Johnson denounced them as intransigents and stepped up the bombing.[26]

Meanwhile, to delude the American public into believing that the Saigon regime was becoming more popular and was therefore worthy of increased support, U.S. leaders helped organize a series of "democratic elections" to legitimize General Nguyen Van Thieu as president and General Nguyen Cao Ky as vice president. The elections were a cruel farce. Thieu and Ky openly used troops and police to intimidate voters and rivals alike. They even dispatched General Nguyen Ngoc Loan, director of the National Police, to force members of the National Assembly to disqualify most serious opponents. Those who were permitted to run were constantly harassed, detained, and treated to all the worst kinds of political dirty tricks.

Even with these tactics, with the exclusion of voters in "insecure" areas as well as those dubbed sympathetic to the NLF, pacifists, or neutralists, and with rampant ballot box stuffing by soldiers and police, Thieu and Ky received 34.8 percent of the national vote. They lost outright in many larger cities such as Saigon, Danang, and Hue. The Assembly's Special Election Committee disclosed in late September that at each of 5,105 polling stations, composing nearly 90 percent of the national facilities, had each committed at least eleven violations. This was, in fact, all the violations provided for in the election laws. According to the elections laws, the National Assembly should have nullified the election if the number of voters at these polling places totaled over 800,000.

On October 1, 1967, the day before the Assembly was scheduled to vote to ratify the election, combat police blockaded all the streets to the National Assembly and General Le Nguyen Khang, commander of the 3rd Military Division, brought his army into Saigon. The following day, General Loan brought his guards into the National Assembly balcony, drew out his pistol, propped up his feet, and began drinking a beer. The implication was clear. Two hours later, Assembly members voted fifty-eight to forty-three to ratify the election. An hour later the body was dissolved. The Johnson administration immediately declared a victory for democracy in South Vietnam and vowed to do all it could to defend the new government.[27]

It was under these circumstances that DRV Politburo members decided to initiate the Tet attacks against southern cities. This was not a desperate gamble but a calculated move designed to persuade U.S. leaders to de-escalate the air war and start negotiations. According to Tran Bach Dang, who planned the 1967 attack on Saigon, the idea of a "general offensive" against urban areas in the South—especially against Saigon, which was the nerve center of the allied war effort—was to create shock waves in the South, and thus, force a turning point in the war. But this plan was not new. It had been conceived as a possible plan of action by NLF leaders as early as 1960.

In 1964, a plan of action similar to the 1968 Tet plan was introduced to the Communist Party's Central Committee. At that time there had been sufficient sapper units in the South to carry out the initial attacks. But the regular and regional forces were still not strong enough to deliver the necessary follow-up assaults. In addition, the political organizations in and around the cities and towns were considered inadequate for providing the necessary support to sustain the attacks. Moreover, in 1964 Communist leaders believed that such a general offensive would have the effect of sucking into Vietnam a huge number of American troops because the American "hawks" would be able to argue that the introduction of U.S. forces would help change the situation in the South. The plan was therefore temporarily shelved by the Central Committee. Instead, they directed southern revolutionaries to lay better groundwork for such an offensive in the future by building up their military and political forces.

By mid-1967 the Politburo and the Central Office of South Vietnam (COSVN/Trung Uong Cuc) ordered that the details of a contingency plan for attacks on Saigon and other cities be worked out. They reasoned that widespread attacks against the urban centers, which were the nerve centers of the U.S.-backed Saigon regime, would compel American leaders to pull back most U.S. forces to defend these southern centers, thereby easing their military pressure on the North. They conjectured that by that time the United States had nearly 500,000 troops in the South. They believed this was very nearly the maximum that the United States was capable of sending. Thus, they reasoned that a general offensive would demonstrate to American leaders and citizens that they had no hope of winning and hence would force them into negotiations and troop withdrawals. Representatives from the Politburo, COSVN, the B-2 Military Command, and the Saigon-Giandinh Regional Party Committee held several meetings from July to October to debate the Politburo decision and to discuss details for the offensive.[28]

Finally, on October 25, 1967, party Central Committee members issued Resolution 14, ordering a "general offensive/general uprising" or "tong cong kich/tong khoi nghia" in the South mainly against Saigon and the upper Mekong Delta provinces.[29] The main aims of Resolution 14 are best summarized by General Tra's aforementioned paper as follows:

The upcoming general offensive/general uprising will be a period, a process, of intensive and complicated strategic offensives by military, political and diplomatic means. . . . The general offensive/general uprising is a process in which we will attack and advance on the enemy continuously both militarily and politically.[30]

At this point Communist planners hypothesized that U.S./ARVN troops would counterattack savagely in order to reclaim important lost positions.[31]

According to most southern revolutionary leaders I interviewed, they defined the offensive as a "process" involving a continuous, protracted, and varying struggle, not just military attacks. They believed that over an extended period this constant and unrelenting pressure would force the United States to enter into negotiations. At this time this concept was repeatedly emphasized in all Communist directives at all levels. Since then it has also been consistently repeated in the writings of many southern leaders and revolutionaries.

Tran Hoan, later minister of information of the Socialist Republic of

Vietnam (SRVN), wrote in 1978 that before the Tet Offensive he was instructed by the secretary of the party Regional Committee of Tri Thien (northern half of Saigon's I Corps), Lieutenant General Tran Van Quang, to send out a directive to all the cadres and soldiers stressing that the

general offensive/general uprising is a process. . . . I repeat, a process. A process of extremely arduous and complicated military combats and protracted political struggles. At present our cadres and soldiers are still quite simplistic in their thinking on this issue. . . . It is wrong and dangerous for them to think that the general offensive/general uprising is a one-blow effort.[32]

In 1986 General Quang, then first deputy minister of defense, delivered a paper to the aforementioned Defense Ministry conference on Tet. It indicates that while no one regarded the upcoming offensive as a desperate gamble, there were considerable strategic and tactical differences of opinion between Hanoi and the people in the field. He recalled that the Ministry of Defense relayed the decision to carry out a general offensive/general uprising in October. When party Regional Committee members from the Military Command of Tri Thien met to discuss it they cited Lenin's dictum that you should not fool around with an uprising and that an uprising means that you have to carry out continuous attacks in order to assure any kind of success.

In spite of these reservations the conferees suggested to the Ministry of Defense that if a general offensive/general uprising had to be carried out, they should wait until April or May 1968 to give the local forces enough time to make the necessary preparations. As far as the Tri Thien area was concerned, the conferees requested that the Ministry supply two additional regiments of infantry, two 105mm artillery battalions, one antiaircraft battalion, and 400 tons of ammunition. The Ministry responded by saying that the party leaders and military commanders of Tri Thien should wait for further decisions to be personally delivered by Le Chuong, the political commissar of the Tri Thien Military Command, who was at the time in Hanoi. Le did not deliver the message until December 3, 1967. It stated that there should be attacks in all areas mainly through the use of local forces, and that Hue should be liberated by its own revolutionary cadres and forces. This, they asserted, would divert enemy forces from the main theater of the war, which was Saigon. Tri Thien leaders also learned that the time for the offensive had been set for sometime during the Tet New Year's celebration of 1968.[33]

General Quang recalled that the Ministry decision was met with both fervor and trepidation by those in Tri Thien. Excitement was high since they were going to take part in a large offensive aimed at the eventual liberation of the South and peace in Vietnam. They were fearful because they were not sure that they had enough power to carry out the task ahead.

Eventually they decided that since their main tasks were to cause diversion and draw enemy forces from Saigon they would try to occupy Hue for five to seven days. For this they believed they had enough resources. General Quang adds that they made this decision because they expected the Ministry to send necessary reinforcements as needed.

Quang claims that on December 25 a representative from the Politburo arrived and reminded local leaders that "the general uprising is a process," resulting in a continual series of attacks. These orders were not well executed. Instead of holding some forces in reserve for the second and third phases of the offensive local leaders threw almost all their forces into the initial attacks in direct contradiction to the scenario envisioned in Resolution 14. Another mistake was the initiation of "such a large campaign with such high objectives without having reserve forces on the spot and relying instead on reinforcements from the Ministry which never arrived while the battlefields were not yet prepared."[34]

The careful wording in General Quang's paper glosses over some very sensitive areas that we cannot go into here, partly because the details involved would require a great deal of time to clarify. However, what emerges from his words is some clear reservation regarding Resolution 14 by the majority of southern revolutionaries. In short, it seemed that a strategy of continual attacks and a general uprising would bring more U.S. pressure, which was contradictory to the Communists' announced goal. General Hoang Van Thao addressed this issue in his summation of the 1986 conference: "On this point, almost all of our comrades agree that it is incorrect both in practice and in theory. We have all clearly seen the results of mounting one phase of general offensive/general uprising against the urban areas when favorable conditions no longer existed."[35]

NO GENERAL UPRISINGS MEANT NO POPULAR SUPPORT?

Another dubious argument forwarded in the United States is the assertion by many that since there was no real general uprising during Tet there was no popular support for the NLF. However, as seen above, there was great popular support for the NLF before the Politburo issued the directive for the Tet Offensive. It is also important to define, especially to my U.S. readers, what the term "general uprising" or "tong khoi nghia" really meant to the revolutionaries at that time, and why uprisings, as understood or interpreted by Americans, did not happen.

At the 1986 Tet conference General Tran Do, the second most senior northern general in the South during the war, said that he had long analyzed the term *tong cong kich/tong khoi nghia*. *Cong kich* is the Sino-Vietnamese equivalent of the Vietnamese *tan cong*, and *khoi nghia* is a classical Chinese translation of the Vietnamese term *noi day*. This tactic of "attack and uprise, uprise and attack," or *tien cong va noi day, noi day va tan cong,* had been used by southerners throughout the war; it meant that military attacks had to involve the support of the population, and with this support there could be more attacks at a future time. The classical Sino-Vietnamese word *tong,* or "general," put in front of *cong kich* and *khoi nghia,* therefore suggested something similar to the regular NLF tactic of "simultaneous uprising" or *noi day dong loat,* which involved military attacks with logistical support by the population over a large area to avoid concentrated counterattacks by the enemy.

What was perhaps different in 1967 was that the term "termination point" or *dut diem,* used as a verb to mean "to take over a target completely," was a favorite term in the South. Hence, General Do said he and other commanders might have been thinking of this term as they began Tet. This was perhaps the reason why, of the three scenarios mentioned in Resolution 14, only the first was what those in the field were thinking about. This is especially true given the fact that by this time everyone was impatient and wanted to bring an end to the war. General Do added that had the Politburo given the campaign a less ambitious name such as "large offensive" or "strategic offensive" and had it stated clearly the campaign's limited objectives, then the people in the field would have been able to come up with better plans for the attacks and would have made better use of the forces available to them.

However, what is even more significant is General Do's explanation of the term *dut diem.* He declared that the southern commanders and population had constantly advised him and the armed forces against adopting this tactic. Their reasoning was that after taking over a target, the PAVN forces had to leave since they could not defend it. This left the local population to bear all the consequences of destructive retaliation by the enemy. Southern commanders had always worked to maintain and assure the safety of the local population in all military campaigns. In other words, the key players in the war in the South had a very different notion of uprising from the northern policy makers or American analysts.[36]

Tran Bach Dang has written that at that juncture in the war, when the United States was dropping bombs on the towns and cities of the South in the hope of driving out the revolutionaries, "uprising" can not be understood by analyzing paradigms drawn from the Russian October Revolution, the French Revolution, or even the August 1945 revolution in Vietnam. It can only be understood in terms of the *dong khoi* or "simultaneous uprisings" in Ben Tre Province in 1959–1960, when the people there used a wide variety of methods to gain political control. Dang added,

"Uprisings" in a war situation had to appear in different forms: the taking over of administrative power in the working-class neighborhoods, the disbanding of the puppet administrations, the patrolling of city streets, the searching out of secret

police and informers, the maintaining of security and order, the organizing of the
population to give direction and supplies to the soldiers, the transporting of weapons and the caring for the wounded. . . . The extent to which these were carried
out differed from neighborhood to neighborhood, but in the entire city [of Saigon]
this unusual atmosphere did occur.[37]

General Quang said that before the offensive against Hue, they had already agreed that there would be no way urban inhabitants could stage
any kind of uprising unless the revolutionary armed forces destroyed the
various types of enemy forces and took complete control of each target.
Even then, he declared, most southern leaders had envisioned an uprising
in which youth groups would go around calling on enemy forces to surrender, local despots would be rooted out, and at the "highest level" armed
bands would be formed to attack enemy forces along with the local fighters.
The general added that during the attack and occupation of Hue NLF
leaders saw their role as rallying from 530,000 to 800,000 inhabitants of
Hue and the surrounding villages to participate in, and give support to, the
Tet campaign.[38]

As far as Saigon was concerned, in 1986 Tran Bach Dang disclosed that
there had been a plan to have several student unions and youth organizations stage a Tet celebration on February 4–5, 1968, with several tens of
thousands of people in the Tao Dan public garden situated in front of the
Saigon Independence Palace. If sappers successfully penetrated the presidential palace and nearby national radio station, then the crowd would be
sent to occupy these grounds. However, the Politburo, for some unexplai-
ned reason, decided to step up the date of the offensive at the very last
minute and gave orders for NLF rebels in Hue to attack according to the
revised Vietnamese lunar calendar date, which preceded other attacks by
eighteen hours.

This was, according to Dang, a colossal mix-up. It not only destroyed
the plan to get the Tet revelers to occupy the two locations, but it also left
the sappers out in the cold without the support of the crack battalions that
were supposed to carry out simultaneous follow-up attacks on key target
areas. These troops were, in fact, still nearly 100 kilometers away from
Saigon when the sappers made their first assault. Consequently, since even
the larger sapper units were composed of only a couple of dozen men—
armed only with submachine guns and grenades—they were not able to
defend the targets that they had occupied for a prolonged period in the
face of counterattacks by the American and Saigon forces using helicopters
and tanks. As a result, the population of Saigon had to use other means to
show their support.[39]

Pham Chanh Truc, later deputy mayor of Ho Chi Minh City, and secretary of the Youth League for Saigon at the time of the Tet Offensive, was
the person responsible for organizing the celebration in the Tao Dan public

garden and other activities for student groups in Saigon. In a 1988 article he wrote that "many comrades" had pointedly "cautioned" (*luu y*) him against saying anything on the Tet Offensive when the senior party leadership had not derived a consensus view on this issue. He says that this left him very frustrated and forced him to restrict himself to citing only a few facts in the article even though he was able to do much more. Even so, he described the profusion of activities by the Youth League in Saigon in detail. He described the daily "rehearsals" (*tap duot*) which began on December 20, 1967, the anniversary of the founding of the NLF. Students raised NLF flags at most schools and university campuses and distributed leaflets throughout the city. When the people's self-defense forces and sapper units simultaneously attacked twenty targets in the center of the city, his forces were in support.

As Tet neared, not only had Truc's group planned an unprecedented celebration known as the "Emperor Quang Trung Tet Festival" (*Hoi Tet Quang Trung*) but throughout the city people were ready to give support to the attacking troops in the target areas. However, since the attack date was pushed up at the last moment, the planned events had to be called off. Instead, each group and individual had to deal with things as they unfolded. Three of the incidents Truc mentions are worth recounting here.[40]

The first was the seizure of the Ban Co–Vuon Chuoi area of Saigon by local inhabitants under the leadership of units of the Section II City Youth League. They chased away all the ARVN local forces and administrators and totally controlled the area until the morning of February 1. Meanwhile, Battalion 2 of the NLF main force had also penetrated the city from the southwest and seized the adjacent area of the city. These two areas were separated only by a traffic island known as Nga Bay. These two forces— the "uprising forces of the city population" and the NLF armed unit, as Truc called them—were literally within "arm's reach" (*voi tay*) of each other. If they had been able to link they would have become a formidable force for the U.S. and ARVN troops to deal with. However, for some mysterious reason which Truc says he still does not understand, these two forces did not know of the other's presence, even though each reported their situation to their respective headquarters. Strange things happen in war, but many southern leaders have told me privately that they had some evidence of betrayal which for several obvious reasons they feared to disclose.

The second example occurred when NLF Battalion 6 penetrated Saigon's twin city, Cholon. The Youth League organized the local population to aid in the capture of a huge area stretching all the way to the district of Binh Thoi. The inhabitants of the area supported the NLF soldiers with all the supplies and intelligence available, while students joined them to fight against enemy counterattacks.

Finally, on the evening of January 31, 1968, with refugees streaming into the city from the suburbs to avoid the cross fire, allied planes attacked the populated areas around the city in order to stop the advance of the NLF attacking forces as well as to preempt popular uprisings. Units of the Youth League immediately set up "support centers for war-displaced refugees" to support these war victims. As a result, the Saigon government was forced to subsidize these activities. In this way, with the support of the people, the Youth League was able to protect their own members and other revolutionary cadres as well as to expand the scope of their activities for months and years to come.[41]

Truc contends that there was plenty of popular support both during and after the Tet Offensive and that whether an "uprising" as defined by some northern Politburo members occurred or not was besides the point. Likewise, almost all the revolutionary fighters that I have talked with over the years have defined both *khoi nghia* and *noi day* in terms of active political support and participation of the population. The southern revolutionaries have constantly reminded me that without this support they would not have been able to recover from this "darkest period" during their long struggle against the most powerful and most destructive war machine in the world. This leads us back to the American argument that the NLF was destroyed by the spring of 1968 and therefore after that the only threat to South Vietnam came from the North.

DID THE UNITED STATES DESTROY THE NLF IN THE SPRING OF 1968?

This assertion is based on the claim that the revolutionary side suffered more than 58,000 casualties from January 29 through March 31, 1968. This is an exaggerated figure since the CIA estimated that the total number of PAVN Viet Cong (VC) participating in the Tet campaign was around 58,000. The U.S. Military Assistance Command, Vietnam (MACV) and General Earl Wheeler estimated that 60,000 enemy troops were involved in the offensive.[42] Certainly not all the NVA and NLF soldiers were killed, and so the NLF could not have been wiped out. Besides, not all the Communist forces present in the South actually fought. This is borne out by what occurred in Saigon.

Saigon, as previously indicated, was the main target of the Tet Offensive and so NLF leaders assigned to it the largest number of attack forces. Besides, the sapper units already in place in the city—fifteen to twenty-two battalions, or 5,400 to 7,700 troops—were used for follow-up attacks on targets in the city once the sappers had breached them. In addition, three divisions of regulars were stationed just outside of Saigon's first strategic defense perimeter in case reinforcements were needed. The attack forces were divided into the Northern Vanguard Command (*bo tu lenh tien phuong Bac*) and the Southern Vanguard Command (*bo tu lenh tien phuong Nam*). The Northern Command, also known as Vanguard 1, was headed by Generals Tran Van Tra, Mai Chi To (political commissar at the time and later interior minister of the Socialist Republic of Vietnam), and Le Duc Anh (later minister of defense of the SRVN). Their forces were supposed to attack the districts of Cu Chi, Hoc Mon, Di An, Go Vap, Lai Thieu, Thu Duc, and Binh Tan and then finally to occupy the ARVN Divisional Headquarters compound at Quan Tre, a portion of Tan Son Nhut Airport, the military base in Go Vap, and the Saigon General Command Headquarters.

The Southern Command, also known as Vanguard 2, was commanded by Vo Van Kiet (later the second-ranking Politburo member and SRVN prime minister) and Tran Bach Dang. The forces under their command were supposed to attack from the south and southwest and then, in coordination with the sapper units, take over the U.S. Embassy, the Saigon presidential palace, the ARVN General Command Headquarters, the National Police Headquarters, the Nha Be petroleum storage compound, a portion of Tan Son Nhut Airport, and a number of other targets.[43]

However, according to a classified study from Long An Province—which supplied most of the forces for the attack on Saigon from the south and southwest—a total of only eight battalions, all of them from the Southern Vanguard Command, penetrated these areas in Saigon. These battalions had brought along mainly light weapons, with only a few B40 grenade launchers, and so none of them was able to break through the heavily reinforced defense structures in the city in order to aid the sappers.[44]

In 1987 General Huynh Cong Than (Tu Than), the commander of the Long An forces, told me that the reason this occurred was that the order for the offensive was not received by the Long An forces until 4:00 a.m. on January 20, 1968. In a period of only eight hours the Long An forces had to march a distance of thirty kilometers through rivers and marshes in order to slip through the defensive perimeter set up by the U.S. 9th and 25th Infantry Divisions and the defensive anchors set up by the ARVN to block the western and southern infiltration routes to Saigon. Had it not been for the active support and participation of several hundred thousand inhabitants of Long An and Saigon it would have been impossible to deliver the 200 metric tons of supplies needed for the attack.[45]

Tran Bach Dang writes that the late attack order caught many of the NLF forces completely unprepared. The troops were out celebrating Tet and the battalion commanders were either still drunk or away on personal business. As a result, it required supreme efforts on the part of Huynh Cong Than and a handful of subordinate commanders to muster enough forces in time for the attack. In the face of the tremendous U.S./ARVN counterattacks with aircraft, tanks, and artillery, which delivered high explosives directly on positions within the city, Dang decided that the offensive should be called off to minimize casualties. He obtained permission from COSVN for the withdrawal of all armed forces from the city to the surrounding areas. As a result, casualties were relatively low. The worst casualties received by a battalion attacking from the outside was 100 killed. In the fiercest battle that the Southern Command engaged in, the equivalent of only one platoon were killed or wounded. Phase 1 of the Tet Offensive officially ended on February 5, the same day Dang left for HQ COSVN for an assessment of Phase 1 and planning of Phase 2.[46] As Gabriel Kolko has documented, "A mere one thousand armed personnel in Saigon, with the aid of local political units, managed for three weeks to hold off over eleven thousand U.S. and ARVN troops and police."[47]

Thus, it is clear that the NLF, for a variety of reasons, did not actually use that many troops during the first phase of the Tet Offensive and, therefore, could not have been depleted militarily, as many American writers have claimed. On the contrary, it actually extended its control of the rural areas after the first phase. During this phase the United States and Saigon were forced to pull back over 100 battalions to defend Saigon alone. As U.S./ARVN troops withdrew to defend Saigon and other urban areas, Saigon regional and local forces panicked and were easily driven off by local guerrillas. The villagers then razed the outposts and bases abandoned by these forces. This helped expand the NLF-controlled areas. In Long An Province, for example, this went all the way up to the doorsteps of Saigon. This situation was repeated in most areas along the Mekong Delta.[48]

This expanded NLF control played a role in encouraging the Politburo and COSVN to decide to launch Phases 2 and 3 of the offensive. General Tran Do recalls that Le Duc Tho arrived in the South as the Politburo representative several days after the first phase ended. After reviewing the situation, Tho, with Politburo backing, ordered the offensive to continue.[49] The initiation of the second and third phases subjected the NLF to increased casualties and hardships, and set the stage for the eventual loss of the bulk of NLF-controlled areas in 1969–1970. But for the rest of 1968, even in areas close to Saigon the NLF was still doing very well.

Two examples illustrate this. One occurred in Ben Tre Province. Ben Tre, known as Kien Hoa under the Diem and Thieu regimes, is eighty-six kilometers southwest of Saigon. It was the birthplace of the "general uprising movement" (*phong tao dong khoi*) in 1960. By the time of Tet, the majority of the 115 provincial villages were under NLF control. For this and other reasons, it was the most bombed province in the Mekong Delta during Phase 1. Kolko notes that "the provincial capital of Ben Tre, with 140,000 inhabitants, was decimated with the justification, as an American colonel put it in one of the most quoted statements of the war, 'We had to destroy the town to save it.' "[50]

Because it had been such a pivotal revolutionary province and because it was so strategically situated that it effectively blocked most of the routes to and from the lower Mekong Delta, Ben Tre became one of the priority provinces for massive counterattacks by ARVN/U.S. forces beginning in July 1968. The entire U.S. 9th Infantry Division was moved into the province to coordinate its attacks with the U.S. 117th Riverine Fleet and half a dozen battalions of southern marines and infantry units. In addition, there were massive B-52 raids and artillery shellings during this period. For example, 5,000 artillery shells were directed against the two villages of Luong Phu and Long My, Giong Trom District, while B-52s bombed these villages six times during the night of July 22, 1968, alone.

According to most of the people I talked with and according to documents I have obtained—the internal documents published by the Military Command of Ben Tre and the provincial party committee report—civilian and military casualties were relatively light throughout 1968. This occurred, in part, because as soon as the counterattacks began, the provincial NLF leaders decided to allow elderly people, women, children, and cadres who had not yet been exposed to move from those liberated areas which they expected to be hardest hit into the relative safety of the areas under the control of Saigon. Another important reason for light casualties was the fact that the NLF still held the initiative and was exacting a heavy toll on U.S./ARVN forces. In fact, in 1968 it managed to liberate an additional thirteen villages with a total population of 72,800, or 10 percent of the total provincial population.[51] By the end of 1968, there were still seventy-two liberated villages which occupied two-thirds of all the land area in the province.[52] As a party document on the province concludes,

By the end of 1968, after more than a year of fighting, the armed forces and people of Ben Tre killed and removed from combat 28,562 enemy soldiers, overran 195 forts and base camps, downed 97 airplanes, sunk and burned 126 boats, and destroyed 96 armored vehicles. In addition, Ben Tre also supplied the Regional Military Command and the Southern Military Command with three full infantry battalions, 10,130 volunteers and new recruits and 58 million dong.[53]

The second example was the case of Long An Province, where, according to its own classified study, NLF forces and civilians received the highest casualties of all the provinces in the South during the three phases of the Tet Offensive. Interviews with southern military commanders and political leaders at the time have generally confirmed this fact. Yet, in late 1968, U.S. government officials still regarded the province as largely under NLF control.[54]

WHEN AND WHY THE NLF LOST CONTROL

In order to understand when and why the NLF lost control of the countryside and what that meant for later years, it is important to understand how the NLF was able to gain and maintain control in the first place. I think that this can be achieved by focusing on only one province: Long An. Here I interviewed dozens of cadres and citizens in the summer of 1986. Since almost everyone I talked with supplied the same details, I will not quote them individually.

Long An is located immediately south of Saigon and was considered by the Saigon regime and the United States to be the gateway to the Mekong Delta or the back door to the city. They regarded this province as one of the most important military and economic centers in the South. The NLF considered Long An to be a crucial staging area for attacks on Saigon from the dangerously accessible southern and western directions. Hence, throughout the twenty-odd years of its involvement in Vietnam the United States determined to control Long An at all costs. The NLF, meanwhile, were just as determined to maintain control of Long An. This meant that the struggle there was one of the most desperate and savage of the war.[55]

As early as late 1959 and early 1960, through a combination of "armed propaganda"—involving the use of many tactics to win over ARVN soldiers—and attacks on ARVN military outposts, the NLF had gained control of the province politically and economically. Militarily, the province already had three battalions of regular troops—Battalions D506 and D508, operating in the eastern half of the province, called Long An due to administrative redistricting by Saigon—and Battalion D504 in the western half, then called Kien Tuong. In addition, the province managed to send one platoon each to operate in the Saigon area and the Nha Be River area, respectively, as well as one squad to fight in the My Tho District of Dinh Toung Province.

The first important military factor contributing to the development and maintenance of revolutionary control in Long An was the building of strong military forces, especially the regular provincial units. In fact, the provincial regular forces were, in 1959, the first to be created and thus had to carry out all the activities that the district units and the village guerrillas were later to perform. By the end of 1961, the province had already managed to train enough district units and village guerrillas to fight on their own at the local levels as well as to coordinate their combat activities with the provincial regular troops. The provincial leadership selected some of the best from its various companies, platoons, and squads to lead the district, village, and hamlet units.[56]

In each district there was an infantry company, a platoon of "special activities" or commando forces, and a platoon of "communication troops" (cong binh) specializing in attacks along the highways or waterways. They were equipped with submachine guns, machine guns, and other automatic weapons. In each village there was a platoon of about twenty-five to thirty guerrillas, and in each hamlet there was a squad of ten to fifteen guerrillas. To all these forces from 1964 on Long An added the so-called intravillage guerrilla units, whose members were picked from the various guerrilla platoons from adjacent villages. These intravillage units had specific duties assigned them by the district unit leaders. In addition, they had to coordinate their activities with all other forces. For example, during the 1964–1967 period the district of Can Giuoc had eighty hamlet guerrilla squads composed of 800 fighters, twenty village guerrilla platoons composed of 500 men, and three intravillage platoons. Intravillage Platoon 1 had thirty-five troops and had the job of cutting off enemy communications and detecting their movements along Route 5. Platoon 2 had twenty men and was assigned the job of harassing and taking the Tan Thanh military post, which protected the district town of Can Giuoc. Platoon 3 was supposed to cut all enemy communications on Route 15.

In the development of these three types of forces the emphasis was always placed on combat quality and not on the number of troops. For example, the official combat duties of these units were defined as follows: (1) The provincial forces had the duty of engaging regular U.S./ARVN troops and being capable of disabling each enemy company and battalion to force the eventual disintegration of a whole enemy regiment or division. At the same time, the provincial troops had to be able to overrun enemy forts and military bases having a battalion or more. (1a) The district forces had the job of attacking and destroying platoons and companies of mobile "security guards"—a type of ARVN regional unit—as well as overrunning forts and compounds held by a platoon of security guards. At the same time, the district forces had to coordinate with the provincial forces in attacking enemy regular troops. (1b) The village, hamlet, and intravillage guerrillas had to place under siege forts occupied by squads or platoons of ARVN "civil guards," or local forces, and to coordinate their activities with the district units in the attacks against the security guards. (2) The commando units could execute attacks against enemy bases, ammunition dumps, artillery positions, and so on. They could act independently or coordinate their activities with the provincial units. (3) The "communication troops" specialized in attacking enemy communications and movements along the highways and waterways.

This clear definition of responsibilities for the various forces contributed significantly to their effectiveness. This effectiveness, however, would not have been possible without the strong provincial troops, which were capable of engaging regular enemy forces entering the province. They provided the district and guerrilla forces with a protective umbrella under which to operate. To enable the regular provincial forces to accomplish all these tasks, supply and training had to be provided. Since the fighting was going on constantly, there was no time for rest, reinforcement, and/or rebuilding. This meant that in order to train new troops the various units had to take turns in combat activities, or training had to be carried out between battles. In order to ensure that each unit received all the supplies it needed, when and where it needed them, the population of Long An had to be organized for specific tasks. The successful accomplishment of all these tasks enabled the NLF to maintain its strength in, and control over, the province.[57]

The second important military factor that contributed to NLF control in Long An was the ability of the NLF forces to destroy all attempts by U.S./ARVN forces to cut up the province and isolate the NLF forces. American and ARVN forces tried to accomplish this goal by stationing their troops in forts and bases along strategic highways and waterways supported by mobile forces using tanks, armored river patrol boats, helicopters, and air and artillery strikes.

The NLF in Long An thwarted these efforts with constant attacks against enemy troops to keep them off balance. In this effort their troop deployments were as follows: (1) The strongest provincial regulars were used against the main enemy forces operating in areas north of Highway 4, where they were strongest. This put the enemy on the defensive and created conditions for penetrating the most vulnerable areas south of the highway to obstruct the enemy's attempt to cut the province in half and to provide protection for their forces in the south. (2) District and guerrilla units were used to fight ARVN security and civil guards who were occupying the hundreds of forts and military compounds along the highways and waterways. This destroyed ARVN and U.S. attempts to divide the territory into smaller pieces in order to further isolate NLF forces. At the same time, these district and guerrilla units served to expand the areas of NLF control to provide it with freedom of movement. (3) Tightly coordinated attacks against main Saigon forces by NLF provincial troops and against forts and compounds were carried out in order to destroy the ability of the mobile ARVN forces and those in forts and bases to protect each other with a coordinated defensive strategy. (4) Commando forces were deployed in all the district and village towns to attack the enemy's nerve centers, their artillery bases, and their supply bases. At the same time, the "communication troops" were used to carry out constant attacks along the highways and waterways, disrupting enemy logistical support and rear areas and thereby limiting the full use of their resources.[58]

In order to be able to carry out the above deployment the NLF had to develop and maintain strong bases in all areas of the province, especially in the region north of Highway 4, since this would provide a staging area for attacks against Saigon. This in turn required that the NLF be able to simultaneously attack enemy forces, defend its own territories, protect the village inhabitants, create strong NLF cadres and followers among the people, and maintain the NLF spirit and political consciousness of the masses. Side by side with development of the base areas and staging areas for attacks, the NLF had to guarantee the constant movement of its various forces.

During the 1964–1967 time frame, when the NLF most tightly controlled

Long An, and when there was actually no gap between the liberated areas, the provincial forces moved around constantly to execute their attacks in both regions. The district units and intravillage guerrillas were also able to move freely in their districts and between villages. This enabled the village and hamlet guerrillas to maintain their infrastructure. This was the reason why enemy forces were always off balance and on the defensive. But this situation changed after the second phase of the Tet Offensive in 1968.[59]

PHASE 2: THRESHOLD TO DISASTER

The second phase of the offensive presented the NLF in Long An with huge problems. The defense of Saigon, for example, was reorganized into three distinct and well-coordinated perimeters. The national police were responsible for the inner city, while ten paratrooper battalions, marines, and special forces occupied the infiltration routes used in the first phase of the offensive; in the outer circle U.S. troops and ARVN regulars constantly carried out their counterattacks, hoping to push the NLF forces further back into the countryside. In spite of the fact that they had to battle the constant counterattacks, the Long An forces managed to cling to the outlying area of Saigon and prepared for the second phase of the offensive against Saigon.[60]

In general, the plan and the directions for the assault remained the same as in the first phase. The attack forces were divided into three contingents, or sections. Sections 2 and 3 from Long An were to attack from the south and southwest and Sections 1, 4, and 5 were to attack from the north and northwest. There were only slight changes in tactics, such as reliance on mortars and rockets and not sappers to attack key targets in the city. However, it was clear from the outset that the mortars and rockets used were not adequate for breaking into a heavily fortified area. In addition, there was no longer the element of surprise. In fact, when the U.S. military command and the Saigon regime learned of the impending attack they placed another brigade and hundreds of pieces of artillery on the routes to the city so that when the NLF forces advanced toward the capital they would be attacked and shelled from behind.

The attack against Saigon by the Long An contingents lasted from May 5 to June 18, 1968. The twists and turns of this six-week campaign are extremely interesting from a military point of view but are too complex to detail here. In general, the attacking forces had to fight every inch of the fifteen to twenty kilometers to Saigon. Along the way they engaged not only various ARVN forces but also the American 9th and 25th Infantry Divisions, which were something that they had managed to avoid altogether during the first phase of Tet, thanks to diversions created by local guerrillas and village inhabitants.

When the Long An contingents arrived at the city the north and northwestern contingents were still being blocked at the outer defense perimeter. Enemy forces were able to concentrate most of their forces against the Long An contingents and pushed them slowly backward. When the northern and northwestern contingents finally managed to enter the city, the Long An units were too depleted and weakened by several days of constant fighting to provide adequate support. As a result, the allies were able to concentrate their forces against Sections 1, 4, and 5. Thus, casualties during this second stage were high. After they were forced to withdraw into the outlying areas of the city, Section 2 found that it had only 775 of its 2,018 troops still in fighting condition, while Section 3 had only 640 left from its original total of 1,430.[61]

American and ARVN forces were able to draw some valuable lessons from the second phase of the offensive. They followed the NLF units closely after the withdrawal into the outlying areas and repeatedly attacked them to prevent NLF forces from regrouping for another assault. Three additional battalions of ARVN rangers were brought in and, along with the U.S. 25th Infantry Division, launched attacks against Section 2. The ARVN 199th Brigade, reinforced by the U.S. 9th Infantry Division, struck retreating troops of Section 3. Five hundred tanks and armored vehicles were placed on Route 4. Three hundred and sixty patrol boats were stationed on the rivers so that there was one every 500 yards. Artillery strikes were increased against all the staging areas of the NLF forces and all suspected escape routes. Chemical defoliants were sprayed on vast areas that had been considered liberated zones. Most devastating of all, massive B-52 raids were conducted daily along the banks of all rivers and waterways as well as on populated areas. In fact, these raids intentionally destroyed the ecological makeup of Long An and other Delta provinces. Moreover, they terrorized the villages in order to deny the NLF sanctuary and base support. Some people have labeled this tactic "My Lai from the sky" because the aim was the same; only the tools differed.

In spite of the heavy losses the Politburo and COSVN ordered Sections 2 and 3 to remain in the outlying areas of Saigon to prepare for the third stage of the offensive. This proved dangerous since they needed to be able to resist the constant counterattacks of ARVN and U.S. forces by dispersing themselves. Instead, they had to remain at the battalion level and coordinate their maneuvers with district and village guerrillas to fight relatively big battles in a number of areas. This created a number of contradictions which had to be resolved. The first was the contradiction between combat and preparation: without fighting back, the various units would not survive; but in fighting back they would absorb heavy casualties and therefore would not have enough strength to mount a third assault on Saigon.[62]

The second contradiction involved the question of troop concentration and dispersion. Maintaining the troops at battalion size would expose them to attrition from the bombing and shelling, but dispersing them into smaller units would not leave them enough strength to resist the mopping-up operations being carried out by the enemy forces. The solution at the time was to dig as many "combat trenches" and build as many strong tunnels as possible to minimize casualties from the shelling and bombing as well as to facilitate counterattacks against the enemy operations. Forces were concentrated quickly to counter the enemy and dispersed quickly to avoid casualties.

While the main forces of Sections 2 and 3 remained in the outlying area of Saigon and fought fierce battles with enemy forces, the guerrilla units in districts and villages, unprotected by regular troops, had to spread themselves out too thinly. Thus, they did not have the strength to attack the remaining enemy outposts in the countryside. As a result, Saigon regional forces regained their confidence, beefed up their units, and, alongside ARVN regulars, began to coordinate attacks against liberated areas. These moves, and the massive destruction of the countryside due to air strikes and chemical sprayings, served to cut off the Long An contingents fighting in the outskirts of Saigon from the rest of the rural areas. Worse still, the organizational division of the Long An forces into Sections 2 and 3 made it difficult to coordinate the activities of the units north and south of Route 4. Everyone I spoke to in Long An—from General Tu Than, Colonel Le Phai and Colonel Le Ky to the district and village leaders—said that this division was a very crucial factor affecting the ability of the Long An contingents in combat as well as the maintenance of their positions in the outlying area of Saigon. The Long An main units were able to remain and fight for half a year in the outskirts of Saigon, launching the six-week third phase of Tet in August. This was largely due to the fact that they were still able to maintain communication lines with the rural areas. But this strategy left the less experienced and more ill-equipped guerrillas in the villages and districts exposed to concerted attacks by enemy forces.[63]

By the end of 1968 and early 1969, the United States had taken advantage of the fact that the Long An main forces were still massing in the direction of Saigon to carry out its "accelerated pacification program." The aim of this program was to move large forces quickly behind the Long An forward positions to take over the liberated areas, thereby isolating these Long An main forces in the outlying areas of Saigon. Against these Long An units Saigon used a combination of forces with the main aim of keeping them occupied and isolated in these forward positions. Meanwhile, an additional 200 patrol boats were deployed on the Vam Co East and West Rivers to facilitate further divisions on Long An to cut off NLF supply and communications lines. After successfully dividing the Long An battlefront, two brigades of the U.S. 25th Infantry Division, the ARVN 25th Division, and fifty rural pacification teams started to retake the liberated areas.

By July 1969, the pacification of the two sections on Long An was basically completed. This created increasing difficulties for the Long An forward units in the outlying areas of Saigon which lasted until the end of the year, when COSVN ordered them to withdraw to the Vietnam-Cambodian border, supposedly to rebuild. This, according to all the Long An commanders to whom I spoke, was the second-biggest mistake made by the leadership because it meant surrendering all the populated areas without a fight. It is of utmost importance in a guerrilla war to maintain contact with your support base. Even when you lose control you should try to maintain what NLF commanders called the "position of adjoining combs" (the *cai lucc*), that is to say, infiltrating the enemy's area in order to get support from the local people and to gain access to enemy territories.[64]

STICKING IT OUT: THE REBUILDING PROCESS

For the reason just stated, the Long An leadership decided to disobey the order from COSVN and sent the provincial forces to the district and village levels to act as local forces and to help rebuild the guerrilla military units there. Political and military cadres thus braved all kinds of sacrifices to carry out the policy of *bam tru,* or literally, "clinging onto the post." The "post" here referred to the land and the people. The NLF's main aim was to get the people to cling to the land, while the NLF cadres clung to the people so tightly that it would be difficult for the enemy, as NLF leaders declared, to "empty the countryside" or to "dry up the ocean to kill the revolutionary fish." Therefore, the NLF also developed a slogan to remind themselves and the population of their determination to stick it out at any cost: *Mot tac khong di, mot ly khong roi. Dan bam dat, can bo bam dan, bo doi bam dich ma danh* (We will not be moved, not an inch, not even a millimeter. People cling to the land, cadres cling to the people, and soldiers cling to the enemy and fight.) Hence, this policy was also known as the *ba bam,* or literally, "three clingings."[65]

For most cadres, "clinging" meant staying close to the people to give them the necessary moral support and political guidance to help them organize into the different types of military forces mentioned earlier and to do political and propaganda work among the enemy's ranks (*binh van* and *dich van*). This often meant living most of the time in tunnels under people's houses, under roads and highways, under paddyfields, and even under the fences of the so-called new life hamlets (*ap doi moi*) and so-called camps for refugees fleeing from communism (*trai ti nan cong san*).[66]

They had to rely on the population to sneak food and water to them. For example, children—especially kids who tended buffaloes—would pretend to go out fishing with bamboo rods and cans of earthworms which they would leave in places where the NLF cadres could pick them up. In reality, beneath the layers of earthworms was fish, meat, or rice. Likewise, the knuckles inside the bamboo canes had all been knocked out and rice, salt, and sesame seeds stuffed inside. Old people were also sneaking food to the NLF troops inside their canes. Peasants put rice and meat in plastic bags and hid them inside their manure carts, which they pushed out into the paddy fields. Fishermen, on the other hand, tied plastic bags full of food under the bottoms of their sampans or junks and rowed them to prearranged places where the NLF cadres and fighters could retrieve them.[67]

On their part, the NLF also crept close to the villages at night to hoe the fields and till the land for the people. During the 1969–1970 period they also planted manioc in the bomb craters, especially those produced by B-52s, in order to provide for themselves and to avoid being wholly dependent on the support of the local population. By planting in the bomb craters they also would not have to prepare the soil and would, therefore, not expose themselves since the ever present enemy reconnaissance planes would be quick to detect changes on the ground. Each B-52 destroyed an area half a mile in diameter and a mile and one-half in length. Such an area was usually covered by an average of fifty to sixty huge bomb craters, each of which could support 150–200 manioc plants. Each plant produced about eight to ten pounds of manioc roots in five to six months. In bomb craters covered with water, the NLF planted bindweed (*rau muong*), which is rich in nutritional value. They also raised fish.

The NLF collected aluminum fragments from downed airplanes, copper artillery casings, and empty shells to exchange for needed supplies. A kilogram of scrap aluminum or copper could fetch enough money to buy about ten kilograms of rice or sugar, one kilogram of pork or fish, eight cans of condensed milk, or five kilograms of soap in 1969–1970.[68]

Clinging to the people and to the enemy was very difficult. There were only a few dozen village guerrillas left in Sections 2 and 3 in 1969. That was the reason why each section in Long An had to bring its main forces back from the Cambodian border area, contrary to COSVN's orders, to rebuild the district and village guerrilla forces. In Section 3 Dong Phu Battalion and D520 Battalion returned to the districts of Can Giuoc and Can Duoc, respectively, and helped rebuild these guerrilla structures. Members of Dong Nai and Phu Loi Battalion and Battalion 1 of Regiment 320 also returned to serve as district guerrilla fighters and commanders. In Section 2 Battalion D264 returned to Duc Hoa District to help rebuild the local guerrilla forces there. This rebuilding effort had to be carried out with the utmost care, with every effort made to conceal the fact from the enemy, with total dedication on the part of many southern political cadres and with support from the population.[69]

The people of Long An and elsewhere in the South told me again and again that the recovery of the guerrilla forces and the revolutionary structures in the South by 1971 was only made possible by the tremendous effort from the southern political and military leaders who returned in 1969–1970. During this period PAVN forces who were sent to the South to help could not function effectively and were killed in large numbers. The people of Long An told me that several thousand regular NVA troops were killed in Long An during this period. Before this period, they said, main force units operating in the South had been well integrated with both southerners and northerners so that the latter could function effectively. On the average, every northern soldier arriving in the South had to receive another year of training before he was battle ready. In addition, regional units and local guerrilla forces provided the necessary political structure and logistical support for the main forces. They also prevented concentrated attacks on main force units through widespread and simultaneous assaults on an entire province or a whole region to occupy and disperse enemy forces. Conversely, main forces had the job of drawing enemy units away from vulnerable areas as well as engaging enemy units too large for the regional and local forces to deal with. The loss of ability to coordinate the activities of these three types of forces, along with other factors, led to what southerners called the "darkest years of 1969–1970." *Bam tru* helped rebuild the regional and local forces and hence necessary structures and coordination lost during these dark days.[70]

The recovery of the southern political and military structures, I was told, was also aided in part by the urban opposition movement which grew in the major urban areas in South Vietnam beginning in 1969. This caused both the Saigon regime and U.S. leaders to spend much attention and energy on dealing with the urban strikes and demonstrations. This was especially true after May 1970, when over 50,000 U.S. and ARVN troops invaded Cambodia in order to "clean up the sanctuaries" and to "dismantle the Vietcong Pentagon."

The invasion of Cambodia also tied up large amounts of U.S. airpower and logistics for several years. In the long run, this helped give the southerners time and space to recover and to take the initiative in many places through coordinated deployments of the previously mentioned three types of forces. In the short run, I was told, the invasion of Cambodia actually interfered with rebuilding efforts in many of the Delta provinces because they had to send reinforcements to the border areas. In fact, both the interviewees and internal documents from Long An contend that the invasion actually caused serious damage to the rebuilding effort. This was because, in order to attack the Parrot's Beak area, where they suspected the NLF headquarters were located, Saigon's 7th, 9th, and 25th Divisions, 3rd Airborne Brigade, and an armored brigade centered their operation in Long An, with full U.S. air and artillery support. Many Long An people, especially political cadres, were killed during this operation because they were taken by surprise and because they were not able to find an effective way to counter such a huge operation at first.[71]

But soon the NLF drew valuable lessons, reorganized themselves, and were able to mount constant counterattacks. From July to October 1970 they fought seventy-five battles, killed 1,750 ARVN soldiers, destroyed

forty tanks, and downed sixteen planes and helicopters. In addition to fighting along the border areas, Long An forces also joined the main forces to
liberate the entire Cambodian province of Svayrieng. After that, Long An
and Kien Tuong sent five delegations of military cadres of about twenty to
thirty to help the people of Svayrieng rebuild their military forces. Together
they were able to form eight full companies of provincial main forces, with
300 soldiers in each. Each was equipped with weapons from Long An and
Kien Tuong. In addition, each district in Svayrieng had one to two platoons
of district forces, while each village had one to two full squads of guerrillas,
all trained by the NLF fighters of Long An and Kien Tuong.

Because of this diversion, it was not until October 1970 that Sections 2
and 3 of Long An again merged into a unified administrative unit, known
as Section 23. After this political and military cadres were sent to the district and village levels to help rebuild the administrative and military structure. Subsequently, the Military Command of Section 23 also reorganized
its main forces into three special full-strength battalions (Battalions D1,
D267, and D269) which incorporated a number of newly arrived northern
troops. The rest of the provincial units were designated K2, K4, K7, and
K9. Two battalions of sappers and one battalion of "communication
troops" were also formed. The Kien Tuong Section reinforced its D504
Battalion with some northern troops and created one company of sappers,
one company of urban commandos, and one mortar and rocket company.
Together the above units and cadres worked among the population and
coordinated their attacks against ARVN forces until the provincial NLF
political and military structures recovered in late 1971 and early 1972.[72]

The people of Long An took pains to point out to me repeatedly that
one of the key things was not how the southern NLF forces were hurt or
weakened, but how they recovered with help and support of the southern
population, both rural and urban. In their opinion, the people were the
biggest assets in any revolutionary war. Stick to the people and you can
survive and gain strength. *Bam tru*, they said, was the key to survival and
success during the 1969–1972 period.

Eric M. Bergerud's recent study of Hau Nghia Province—next to Long
An and just southwest of Saigon—supports most of the above conclusions.
He observes,

Without doubt, 1969 was the best year for the allies both in Vietnam overall and
in Hau Nghia province. Perhaps it would be more accurate to describe 1969 as the
worst year for the Front because, regardless of the outward manifestations of progress, GVN again failed to win the freely given support of the rural population in
Hau Nghia province. . . . The allies again failed miserably to attack the Front's
political apparatus in an organized manner. This was a great disappointment for
CORDS [Civil Operations and Revolutionary Development Support] because 1969
was the first year during which the attack on the enemy apparatus was given top
priority in practice as well as in word.[73]

CONCLUSION

In summary, several points can be made. The Tet Offensive, though it did not overthrow the Saigon government, was successful in accomplishing its main objective of forcing the United States to de-escalate the war in North Vietnam and to begin negotiations that would eventually lead to a peace agreement based on NLF terms in January 1973. The offensive also dealt a devastating blow to the Saigon regime, making it absolutely clear that the government would never be able to survive on its own without massive U.S. aid. Significantly, the offensive set off dynamics in South Vietnam which led to the development of a vast urban peace movement and a widespread sentiment for peace throughout the South that would play a critical role in 1975.

Tet might well have had even greater results for the NLF had their troops returned to their rural bases after the first or second phase instead of trying to carry out all three phases. If the troops had returned to protect their rural bases they would probably still have achieved the original purposes of the offensive and would have emerged from it much stronger. Far fewer cadres and civilians in the countryside might have been killed in the 1969–1972 period.

Instead, the NLF forces from Long An stayed massed around Saigon; thus, enemy troops were able to inflict high casualties on both NLF and guerrilla units. Worse still, the Politburo and COSVN made the strategic mistake of ordering the NLF forces in Long An and many other provinces to leave for the border areas. As a result, 1969–1970 became the most difficult years of the war for the Communist cause.

Even so, due to popular support, the NLF was not destroyed. Instead, it managed to rebuild itself through the strategy of "three clingings." It was this recovery that led to the military successes of 1971 and 1972. It made it possible for northern forces to operate in the South again without getting into danger.

In short, the story of Tet and its aftermath demonstrates that popular support in the South allowed the NLF to rise from the ashes of defeat like the phoenix in spite of American efforts to destroy it, including the infamous Phoenix program. To claim that the NLF was defeated after the spring of 1968 never to recover again ignores or distorts the facts. In this connection, one may note that accounts of Tet and its aftermath often overemphasize the role of national leadership and directives, and fail to recognize the role of local leaders, organizations, and initiatives.

NOTES

The original version of this chapter was written in early 1988 and was published in the January–February and March–April issues of the *Indochina Newsletter*. The entire work was presented to a conference held in Hanoi during November 25–27, 1988, at which scholars from the United States and Vietnam met for the first time since the war to discuss its history. The conference was originally called the "Conference on the History of the American War in Vietnam" by the Vietnamese hosts.

1. A copy of the book was smuggled out of Vietnam and published in the United States. See Foreign Broadcast Information Service, *Vietnam: History of the Bulwark B2 Theatre,* Volume 5, *Concluding the 30-Years War in Southeast Asia Report,* No. 1247, JPRS 82783, February 2, 1983. The book still can not be legally read in Vietnam.

2. The conference was entitled "Hoi Thao Khoa Hoc Tong Ket Xuan Mau Than 1968." Presentations and proceedings of this meeting were sent to the Institute of Vietnamese Military History (Vien Lich Su Quan Su Viet Nam) of the Department of Defense in Hanoi. Excerpts of some papers were published as *Tap Chi Lich Su Quan Doi: So Dac Biet 20 Nam Tet Mau Than* [Journal of Military History: Special 20th Anniversary Issue on the Tet Offensive], February 1988. General Thao's summary is entitled "May Van De ve Chien Luoc trong Cuoc Tien Cong va Noi Daty Xuan 1968" [Some Strategic Questions in the Offensive and Uprising of Spring 1968], p. 35.

3. Tran Bach Dang, "Mau Than: Cuoc Tong Dien Tap Chien Luoc" [Mau Than (Tet Offensive): A Strategic Rehearsal], *Tap Chi Lich Su Quan Su,* February 1988, pp. 57–64 [hereafter "Mau Than"].

4. The interviews were conducted after careful study of most of the published Vietnamese and American sources. Interviewees included leading policy makers, military leaders and troops, and provincial, district, local, and village leaders and citizens. I asked top leaders about specific policies, programs, and events, while I focused on the personal histories of provincial leaders and local revolutionaries. Besides talking with top leaders in the South who were living in Hanoi or Ho Chi Minh City at the time, I also conducted extensive interviews with hundreds of leaders and revolutionaries in key provinces such as Long An, Ben Tre, Quangnam-Danang, and Minh Hai. Among the national figures interviewed were National Assembly President Le Quang Dao, who became a lieutenant general in 1961 and was the overall political and military commander of the Quang Tri–Khe Sanh region during Tet; Lieutenant General Nguyen Chanh (Tuong Binh), director of the General Office of Military Logistics, who fought against the U.S. 1st Cavalry Division during Tet; General Tran Van Tra; General Tran Bach Dang; General Nguyen Van Chinh (Chin Can), the deputy prime minister for official discipline and organization at the time of the interview; Major General Huynh Cong Than (Tu Than), overall military leader in Long An Province during the entire war and commander of the contingents that successfully penetrated Saigon during Tet; and Major General Hoang Van Thao, director of the High Military Commission in the Southern Region (Vien Quan Su Cao Cap Mien Nam). Hundreds of other national, provincial, and local leaders and revolutionaries were also interviewed. The list is far too long to include here. Those who are interested in a complete list of these individuals may write the author. Much of the general information about Tet gleaned from these interviews has been used without undertaking tedious and continuous citings throughout the remainder of the paper. This is especially true in the

general discussion of Tet itself. The information derived from the sources cited in notes 28–41, 43–46, 48–49, and 51–72 was complemented by knowledge obtained from these interviews.

5. General Cao Pha, "The Year of Mau Than: Turning Point in the Vietnamese People's War of Resistance against U.S. Aggression and for National Salvation"; General Hoang Phuong, "For Nixon: The Highest Escalation of the War and the Most Disastrous Defeats."

6. The original article was divided into four parts. Due to a lack of space only Part 4 was published in the February issue as Tran Van Tra, "Thang Loi Va Suy Nghi Ve Thang Loi" [Victory and Thoughts about Victory], *Tap Chi Lich Su Quan Doi* [Journal of Military History], February 1988, pp. 36–45 [hereafter "Thang Loi"]. The first three parts were published under the title "Tet Mau Than: Chien Cong Hien Hach" [The Glorious Victory of *Tet Mau Than*], *Tap Chi Lich Su Quan Dai*, April 1988, pp. 8–23.

7. Tra, "Thang Loi," pp. 42–44.

8. Ibid.

9. Ibid.; see note number 6.

10. Tran Vu, "1971: Nam Phan Thang Loi Gianh Quyen Chu Dong Chien Truong" [1971: A Year of Successful Counteroffensives That Regained Initiatives on the Battlefronts], *Lich Su Quan Su*, April 1991, p. 4.

11. Ibid., pp. 4–5.

12. Some examples of the exceptions are an ambitious and excellent analysis of Tet and its aftermath by Gabriel Kolko, *Anatomy of a War: Vietnam, the United States, and the Modern Historical Experience* (New York: Pantheon Books, 1985) [hereafter *Anatomy of a War*]; and a detailed treatment of what happened in the area southwest of Saigon during Tet in Eric M. Bergerud, *The Dynamics of Defeat: The Vietnam War in Hau Nghia Province* (Boulder, Colo.: Westview Press, 1991) [hereafter *Dynamics of Defeat*]. Although both authors basically agree with my conclusions their emphasis on official documents has put off many southern revolutionaries.

13. George Donnelson Moss, *Vietnam: An American Ordeal* (Englewood Cliffs, N.J.: Prentice-Hall, 1990), p. 243.

14. Ibid., p. 252.

15. Ibid., pp. 252–253.

16. James J. Wirtz, *The Tet Offensive: Intelligence Failure in War* (Ithaca, N.Y.: Cornell University Press, 1991), pp. 2–3 [hereafter *Tet*].

17. Ibid., p. 2.

18. Quote in Stanley W. Cloud, "Exorcising the Old Demons," *Time*, March 11, 1991, p. 52.

19. "NLF in Vietnam," Associated Press, February 4, 1967.

20. *Le Figaro*, February 15, 1967, p. 1.

21. "South Vietnam Situation Today," Reuters News Agency, March 11, 1967. Long An Province is immediately south of Saigon.

22. "Who Holds What in Vietnam Now," *U.S. News and World Report*, March 22, 1967, p. 35.

23. Tom Buckley, "Pacification Report Stalled in 3 Vietnam's I Corps Region," *New York Times*, May 24, 1967, p. 2.

24. R.W. Apple, Jr., "Vietnam Signs of Stalemate," *New York Times,* August 7, 1967, pp. 1, 14.

25. See *The Pentagon Papers,* Senator Gravel edition, Volume 2 (Boston: Beacon Press, 1971), p. 507.

26. Ibid., Volume 4, pp. 349–351.

27. For an account of the election, see Francis H. Craighill III and Robert C. Zelnick, "Ballots or Bullets: What the 1967 Elections Could Mean," in *Vietnam: Matter for the Agenda* (Los Angeles, Calif.: Center for the Studies of Democratic Institutions, 1968). For reports in the Saigon press, see *Than Chung,* August 16, 1967; *Chang Dao,* October 3, 1967.

28. Dang, "Mau Than," *Tap Chi Lich Su Quan Su,* pp. 57–63.

29. *Mau Than Saigon* [The Tet Offensive in Saigon] (Ho Chi Minh City: Nha Xuat Ban Tre, 1988), p. 4.

30. *Tap Chi Lich Su Quan Doi* reprinted most of Resolution 14 in its February 1988 issue on pp. 2–3, but says that the document (Emperor Quang Trang Resolution) was issued by the Central Committee on January 1, 1968.

31. Ibid.

32. Tran Hoan, "Xung Quanh Ham Chi Huy" [Around the Command Tunnel], in *Hue Nhung Ngay Noi Day* [Hue during the Days of Uprising] (Hue: Sach Giao Khoa, 1979), pp. 31–32. Tran Hoan explained to this writer the impact of the concept of process on the conduct of the offensive and its aftermath in April 1980 in Hue and in November 1989 in Hanoi.

33. Tran Van Quang, "Hue 25 Ngay Dem" [Twenty-Five Days and Nights in Hue], *Tap Chi Lich Su Quan Su,* January 1988, pp. 25–28.

34. Ibid.

35. Ibid., p. 24.

36. Tran Do, "Tet Mau Than: Tran Tap Kich Chien Cuoc" [Tet 1968: A Strategic Offensive], *Tap Chi Lich Su Quan Su,* February 1988, pp. 48–54.

37. Tran Bach Dang, "Ben Them Mot Vai Khia Chanh Cua Cuoc Tong Dien Tap Chien Luoc Mau Than 1968" [Additional Remarks on Several Facets of the General Strategic Rehearsal of Mau Than 1968], *Tap Chi Lich Su Quan Su,* July 1988, p. 3.

38. *Tap Chi Lich Su Quan Su,* February 1988, p. 27.

39. Tran Bach Dang, "Nhat Ky Mau Than" [Mau Than Diary], in *Mau Than Saigon,* p. 36.

40. Pham Chanh Truc, "20 Nam, Them Mot Lan Suy Nghi" [Twenty Years, Yet Another Occasion to Ruminate], in *Mau Than Saigon,* pp. 9–12.

41. Ibid.

42. Wirtz, *Tet,* p. 249.

43. *Mau Than Saigon,* pp. 4–5.

44. *Bao Cao Dien Bien 21 Nam Khang Chien Chong My Va Nhung Bai Hoc ve Toan Dan Danh Giac cua Long An* [Report on Developments in the 21 Years of Resistance against the Americans and the Lessons of the Entire Population Fighting the Enemy in Long An] (Long An: Ban Tong Ket Chien Tranh Tinh Long An [Committee on Assessment of the War in Long An Province]), pp. 98–100 [hereafter *Bao Cao . . . Long An*].

45. Ibid., pp. 96–100.

46. *Mau Than Saigon,* pp. 36–44.

47. Kolko, *Anatomy of War*, p. 308.

48. *Bao Cao . . . Long An*, pp. 101–102.

49. *Tap Chi Lich Su Quan Su*, p. 52.

50. Kolko, *Anatomy of a War*, pp. 308–309.

51. "Bo Chi Huy Quan Su Tinh Ben Tre" [The Military Command of Ben Tre Province], in *Cuoc Khang Chien Chong My Cuu Nuoc Cua Nhan Dan Ben Tre* [Resistance against the Americans for National Salvation of the Population of Ben Tre], 1985, pp. 190–196. Foreword by General Hoang Van Thai.

52. Ibid., p. 194.

53. A detailed discussion of and statistics on these facts are also found in ibid., pp. 190–196. The main source of these facts is *Lich Su Dang Bo Dang Cong San Viet Nam Tinh Ben Tre, 1930–1985* [History of the Communist Party Provincial Committee of Ben Tre, 1930–1985] (Ben Nghien Cuu Lich Su Dang Ben Tre [Party Historical Research Committee of Ben Tre], 1985), p. 188.

54. *Bao Cao . . . Long An*, pp. 106–110, 174.

55. Ibid., pp. 122–127.

56. Ibid., pp. 122–123.

57. Ibid., pp. 106–127.

58. Ibid.

59. Ibid.

60. Ibid.

61. Ibid.

62. Ibid.

63. Ibid.

64. Ibid.

65. Ibid.

66. Ibid.

67. Ibid.

68. Ibid.

69. Ibid.

70. Ibid.

71. Ibid.

72. Ibid.

73. Bergerud, *Dynamics of Defeat*, pp. 254–255.

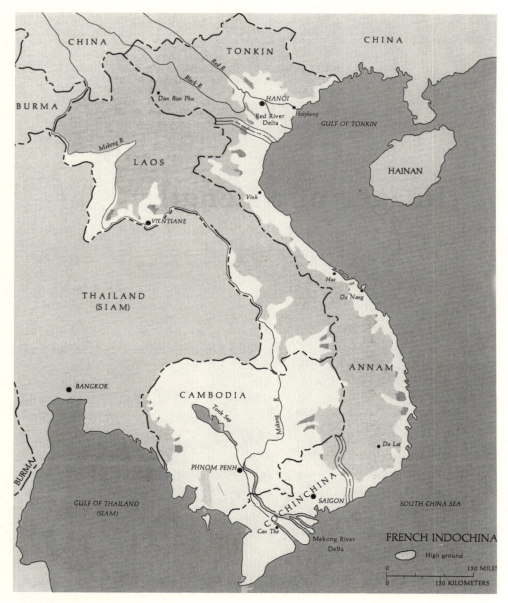

Map of French Indochina
From official U.S. Army History (*Images of a Lengthy War*: *US Army in Vietnam*, by Joel
D. Meyerion).

Map of the Tet Offensive, 1968
U.S. Army History.

Vo Nguyen Giap during Tet was Minister of Defense and number three on the SRVN politburo. Seen here in the summer of 1967, Senior General Giap, although philosophically opposed to the Tet Campaign, had already begun planning the offensive most leaders hoped would shorten the War. U.S. Army History.

Fifth U.S. Marines patrolling the war torn streets of Hue following a 25-day struggle for control of the old Imperial Capital. U.S. Marine Corps.

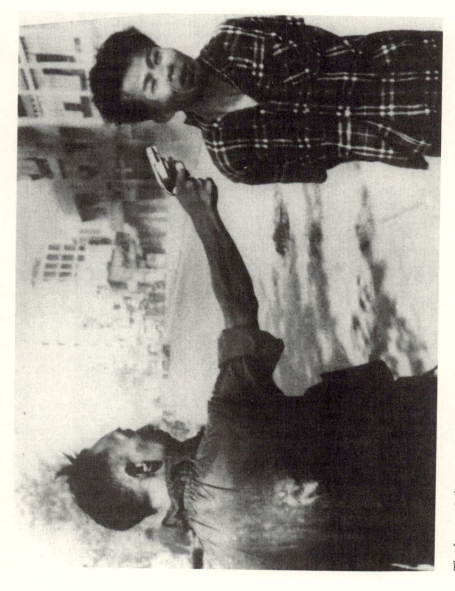

The famous *Life* Magazine photo by Associated Press photographer Eddie Adams shows the street execution of a VC lieutenant by South Vietnam's National Police Chief Nguyen Ngoc Loan. The photo won the Pulitzer Prize.
U.S. Army History.

Paying last respects to loved ones murdered at Hue. Skulls and bones of Tet massacre victims recovered from mass graves are laid out in a small village school house on the outskirts of Hue. U.S. Army History.

Marines waiting during a folly morning for a PAVN attack that didn't come; this time. U.S. Army History.

President Johnson and his advisors in the war room located in the basement of the White House viewing a terrain model of Khe Sanh. U.S. Army History.

March 31, 1968, President Johnson under public and media pressure as a result of Tet announces he will not seek reelection and calls on SRVN leaders to negotiate a settlement to the conflict. U.S. Army History.

7

My Recollections of the Tet Offensive

Ambassador Bui Diem

Time flies! The Vietnam War ended almost twenty years ago, the Tet attacks occurred twenty-eight years ago, and here I am, looking back at what happened then. I am, along with so many others, still trying to learn more about that war and the momentous event known as the Tet Offensive. In the process I hope something useful for the future may come out of this effort.

During the past few years, I have had the opportunity to participate in many seminars and conferences on the Vietnam War. I am convinced that with more facts, more research, more perspectives from each of us, historian, scholar, researcher or writer, all of us now have a better understanding of the many "whys" and "hows" of the war. But, as all of us know, facts are not all that count. In politics, quite often perceptions count more than facts and contribute in no small part to the making of history. The Vietnam War is not an exception in this respect, and the Tet attacks of 1968 are a perfect illustration of this particular fact of life. My brief chapter is about this special aspect of the war.

In 1968, during these critical days, I was a Vietnamese who happened, due to the circumstances of his professional career, to be an eyewitness to the actions and reactions of American leaders in Washington and Vietnamese leaders and citizens in Saigon. As such I would simply like to offer the reader some of my personal recollections on this episode of the war. I sincerely hope that, in some way, my memories will contribute to our quest for wisdom that, according to Henry Kissinger, "America owes to itself if Vietnam is to leave any useful legacy."[1]

This chapter is divided into three parts. First I will try to present briefly some facts about Tet I consider irrefutable, given the many books and articles that we now have—especially the very candid admissions by the Communist authorities themselves in relation to these facts. Then I will try to describe how these facts were perceived at that time. Finally, my conclusion will discuss how these perceptions contributed to the important decisions of all the parties to the war, decisions which in many ways influenced the outcome of the war.

Don Oberdorfer of the *Washington Post,* in his classic book about Tet, called Mau Than Tet the turning point of the war. It was, indeed, and in my personal opinion if the coup in November 1963 against President Ngo Dinh Diem was a turning point in the history of the U.S. involvement in Vietnam, Tet 1968 was a turning point in the U.S. military effort in Vietnam. Clearly, before Tet American strategy was still focused on winning the war, but after Tet, even though the war would continue for one more year under the Johnson administration and four more years under the Nixon administration, it would become more of a holding action to permit a U.S. withdrawal from the war than the reflection of a political will to pursue the war to a victorious end.[2]

For a full understanding of this pivotal event, here are some basic facts. The Communist preparations for a spring offensive in 1968 were known weeks in advance by Americans and South Vietnamese, yet when the attacks began on the night of January 31, 1968, it was almost a surprise. Indeed, the timing of the attacks was totally unexpected, and the strategy, which consisted of launching attacks simultaneously against all thirty provincial capitals and more than seventy district towns throughout the country was so audacious that by itself it was a surprise.[3]

For all the Vietnamese, Tet is more than a traditional holiday. It is a symbol of hope, a combination of Christmas, New Year, Thanksgiving, and the Fourth of July. So throughout the years of the war, with or without formal agreement, both sides tacitly observed a kind of truce during the three days of Tet, and if occasionally there were violations they were of no consequence. Obviously that was not the case in January 1968. On the first day of the Vietnamese New Year—the Year of the Monkey—throughout the land families got together in a relaxed mood for celebration. However, no sooner had the sounds of the first firecrackers of the traditional Tet celebration died down than the Communists detonated their own deadly fireworks as they attacked in a well-coordinated general offensive against not only the old capital of Hue and the new capital of Saigon, but also almost all the provincial capitals and district towns throughout the country.

At first the civilian population did not realize that it was a Communist attack. To many the crackling noise of the machine guns sounded like people celebrating the new year with more firecrackers than usual. Moreover, the very idea of attacking cities, where allied troops, American and South Vietnamese, were supposed to have all the advantages, was so incredible and daring a gamble that the first reports of the attacks were dismissed as jokes. But it was a real attack, which forced the South Vietnamese into a national state of shock and awakened them to the realities of war at their doorsteps on this first day of Tet, when normally even the guns remained silent to leave room for the traditional joyful greetings.

As Communist prisoners later confirmed, they were able to infiltrate men and weapons into Saigon through ingenious and meticulous preparations several days before the attacks by taking advantage of the busy Tet celebration atmosphere, during which the whole population prepared for the festivities of the new year. They even staged fake funerals to smuggle heavy weapons inside empty coffins covered with flowers into Saigon. I was not in Saigon when the Tet Offensive began, but I returned home four days later. My mother, sister, and other relatives told me that the attacks had been really spectacular.

Commando units (mostly sappers) aided by infiltrated agents made the first assaults in the capital area, attacking specific targets such as the presidential palace, the U.S. Embassy, the police and navy headquarters, the radio station, and the Joint General Staff compounds. Next, the main force units, believed to be between 4,000 and 5,000 strong, reinforced the initial assault by attacking at dawn, from both the northern and southern suburbs. The attacks were spectacular. Suddenly the city found itself in the midst of a ferocious street war, and the attacks succeeded in many cases in penetrating to the inner defense areas of their targets; but the attackers could not hang on. The U.S. Embassy in the downtown area, one of the main objectives of the surprise offensive, was a case in point. The small group of sappers and commandos (approximately two platoons) succeeded in blasting a hole in the wall of the Embassy, got into the compound, and killed five defending Marines, but were quickly eliminated after a few hours of fighting. The whole area was retaken by mid-morning, when Ambassador Ellsworth Bunker, accompanied by TV cameras and newsmen, came to his office to inspect the grounds still littered with the bodies of dead enemy soldiers.

All around town the same situation prevailed, and after a night of fierce fighting the only place where the Communists could hang on until daylight was the radio station. By noon the next day they had also been crushed, by the large reinforcing units of the South Vietnamese Army and especially of the Police Forces, which had reacted swiftly and vigorously in spite of being caught off guard. Either through lack of coordination or because the main force units could not come in time to link up with them, these commando units quickly became suicide squads and in many places did not survive the day. The main force units, for their part, fared better. They came in larger units and fought in the suburbs, mixing themselves with the civilian population; but the government troops, strongly backed by the air and artillery power of the United States, pushed them back from the center of the city.

After four days of confused fighting which caused many casualties among the civilians, it became clear that the back of the attack was broken. All in all, the attacks lasted approximately a week, after which the situation returned almost to normal, except for some occasional sniping from isolated Communist elements who had hidden themselves among the population. The physical destruction in the capital, given the scope of the Communist attacks, was not considerable. However, the disruption of the normal flow of life was nearly complete during the first three days of fighting, and the casualties among the civilians were serious, with more than 500 killed and 3,000 or 4,000 wounded. As for the uprising of the population that Communist leaders had counted on, and so often referred to in their statements and indoctrination documents before the attacks, to their disappointment there was none in Saigon nor elsewhere throughout the country, not even in the old imperial city of Hue, where the Communists gained control for almost a month.

The Communists synchronized their attacks against Saigon with other attacks against all the important provincial capitals in the Delta area to the south and in the northern part of the country, but nowhere was the fighting as ferocious as in Hue. There, more than in any other place, the Communists revealed the true character of their implacable brutality. They controlled the city for only three weeks, yet during this short period of time, they shot, clubbed to death, or buried alive more than 4,000 people, including military personnel, foreign doctors and missionaries and, in most of the cases, harmless civilians who were simply suspected of having connections with the government. Mass graves were in fact discovered after the Communist departure. As members of the victims' families later testified, those who were killed belonged to a wide cross section of the population, including intellectuals, schoolteachers, businessmen, and even clergymen. It was a pure and simple bloodbath which, along with other material destruction, left Hue in ruins for many years to follow.

The whole Communist offensive lasted approximately a month, then fizzled out in spite of predictions in many quarters that there would be a second wave. It caused widespread destruction in every important city and town where the fighting occurred. It occasioned disruption not only of the normal life of the population but also of all the governmental programs which represented the patient efforts of the previous years. The losses, in terms of human lives, were severe, with 5,000 allied combatants killed and more than 15,000 wounded. In addition, there were tens of thousands of South Vietnamese and American civilian victims. Estimates of Viet Cong and NVA casualties have been placed as high as 40,000. Militarily, these losses were important in the sense that they affected, at least temporarily, the balance of forces between the two sides. But, even more important than these losses was the impact that the offensive had on the whole course of the war. To measure this impact, clearly the military factor was only one part of the equation.[4]

The Tet Offensive of 1968, as seen through its synchronized efforts, had been planned long in advance by Vo Nguyen Giap and the North Vietnamese strategists.[5] What did they have in mind when they launched this offensive, which they should have known was at best a high-risk gamble? Was it a "go for broke" attempt to break the stalemate and force the Americans "into the sea" or at least to divert U.S. airpower away from its northern bombing campaign? Was it to influence public opinion in the United States? Obviously, the Communists had many objectives in mind, both political and military, but as a senior Communist Vietnamese general, Tran Van Tra, later admitted in a candid 1982 report, "These objectives were beyond our actual strength and founded in part on an illusion based on our subjective desires."[6] They assumed particularly in this respect that the people in the cities of South Vietnam would welcome them with fervor and in a general "popular uprising" would topple the "puppet government" of South Vietnam. Their cadres and combatants were even told in advance that the South Vietnamese forces would desert or join them once the offensive began. And, as if they believed their own indoctrination and propaganda, during the night of January 31 Radio Hanoi broadcasted appeals to the population of South Vietnam calling for the establishment of "people's committees," ostensibly aimed at the formation of a "people's government" for the liberation of South Vietnam. The realities turned out to be vastly different from their wishful thinking. There were no popular uprisings, and the governmental troops, instead of deserting, fought back aggressively. It was probably this shattered illusion that Tran Van Tra alluded to.[7]

In strictly military terms, the Communists did not fare well. The one exception was the old imperial city of Hue, where they dug in for twenty-four days and perpetrated the most horrible bloodbath of the whole war. Their commando units in all other places were killed or captured within days, and their main force units could not stand up against the overwhelming military power of the allied troops. Although there was no way to obtain accurate figures, the general consensus described their casualties as devastating. In fact, between 35,000 and 40,000 of their men died or were wounded during the first month of the offensive. Such casualties for only limited military rewards, even considering the Communists' customary disregard for their own casualties, was too heavy a price—unless, as some analysts speculated at that time, they had deliberately sacrificed the cream of the southern NLF forces with the unavowed Machiavellian purpose of eliminating a potential future threat to themselves.[8]

Thus, we have the facts the way they have been broadly interpreted by almost all the historians on both sides of the war. However, as we have seen in later years, facts do not necessarily coincide with perceptions. If the war in Vietnam had been confined only to the cities and battlefields of South Vietnam then the Tet Offensive of 1968 would have been considered a devastating Communist military defeat. But such was not the case. The Communists failed to achieve results in the military field but by the sheer audacity of their attacks they succeeded in provoking a traumatic shock in the United States and the world, impacting U.S. public opinion at a vulnerable moment in time. In fact, public support for the war was already on a downward trend, just when the primaries preceding the U.S. presidential campaign of 1968 began.

In a sense the shock effect of the enemy offensive was created in part by Washington itself. In a series of appearances during the fall of 1967, including a speech before a joint session of Congress and in TV interviews, General William C. Westmoreland had conditioned the country into believing victory was at hand. In this rosy mood of confidence the U.S. public assumed—despite a certain dose of skepticism in some quarters—that a major enemy offensive could no longer happen. Then in January 1968, in plain view on everyone's TV screens, the evening news showed scenes of ferocious fighting at the U.S. Embassy and other places in downtown Saigon. It shocked American viewers. The war with its ugly face of blood and destruction, of dead lying in the streets while American and South Vietnamese units blasted enemy centers of resistance—all this was suddenly brought into the home of every American family. It was real carnage in vivid colors on the TV screen, and the reaction in the public mind was, to say the least, one of consternation.[9]

During the first three or four days of the offensive, when South Vietnamese forces were still fighting hard to clean out the Communist pockets inside Saigon and push their main force units back into the suburbs, there was real concern in Washington as to whether the South Vietnamese would be able to withstand the invaders and provide security in the capital and other cities so that normal life could return for the civilian population.

But as soon as it became clear that the back of offensive had been definitely broken, even though ferocious fighting continued in Hue, the concern switched to the less urgent but more serious problem of the effect of the offensive on U.S. public opinion. It was in this domain that the Communists were more successful. The audacity of their offensive stunned public opinion. But despite the serious setback suffered by the Communists, little by little the implications of their offensive began to exert a different effect in Washington. In particular, Americans were struck by the contrast between the enthusiasm of President Johnson's public relations campaign and the reality of enemy capabilities. Westmoreland and Bunker had been optimistic during their recent tours, but now it seemed as if all the talk about progress and being "in control" had been either blatantly mistaken or intentionally deceptive.[10]

In Congress and among the press, people started asking questions. If the military situation was supposed to be under control, how could the Communists launch such a well-synchronized and widespread operation without our intelligence people detecting it? Why was it that with half a million American soldiers in the country, the Vietcong was still able to penetrate the major cities in force, even to attack the U.S. Embassy? Slowly it became clear that whatever the military results, psychologically the Tet attacks had undermined the Johnson administration's credibility. It made people distrust the government's assessments, its judgment. And in so doing it cast doubt on the entire war policy. The devastating losses on the enemy side were one thing, but the perception in the minds of people on "main street" was another; and a serious military defeat for the Communists was transformed into a psychological victory helping them beyond their own expectations to impose on the Americans their well-known "fight and talk" strategy, which led to the negotiations in Paris a few months later. In that sense, the Tet Offensive of 1968 was clearly a turning point of the Vietnam War. It marked the beginning of the collapse of both political will in Washington and of national support for the war.[11]

The irony of the situation was even more visible with the difference of moods between Washington and Saigon in the aftermath of the Tet attacks. In Washington the atmosphere was clearly an atmosphere of doom and gloom, while in Saigon, strangely enough, in spite of all the destruction and disruption of normal life, the mood was exuberant. The South Vietnamese had heard a lot about the Viet Cong but had no precise idea about their strength, so their first direct contacts with the men from the jungles occurred during the days of the Tet attacks and they were not much impressed. They had discovered that after all these Viet Cong were not ten feet tall. Besides, there was no uprising of any kind which could confirm the Communist claim that the people of South Vietnam were on their side. For its part, instead of collapsing, the Saigon government came out of the crisis with more confidence than ever before, and almost doubled its military strength through a general mobilization supported by massive U.S. economic and military aid.[12]

However, in 1968 continued American support for South Vietnam was critical, and for whatever the reason American attitudes on this issue changed dramatically after Tet. During my meetings with President Johnson in March I soon came to realize, even before he announced that he would not seek reelection, that the course of the war was changing. No matter where I was at the time, something had changed. You know that sometimes there are moments when somehow, due to the circumstances in which you are involved, you realize that you are in the midst of one of the most significant moments in history. I can say for sure that on March 18, 1968, when I met with President Johnson, even though he did not mention anything about stopping the war, I felt in my heart that to U.S. leaders the entire course of the war had changed. Remember, this was just barely six weeks after the initial Tet attacks.

Of course, as most readers realize, the ambassador of a foreign state in Washington does not meet with the president every day. Once a year there is a ceremonial banquet for all the ambassadors, separately or all together, and there is a lot of chitchat—that is, under normal circumstances or in normal times. However, Vietnam was not going through a normal time. It was about as unusual as it could get. This is why I received an invitation to meet with the president.

In fact, just a few days earlier I had asked for an appointment to see the president, not really expecting to see him anytime soon. Nonetheless, two days later, a friend of mine conveyed to me that the president wanted very much to see me. So I went to see him, hoping to take advantage of this important opportunity to convince him in any way I could to maintain his present policies in Southeast Asia. I wanted to see if I could gauge his feelings and report them back to my government in Saigon. To me this was the most important meeting I'd ever had with President Johnson.

I did not come in through the front door. Instead, I came through the adjoining office of my friend to avoid the press. From there I went into the Oval Office, where I saw a man . . . how shall I say it . . . completely lost! He was rocking slowly in his rocking chair waiting for me. Before, I had always seen him in a jovial or active mood, doing this or that, everywhere at once. But this day he was very different. He asked me to tell him what my read on the situation in Saigon was and what the views of the government were. He seemed to be very pleased about the way the Saigon government was holding up and the way I'd reported things to them. I said that it was "a dangerous time for Saigon but that somehow we could and would get through this crisis just as we had so many others before." I also explained that I and they understood the political situation inside the United States, but I emphasized our need for an immediate resupply of weapons and supplies to fight off any future enemy attacks.

Even though he assured me that he would do his best to resupply needed weapons and promised continued support, his gray and melancholy appearance made it very clear to me that Tet had meant the beginning of the end of American commitment to South Vietnam. I told this to Saigon. Sadly, I was right! As we can see, by all accounts the Tet Offensive was a big event in the course of the Vietnam War. It was perceived by public opinion, the news media, and the Congress in the United States not as a serious military defeat for the Communists, but as a revelation about their strength as well as about U.S. and allied vulnerability. This was perhaps a distortion of what really happened in the military balance of forces on the battlefield, but it was a fact of life in the political atmosphere of Washington at this particular juncture of the war and as such impacted heavily on governmental decision making.

As I noted earlier, the leadership in Saigon was optimistic after the initial Tet phase passed. When I arrived, four days after the attacks, the first thing I noticed in Saigon was the complete disruption of normal life. There was still fighting going on in the streets of Saigon not too far from my home at the center of the downtown area. To be very honest, there was still a lot of uncertainty about whether the enemy would attack again. During the day and night we could hear gunfire and explosions in the distance. In short, there was still a lot of concern, even though we now know that the fighting had actually been confined to only one or two isolated pockets.

I reported the full situation in Washington very candidly. This was particularly true with regard to my March 18 meeting with President Johnson. I told them that the U.S. commitment was not endless and that since Tet I had believed they would begin to pull back. These words proved prophetic. The gradual draw-down of American combat troops and material support began soon thereafter.

I tried to convey the president's changed attitude to President Thieu and other leaders. They listened but, in retrospect, they did not fully grasp the total impact of what I was saying. They had been speaking to U.S. officials and military leaders in Vietnam and these officials were still committed to American support of the war. It took a long time for them fully to comprehend what was happening after Tet. Even after the president's announcement to end the bombing and not seek reelection, and after General Westmoreland was reassigned, they did not completely realize that the United States might pull out. However, by the end of the year and by the time President Nixon took over things were much more obvious.

By this time almost everyone understood that the Americans would leave. Our leaders scrambled to make the best of this situation, but it seemed to many of us that during those last years events were out of our hands. They occurred out of our control. Tet made this so. Maybe it should not have but it did.[13]

Indeed, the changes I feared after my meeting with President Johnson came to pass just a month later with the decision from the president not to seek reelection, to stop the bombing, and to open negotiations with the Communists. The war did not end then, but the whole course of the war was changed irreversibly. Not long after, it became clear to me that the complete withdrawal of U.S. troops from Vietnam would be only a matter of time and modalities. In that sense, the Tet attacks of 1968 could well be considered a prelude to the end of the war five years later. Thus, Tet was the climax of the Second Indochina War. Indeed, to me, Tet was the time when U.S. public opinion and misconception snatched defeat from the jaws of potential victory.

NOTES

1. Dr. Kissinger's remarks come from Henry Kissinger, *The White House Years* (Boston: Little, Brown, 1979).

2. See Donald Oberdorfer, *Tet!* (Garden City, N.Y.: Doubleday, 1971), [hereafter *Tet!*].

3. Ibid.

4. The aforementioned general facts on the Tet Offensive come from ibid.

5. For more information on the Communist planning of the Tet Offensive, see ibid.; Vo Nguyen Giap, *"Big Victory, Great Task"* (New York: Praeger, 1968).

6. This quote can be found in Tran Van Tra, *Vietnam: History of the Bulwark B2 Theatre,* Volume 5, *Concluding the 30-Years War* (Ho Chi Minh City: Van Nghe Publishing House, 1982).

7. Ibid.

8. Tra's book mentioned above alludes to such a suggestion.

9. For views on the effects of the U.S. media on the war and on how Tet was perceived see Peter Braestrup, *Big Story!,* 2 volumes (Boulder, Colo.: Westview Press, 1977). In his memoirs Westmoreland discusses his role in Tet and his belief that Tet was a great victory which could have led to complete victory with 250,000 additional troops; see *A Soldier Reports* (New York: Doubleday, 1976).

10. Johnson's attitudes and his "public relations" effort before Tet can be found in his autobiography *The Vantage Point: Perspectives of the Presidency, 1963–1969* (New York: Holt, Rinehart, and Winston, 1971) and Larry Berman's *Lyndon Johnson's War: The Road to Stalemate in Vietnam* (New York: Norton, 1989) [hereafter *Lyndon Johnson's War*]. Another excellent source for these issues is *The Pentagon Papers: The Defense Department History of United States Decision Making in Vietnam,* U.S. Senator Gravel edition (Boston: Beacon, 1971).

11. For details on Tet as a psychological turning point see Oberdorfer, *Tet!*.

12. For an extended view of the mood in Saigon following Tet, see Bui Diem and David Chanoff, *In the Jaws of History* (Boston: Houghton Mifflin, 1987). For a detailed view of the mood in Washington see Berman, *Lyndon Johnson's War.*

13. In her analysis, *The Viet Cong in Saigon: Tactics and Objectives during the Tet Offensive* (Santa Monica, Calif.: Rand Corporation, 1969), Victoria Pohle agrees that the Saigon leadership was very confident immediately following Tet. However, she believes that they came to understand that the United States might pull out sooner, and with fateful results. In any case, once this was understood everyone realized that without the United States, as things stood in 1968, it would be very difficult to preserve the South Vietnamese government.

8

The Tet Offensive and Middletown: A Study in Contradiction

Anthony Edmonds

Although much controversy still swirls around the Tet Offensive, most observers seem to agree on one broad proposition: Tet was probably instrumental in causing a major reassessment of U.S. policy, given the official perception that the offensive had caused a shift in public opinion. In other words, Tet helped push the American public toward a deepening pessimism about the war and America's role in it; this pessimism, then, was instrumental in causing an alteration in U.S. policy.

The journalist Don Oberdorfer, in his early and still valuable account of the offensive, argues that Tet "was a pivotal event, one of the great turning points of our day."[1] He emphasizes Tet's "powerful impact on American public attitudes and governmental decision-making" and concludes that "the American people and most of their leaders reached the conclusion that the Vietnam War would require greater effort over a far longer period of time than it was worth."[2]

Writing two decades later, James Olson and Randy Roberts make the same point in their superb textbook, *Where the Domino Fell:* "Tet was an overwhelming strategic victory for the Communists. . . . Americans were no longer in the mood for more talk about victories."[3] For Olson and Roberts, Art Buchwald's column entitled "We Have the Enemy on the Run, Says General Custer" aptly symbolizes the public's Tet-induced pessimism about the war.[4]

Finally, the most recent specialized scholarly account of Tet, James Wirtz' masterful *The Tet Offensive: Intelligence Failure in War,* echoes the views of Oberdorfer and Olson and Roberts. Wirtz proclaims at the outset that

The Tet offensive was the decisive battle of the Vietnam War because of its profound impact on American attitudes about involvement in Southeast Asia. In the
aftermath of Tet, many Americans became disillusioned. . . . To the American public and even to members of the administration, the offensive demonstrated that U.S.
intervention . . . had produced a negligible effect on the will and capability of the
Vietcong and North Vietnamese.[5]

Tet, finally, "contradicted the claims of progress . . . made by the Johnson
administration and the military."[6]

I want to test this proposition in a local context—that of Muncie, Indiana. I choose Muncie for two reasons. First, I live and teach there. More
importantly, Muncie has a long history of being singled out as a microcosm
worth studying. From the Lynds' pioneering *Middletown* works of the
1920s and 1930s through a recent *Chicago Tribune* feature on politics in
Muncie, this medium-sized city of 80,000 souls has been under the micro-
scope for eight decades. It is "the nation's most studied city" and therefore
has a kind of cachet as a starting point for local history.[7]

Did the Tet Offensive tend to make Munsonians pessimistic about the
war? Did they call for a change in policy downsizing America's commitment? Unfortunately, no public opinion poll data exist specifically for Muncie during Tet. Thus, I will rely on two traditional types of sources in this
exercise: two local daily newspapers as well as the local university paper
and a series of interviews about the war with local citizens. By carefully
examining the front pages and editorial pages of papers and listening to
the oral histories, we might have at least a tentative sense of public attitudes
and public discourse.

Based strictly on quantitative evidence, Tet must have had some impact
on Munsonians. During February 1968, ninety-six front-page articles on
the Vietnam War (the majority of them on Tet or related issues) appeared
in Muncie's daily newspapers, the morning *Muncie Star* and the afternoon
Muncie Evening Press. Moreover, twenty-one of the articles were "banner
headline" lead articles.[8] In addition, twenty-four letters to the editor,
twenty-two columns by national pundits, twelve editorials, and ten political
cartoons related to Tet and the war appeared on the editorial pages of the
two local papers during February. Even the *Ball State News* weighed in
with four front-page articles, three letters to the editor, three editorials, two
cartoons, and one "outside pundit" column in its abbreviated February
run.[9]

Certainly, much of the considerable attention devoted to the Tet Offensive did seem to indicate a degree of pessimism among letter writers, edi-
torialists, cartoonists, and columnists. At one end of the spectrum, some
readers became convinced that those who protested against the war, the
draft, and American hypocrisy might well have a valid point. Ball State
student Mary Mayfield, for example, used Tet to launch a spirited defense

of all who condemned the war. They were rightly protesting "the loss of innocent lives in Vietnam [and] the unfairness of United States draft laws (and the draft itself)."[10] One James Keating indeed saw the elimination of most draft deferments as potentially more dangerous than the war itself: "Artists will use their hands for combat rather than advancing culture," he complained. "This . . . draft ruling wears away the fabric of American strength."[11]

Other letter writers argued that South Vietnamese and American hypocrisy undercut the United States' attempt to occupy the moral high ground. Carl van Buskirk (a "registered Republican") wrote that he could "not support a government [Saigon] who arrested members of the opposition party," while Ball State professor David Scruton contended that the enemy's actions, no matter how "bestial" during Tet, could in no "way serve as a moral justification for what we may do if our acts are unwise, intemperate, or inconsistent with our national ideology."[12]

More common, however, were sentiments of bewilderment, disappointment, and concern over the real possibility of a protracted war and stalemate. Partly, this feeling derived from a sense that events beyond American control were closing in. The North Koreans had captured the *Pueblo* a week prior to Tet; the trade deficit was growing; Charles DeGaulle was increasingly a thorn in America's side. One cartoon in the *Press*, for example, poignantly showed a bewildered and wounded LBJ in an arm sling named "Viet Nam" and a foot cast labeled "Korea." He stood in front of George Washington at Valley Forge, complaining, "Talk about a Rough Winter."[13]

But many observers were not so sympathetic toward the president. More representative of this sense of pessimism and loss are three other editorial cartoons suggesting administrative mendacity and false optimism. One in the *Star* showed Johnson in a track suit, running furiously in place with bullets knocking his hat from his head. Title: "We're Advancing on All Fronts."[14] Johnson here is clearly misleading his public. A Bill Mauldin cartoon in the *Ball State News* echoed this sentiment from a grunt point of view. As rockets fall around two soldiers in a foxhole, one says to the other, "Maybe They Have Had Enough and Are Being Inscrutable about It."[15] Finally, a cartoon in the *Press* made disillusionment manifest. A sandaled foot named "Viet Cong Offensive" steps on eyeglasses labeled "Official U.S. Optimism." Title: "Rose Colored Glasses."[16]

Several nationally syndicated columnists published in Muncie papers also expressed this sense of disillusionment engendered by Tet. Not that they urged unilateral withdrawal or a negotiated settlement on enemy terms. Rather, we get a sense of futility, stalemate, and an uncertain future. Rowland Evans and Robert Novak, with great prescience, suggested only two days after the initial Communist attack that the battle might end in a "stalemate" with the United States faced with the need for "an agonizing reappraisal" of its policy.[17] Bruce Boissat expanded this view when he noted that America's "bargaining position" was "seriously weakened" because of the offensive,[18] while Michael Padev took a slightly different tack, viewing Tet from the point of view of U.S. credibility: "The Communist attacks . . . have politically defeated the basic purpose of American policy in Vietnam— to show the South Vietnamese people that they would be safe from Communist aggression and terror."[19] If South Vietnam could trust the United States less, its own reconstruction tasks were almost insurmountable after Tet. According to Evans and Novak, "Saigon now has to perform the near miracle of physical reconstruction, internal reform, and pacification. . . . [There] is scarcely reason for general optimism about Saigon capitalizing on its last chance."[20]

If this was a barely tenable final opportunity, then the columnist Henry Taylor perhaps best summarized why many pundits seemed so pessimistic. He wrote of an old Chinese proverb, "Well, a full 4,000 years ago a Chinese general observed: 'In shallow water the dragon is eaten by the minnows.' "[21] And it was surely clear after Tet who the dragon and minnows were, respectively.

Sometimes, local editorial writers joined this chorus of doubters. An editorial in the *Star,* for example, noted the government's "official" line "that the Communists have suffered such heavy losses in the offensive" that they clearly experienced a military defeat. "But," concluded the editorial, "what if" this version "is wrong?"[22] Peggy Howard, editor of the *Ball State News,* certainly felt that the official story omitted a key fact: "In spite of claims that the enemy has lost a great number of troops," she wrote, "this has been a great psychological victory for North Vietnam."[23]

Part of this "victory" for the enemy involved a sense of powerlessness on the part of U.S. strategists. An editorial in the *Star* argued that "the recent offensive . . . by the Communists . . . has demonstrated that they still call the shots."[24] Indeed, they were able to control the tempo of the war in part because of cooperation from the South Vietnamese. An editorial in the *Press,* for example, noted that, although there was no massive "popular revolution among the South Vietnamese" during Tet, the Viet Cong would not have been able "to infiltrate men and weapons into so many South Vietnamese cities" without "some aid from the populace" of the South.[25]

A powerful editorial in the *Star* on February 11, about halfway through the offensive, best summarized this sense of pessimism and foreboding. Entitled "1984," the piece painted a nightmare scenario in which 2,500,000 American troops fight another Tet in that Orwellian year. There were, of course, "light casualties" for U.S. troops and "heavy" ones for the Viet Cong. The American forces would have done even better had ARVN forces not been "in recreation areas celebrating the New Year."[26]

For some Munsonians who read and wrote to the local press, Tet did seem to engender that sense of gloom posited by the conventional wisdom.

But for many others, the dominant response was one of guarded optimism. The massive Communist losses, if combined with renewed determination to commit fully to winning the war, provided an opportunity for victory.

The columnist Roscoe Drummond argued that the Tet Offensive actually played to America's military strength. Hanoi "abandoned . . . guerilla tactics and embraced direct conflict with U.S. and South Vietnamese forces." In spite of some initial surprise created by the assault, Drummond argued that the enemy had not "been able to hold their gains and . . . [had] suffered punitive losses of men." Tet then became "a turning point in the war," favorable to the American side.[27] H. O. V., writing to the *Press*, echoed Drummond's point: "The Viet Cong . . . have paid and will pay [for Tet] with huge losses."[28] Finally, a major editorial in the *Press* made clear the sense of U.S. victory and Communist defeat:

> The communist leaders of North Vietnam made a big mistake in their recent offensive against the cities of the South.
> The idea of the Red Campaign was to achieve some stunning victory and break American will to resist. As Dien Bien Phu finished the French in Vietnam, it was hoped, some single military stroke would accelerate the spread of dovish sentiment in America and force a withdrawl.
> So far the result has been exactly the reverse. The American people were indeed shocked and angered by the assault on the cities, and became unsettled about the course of U.S. policy in Vietnam. But their discontent has fueled a demand that military efforts be increased rather than diminished.[29]

Of course, the key assumption in this clarion call was that the United States would increase its "military efforts." And manifestly, a substantial body of local opinion supported the option of more force, not less. For example, the same *Star* editorial which bemoaned the fact that Communists "still call the shots" in Vietnam claimed that the United States could "prevent" an enemy victory if it really "tried to win."[30] Indeed, American success in recapturing Hue provided a model for future strategy. According to a *Star* editorial, "We used all-out force" to dislodge the enemy from Hue. Therefore, "isn't it ridiculous to refrain from using full firepower against the enemy and his supply route through Laos?"[31] In fact, as early as February 2, only a few days after the initial Tet assaults, when Saigon was still in chaos and Hue under firm enemy control, the *Star* offered its own blueprint for military victory in the wake of Tet. It called for "a declaration of war against North Vietnam; the closing of Haiphong Harbor; invading North Vietnam; destroying all targets of consequence; warning China and Russia that . . . any attempt to supply [North Vietnam] with arms will be answered militarily."[32] (No pessimistic stalematism here.)

If anything, letter writers to the local press were more militant than columnists and editorial writers. Mrs. B. E. F., for example, wanted to throw the United Nations off American "soil" because it continued "to condone the murder of our boys in Vietnam."[33] In a considerably weirder vein, John C. Roberts wrote that the United States was "terrorized" by "small" Communist countries "because we have lost God out of our national life," a loss which resulted in America's being possessed of "evil spirits." Presumably, a forceful domestic exorcism would lead to spiritual uplift and the kicking of some commie butt.[34]

The "evil spirits" killing U.S. troops in Vietnam also deserved a dose of exorcism, apocalyptically Kurtzlike, in the eyes of some locals. P. J. P. wrote bitterly that the United States had been too "lenient" with North Vietnam. We needed to "give them some of their own medicine," specifically, "kill women and children."[35] Two letters went so far as to call up the nuclear option. P. H. said that Tet showed America as "weak." We could still win if we weren't afraid of "provoking a nuclear confrontation."[36] Like-minded Leonard Sherry pulled out all the plugs:

President Johnson should use nuclear weapons without delay. Failure to do so makes him look chicken. Blast Haiphong, Hanoi, North Vietnam, Ho Chi Ming [sic] to Hell and back if that's what it takes to win. . . . Fulbright should be tried for treason.[37]

Although clearly situated on the margin (if not over the edge), Sherry's advice might well have represented the deepest, unstated sentiments of a substantial number of the citizens of "Middletown." Deeply patriotic and fervently unwilling to admit defeat, many Munsonians saw in the Tet Offensive a window of opportunity rather than a door closing.

Thus, in light of such contradictory evidence, it would be ludicrous to argue that there was a Muncie consensus on the Tet Offensive. On the basis of the best evidence possible, we may conclude that confusion, ambiguity, and contradiction marked Muncie's response to this most crucial event of the war. While some cried doom, gloom, and stalemate, others saw a chance to apply maximum force for maximum results. The conventional wisdom that there was a national *cri de coeur,* a sense of pessimism over the obvious psychological victory of the enemy during Tet, may well be true. But this modest local study does not prove the case.

An epilogue: although Munsonians appeared to notice Tet and be concerned about it, the offensive was certainly not the main focus of local life in early 1968. I read more than a score of interviews dealing with the Vietnam War as remembered by citizens of Muncie. Not one even mentioned the Tet Offensive (Vietnam War Oral History Collection, Ball State University Archives, University Library, Muncie, Indiana). Clearly, by the last two weeks in February 1968, Muncie newspapers were much more concerned with local issues than with international crises like Tet. An editorial cartoon in the *Evening Press* forcefully illustrates this point. A group of "world problems," prominently featuring Vietnam, stands outside a locked door labeled "Indiana." A sign hanging from the door warns, "Hoosier Hysteria: Do Not Disturb" (*Evening Press,* February 21, 1968, p. 4). (For the uninitiated, "Hoosier Hysteria" refers to the annual state high school basketball tournament.) Something as "insignificant" as the major event in America's longest war could hardly compete with high school hoops in the heart of the heart of the country.

NOTES

Portions of this article originally appeared in an article by the author entitled "Nobody Gets Off the Bus," *Viet Nam Generation* (1994), pp. 119–122.

1. Don Oberdorfer, *Tet!,* reprint edition of the original 1971 volume (New York: Da Capo Press, 1984), p. 329.
2. Ibid., pp. ix, 331.
3. James S. Olson and Randy Roberts, *Where the Domino Fell: America and Vietnam, 1945–50* (New York: St. Martin's Press, 1991), p. 186.
4. Ibid., p. 187.
5. James J. Wirtz, *The Tet Offensive: Intelligence Failure in War* (Ithaca, N.Y.: Cornell University Press, 1991), pp. 1–2.
6. Ibid., p. 2.
7. *Muncie Star,* August 11, 1982, p. 2. Quoted in Anthony O. Edmonds, " 'Middletown': A Community Reacts to Social Science," *Proceedings of the Indiana Academy of the Social Sciences,* 3rd series, 19 (1984): 87.
8. I fully realize that newspaper editorials, columns, and letters to the editor provide only tentative evidence of public views. Given the lack of public polling data, however, they at least give us the best approximate indication available.
9. Only thirteen issues of the *Ball State News* appeared in February because of the exam period and spring break.
10. Letter, *Muncie Evening Press,* February 2, 1968, p. 4.
11. Letter, *Press,* February 23, 1968, p. 4.
12. Letter, *Star,* February 29, 1968, p. 4; Letter, *Star,* February 28, 1968, p. 4.
13. *Press,* February 22, 1968, p. 4.
14. *Star,* February 20, 1968, p. 4.
15. *Ball State News,* February 15, 1968, p. 2.
16. *Press,* February 8, 1968, p. 4.
17. Ibid., February 1, 1968, p. 4.
18. Ibid., February 17, 1968, p. 4.
19. *Star,* February 11, 1968, p. 4.
20. *Press,* February 13, 1968, p. 4.
21. *Star,* February 9, 1968, p. 4.
22. Ibid., February 17, 1968, p. 4.
23. *Ball State News,* February 15, 1968, p. 2.
24. *Star,* February 17, 1968, p. 4.
25. *Press,* February 13, 1968, p. 4.
26. *Star,* February 11, 1968, sec. A, p. 4.

27. Ibid., February 24, 1968, p. 4.
28. Letter, *Press,* February 28, 1968, p. 4.
29. Ibid., February 17, 1968, p. 4.
30. *Star,* February 17, 1968, p. 4.
31. Ibid., February 21, 1968, p. 4.
32. Ibid., February 2, 1968, p. 4.
33. Letter, ibid., February 13, 1968, p. 4.
34. Letter, ibid., February 2, 1968, p. 4.
35. Letter, ibid., February 2, 1968, p. 7.
36. Letter, *Press,* February 8, 1968, p. 4.
37. Letter, *Star,* February 25, 1968, p. 4.

9

The Warning That Left Something to Chance: Intelligence at Tet

John Prados

Two meanings of the word "chance" are relevant to our present purpose. One is chance as a random factor—for this subject the accidental conjunction of chance occurrences that could have furnished warning of a large-scale nationwide North Vietnamese and Viet Cong (VC) offensive in Vietnam at Tet in 1968. The second relevant meaning is chance as risk. I believe the reasons for the continuing controversy over whether there was a "surprise" at Tet have much to do with these forms of chance.

"Surprise" is a loaded word in the intelligence business, and is but slightly less pejorative when applied as historical interpretation. Thus, whether the attack at Tet represented a surprise—and intelligence failure— has ever after remained a fervid question, often lurking in the wings of Vietnam discussions, provoking numerous arguments, even forming part of a court case, when the Tet intelligence question became enmeshed in the larger dispute over whether falsification occurred in compilation of the North Vietnamese Army (NVA) and VC order of battle.

The extremes of the Tet intelligence controversy are represented by senior army officers themselves; there is no need for looking under rugs for perverse, so-called revisionist historians purportedly trying to overturn some conventional wisdom. At one extreme is General David R. Palmer, who in a text used at West Point held that Tet had been an intelligence failure comparable to Pearl Harbor.[1] At the opposite end of the spectrum are the officers who held command and intelligence posts in Vietnam in January 1968, arguing that Military Assistance Command, Vietnam (MACV) knew all about the Tet Offensive. For the moment we can take as representative of this view a statement before a congressional investigating committee on December 3, 1975, by General Daniel O. Graham, who at Tet had been a colonel assigned to MACV intelligence. "We were not surprised by the fact of the Tet Offensive," Graham told the legislators. "We were not surprised by the massiveness of the numbers of troops committed. What surprised us was the rashness of the Tet attacks."[2]

One view or the other, as these labels are applied in history, will ultimately lose the battle of interpretation and be called revisionist. Whoever the revisionists turn out to be, however, they will be senior officers of the U.S. Army who held responsible positions in the military hierarchy. It is time to move forward on interpretation of this history, and a good place to begin is to look at where the idea for an offensive came from and what the United States found out about it.

WHAT DID WE KNOW AND WHEN DID WE KNOW IT?

The record and pattern of military operations across South Vietnam indicate that Hanoi and the Viet Cong began planning for the Tet Offensive sometime in the summer or early fall of 1967. General William E. Westmoreland, commander of MACV, dates the moment from the time in July that a B-52 bombing mission near the Cambodian border caught a top NVA headquarters and gravely wounded General Nguyen Chi Thanh, senior NVA field commander in the South. Westmoreland's intelligence, or J-2, chief, Brigadier General Phillip B. Davidson, repeats this assessment and relates the strategy to a power struggle he alleges among the top North Vietnamese leadership.[3]

In truth a great deal remains to be learned about the Vietnamese side of the war, and there is no way to assert with confidence that this was Hanoi's path to a decision. General Thanh's loss was certainly a grievous one, but coincidental in terms of Hanoi's timing of its offensive, which depended much more on immutable factors such as the time necessary to assemble the required troops and supplies and move them down the Ho Chi Minh Trail, or infiltrate them by sea into Cambodia. The necessary preparation time was considerable. Just to move replacements or troop units to the northernmost portion of South Vietnam, the Khe Sanh area, required thirty days or more. Sending troops further south took longer. At some point these movements became detectable—"observables" in the intelligence jargon. In turn it was possible for the observables to lead to an estimate of Hanoi's intentions.

Another avenue making possible some prediction of an offensive was combat intelligence, the day-to-day process of taking and interrogating prisoners, capturing and translating documents. Here too there would be indicators of forthcoming operations that MACV J-2 analysts, not to mention South Vietnamese or those of the joint organization maintained by both, the Combined Intelligence Center Vietnam (CICV), would be able to interpret.

Finally, there was the area of overt behavior. Hanoi's actions and words supplied indications of its intentions. Separately or together, all or any of these sources could have furnished the key necessary to predict the Tet Offensive, the nature of that operation, and the required preventive measures. A survey of the record and a comparison with the predictions that were actually made lead to better understanding of the Tet intelligence controversy.

First to the observables. Official retrospective figures for North Vietnamese infiltration into the South for the months before the offensive are not that large; none matches the peak for calendar 1967 of 12,124 set in June, supposedly before Hanoi ever made its decision to attack. Specifically, 8,152 is the figure for September, 5,290 for October, 6,892 for November, and 8,712 for December. These numbers themselves became controversial in 1982 when CBS Television broadcast a documentary report, "The Uncounted Enemy: A Vietnam Deception," which claimed evidence of infiltration levels of 20,000 to 25,000 for the last five months before Tet.[4] What order of battle analysts accepted for January 1968, 22,820, does mark a clear departure from the previous data and an indicator of impending action.

These retrospective figures may but do not necessarily equate to the estimates made at the time; however, another observable obviously reflecting North Vietnamese activity is the volume of shipments down the Ho Chi Minh Trail. Here the trend was recognized as it occurred. For example, in September 1966, 55 trucks were reported by one source and 192 by another along Trail routes in Laos, but the sightings from the same sources in September 1967 were 256 and 201. October truck sightings included 992 by one method and 148 by another, far higher levels than in 1966, while the December 1967 sightings were of 4,235 trucks by one source and 695 by another.[5] This was a level many times the rate of the previous year and clearly looked like a major push, leading to curiosity as to what the movements portended.

Observables (other than communications intelligence) suggested Hanoi was increasing its capabilities, but they did not reveal intentions. Combat intelligence proved more useful in that regard. One document captured as early as August 1967 is suggestive in refuting the arguments of those who assert the North Vietnamese were thinking entirely on a military plane, not aiming at American public opinion: "We can realize that although the Americans are very strong economically and militarily, their aggressive war has been taking place in an international situation in a country full of repugnances. These repugnances are stronger than American money and weapons."[6] In March 1967, almost a year in advance, troops of the Army of the Republic of Vietnam (ARVN) captured a document with the first recorded reference to a direct attack on Saigon. Then, in October, ARVN III Corps units found another document which discussed sapper training and preparations for VC and NVA personnel to use ARVN mechanized equipment. This paper was reportedly a product of the elusive Unit 16, then the command for NVA armored forces assigned to the Central Office of South Vietnam (COSVN), the VC/NVA high command.

On October 16, ARVN units carrying out Operation Xay Dung in the Mekong Delta area encountered a three-page memorandum from the regional party committee secretary of COSVN'S Military Region 2, a document dated September 2, which for the first time used the phrase "winter-spring campaign" and discussed preparations for it. The general concept given in the document was that main force, province and district local, engineer, and sapper units "must increase attacks on major units, cities and towns, base areas, airfields and lines of communication."[7]

Another ARVN document capture in Tay Ninh Province on October 25 produced an instructional notice for middle-level cadres outlining a political program leading to a coalition government and triggered by a three-pronged offensive designed to defeat ARVN, destroy the U.S. political and military "institutions," and catalyze a countrywide insurrection of the popular masses.[8] Appearing here for the first time was the slogan "general offensive/general uprising" (*tong cong kich/tong khoi nghia*) or TCK/TKN, which some have called a code name but which conforms rather more closely to Vietnamese usage of slogans.

A series of document captures during November very clearly puts details into the vague references so far elicited. Several key documents were captured in the Central Highlands during the battle of Dak To that month. Possibly the best-known capture of the entire pre-Tet period was a military directive issued by the COSVN B-3 Front Command, the formation controlling North Vietnamese and VC activity in the central portion of the country. General Westmoreland made this a subject of comment at a press conference he held in Washington on November 22 in the course of a visit to the United States to help increase support for the war effort. Like the old adage about the number of fathers of victory and defeat, the United States and South Vietnam, both of which would claim Tet as a major military victory, claim to have discovered this B-3 Front directive. Americans say the document was retrieved by U.S. forces in the Dak To area on November 6, while the leading South Vietnamese authority on the subject maintains that ARVN captured the document northwest of Kontum three days earlier.

The B-3 directive called for "many large scale, well-coordinated combat operations" to "destroy or disintegrate a large part of the Puppet [ARVN] army," to improve NVA combat techniques, to liberate an important area, and "to effect close coordination with various battle areas throughout South Vietnam."[9] One special objective of immediate interest—this was, after all, during the battle of Dak To—was to "annihilate a major U.S. element in order to force the enemy to deploy as many additional troops to the Western highlands as possible."[10] Westmoreland commented on each of the B-3 Front objectives, as did MACV deputy commander General Creighton W. Abrams in an earlier cable reporting the document to Westmoreland.

Three days before Westmoreland's Washington session with the press, Company B of the 2nd Battalion, 327th Airborne Infantry, in Quang Tin Province, captured a thirteen-page notebook from which a document was extracted. The new item bore the electrifying title "Ho Chi Minh's Order for Implementation of General Counteroffensive and General Uprising during 1967 Winter and 1968 Spring and Summer." The notebook, belonging to one Vu Sinh Vien, contained notes from a November 12 meeting held to promulgate a Hanoi decision embodied in the so-called Resolution 13, adopted by the Central Committee of the Lao Dong Party. Not only did the title electrify, but the text contained this: "The time for a direct revolution has come and . . . the opportunity for a general counteroffensive and general uprising is within reach. . . . The entire army and population is ordered to implement a general counter offensive and general uprising in order to achieve a decisive victory for the revolution with the [campaign season]." Since this language was emphasized by the translators at the Combined Documents Exploitation Center (CDEC), it is clear that American intelligence did not miss the message.[11] Moreover, CDEC not only summarized the Vien notebook in its December 6, 1967, bulletin, it circulated a full translation on December 15, and the intelligence became the subject of a Defense Intelligence Agency memorandum on January 3, 1968. Two days later the U.S. Embassy in Saigon even put out a press release containing a number of details from the notebook.[12]

In April 1968, after fighting had subsided, the U.S. Embassy published a further intriguing indication of COSVN intentions in its series *Vietnam Documents and Research Notes*. This item, provenance not indicated, was the November 1 directive issued by a provincial standing committee:

Our troops are continuously attacking the enemy everywhere, especially in district seats and province capitals. We have started a partial uprising in the city. Several province capitals and district seats have changed hands three or four times. The enemy troops in several districts and provinces have been confused and disorganized. . . . The rural people, together with town people, are rising up to fight the U.S., overthrow the puppet government and seize power. . . . The time is now more favorable than ever before. This is to notify you that an offensive and uprising will take place in the near future and we will mount stronger attacks on towns and cities, in coordination with the widespread movement in the rural areas. The enemy will be thrown into utmost confusion.[13]

Another interesting document, captured by the ARVN 25th Division on November 7, although it did not reach CDEC until mid-December, was a directive to personnel in Long An Province the VC classified top secret. The order instituted a program to place agents in Saigon and covered their selection, training, and infiltration. The rationale given was weakness in the quality and number of urban cadre, which required their reinforcement by rural revolutionary forces. A COSVN decision was cited specifically in connection with the order. The objective given was "making preparations to topple the 'Puppet' Government." Tellingly, the order directed that "every effort . . . be made to complete the placing of agents by late January [1968]."[14]

One more alarming capture was made in Quang Nam Province on December 4 by the 198th Light Infantry Brigade, a U.S. unit. The document arrived at CDEC on December 19 and a summary circulated on December 23. The item was a directive announcing the twin strategic objectives of an all-out effort to destroy a major enemy force plus a deployment of VC organizations in urban areas to serve the aim of an uprising in cities and towns. Local units were enjoined to raise at least 4,950 hard-core members to act among a group of participants expected to number 22,800. Most striking about this order is the large number of participants estimated for an area of just a few districts or villages; at the national level there could not be an action of this dimension without a so-called general uprising. The directive was dated November 16, which fit closely with the indication in the Vien notebook that COSVN was beginning to act upon Resolution 13 during the second week of November.

The South Vietnamese Marine Corps made a further contribution to combat intelligence in the Mekong Delta, where it captured a December 16 directive by a province military affairs committee. This document was unusual in mandating *strict compliance* with the cease-fires planned for Christmas, New Year, and Tet. It did expect "most advantageous use of the truce period" to move supplies and train troops, however, and this aspect seemed the most salient to American authorities, who made it the subject of a January 8, 1968, press release. The publicity item was titled "Captured Document Indicates Viet Cong Plan to Take Advantage of Cease-Fire."[15] That title would seem rather ironic in the wake of the Tet Offensive.

Moving right up to eve of Tet, a scout company of the ARVN 23rd Division found yet another document relevant to warning on January 18, 1968, of which CDEC circulated a full translation on January 28. The undated set of notes, opening with a discussion of intentions, began thus: "Launch heavy attacks in order to destroy the enemy; material resources; capture high ranking enemy cadre and simultaneously attack American installations. Besiege and isolate American strong points; limit the U.S. soldiers' movements and capture them to demand compensation for war damage." Clearly looking toward some kind of war-winning action, the document recorded the need to "properly manage the timely takeover of the [South Vietnamese] administration and organize a government." Finally, among the items listed as important for fulfillment by leadership cadre were the following: "The party committee echelons must take the command; assault units must be set up and have the responsibility of occupying the targets; in cities, we must try to motivate the people by all methods; when the people go out they must be armed; we should rapidly occupy key positions, prepare a proper plan for the 'three prong' attack and capture important officials when ordered."[16] A summary of these notes circulated on January 25 in *CDEC Bulletin* No. 9184.

To add a few more bricks to the pile, we may note a COSVN transportation section document captured in January in the ARVN III Corps area that detailed a reorganization of the adversary's Military Region 4, which included Saigon and Cholon, into a novel configuration rather like a pie in which each slice, corresponding to one of the region's five subdivisions, extended right into the Saigon metropolitan area. There will be more to say about this particular indicator later. Near Dak To on January 4, the U.S. 4th Infantry Division captured a copy of an operations order providing details for an attack on Pleiku city in the Central Highlands. In mid-January a 101st Airborne Division unit came up with a document from a VC regiment giving plans for attacks on the capital of Binh Duong Province and the headquarters of the ARVN 5th Military Division and associated 1st Armored Cavalry Squadron. On January 20 units of ARVN II Corps captured specific plans for attacks on the cities of Ban Me Thuot and Qui Nhon. In Qui Nhon, on January 28, the South Vietnamese Military Security Service, a national counterintelligence agency, apprehended eleven VC cadres carrying tape recordings, evidently for broadcast on a local radio station, that asserted that the Viet Cong controlled Hue, Danang, and Saigon. Under interrogation the cadres themselves confirmed that Qui Nhon was on the list for attack as well.

As in the last example, where interrogation confirmed a documentary source, human intelligence formed an important part of the information base warning of Tet. As early as May 1967 the Vietnamese national police arrested a senior cadre from the Saigon area who admitted his mission was to recruit members for a prospective coalition government. In September the police detained another agent who was discovered to be circulating between the U.S. Embassy and COSVN in one of the many exploratory diplomatic feelers of this period. South Vietnamese officials feared the Americans making some private agreement with the Viet Cong and were outraged when the Embassy and its CIA station insisted upon the release of the go-between, whom they classified as a double agent. What else the CIA may have learned from this agent is not yet known.

Another CIA source, according to Robert Brewer, an intelligence officer who was province senior advisor in Quang Tri at this time, was a North Vietnamese walk-in who became a CIA double agent in about September

1967. Brewer did not entirely trust the agent, who was dubbed X-1, but the walk-in did furnish apparently authentic copies of Resolution 13 and of the updated revision of November. South Vietnamese intelligence expert Colonel Hoang Ngoc Lung also states that ARVN intelligence learned of Resolution 13 through its own agent network in October. As if that were not enough, in mid-August the U.S. 1st Marine Division captured a copy of a resolution passed by a party committee in Quang Nam Province that was "based" upon Resolution 13, while on August 27 the 1st Brigade, U.S. 101st Airborne Division, captured some cadre's notes taken while studying the original Resolution 13. In short, documentary indications of a Hanoi decision seem to have been explicitly confirmed by agent intelligence.

On December 7, the fateful anniversary of Pearl Harbor, a Vietnamese who apparently wished to become an American agent was debriefed at Hue by U.S. military intelligence officers. The prospective agent provided an account of a mid-November meeting of high-level VC cadre and NVA officers at nearby Nam Dong to discuss future plans. According to the source, the "Autumn-Winter Offensive" had scored good results for heavy losses, but plans for the spring offensive now called for large-scale attacks of battalion and regiment size, to be launched simultaneously to prevent allied reactions. Every battalion was to participate, there would be a reinforcement of a battalion with "modern weapons" and "supported by experts," and guerrilla units in particular were "to disturb the safety of Hue City by sabotage operations." The source reported this "Spring Offensive" was to begin sometime after Christmas 1967.[17]

In mid-January, as Tet approached, a Chieu Hoi rallier [former VC who helps the U.S. or RVN] from the 273rd Regiment of the VC 9th Division supplied the South Vietnamese with data confirming other documentary sources. In this case he corroborated evidence that the COSVN planned an attack on the provincial capital of Binh Duong. On January 28 at Bien Hoa, headquarters of the ARVN III Corps, human sources revealed movement of a VC artillery regiment and two infantry ones into attack positions near that city. The next morning residents of a suburban district confirmed the presence of a VC unit near them as well, and there was an incident in which a reconnaissance party of Viet Cong officers was spotted near the base.

Naturally none of the documents or any of the agent or defector reports could provide warning as graphic and immediate as the North Vietnamese and Viet Cong themselves when, a day in advance of the big offensive, some of the forces attacked prematurely. Still, for now the point is that there was a good deal of intelligence available to MACV and ARVN estimators and some of it was very explicit.

In the case of Tet the secret intelligence dovetails in an interesting way with the overt, incontrovertible evidence of what the North Vietnamese and Viet Cong were doing and saying. The most obvious things said were

by General Vo Nguyen Giap, North Vietnamese defense minister, master-
mind of the victory in the Franco-Vietnamese war of 1945–1954. Giap
authored a series of articles broadcast over Hanoi Radio and published in
the party and army newspapers in September 1967. Collectively known as
Big Victory, Great Task, the series appears to have been intended to provide NVA and VC political officers with a detailed prospectus helping them
to explain the great demands about to be made upon their men.[18]

Warning that a *big* victory would surely prove a *great* task, General Giap
wrote that President Johnson's approvals of further troop deployments
would give the United States more than half a million soldiers in Vietnam
by mid-1968. Giap also noted an element of opportunity, however, since
"the present mobilization level has far exceeded initial U.S. forecasts and
is at sharp variance with U.S. global strategy." Giap thus recognized both
near-term risk in the growth of MACV forces and an opportunity to confront Washington with the dilemma of its Vietnam policy versus its global
commitments. This sounds very much like the recipe for an offensive, one
which had to occur before all those extra reinforcements reached Westmoreland—one, in fact, at Tet.[19]

Most strikingly, the cadre notebook study of Resolution 13 that the U.S.
1st Marine Division captured on August 16, 1967 (already mentioned) specifically recorded an allied capability to increase the U.S. troop contingent
to 600,000 or 700,000 by the end of 1968. (General Westmoreland's Program 5 troop request, had President Johnson accepted it, would have done
exactly that.)

The cadre studying Resolution 13 concluded that the general mission of
both North Vietnam and the Viet Cong had to be "to destroy a part of the
U.S. troops and an important part [of ARVN] in order to create favorable
conditions for an offensive and a general uprising in a relatively short period of time."[20] General Giap's prescription in *Big Victory, Great Task* was
that the NVA and VC should "repeatedly harass the enemy and destroy
many large U.S. and rebel units . . . scattering the enemy in order to fight
him." Large-scale battles were by no means ruled out, but the military
effort was termed a "bugle call" to urge the southern people "to take advantage of their victories to surge forward."[21]

Either there is an uncanny coincidence here, or North Vietnamese military operations in the fall of 1967 quite deliberately followed the prescribed
pattern. First there was a battle at Song Be in the III Corps zone, where on
October 27 the NVA 88th Regiment attacked a battalion command post
of the ARVN 5th Division. Two days later the town of Loc Ninh faced an
attack from the 273rd Regiment of the VC 9th Division. Countered by
ARVN and U.S. troops, instead of fading away the Viet Cong came back,
feeding in their 272nd Regiment, followed by the 141st and 165th NVA
Regiments. The Loc Ninh battle represented the first time COSVN had
staged coordinated attacks by large units from different divisions.

Then, before the Loc Ninh battle petered out, on November 4 the Dak
To battle opened in the Central Highlands when a U.S. patrol ran into
North Vietnamese troops dug in on a ridge southwest of the village. Again
the North Vietnamese stood, committing elements of the NVA 1st Division
and two other regiments to an engagement which lasted more than two
weeks. The general impact of these operations was to draw U.S. and ARVN
troops away from the populated lowlands and into areas along South Vietnam's borders or the Demilitarized Zone (DMZ).

A further border operation that was not brought to the point of contact,
at least at this time, was the North Vietnamese investment of the American
combat base at Khe Sanh, in the northwest corner of South Vietnam. More
and more signs of NVA troops in the vicinity accumulated, with telling
effect on allied intelligence predictions, as shall be seen presently.

In a now celebrated incident, on January 2, 1968, a party of North
Vietnamese officers making a personal reconnaissance of the Khe Sanh perimeter were discovered and shot down. The impression that they had been
on a scouting mission was taken as evidence of imminent attack on Khe
Sanh. Province advisor Bob Brewer describes a virtually identical episode
which occurred in a lowland residential district of Quang Tri, and there
was also the Bien Hoa incident already referred to. When combat actually
began Khe Sanh would not be attacked, while Quang Tri town and Bien
Hoa became the scenes of fierce fighting.

Shortly after noontime on January 21 Radio Hanoi broadcast on its
home service the NVA General Staff instructions for observation of the Tet
festival, essentially similar to those contained in a captured document, but
without any indication of timing. We know from other sources that North
Vietnam moved its Tet celebrations a few days ahead for 1968 so that the
holiday there no longer coincided with the planned offensive at Tet in the
South. Ominously, however, Hanoi Radio reported that Premier Pham Van
Dong had declared 1968 the year of the "fight and win" Tet. Later in the
broadcast announcers remarked that the General Staff instructions stressed,
among other things, the need for army and people to "heighten their enthusiasm, fulfill their tasks satisfactorily, and strive for emulation *in re-
cording combat achievements* with which to greet the victorious spring and
the Party's anniversary on February 3rd."[22]

In a report that in retrospect clearly seems intended to lay a foundation
for a view of the Tet Offensive as a reciprocal response, on January 25 the
party newspaper *Nhan Dan* published a commentary alleging and con-
demning U.S. and South Vietnamese violations of the cease-fires at Christmas and New Year. The commentary also criticized South Vietnam's
recently announced decision to shorten its planned Tet cease-fire. The *Nhan
Dan* commentary was repeated that night by Radio Hanoi in its English-
language service.

When, on January 30, the United States went ahead and completely canceled its own Tet stand-down, Radio Hanoi broadcast the critical statement from the North Vietnamese Foreign Ministry that resulted. Forty-one minutes earlier, at 11:56 p.m. on January 30, Radio Hanoi broadcast in English a New Year (Tet) poem by President Ho Chi Minh that had appeared on the front page of every Hanoi daily newspaper earlier in the day:

> This spring far outshines the previous springs.
> Of victories throughout the land come happy tidings.
> The South and North emulate each other in fighting the U.S. aggressors!
> Forward!
> Total victory shall be ours.[23]

Interrogation of prisoners and defectors later established that, like BBC radio broadcasts to the French Resistance before the Normandy invasion, the Radio Hanoi transmission contained a hidden meaning: It was an order in open code to begin the attacks of the Tet Offensive.

WHAT DID WE MAKE OF WHAT THERE WAS TO KNOW?

Summarized above are the intelligence observables, the combat intelligence, and the overt data of action and declaration pertinent to warning of the Tet Offensive. In fact, the record is even broader than indicated since, for reasons of space, a number of additional captured documents and cables recounting either documentary finds or interrogations have not been detailed. Suffice it to say that the indicators are numerous, that the stream of them began relatively early in the cycle of preparations for the offensive, and that many of the reports were complementary and built upon each other.

In the case of Pearl Harbor, a classic instance of intelligence failure, the accepted explanations are that the fact of an attack against this major U.S. base was either not knowable, due to the adversary's careful precautions and technical accomplishments, or that the "signal" that might have warned the Americans was lost in the "noise" of developments related to more obvious and more widely expected adversary threats. There is a little of these explanations that is relevant for Tet but not very much. Tet represented a technical achievement for a COSVN command that had hardly ever coordinated attacks by two different units, much less disparate forces throughout South Vietnam. But Loc Ninh and Dak To, not to mention the well-coordinated investment of Khe Sanh, showed that COSVN was moving in that direction and had attained the capability. Captured documents demonstrated intent to coordinate even more widely.

The signal-versus-noise question gets us into the realm of perception, reception, and deception, and the role of Khe Sanh in North Vietnamese planning for Tet. Combat intelligence provided numerous indications of interest in countrywide objectives and attacks on towns and cities. Observable intelligence, particularly radio intelligence, showed a military buildup around Khe Sanh plus a massively increased scale of logistic support. Internally, however, the different streams of intelligence seemed remarkably coherent and consistent, with few contradictory indicators to provoke disbelief. Put differently, the question was, in which stream of intelligence could one repose more confidence?

The combat intelligence echoes in the reporting by the Central Intelligence Agency. A draft study completed in late November and sent to Washington on December 8 has been cited by President Johnson's national security adviser, Walt W. Rostow, as evidence the United States knew about Tet.[24] The trouble with that is that few believed the CIA Saigon station report, by a team consisting of Joseph Hovey, Bobby Layton, and Carl Ogle. In fact, there is a story in CIA lore that a senior officer, just back from the Saigon station, was being told his own similar theory was sadly mistaken when the first cables came through reporting the U.S. Embassy in South Vietnam under attack.

For what it is worth, the CIA team referred specifically to numerous recently captured documents, and they predicted a three-phase campaign (October–December 1967, January–March 1968, and April–June 1968) with "military and political ambitions which surpass any thing previously attempted in such a relatively short period of time." Their analysis expected an "all-out attack," with efforts on all battlefronts, and explicitly referred to the concept of "general offensive and general uprising." The Hovey team predicted "widespread guerrilla attacks" on large units in "rural/heavily populated areas" as well as attacks on key "agencies and rear service bases." The Saigon station's summary conclusion was, "The war is probably nearing a turning point and . . . the outcome of the 1967–68 winter–spring campaign will in all likelihood determine the future direction of the war."

Yet even the CIA felt the pull of the observables. Given the experience of Loc Ninh and Dak To, the agency's analysis also emphasized that the VC/NVA would "conduct large-scale, continuous, coordinated attacks by main force units, primarily in mountainous areas close to border sanctuaries," with the intention of forcing MACV and ARVN to redeploy major forces to those regions.[25] All this fell short of an exact prediction of Tet but it came closer than most others.

Another CIA Saigon station report, sent on December 10, gives us more flavor for the evidence agency analysts considered persuasive. This self-styled "think piece" based itself on recent combat actions, movement of possibly two additional NVA divisions toward South Vietnam, and evidence from agents, interrogations, and documents. The report cited prisoners taken at Loc Ninh and in Long An Province who had been told, in essence, "Now is the time." A certain amount of that was to be expected, but, "To be sure, it is standard practice for VC indoctrinations to stress the importance of upcoming campaigns, but this time there are differences. There is a 'this-is-it' tone, and there are implications—even some apparently explicit statements—that the winter-spring campaign is the great final effort." Moreover, "The costly head-on clashes at Loc Ninh and Dak To reflect exactly what the exhortations for the great winter-spring offensive call for." The CIA believed Hanoi's view was a serious misapprehension and based on an impression "that if he strikes some effective blows in the next few months the United States will be so eager to get out of Vietnam it will accept a VC-dominated 'coalition government,' " and that VC/NVA losses were so great as to require a proximate end to the war. The CIA concluded, "We believe he has drastically misread the situation. . . . If he continues his planned offensive, he will cause us some painful losses but his losses will be staggering. . . . He has taken a gamble that is almost certain to fail, and that failure will have a crushing effect on his forces."[26]

All those things came to pass, yet the outcome would be the opposite of that expected by the CIA. One can only conclude that the agency had misread the political aspect of the situation and misunderstood the impact of VC/NVA losses.

At the White House, Walt Rostow was concerned about this CIA reporting and asked George Carver, the CIA's special assistant for Vietnam affairs (SAVA), in effect the agency's senior official concerned with Vietnam, to comment on the station's reporting. The SAVA found little that was objectionable about the report other than low numbers projected for the VC/NVA order of battle (a reflection of an intense dispute on this subject which continued throughout the period). The SAVA evaluation went to the White House on December 15, 1967. Rostow sent both the report and the SAVA comments on it to LBJ the next day, adding his own spin that Hanoi was talking as if it were bucking for a general uprising or restaging the battle of Dien Bien Phu at Khe Sanh. Here Rostow too showed himself drawn like a moth to the flame of observable intelligence.

Soon after seeing the Saigon CIA report, President Johnson flew to Australia for the funeral of Prime Minister Harold Holt, who had drowned while swimming. Given the privilege of addressing the Australian cabinet, Johnson warned of dark days ahead in Vietnam, even the possible use of "kamikaze" tactics by the adversary in their attempt to achieve a breakthrough. Rostow likes to use the episode to assert Washington's prescience in expecting an offensive, but it was Dien Bien Phu that LBJ was encouraged to believe in. This is demonstrated indirectly by the question an Australian cabinet minister posed regarding the NVA divisions closing in upon Khe Sanh. *That* was the threat the Americans emphasized, not any threat to Saigon, near which Australia had deployed troops whose security was no doubt of interest to the ministers.

Following Rostow's lead, President Johnson focused upon the observables. Intelligence MACV was exactly the same. J-2 was embroiled during this period in a dispute over the size of the North Vietnamese forces in the South. As part of a campaign to win political support for the war, General Westmoreland was arguing that America had reached the "cross-over point" at which VC/NVA casualties were greater than their rate of replacement, so that the light at the end of the tunnel (victory) had become visible and withdrawals could begin sometime in 1969. General Davidson's J-2 supported this assessment in intelligence briefings. Naturally the briefings carefully noted that one possible response by the adversary to losing the war was a go-for-broke offensive, but they also discussed the possibility of the VC/NVA giving up mobile warfare with large units and reverting to strictly guerrilla operations. A late November estimate of the current enemy situation predicted that major NVA units in the Dak To area would withdraw across the Laotian border, that activity in the Saigon area (III Corps) "will continue until the holiday stand-downs, when it will probably end for logistical reasons," and that actions near the DMZ (Khe Sanh) and Thua Thien Province (Hue) "will probably increase in January and after the Tet buildup."[27] The November 1967 "Periodic Intelligence Report" (PERINTREP), whose analysis of potential VC/NVA courses of action was repeated word for word in the quoted estimate, credited the North Vietnamese with an intention of conducting war from the peripheral sanctuaries with a reinforcement potential of two or three divisions plus 25,000 to 30,000 replacements.[28]

What appears clear from these estimates is that J-2 expected a threat in the Khe Sanh–DMZ area, a rush of supplies rather than an offensive at Tet, and no particular threat to Saigon.

General Westmoreland commented directly upon the possible offensive on December 20 in a cable to Washington sent while Lyndon Johnson was en route to Australia. He perceived an intensified effort, maybe even a maximum one, over a relatively short period of time. But, according to Westmoreland, the adversary was fighting exactly the battle *he* (Westmoreland) preferred. That is, as long as the fight centered along the DMZ or South Vietnam's borders, the allies were able to employ their massive firepower away from population centers while exploiting tactical mobility to get the most out of the available troop formations. "I can see absolutely no psychological or military advantage to a strategy that would intentionally invite the war east towards the coast," General Westmoreland cabled the chairman of the Joint Chiefs of Staff on December 10, 1967. "It would be retrogressive, costly in casualties and refugees, and almost certainly prolong the war."[29]

Here is a key clue as to how Hanoi's deception could be successful. General Westmoreland *intended* to fight along the borders and was prepared to believe in a threat to Khe Sanh. In particular, a victory at that place in a pitched battle might win MACV approval for an invasion of Laos (as an exploitation) which General Westmoreland had previously failed to secure from President Johnson. When Hanoi began to threaten Khe Sanh, Westmoreland made it not merely important, but the centerpiece of his concept of North Vietnamese strategy. That, as reported by Westmoreland after Tet had begun and by Davidson in his book on the Vietnam War, was a three-phase offensive with the first being the Loc Ninh–Dak To battles, the second Tet itself, and the last the assault on Khe Sanh.

Evidence of General Westmoreland's overwhelming focus on the Khe Sanh area is his plan in January, still before Tet, to shift two battalions of ARVN paratroops and two brigades of the 1st Air Cavalry Division to the northern provinces while accepting a calculated risk around Saigon.

There were some American officers not at all happy with Westmoreland's plans. Among them was Lieutenant General Frederick C. Weyand, commanding the II Field Force. Weyand insisted upon authority to reposition his units closer to Saigon in anticipation of some VC action. He did this despite the fact that senior intelligence officers in his command had gone along with unsubstantiated reductions in order of battle holdings for the III Corps area during the dispute on that subject, so that the intelligence now did not seem to support any prediction of a VC threat in the zone.

Weyand also brought up the threat to III Corps during the meetings on the Weekly Intelligence Estimate Update (WIEU) held every eight days, usually attended also by General Westmoreland, General Davidson, and others. Weyand mentioned the possibility of urban attacks and a special threat for Saigon, and was supported by Colonel Charles A. Morris, Davison's own chief of production. They were opposed by other officers. In retrospect Davidson himself points to the WIEUs as the evidence Tet was not a surprise. If so, the principal credit belongs to Weyand and Morris.

General Weyand's basis for his suspicions was a document showing a realignment of the command sectors for COSVN's Military Region 4, an indicator referred to earlier. The COSVN administrative document, whose main function was to advise supply authorities and designate post office destinations, also revealed the sector boundaries revised to aim at Saigon like daggers. This document was dutifully logged and translated at CDEC, and both a cable summary and a *CDEC Bulletin* entry on it circulated throughout the U.S. chain of command, even reaching the White House. As yet, however, there is no evidence in the declassified records that anyone other than General Weyand took notice of it. Westmoreland himself terms Weyand's intelligence basis for his suspicions "various bits" that were "tenuous" even though "disturbing."[30]

South Vietnamese officers harbored a number of suspicions. One, General Tran Ngoc Tam, turned to Westmoreland at a cocktail party and confided his feeling that the other side was planning "such a blow . . . that we might be unable to 'win the victory.' "[31] General Vinh Loc, commanding II Corps, told an American division commander he had indications of activity in his area, but did not cancel plans to go to Saigon for the holiday.

Down in the depths of the Combined Intelligence Center Vietnam, when an American enlisted analyst put together the indications of widespread urban attacks and drew that conclusion, his lieutenant queried the ARVN counterpart in their office. The Vietnamese officer answered in the affirmative when asked if the VC planned to attack during Tet, and when asked if that meant cities, other corps, or Saigon, the ARVN lieutenant replied, "Yes, all cities. All corps. Especially Saigon."[32] That conversation appears to have occurred around mid-January.

Colonel Hoang Ngoc Lung reports that South Vietnamese president Nguyen Van Thieu was told of each of the developments intelligence came up with as they occurred. Lung cites various shortcomings in South Vietnamese intelligence, of which perhaps the major ones were that reports were never assembled into a comprehensive mosaic (something like a U.S. National Intelligence Estimate) and that the Vietnamese agencies had very little coordination among one another.

A most important development, for example, was the Vietnamese capture of one Nam Dong, reportedly the political officer of COSVN Military Region 4, taken from ambush when returning from a conference at COSVN headquarters. According to Lung, the interrogation revealed that COSVN was shifting from a protracted war strategy to one of general offensive/general uprising. The MACV J-2 chief, General Davidson, reports that he first learned of this intelligence from reading Lung's postwar monograph written for the U.S. Army. Lung himself notes that the agency which captured the VC official never circulated the intelligence to the J-2 section of the Vietnamese Joint General Staff.

President Thieu refused to cancel the Tet cease-fire when Westmoreland and ARVN Chief of Staff General Cao Van Vien visited to urge him to do so. There was never any countrywide ARVN alert, though individual units did take some precautions, and half the Vietnamese personnel were granted leave for Tet. Many units were at only 10 or 20 percent of their authorized strength when the offensive began.

Even those Americans who expected an offensive figured it would come before or after, but not during, Tet. On January 22 General Westmoreland reported enemy actions during the preceding forty-eight hours, which had included the first large-scale shelling of Khe Sanh, as "the initial attacks of the expected enemy offensive in northern I Corps." The MACV commander viewed these actions as "probably" preliminary to a full-scale attack on Khe Sanh, though he did note, "I believe that the enemy will attempt a countrywide show of strength just prior to Tet, with Khe Sanh being the main event." Westmoreland also reported danger to Pleiku and Kontum, three combat camps in the Central Highlands, and provincial towns in III and IV Corps which would be "likely targets for renewed attacks by fire." This cable, MAC 01049, also contains the first specific mention of Saigon: "Terrorism will probably increase in and around Saigon."[33] That was the closest MACV came to predicting the real Tet.

A second cable, MAC 00P67, sent "eyes only" the same day, reported the adversary displaying a "very unusual sense of urgency." The report believed Hanoi planned "a coordinated offensive designed to seize and hold key objectives in the northern two provinces." Westmoreland added Hue and Quang Tri to the list of localities reported to be in danger. He cited odds among those who felt the offensive would come before Tet and after Tet.[34] Later MACV reported that January 25 was shaping up as the big day.

Nowhere did General Westmoreland predict an urban offensive, or any countrywide activity beyond a "show of force." At each stage his intelligence predictions were of Khe Sanh plus whatever towns and cities intelligence had identified as specifically threatened. This is distinctly different from the passage in Westmoreland's memoirs in which he quotes one of the captured documents that details the intention to attack cities and towns and then implies that it was American officials and reporters who did not believe in the threat.[35] General Westmoreland also quotes Davidson to the effect that the real Tet "was so preposterous that I would have been unable to sell it to anyone."[36]

In truth MACV never attempted to do so. Finally comes Westmoreland's plaintive cry: "Yet who would listen? How to alert anybody when press, Congress, and White House were preoccupied with Khe Sanh,"[37] implying that MACV itself was well aware of the true threat. The facts are that General Westmoreland and MACV intelligence were both *leaders* in the rush to make Khe Sanh the primary place of confrontation. The truth is that Westmoreland took a chance on a certain interpretation of the intelligence and was caught out. It's just that simple.

After MACV reports on January 21 that the offensive had begun and later that the twenty-fifth was shaping up as the key day, both those days came and went. Nothing happened. Then on the night of January 29 Viet Cong forces, apparently unaware that COSVN had ordered a twenty-four-hour postponement, began attacks on six towns in the II Corps region. By itself that degree of coordination was unprecedented, but in combination with the many indications previously cited, these events removed most officers' doubts that something was really happening.

At 11:25 a.m. on January 30 the MACV chief of staff, General Walter T. ("Dutch") Kerwin, sent out a special alert order to U.S. forces. American troops got instructions to take special precautions to protect command posts, to go on alert, to cancel the scheduled Tet cease-fire. General Westmoreland got on the telephone to call each of his key subordinate commanders. These measures along with Westmoreland's previous efforts to get the Tet cease-fire canceled have been presented as the evidence that MACV was not surprised at Tet.

Even if this were true, the only surprise that could be avoided at this stage was tactical. Strategic surprise could not be avoided because MACV was prepared to believe only in Khe Sanh–plus, not in the Tet Offensive that occurred. Dutch Kerwin's alert order did nothing to prepare American forces for fighting of the scope and depth that followed.

The last-minute preparations also contain ambiguous elements which bear on whether tactical surprise was avoided. General Earle Wheeler sent the White House a copy of a Westmoreland cable to the commander in chief Pacific (MAC 01333), an "eyes only" secret one, received at an hour that indicates it must have been sent about the time of the Kerwin alert order. The cable reports, "There are indications that the enemy may not cease military operations during Tet."[38] If, at this late date, just hours before the countrywide Tet attacks, MACV voiced warnings with such lack of assurance, the conclusion must be that Westmoreland had not avoided surprise. Moreover, there does not seem to have been enough surety at MACV to inform ARVN of the action.

General Westmoreland's other last-minute actions also contain an element of ambiguity. He tried to get the Tet cease-fire canceled or reduced, but Westmoreland had attempted to do that at *every instance of a cease-fire* since the notorious "bombing halt" of 1965–1966, when Hanoi took advantage of a cease-fire to reinforce and reprovision its troops. Telephoning key subordinates was ambiguous since Westmoreland's practice was to do this often, including on such routine occasions as his own arrivals or departures from South Vietnam.

To turn the question around, approaching it from an intelligence standpoint, there were certain measures that MACV would surely have taken *had it been certain of imminent attack*: cancellation of leaves, recall of soldiers from local liberty, halting routine chores that detracted from combat readiness. Even if, as a security measure, one wished to avoid those actions, there were quiet but key things to be done like generating aircraft readiness rates to provide instant aerial firepower. The record contains no indications that any of these things were done. This author has discussed the night of Tet with a number of combat veterans, including some who manned key positions: one a marine in one of the guard towers at Danang; another an air force security guard on the line at Tan Son Nhut; a third a radio operator near Bong Son. None of these soldiers got any briefing to be especially alert that night. Even at MACV intelligence, at headquarters in the Tan Son Nhut complex, no one was especially alert in spite of the intense interest engendered by the attacks the previous night. Lieutenant Bruce E. Jones, on duty for a special intelligence staff monitoring Khe Sanh, was scoffed at by a more senior officer when he reported a bar girl's warning that they would be attacked. The headquarters complex had a total of four military policemen positioned outside.[39]

There is one key indicator involving MACV headquarters itself. General

Davidson notes how senior MACV officers armed themselves for that night as if it showed they were aware of the attacks; Don Oberdorfer also mentions this in his fine Tet account. But who ever heard of a command headquarters that went off duty the night of the big attack?

The proof of the pudding is in the eating—let us take a look at what happened to MACV senior officers the night of Tet. General Westmoreland was at home on Tran Quy Cap Street. There was shooting near enough to hear; he sat by the phone waiting for word. General Abrams was at home down the street from Tan Son Nhut; aides tried to avoid disturbing his sleep because they knew he would need the rest to meet the challenge. General Kerwin was at home, and next morning, trying to get back to MACV headquarters, he was held up by an ambush. General Davidson prepared to defend his house with his orderlies and housemates. Major General John Chaisson, just back from leave in Maine, was awakened by shooting outside his window. Chaisson was the chief of MACV's combined operations center. Colonel Daniel Graham, then a senior intelligence official, was routed from his bunk at a downtown bachelor officers' quarters to form part of an ad hoc combat unit of field rank officers trying to defend their area. At Danang, marine general Robert C. Cushman was in his quarters too.

Nor was it just the U.S. military who succumbed to this surprise. President Thieu was at My Tho in the Mekong Delta with his wife's family. Vice President Ky was at his home at Tan Son Nhut. Joint General Staff chief General Cao Van Vien was at home in Cholon and could not get across the city to ARVN headquarters until after dawn. Ambassador Ellsworth Bunker, in his villa away from the U.S. Embassy, had to be brought back using an armored personnel carrier. Ambassador Robert Komer, MACV's deputy for pacification operations, recalls he was asleep in bed that night. Colonel George Jacobsen, a senior CIA official whose home was on the U.S. Embassy grounds, had to defend himself with a pistol when Viet Cong commandos broke into the house.

At all these places, including the U.S. Embassy, which was attacked with enormous public relations consequences, Vietnamese guards supposed to provide security did not show up for work that night. These lowly Vietnamese seem to have had better intelligence than MACV J-2. As General Davidson puts it, "The most common question the senior American officers stationed in Saigon during the Tet offensive have asked is, why didn't the Viet Cong sappers attack the billets of these senior officers as part of their attacks against Saigon? . . . By so doing, Giap could have gained not only a major propaganda victory, but at the same time could have paralyzed MACV's reaction to the Communist attacks until senior officers from the subordinate commands could have come to Saigon."[40] Again, turning this question around, how could MACV possibly have taken the chance, assumed the risk of this happening, if it was well aware of the imminent Tet

Offensive? "I was there at Westy's elbow," Bob Komer later told an interviewer, "boy was it a surprise, lem me tell you!"[41]

In sum, the picture is not a pretty one for those who would have it that the United States knew all about Tet or, as it is sometimes quaintly put, that the only surprise about Tet was the extent of Hanoi's folly. There were numerous indications long before the offensive began, straws in the wind that could be read by astute analysts and sometimes were. The indicators included observable intelligence, combat intelligence, and overt behavior or declarations. Interpretation of the indicators was not clouded by discrepant information, as is sometimes the case; rather, adversary actions created a deception—an alternative interpretation of some plausibility. American commanders chose to believe in that other interpretation. To some degree the adversary achieved surprise, both strategic and tactical.

It is possible to postulate a reason why MACV succumbed to the alternative interpretation also. The Khe Sanh offensive and later Khe Sanh–plus interpretations conformed to the preferences of senior commanders for their own strategy. Those preferences created a predisposition against believing intelligence analysts who based themselves on the combat intelligence. In addition, there was a seductive attraction in the observables, particularly the communications intelligence, because of the presumption that the adversary's own communications were an automatic gauge of his secret intentions. There is as yet no evidence that either commanders or intelligence specialists faced the question of why adversary communications should be any more authoritative as sources than adversary secret documents. Yet MACV J-2 consistently depended on the intercepts over the documents and interrogations, in effect ignoring some of the pillars of intelligence. It is especially poignant, given this context, that the Westmoreland memoir should quote an adversary's *document* to claim foreknowledge of Hanoi's real plans.

So it is that the warning left something to chance. There was a chance, a certain probability, that the Tet Offensive would be discovered in advance. Hanoi seems to have confronted this truth enough to realize that an operation of the dimensions planned could not but throw off a certain number of indications. Hanoi appears to have structured a second plausible interpretation to face their adversaries with the conundrum of choice. Westmoreland took a chance; he focused upon a certain facet of the evidence which supported his strategic preferences and resisted expanding his interpretation to encompass all the evidence. Even at the last moment, MACV continued to take chances, assuming risks entailed in conducting business as usual in Saigon. Having taken these chances, MACV was caught out and disaster followed. That Hanoi also made mistakes and incurred tremendous losses in the battles of Tet should not be allowed to obscure the intelligence failure that occurred.

NOTES

A variant version of this chapter under the title "The Warning That Left Something to Chance: Intelligence at TET" originally appeared in *The Journal of American-East Asian Relations,* Vol. 2, No. 2 (Summer 1993), pp. 161–184. Material from that article is reprinted here with permission of Imprint Publications, Inc.

1. Dave Richard Palmer, *Summons of the Trumpet: A History of the Vietnam War from a Military Man's Viewpoints* (San Rafael, Calif.: Presidio Press, 1978), p. 228. Among other recent works with varying views on intelligence matters during the Tet period are Thomas L. Cubbage III, "Intelligence and the Tet Offensive: The South Vietnamese View of the Threat," in Elizabeth Jane Errington and B. J. C. McKercher, eds., *The Vietnam War as History* (Westport, Conn.: Praeger, 1990), pp. 92–116 [hereafter "Intelligence and Tet"]; Ted Gittinger, ed., *The Johnson Years: A Vietnam Roundtable* (Austin, Tex.: LBJ Library, University of Texas Press, 1993), pp. 115–122, Appendices IV and VI.

2. U.S. Congress, House Select Committee on Intelligence, 94th Cong., 1st session, *Hearings: U.S. Intelligence Agencies and Activities: The Performance of the Intelligence Community* (Washington, D.C.: U.S. Gov't Printing Office, 1975), pt. 5, p. 1653. A similar view is found in Cubbage, "Intelligence and Tet." For a more comprehensive analysis, see James J. Wirtz, *The Tet Offensive: Intelligence Failure in War* (Ithaca, N.Y.: Cornell University Press, 1991). Cubbage, for one, remains unconvinced, as shown by his review of the Wirtz monograph in *Conflict Quarterly,* Vol. 13, No. 3 (Summer 1993).

3. Phillip B. Davidson, *Vietnam at War: The History 1946–1975* (Novato, Calif.: Presidio Press, 1988), pp. 418–422, 434, 439–450 [hereafter *Vietnam at War*]. A finely detailed analysis of Hanoi's decision making which, however, also takes the view that U.S. intelligence was unable to interpret correctly the data it had in hand, is in Ronnie E. Ford, "Tet Revisited: The Strategy of the Communist Vietnamese," *Intelligence and National Security,* Vol. 9, No. 4 (April 1994). For a collection of translated source materials, see Patrick J. McGarvey, ed., *Visions of Victory: Selected Vietnamese Communist Military Writings, 1964–1968* (Stanford, Calif.: Stanford University Press, 1969).

4. George Crile et al., *CBS Reports,* "The Uncounted Enemy: A Vietnam Deception." Television broadcast, January 23, 1982.

5. "Fact Sheet: Comparisons of Truck Sightings in the Lao Panhandle," December 7, 1967, folder: "Laos, v. 17," Box 271, Country File: Laos, National Security File, Lyndon Baines Johnson Papers, Lyndon Baines Johnson Library, Austin, Texas [hereafter CF:NSF:LBJP or NSC History].

6. MACV Combined Documents Exploitation Center (CDEC), Translation 08-0501-67, "The Success of the VC 'War of Liberation,' " folder: "Captured Document Cables," Box 153, CF: Vietnam, NSF, LBJP.

7. MACV-CDEC, Translation 11-1754-67 in summary in *CDEC Bulletin,* No. 8014, November 15, 1967, folder: "CDEC Bulletins, vol. 2," Box 153, CF: Vietnam, NSF, LBJP.

8. Hoang Ngoc Lung, *Indochina Monograph: The General Offensives of 1968–1969* (Washington, D.C.: Office of Chief of Military History, 1976), pp. 33–34.

9. MACV-CDEC, Translation 11-1591-67, "1967–68 Winter–Spring Campaign by B3 Front," November 14, 1967, folder: "CDEC Bulletins, vol. 2," Box 153, CF: Vietnam, NSF, LBJP.

10. Ibid.

11. MACV-CDEC, *CDEC Bulletin,* No. 8319, December 6, 1967, folder: "CDEC Bulletins, vol. 2," Box 153, CF: Vietnam, NSF, LBJP.

12. U.S. Mission to Vietnam, press release: "Captured Document Indicates Final Phase of Revolution Is at Hand," January 5, 1968, folder: "Press Releases on Captured Documents," Box 143, CF: Vietnam, NSF, LBJP. Widely quoted by Oberdorfer, Palmer, Davidson, Westmoreland, and others. The most likely explanation for why this key enemy document was given public circulation is itself a suggestion as to how the Viet Cong and North Vietnamese were able to achieve surprise at Tet: American officials and officers could not or refused to understand the basic thrust of adversary strategy. Had they done so, it would have been important to the response to keep their knowledge of VC/NVA plans secret and this press release would never have been handed out.

13. U.S. Mission to Vietnam, "The Decisive Hour: Two Directives for Tet," *Vietnam Documents and Research Notes,* No. 28/29, April 1968.

14. MACV-CDEC, *CDEC Bulletin,* No. 8468, December 14, 1967, folder: "CDEC Bulletins, vol. 2," Box 153, CF: Vietnam, NSF, LBJP.

15. U.S. Mission to Vietnam, press release: "Captured Document Indicates Viet Cong Plan to Take Advantage of Cease Fire," January 8, 1968, folder: "Press Releases on Captured Documents," Box 153, CF: Vietnam, NSF, LBJP.

16. MACV-CDEC, CDEC Report No. 6-027-0789-68, January 28, 1968, folder: "CDEC Bulletins, vol. 2," Box 153, CF: Vietnam, NSF, LBJP.

17. Department of Defense, Intelligence Information Report No. 6-028-6244-67, December 14, 1967, ibid.

18. Vo Nguyen Giap, *Big Victory, Great Task* (New York: Praeger, 1968), p. 19 [hereafter *Big Victory*].

19. Ibid., pp. 81–99, esp. pp. 89, 94; quoted from p. 90.

20. MACV-CDEC, *CDEC Bulletin,* No. 7009, n.d. [ca. August 25, 1967], "Captured Document Cables," LBJP.

21. Giap, *Big Victory,* p. 104.

22. "North Vietnamese Instructions on Tet Celebrations," January 24, 1968, *BBC Summaries of World Broadcasts,* pt. 3: FE No. 2677-A3, p. 1.

23. "North Vietnam Press on Tet Festival," February 1, 1968, ibid., FE No. 2684-A3, p. 4.

24. Walt W. Rostow, *The Diffusion of Power: An Essay in Recent History* (New York: Macmillan, 1972), pp. 463–464.

25. Ibid., pp. 462–463.

26. Central Intelligence Agency, Saigon Station Report No. 65/67 (December 3–9, 1967), December 10, 1967 (FOIA).

27. Department of State, Saigon, Telegram A-324 and attachment, "An Assessment of the Current Enemy Situation," November 25, 1967, folder: "General Military 2(c) vol. 1," Box 68, CF: Vietnam, NSF, LBJP.

28. MACV J-2 Periodic Intelligence Report (PERINTREP), November 1967, attached to note, McCafferty to Rostow, January 9, 1968, folder: "General Military 2(c)3," Box 69, CF: Vietnam, NSF, LBJP.

29. Westmoreland to Wheeler (MAC 11956), December 10, 1967, folder: "History File vol. 26," Box 15, William C. Westmoreland Papers, LBJP.

30. William C. Westmoreland, *A Soldier Reports* (Garden City, N.Y.: Doubleday, 1976), p. 318 [hereafter *A Soldier Reports*].

31. Ibid., quoted from p. 314.

32. Bruce E. Jones, *War without Windows* (New York: Vanguard Press, 1987), quoted from p. 159 [hereafter *War without Windows*].

33. Westmoreland cable (MAC 01049), retyped version, January 22, 1968, folder: "vol. 2-Tabs A-Z and AA-ZZ," Box 47, NSC History: March 31st Speech, LBJP.

34. Westmoreland cable (MAC 00967 "eyes only"), retyped version, January 22, 1968, ibid.

35. Westmoreland, *A Soldier Reports*, p. 316.

36. Ibid., quoted from p. 321.

37. Ibid., p. 322.

38. Westmoreland to Sharp (MAC 01333) January 1968, NSC History, LBJP.

39. Jones, *War without Windows*, pp. 170–71.

40. Davidson, *Vietnam at War*, p. 482.

41. Kim Willenson, ed., *The Bad War: An Oral History of the Vietnam War* (New York: New American Library, 1987), p. 95.

10

Don't Bother Me with the Facts; I've Made Up My Mind: The Tet Offensive in the Context of Intelligence and U.S. Strategy[1]

Larry Cable

In recent years, much of the debate over the origins and impact of the Tet Offensive has focused on whether or not Tet caught American strategists by "surprise" due to a so-called failure of intelligence. This debate is often placed in a revisionist framework: if American evaluation of the intelligence data available before Tet had been more effective, the damage done to the allied war effort could have been obviated or better contained.

Both this debate and its revisionist implications are, however, scarcely relevant to the subject. American strategic thinking in Vietnam was so flawed as to prevent any effective evaluation of the enemy's strategic intentions. These flaws not only blinded American strategists to the intelligence data before them, but also helped produce a strategic posture that invited the enemy to launch a general offensive under circumstances that would be as devastating to the American and Republic of Vietnam's war effort as it was unexpected in its size and scope. In sum, flawed American strategic evaluation of the ways, means, and ends of American and Vietnamese political intentions and military operations in Vietnam precluded effective intelligence exploitation and made the debacle that was Tet Mau Than inevitable.[2]

The concept of historical inevitability, though unfounded and unjustifiable, nonetheless has a compelling reality when applied to the dynamics of policy formulation, implementation, and evaluation as a result of several phenomena. Among them are a shared intellectual heritage on the part of decision makers and senior-level implementors; the power of institutional imperatives, including those arising from the domestic political culture; and a pervasive unwillingness to accept intelligence that runs counter to personal predilections, prejudices, and beliefs such as to constitute a variant of the common psychological occurrence called cognitive dissonance. The Tet Offensive, or more properly, the combination of the Tet Urban Offensives and the siege at Khe Sanh, represent a dramatic and pivotal event in which the larger, more accurate understanding of historical inevitability can be seen at work.

The policy process consists of three distinct but connected stages; formulation, implementation, and evaluation. Of these, evaluation comprises the necessary point of departure, because without an accurate and comprehensive understanding of the dynamics operating within an area of concern it is impossible to formulate, let alone implement, policy that is relevant to the interests of the intervening and host states.

Effective formulation, particularly within the context of military intervention, requires the establishment of a goal toward which, if necessary, force will be directed. It also requires the defining of success or victory in terms of the desired goal, so that progress toward that goal might be effectively measured. In addition, it is necessary to develop a theory of victory that considers the strengths and weaknesses of both intervenor and host and those of the opponent, as well as to appreciate the various features of the actual battlefield of internal war and the actions of the intervenor.

Proper policy implementation requires that all senior implementors understand and agree on the goal, definition, and theory of victory, so that they might take full advantage of the necessary operational and tactical flexibility that is formally or de facto granted by a national command authority. Furthermore, effective implementation is considerably enhanced by an effective meshing with the mechanisms of evaluation; either those of operational review or external intelligence production.

If the process is to work, several conditions must be met. The first is purely intellectual: the goal, definition, and theory of victory must be internally consistent, coherent, and flexible enough to permit adjustment in one to be reflected by appropriate changes in the others and, most importantly, relevant to the realities on the ground. The second condition is process oriented: the mechanisms for evaluation allow formulators and implementors alike to have access to a coherent picture assembled from complementary systems focusing on internal operational review such as military after-action reports and periodic reports, as well as those whose purview is the opponent, the host, and the uncommitted generally conducted by the intelligence community. The third condition is rooted in personality: commanders, leaders, and decision makers alike must not seek to impose an artificial understanding on either the nature of the arena and the contest being waged or the nature, character, and effectiveness of the intervention. They must be willing and able, quite possibly in the face of domestic political or institutional imperatives, to accept the realities as they emerge.

These conditions are difficult enough to secure in a conventional, interstate war between peer opponents. It is far more vexing to achieve them in the setting that existed in Vietnam where there were not only four parties— no two of which constituted peers—but also a war that mixed aspects of insurgency, partisan war and conventional interstate war. From the beginning, U.S. policy makers in Vietnam failed to recognize that the three conditions described above were relevant to success or failure. At this juncture the first move was made to assure the coming of the Tet Offensive.[3]

The war that emerged incrementally in South Vietnam between 1956 and 1964 was an insurgency, the armed expression of organic, internal political disaffiliation. The repeated misuse of its initiative by the regime of Ngo Dinh Diem had served to provoke and widen a perception that the Saigon government lacked functional legitimacy. This condition was significantly exacerbated by its fundamentally Northern character and concomitant absence of existential legitimacy. The guerrillas in the south were just that, southerners pursuing a southern political agenda that focused on the removal of a palpably illegitimate regime, and not an immediate federation with North Vietnam. Former members of the Viet Minh were present within the guerrilla organization (ultimately dubbed by the South Vietnamese government the Viet Cong or Vietnamese Communists or VC), but this in no way enervated the reality that opposition to the government had arisen and broadened for reasons quite organic to the southern contemporary realities. As a result, Northern complicity or assistance was as irrelevant as it was nonexistent in the constant development of the armed opposition and its final political umbrella, the National Liberation Front (NLF).

Numerous intelligence materials, primarily from the Central Intelligence Agency (CIA) and also including products of the State Department's Bureau of Intelligence and Research (INR), as well as some components of the military's intelligence organizations, demonstrate that both the Eisenhower and Kennedy administrations were properly informed regarding the southern war. Similarly, both administrations were repeatedly briefed concerning the internal difficulties that plagued North Vietnam during the same period and effectively precluded Hanoi from exercising any ambitions that may have been held by Ho Chi Minh and his coterie regarding unification.[4]

It is equally obvious that the intelligence mosaic was not effectively or properly employed in formulating and executing policy during this period, for several reasons. First, domestic political imperatives pushed first the Eisenhower and then the Kennedy and Johnson administrations into an overt commitment to the South Vietnamese government which exaggerated Vietnam's apparent importance as a test case of the United States' political and military capacity to act as global guarantor of containment. It also served to limit progressively the options available to the United States, including its capacity to decommit, which in interventionary diplomacy constitutes the ultimate lever of influence over the policies and behaviors of the host government.

The second reason is to be found in the imperatives at work in both the military and civilian components of the U.S. government, including the emphasis on rapid and definitive ending of the guerrilla threat and the belief that high firepower, high-mobility air and ground combat operations constituted the only certain avenue to victory.

The third was the civilian and military leaders' prevalent use of incorrect and misleading analogies, ranging from the Munich Conference to the efficacy of strategic air operations in World War II to the retrospective belief that the guerrilla partisan actions of the South Korean Labor party in 1949 and early 1950 constituted an early warning of looming conventional cross-border invasion by the North Korean Peoples' Army in June 1950.

The fourth reason arose from the inability of many U.S. policy formulators and implimentors to work effectively across the cultural gap that separated an American from his South Vietnamese counterpart, coupled with the paradoxical belief that North Vietnamese government decisions proceeded from the same calculus of rationality as those of the U.S. government. Taken collectively, these reasons compelled U.S. decision makers to adopt an understanding on the war in South Vietnam which progressively emphasized the crucial importance of the North Vietnamese in the increased success of the southern guerrillas and gave primacy to the imposition of public order in South Vietnam through conventional military mechanisms. In this way, it was argued, the climate necessary for the effective development of national political, economic, and social institutions within the nation leading to long-term stability might be provided. At this point the second step down the long, dark hallway toward Tet had been taken.

The first step was taken in 1964 not by the Politburo or Central Committee in Hanoi but by policy makers in the Johnson administration. Without regard to the intelligence matrix following the November 1963 coup against President Diem and the concomitant growth of the VC/NLF, and without any but the most dubious military and political support on the battlefields within that insurgency-racked country, various senior administration personnel, including McGeorge Bundy and John McNaughton, focused on the use of air power to cut off the flow of men and supplies from the North to the South. This strategic concept was variously dubbed "progressive squeeze and talk," and "graduated escalation of overt military pressure" and it centered on the use of U.S. air assets in an interdiction role directed against both the North Vietnamese logistics bases and the web of trails running through Laos. It was assumed that the strength of the Viet Cong flowed along those trails. More importantly, the concept was aimed directly at the military infrastructure so as to demonstrate that the United States had both the political will and the military capacity to inflict damage disproportionate to any benefits that Hanoi might gain in the South. The program was implemented incrementally through 1964 and culminated in Operation Rolling Thunder early in the following year.

This concept completely ignored all of the intelligence regarding the enhanced existential and functional legitimacy of the VC/NLF within a growing percentage of the Southern population, the extreme turbulence within the Saigon regime, and the lack of any substantial political will within the northern population for a southern adventure. It also ignored the long-standing regional antipathies that constituted a recurrent theme of Vietnamese history. These antipathies had most recently manifested themselves in the robust resistance the insurgents offered to Hanoi's repeated attempts to seize political control of the indigenous organization. Furthermore, U.S. formulators and executors alike failed to consider this concept in conjunction with a recurrent southern theme enunciated by the newest chief of the South Vietnamese state, General Nguyen Khanh: the need for all southerners to unite against a common enemy, the North. Not surprisingly, the North Vietnamese government viewed the mix of U.S. policy with the increasingly truculent rhetoric of the Khanh government as a credible threat, with the result that North Vietnamese regulars from the Peoples' Army of Vietnam (PAVN) were deployed in limited numbers across the border. These dispositions could be seen as either defensive or the preparations for a conventional attack. Given the synergistic operation of U.S. military doctrine, domestic political imperatives, and the willingness of decision makers to ignore or misinterpret intelligence, it is not surprising that U.S. planners believed that only U.S. ground combat forces could help avert the collapse of the South.[5]

The CIA reported in a timely, accurate, but ultimate ineffectual fashion on the probable consequences of the air campaign as well as the sources of North Vietnamese and VC/NLF conduct and success. Eventually, even Air Force intelligence and the Rand Corporation pronounced the air campaign a counterproductive failure. Moreover, reports from the U.S. Embassy and Operations Mission in Saigon clearly pointed out the irrelevance of the North Vietnamese to the growth of the southern insurgents. The decision to focus on the wrong opponent was predicated not on intelligence but on the Johnson administration's and the U.S. military's imposition of a purely American concept as to what the war ought to be based upon: U.S. politico-military doctrine, the world view and imperatives of the domestic political culture, and the evil twins of cognitive dissonance and mirror imaging. Policy was formulated and implemented without regard to evaluation either before or after operations began.

With the palpable failure of the air campaign, including Rolling Thunder and the introduction of PAVN elements on and across the common Vietnamese border, the United States took a further, giant step toward escalation. The introduction of U.S. ground combat forces in April 1965 and the subsequent increase in military personnel altered the relationship between the VC/NLF and Hanoi by helping to transform an insurgent entity into one of a partisan nature.

It therefore became likely that the southern guerrillas would not only lose their status as independent politico-military actors, but that they would also be incrementally reduced first to the role of partisans and ultimately to expendable bullet catchers. In late 1965 and early 1966 both the INR and CIA recognized this potential. The real and developing perception within the North Vietnamese population was that its government must directly and effectively enter the war so that a reward commensurate with the perceived sacrifice imposed by the bombers of Rolling Thunder might be achieved. Finally, the Embassy, USOM, INR, CIA and, to a significantly lesser extent, the intelligence section of the U.S. Military Assistance Command, Vietnam (USMACV) recognized that introducing U.S. ground combat forces would not only relegate the armed forces of South Vietnam (ARVN) to the sidelines but could also severely disrupt the whole fabric of rural South Vietnam. All of these understandings and warnings went unheeded by policy formulators and implementors alike whether military or civilian.[6]

The intelligence products emanating from an increasingly divisive intelligence community warned that combat operations by high-firepower, high-mobility U.S. forces would ultimately cause severe disruption within the South Vietnamese population. In the end, it was reasoned, only the VC/NLF or North Vietnam could benefit. This rationale was reinforced both by dispatches from the Embassy and Operations Mission and the combat after-action reports (CAAR) of U.S. units in the field. The CAAR would have been particularly instructive to senior formulators and implementors if only they had been read and heeded. That they were not constitutes a severe indictment of the U.S. commanders and political leaders in the long months between April 1965 and January 1968. For nearly three years the single best source of internal assessment regarding the use of U.S. ground combat operations was widely distributed but apparently ignored. The direct observations and experiences of U.S. maneuver battalions and their subunits provided excellent, comprehensive, and relatively timely validation of intelligence evaluating the general condition of South Vietnam. In short, the confirmatory value of the CAAR record, particularly as it reflects the experiences of brigades and battalions, presents a picture of both counterproductive failure and the changing nature of the enemy in I, II, and III Corps Tactical Zones (CTZ). This should have been compelling even to senior personnel who increasingly through 1966 and 1967 distrusted the CIA's nonteam playing.

Had the combination of CAARs, the myriad of intelligence reports, and other related evaluation mechanisms been assimilated or even cursorily inspected by senior leadership, two realities would have been quickly and compellingly apparent. The first would have been the hopelessly bankrupt nature of the implementation concept that governed the use of U.S. combat forces. Put briefly, U.S. ground forces were to be employed to increase the VC and PAVN requirements for external origin supplies. Thus, the North Vietnamese infrastructure and associated lines of supply were rendered more vulnerable to air attack. Ground operations were intended as a force multiplier for the several interlocking air campaigns in both Vietnams and Laos.

The second reality was the identity of the victims of U.S. firepower. While the primary operational focus was not killing, U.S. operations did kill people, and a substantial number of them. The organizational affiliation of the dead was important not to augment the body count box score, but so that U.S. and South Vietnamese decision makers might have an accurate understanding of the relationship between the indigenous Viet Cong and the interventionary North Vietnamese. No mistake should be made: by late 1965 there were two indigenous and two interventionary belligerents fighting in South Vietnam. The two local contestants who by this time were losing control of their own destinies or at least political agendas were the government of South Vietnam (GVN) and the VC/NLF. The precise nature of the relationship between each intervenor, the United States and North Vietnam (DRV), and its nominal host had become central to the evaluation, formulation, and implementation triad.

By mid 1966 combat after-action reports made it clear that U.S. efforts had failed. At the same time, the PAVN presence had grown significantly during the first fifteen months of U.S. ground operations, despite the increase in air and ground attacks. The only legitimate conclusion was that the CIA's extremely dour appreciation of U.S. strategy and its operational implementation had been amply borne out by the changing realities on the ground. At the same time, reports from the Embassy, USOM, USMACV, CAARs, and the CIA revealed that U.S. ground operations had produced an extremely destabilizing effect on the rural population. Roughly 25 percent of the population had become refugees at least once during the period. The number of refugees had grown so large that USMACV defined refugee generation as an indicator of success to be employed by commanders in constructing a CAAR. Furthermore, the increased employment of American forces had relegated ARVN to a marginal role. This undercut not only its combat efficiency but also the perceived legitimacy of whatever Saigon regime had emerged temporarily at the top of the GVN tree. The overall picture was one of policy failure. Unfortunately, this was a picture that senior military and civilian officials did not accept.

Without doubt, U.S. forces had a highly lethal effect during the first eighteen months of major operations. But other than the peasant who had copped a frag addressed, "to whom it may concern," what was the political or other affiliation of the victims of U.S. fire and what did this imply both about the relationship between the VC and Hanoi and any changes in the North Vietnamese theory of victory? Clearly, U.S. forces were killing Viet Cong even when they encountered PAVN units. This was dramatically underscored in the 1967 Battle of Dak To where U.S. forces acting on information from a Viet Cong defector, Sergeant Vu, diverted from the original concept governing a multibrigade search and destroy sweep in the central highlands to attack a well-emplaced PAVN force. Both CAARs and intelligence noted that the vast majority of the northern units withdrew in good order and with minimal casualties across the Laotian border. The VC main forces that had been brigaded with PAVN took the brunt of the losses, and several were virtually destroyed. This fact should have served to reinforce earlier, smaller versions of the same dynamic: when fighting PAVN the Americans were killing southern guerrillas. Why was this occurring, and what strategic or political inferences can be legitimately and properly derived from the observed phenomenon?[7]

Had these questions been raised by USMACV and higher echelon commanders and decision makers, the Tet Urban Offensives could have been averted and might also have provided the basis for a reorientation of at least the psychological operations directed against the VC/NLF and their mass support base. Unfortunately, neither theater commanders, including General William Westmoreland, nor the U.S. ambassador, nor higher levels of the U.S. politico-military command structure either asked the question or even had the basis to understand that the question needed to be asked. Similarly, they lacked the intellectual context necessary to understand the significance of the following phenomena observed between mid-1966 and the final quarter of 1967: the reduction of enemy-initiated actions; the deployment of significant PAVN forces in northern I CTZ and the central highlands of II CTZ where they directly threatened major urban centers; the continued combat capacity of the VC in II, III, and IV CTZ coupled with the ineffectiveness of both U.S. and ARVN units in counterinsurgency, or as it had been renamed, "pacification support"; the increase of unregulated refugee streams and shanty towns within or on the outskirts of every major South Vietnamese city north of IV CTZ; the cultural unpalatability and concomitant anomie within the U.S.-designed and -constructed refugee relocation villages; the utility of Rolling Thunder in maintaining and enhancing the political will of the North Vietnamese population; and, last but certainly not least, indicators arising from human intelligence sources close to the Central Committee and Politburo in the late summer of 1966 that the decision had been made to proceed toward the unlimited goal of unification.

Taken in conjunction with the other observed and reported occurrences, these indicators should have led to one conclusion: the North Vietnamese had resolved to achieve a reward commensurate with the sacrifices made since early 1965, namely, unification. As a result, Hanoi faced two adversaries, the US/GVN and the VC/NLF. Even a cursory awareness of Vietnam's cultural, political, and social history would have provided the necessary matrix in which to properly place the several sets of critical observations.

Had the commanders and policy formulators accepted the assessment from intelligence that a general uprising led by VC combatants could automatically ignite broad support from a population alienated from the Saigon government, disaster could have been halted in midstride.

The fundamental American error was the failure to understand that the United States was not fighting a monolithic enemy. This had been evident at the beginning when military and administration alike had assumed that the southern guerrillas were northern partisans, with the result that U.S. strategy had focused on the North as the main enemy, relegating the VC/NLF to a subordinate, even marginal status. Policy formulators in Hanoi had not committed the same error. Rather, they correctly saw that they faced two rivals who had to be eliminated in order to achieve the 1966 goal of unchallenged hegemony. While the North possessed the necessary human and material resources to continue the war regardless of the U.S. intervention, it did not have the capacity to defeat its two enemies either serially or conjointly. As a result, the obvious option was to employ the United States and its junior associate, the GVN, to destroy the VC/NLF while progressively reducing or enervating the American will to continue the war. Thus, the ability to accept casualties and damage became far more important than the capacity to inflict casualties and damage.

It now behooved Hanoi to shift the burden for the war as much as possible on the VC/NLF forces. This would achieve two ends simultaneously: reduce the combat potential and political potency of the VC/NLF as a result of U.S. operations and effective conflict protraction without imposing unacceptable cost on the northern population. The implementation of this strategic approach became increasingly apparent, although it was not properly appreciated at the time through 1966 and by 1967 it became clear that the VC had been reduced from partisan auxiliaries to expendable bullet catchers whose deaths constituted a net advantage to Hanoi. The PAVN's losses, combined with the physical and psychological effects of Operation Rolling Thunder, assured the gradual strengthening of North Vietnam's political will, with the result that Hanoi had minimum problems assuring its own population that it could pursue a conflict protraction approach.

Finally, as VC/NLF losses mounted in I, II, and III CTZ and the population dislocation increased, the politico-military leadership of the southern guerrillas increasingly found the idea of a general uprising ever more attractive. Three reasons were adduced in support of an uprising: the losses within the ranks of the best trained and equipped and most experienced main force units were becoming unacceptable; the creation of the Civil

Operations and Revolutionary Development Support (CORDS) program under Ambassador Robert Komer would probably reinvigorate the moribund U.S./GVN counterinsurgency program; and both PAVN and VC units had alienated previously supportive, or at least uncommitted, members of the rural population. Thus, time was no longer on the guerrillas' side, a consideration that was reinforced by an increasing awareness that the southerners were becoming all too dependent on northern resources and thus were at real risk of losing their independence.

U.S. Commanders and decision makers did not act on the indicators noted by the intelligence agencies or the conclusion that a general uprising focused on the urban centers was increasingly likely after late 1966. They ignored all signs even after the warnings were renewed with increasing definiteness through 1967. While no one could state with utter certainty that some kind of general uprising would occur at or near Tet in 1968, their import was unmistakable: the Viet Cong, through the mechanism of a general uprising, would attempt to achieve, if not an ending to the war which gained the political goals of the core southern NLF, then sufficient politico-military leverage to begin a conflict resolution process that would not allow Hanoi to attain operational dominance over the South. This potential was passed over by U.S. commanders and ignored by an administration which by mid-1967 was attempting to convince an ever more skeptical and divided domestic constituency that two years of effort were producing not merely a growing mound of body bags but a successful outcome that justified the expense, deaths, and domestic turbulence.[8]

Hanoi and PAVN's role was to create a strategic conundrum for the United States that would facilitate implementation of the emerging concept of the Americans and the VC eating each other up. The heavy PAVN forces stationed just south of the Demilitarized Zone (DMZ) in I CTZ and in the central highlands along and near the international border in II CTZ provided the basis for the requisite conundrum. Unless large U.S. contingents were stationed opposite these concentrations, the way was open for the PAVN regulars to stage what was referred to in intelligence, USMACV, and Embassy documents as an "urban spectacular." This implied the overrunning of the major population centers in the northern third of South Vietnam, with vast, negative effects on the political will of the U.S. and South Vietnamese publics as well as the perceptions of American effectiveness globally. However, insofar as General Westmoreland concentrated American combat power on blocking or attacking and defeating the PAVN forces, he opened the rest of South Vietnam to Viet Cong-initiated actions. As ARVN had both been relegated to the backwaters of the war and only partially retrained and reoriented toward counterinsurgency or pacification support efforts, the South Vietnamese capacity to cover, let alone preempt, the VC in the so-called other war was limited. If the U.S. commander reacted to increasing VC successes by drawing down the maneuver battalions in I and II CTZs, he then invited the feared "spectacular."

Since intelligence appreciations, both civilian and military, had warned of this dilemma, it is unlikely that either USMACV or the administration was unaware of the danger presented by the interlocking of PAVN and VC threats. Nor is there any credible evidence to support the idea that either local commanders or their superiors in Washington were blind to the critical vulnerabilities of the urban centers, whether attacked by PAVN or VC formations. General Westmoreland demonstrated conclusively that he had been given a full and timely strategic picture represented by the PAVN divisions in I and II CTZ when he formed Task Force Oregon. More importantly, he requested in mid-1967 that the air and ground forces be added to his command.

The Joint Chiefs of Staff (JCS) approved Westmoreland's request, demonstrating that the senior military command focused on the PAVN regulars and the chance to destroy a significant portion of their combat capacity in a relatively short campaign.

Neither USMACV nor the JCS gave any credence to intelligence assessments from civilian and military sources which pointed to the probability of a VC/NLF general uprising and the necessary conclusion that any urban spectacular was more likely to be achieved by southern rather than northern forces. This reflected the long-standing unwillingness of U.S. policy makers to accept evaluations which suggested that the United States was facing not one but two quite disparate opponents. It also reflected the prejudice of U.S. military commanders against irregular forces. Bluntly, U.S. doctrine and shared intellectual heritage alike conspired to assure that the Viet Cong, being irregular, guerrilla forces, would not be seen as critical a threat or as lucrative a target as the presumably more competent PAVN "hard hats."

The Tet Urban Offensives should not have been a surprise within the U.S. military and administration, for there had been no intelligence failure, no absence of warning and prediction. There also was no need for specific warning intelligence for American decision makers, theater commanders, and their subordinates or the South Vietnamese government and military to have not only met but to have anticipated and prevented or preempted the Offensive. The periodic reports of the Embassy and USOM as well as the overlooked CAARs clearly demonstrated that the relationship between the VC/NLF and the DRV had changed twice between mid-1965 and mid-1967. In particular, by summer 1967 the CAARs showed that the VC had become an expendable shield covering PAVN, so even a half-alert observer should have been aware of the changed nature of the game from Hanoi's perspective. PAVN's operational disposition served to alert all hands to the attractive potential of an "urban spectacular," while the increased emphasis on the desirability, even necessity, of the general uprising, which increasingly marked the public and private rhetoric of the NLF leadership after fall 1966, should have put Saigon and Washington on notice that the VC were as capable and prepared as PAVN to undertake the "spectacular," and perhaps on an even larger scale. The absence of sufficient U.S. and GVN forces to guard against both PAVN and the VC simultaneously should have reinforced the urgency of the twin warnings.

Finally, the continued strengthening of North Vietnam's political will with the concomitant demand throughout the northern domestic political culture should have oriented U.S. formulators and implementors to the emergence of a theory of victory based on conflict protraction and to the DRV's commitment to the goal of forced operational dominance of all Vietnam. If the Vietnamese historical experience had been factored into the evaluation process, the necessary conclusion would have been that the DRV and the VC/NLF were in a race to eliminate the United States and its GVN client. The onus of time was most clearly on the southern guerrillas to maintain their status as independent political actors, and to prevent an unacceptable outcome: northern domination.

If the overall record is considered, the necessary conclusion that emerges is that U.S. intelligence had been excellent. First, the CIA and INR had correctly identified the character of the war in South Vietnam between 1956 and 1964; second, the CIA had correctly foreseen the role played by the Diem regime as well as the turbulence that would follow its overthrow. The irrelevant, ineffectual, and ultimately quite counterproductive air war had been both predicted and retrospectively evaluated not only by the CIA but also by other components of the intelligence system, which by 1967 had become so unwieldy that any commander or decision maker could find the right product to meet his requirements. Despite the morass of too many choices, it was still quite clear that ground operations were inherently so destabilizing for South Vietnam as to assure the growth, if not of DRV influence, then the size and potency of the VC/NLF. Finally, the CIA correctly deduced the changing nature of DRV's goals, theories of victory, and relationship with the VC/NLF. As a result, the periodic warnings of an "urban spectacular" that would be the centerpiece of a general uprising by the southern guerrillas probably at the Tet festival should have been taken seriously.[9]

The key question is why were these warnings not heeded and acted upon? The answer is to be found in the nature of the U.S. decision-making process. The process itself was intellectually contaminated in several critical aspects. The most basic level of contamination occurred in the shared intellectual heritage of senior commanders and leaders who had specific visions regarding the war in South Vietnam and the U.S. military's capacities to operate within that venue. They imposed a specific architecture on the Vietnam War, regardless of the intelligence picture which showed their ideas to be utterly without merit or factual support. These same personalities were unable to understand that they were intervening on human terrain vastly different from that of the United States. Unable to accept the Vietnamese, whether as hosts, opponents, or uncommitted middle, as nothing more than round eyes with a fondness for rice and nunc mam, senior U.S. officials engaged in never-ending exercises of mirror imaging.

Yet another limitation was that of U.S. military doctrine which, as repeatedly shown by the intelligence and other components of the system, was massively irrelevant to the realities that emerged on the ground in Vietnam. As a consequence, American strategic and operational implementation modalities served both to transform the character of the war and to invite a second, hostile intervenor, North Vietnam, into the conflict. While all governments' foreign policy are affected by inducements and constraints placed upon them by domestic political imperatives and by the dictates of various institutions that are exogenous and often injurious of the policy goals at stake, the U.S. government demonstrated less skill than its opponents in Hanoi in subordinating these to the requirements of successful politico-military struggle. Linking all of these is cognitive dissonance: an ability to see only what one wishes to see or to justify the dismissal of information or perspectives that run counter to one's desires.

This phenomenon was rampant throughout the U.S. involvement in Vietnam and reached a high point in the fall of 1967 when Secretary of Defense Robert McNamara, having again reviewed all of the evaluations regarding the war and its intellectual architecture came to the conclusion that the U.S. course of action for three and a half years had been wrong and needed to be severely modified. This assessment could not have come at a worse time for the Johnson administration, which had been engaged in a prolonged full-court press of public relations in an attempt to calm and reassure an increasingly restive American citizenry that the United States was achieving its goals in South Vietnam and would not have to stay the course much longer. Given this context, it is no surprise that indications of a Viet Cong urban spectacular were not welcome.

There was no intelligence failure involved in the Tet Urban Offensives or in the siege of Khe Sanh. Rather, the failure was one of strategic conceptualization, which in turn was the product of the polluted policy process. The willful absence of an appropriate intellectual matrix for that process, exacerbated by the dearth of comprehensive evaluation systems that properly integrated the products of the intelligence community with the internal assessment mechanisms of the military services and the foreign policy bureaucracies, assured that decision makers and military commanders would assume the role of patsy.

NOTES

1. It should be noted that slightly over 425 primary source documents from a variety of archives and holdings, most declassified since 1990, were used directly in the preparation of this article. Due to space and sensitivity limitations, only brief

and general citations are offered. However, a complete bibliographic rendition will be provided by the writer upon request. Most of these sources are Combat After Action Reports (CAARs) from the CIA. Many are located at the Center for Military History, Washington, D.C., [hereafter cited as CAARs-CIA-CMH].

2. This introduction has been provided by the editors with the consent of the author.

3. For a detailed statement of this above analysis, see Larry Cable, *Unholy Grail: The United States Army and the Wars in Vietnam, 1965–1968* (London: Routledge Press, 1991), especially the author's introduction entitled "Inbrief" and the conclusion entitled "Outbrief," [hereafter cited as *Unholy Grail*].

4. For more on the CIA and State Department INRs in the Eisenhower and Kennedy years, see ibid., Chapters 1 and 2. For a more extensive analysis of the Viet Cong and NLF, see Douglas Pike, *Vietcong: The Organization and Techniques of the National Liberation Front of South Vietnam* (Cambridge, Mass.: MIT Press, 1966).

5. The events and analysis covered above can be found in greater detail in Cable, *Unholy Grail*, Chapters 3–5; Douglas Pike, *PAVN: People's Army of North Vietnam* (Novato, Calif: Presidio Press, 1986). It should be noted that General Khanh restated this above point and concept to the author and many others during a Vietnam Roundtable held at Texas Tech University, in Lubbock, Texas, between March 30, and April 1, 1995. Moreover, he also made similar pronouncements to the author privately on several occasions.

6. For more details on the above analysis of the use of U.S. air and ground forces, see Earl H. Tilford, Jr., *Crosswinds: The Air Force's Setup in Vietnam* (College Station, Tex.: Texas A & M University Press, 1993); for ground forces, Andrew F. Krepinevich, *The Army and Vietnam* (Baltimore: Johns Hopkins University Press, 1986).

7. The vast majority of the above material has been derived from the previously mentioned CAARs-CIA-CMH files. Please refer to note 1.

8. Ibid.

9. Ibid.

11

Tet beyond the Wire: TCK/TKN, the General Offensive/General Uprising

Robert Nourse

The general uprising phase of the Tet Offensive of 1968 has often been portrayed as a spontaneous event that the enemy hoped would accompany and assist the offensive's wider strategic and tactical objectives. However, at least in I Corps, the northernmost military region of the Republic of South Vietnam, the general uprising phase of the Tet Offensive followed a detailed plan that left little to chance. A series of preparatory attacks in I Corps during December and January 1968 were launched as part of an effort to weaken the will and destroy the confidence of local peasants in the South Vietnamese government. These attacks were designed to ensure that subsequent main force VC and NVA operations would both complete the revolutionary education of the masses and employ them in support of what Hanoi and the NLF hoped would be the decisive action of the war. The relationship of these localized attacks and their sequels during the Tet Offensive were made apparent to me as the American in Ly Tin District of Quang Tin Province in I Corps during the months immediately before and after the Tet Offensive.

In December 1967 the 1st Battalion, 46th Infantry, was operating in my area of Quang Tin Province. On December 4 they captured an enemy document that gave more specific guidance to the local VC cadres than had as yet been seen in higher-level documents previously obtained by American military intelligence. This document, described in MACV Bulletin No. 8613, dated November 17, 1967, instructed the VC cadres

to intensify proselyting activities and concurrently promote political struggle among the population within their respective areas. The document announced that the "strategic objectives" set forth by the Party consisted of: 1. An all-out effort to destroy a major 'enemy' (FWMAF/RVNAF) vital force in conjunction with an attempt to disintegrate the RVNAF. [FWMAF—Free World Military Assistance Force; RVNAF—Republic of Vietnam Armed Forces.] 2. Development of VC organization in urban areas so as to serve the ultimate aim of uprising (by the people) in cities and towns. These could be achieved by constant attacks to [*sic*] directed at the FWMAF/RVNAF rear bases in an attempt to provide effective support to the political struggles by the population both in urban and rural areas.[1]

In retrospect, the response of the local VC cadres to this directive was a series of preparatory raids on five neighboring districts in Quang Tin and Quang Ngai Provinces, including my own district of Ly Tin. On December 3 Binh Son District, a few miles south of Ly Tin, was overrun. On January 2 the military compound at Ly Tin on the coast of Quang Tin Province very nearly met the same fate. It was saved mainly by a variable-time barrage I called in on our position. We were spared, but the enemy left forty-six dead and had carried away many more. At the time, however, the origin, significance, and ferocious nature of these raids were not entirely understood. Events in Ly Tin later that month enhanced my understanding of their purpose.

On the eve of Tet, the military compound at Ly Tin prepared for a VC attack expected because it was the period of the dark of the moon, which left the outpost virtually blind. I placed my advisor team on alert and ordered them into the sandbagged bunkers that flanked the command post where I remained with my watch personnel. Captain Nguyen Duc, chief of Ly Tin District, closely monitored his popular forces (PFs), who manned the outer bunker line that protected the rectangular compound, as if to acknowledge their questionable training and quality; however, they could put up a good fight and had stood the test during a night attack just four weeks before.

We Americans fidgeted and dozed in our bunkers, startled fully conscious now and then by sounds in the three rows of barbed wire that surrounded the compound, but the night remained unusually quiet. Absent, too, were the usual illumination rounds that constantly "popped" overhead and then drifted to earth, bathing us in an eerie, flickering light.

I retired to our living quarters adjacent to the command bunker to rest and await a call. I knew I would soon be up again. The VC ruled the nights, striking here and there throughout the district with elusive suddenness. It was my responsibility to answer pleas for help from friendly forces in the field and call in artillery on coordinates that crossed at unseen spots somewhere in the night.

I rested fitfully, listening to the distant crackling of voices on the radio and waiting for the thumping impact of mortar rounds that might signal an attack. I must have dozed for more than an hour when suddenly I was awakened. I jumped from the bunk and glanced at my watch. It was just past midnight. The noise came again, then again—whoooooosh, whoooooosh—it was unlike the sounds of war on a typical Vietnamese night.

"Incoming . . . !"

I heard the alarm being repeated by my team members.

"Rockets incoming!"

The first rounds had found their mark as distant explosions rumbled in the night. I ran outside to observe the sparkling trails of 122mm rockets roaring and sizzling in great arcs through the cobalt sky. Flashes burst, then died on the horizon around Chu Lai.

I rushed into the command bunker to monitor the radio. Dozens of voices were calling for support. Explosions rocked the area and bursts from more distant hits lit up our area. The rocket fire continued intermittently as VC crews set up in an area we dubbed the rocket pocket, fired, then hustled to other prearranged firing spots in the ravines west of us and just ahead of American counterartillery fire.

In the first minutes, the sky over Ly Tin District was strangely empty of American choppers, but within half an hour the air was filled with the throb of rotor blades as gunships began maneuvering stealthily in the blackness above, awaiting an opportunity to strike.

Soon, orange tracers were flashing toward the ground as the gunships homed in on targets below. Flares dangled as if from unseen strings as their gleaming white light lit distant areas of the district. A few mortar rounds burst at intervals within our wire, and my advisor teammates, Sergeant Pasqua and Specialist Eitel, prepared to return fire from the mortar pit behind the command bunker. The others awaited the VC, who we were certain would be coming.

The fighting raged throughout the district, and the rockets continued arcing toward the Americal Division (23rd Infantry Division) headquarters and marine air installation at Chu Lai several miles away from the coast. Strangely, the expected attack on our compound had not come, and every minute nearer dawn brought us closer to safety. We grew curious and bold even as explosions sent vibrations through our feet.

I climbed to the top of the command bunker and peered east toward Chu Lai. My men stuck their heads out, and PFs along the bunker line came out to watch. More rockets rose in fiery streaks and roared off. I watched casually from my perch with members of my team as though these were Fourth of July fireworks. Light flickered and explosions rumbled like distant kettledrums. We were detached from the blast that ripped through the Americal's base, and I wondered how the thousands of noncombatant American troops fared in this taste of war.

Suddenly the eastern sky was lit by a huge fireball, as bright as the sun and as intense as the blast of a nuclear explosion. Flame, thick and bilious, burst skyward, and the shock wave hit our compound with a primordial bang. An aviation fuel dump had been hit, and the fires raged through the early morning hours, then began to fade into the amber dawn rising over the South China Sea. Slowly the darkness lifted; the mortar and rocket fire subsided, and the tension drained from our bodies as the night retreated before the blaze of early morning color. We had survived another night.

The enemy had struck widely throughout Ly Tin District and I Corps, blowing up bridges, attacking outposts, and launching rockets. We did not learn until later the next day that the VC were attacking in force throughout the country in a campaign that has come to be called the Tet Offensive. They had bypassed our compound, however, and now the light of a new day brought safety. Perhaps it was the terrible defeat they had suffered nearly a month before when they attacked our compound that kept the VC away this night. In early January, we had been nearly overrun, saved mainly by a variable time barrage I called on our position. We were spared, but the enemy left forty-six dead, twisted and shattered in and around the compound and had carried away many more.

I remained close to the radio as the sun's rays bronzed the interior of the command bunker, when Captain Duc hurried through the passageway that connected his bunker with mine.

"Big trouble," he said breathlessly. "Many people come."

He motioned me outside and quickly we climbed to the top of the bunker. I did not know what to expect since the VC seldom attacked in force during daylight hours. Captain Duc pointed west over the rice fields. The sun illuminated the mountain peaks some three miles away that rose like pinnacles from the coastal plain. Below, the rays of light barely lit the jungly and spiny ridges that flowed down to the rice fields.

The outlines of Khong Hiep, the hamlet closest to the compound, began to emerge, and light warmed the crest of Hill 69, base camp for 1st Battalion, 46th Infantry of the America's 198th Light Infantry Brigade.

I looked out over the gridlike pattern of rice paddies on the plain. In the distance, indistinct and obscured by morning mist, moving forms approached. They came slowly, cautiously and in single file down the dikes that separated the rice fields. I peered through my binoculars, but the light was still too dim. I would catch a shadowy figure only to lose it as it disappeared behind a tree line.

The light grew and the forms came closer, and we could see now they were peasants. This was Tet morning, and they were dressed in their best clothes. They carried the traditional Tet baskets that bore gifts for friends and relatives.

As the crowd approached, their features became more distinct, faces taut in anxiety, bodies erect and tense. The children did not dodge around their parents' feet but hung closely by their sides, docile and downcast. Even we Americans realized this was an unusual scene, something akin to the population of a small American town assembling in front of city hall on Christmas morning. Instinctively, we knew the VC were involved, but what were they up to?

I conferred with Captain Duc, and we decided not to fire into the crowd. I ordered Sergeant Pasqua to break out two tear gas grenades for each American to use to disperse the crowd. The sun was now above the horizon as the villagers approached unimproved and rutted Route 1—dubbed "Street without Joy" by the French—the main Vietnamese north-south highway that passed within twenty feet of the compound's entrance.

The crowd faltered on either side of the road, then began to move across it, pushed by unseen hands. I estimated there were about 400 villagers as they funneled into the path that led up to a compound gate, a thin band of barbed wire on a flimsy wooden frame.

Captain Duc ordered the PFs up to the compound's west rim, and I told my men to space themselves at intervals, tear gas grenades at the ready. Normally at this hour, the PFs would have been dismissed to return to their fields, but Captain Duc wisely had kept them on duty to guard against possible attack.

The people came on, slowly, frightened, their eyes darting from side to side. These were not the enemy. They were poor peasants barely able to eke out a living from the soil. I recognized several of them from my trips into the hamlets. One was a young women of about seventeen who frequently visited Captain Duc in his quarters. She was graced with typical Vietnamese beauty—fragile with clear skin and dark eyes.

Captain Duc's men stood in silent skirmish line, rifles pointing up and out. My own men, bigger and huskier, were easy to identify among the PFs. The quiet was broken only by the shuffle of feet as the people pushed forward, spreading out along the bunker line. They could go no farther and came to a halt. The morning air was warming as the sun rose higher in the sky, its rays glancing off Route 1.

Occasionally a child cried, and I heard low murmuring as the crowd faced us without moving. The impasse lasted about three minutes, and I was prepared to give the order to throw the tear gas. Suddenly Captain Duc shouted to his men. I did not comprehend, but his message was clear. The PFs opened up, their carbines and M1s popping and rattling with fury, their shouts primitive and joyous as they fired over the heads of the crowd.

I gasped as the villagers screamed and scattered, lunging away from the bunker line, dropping to the ground in piles. The PFs continued to fire and charged out the front gate to engage a platoon-sized band of men who had remained.

For a second, I was confused. Why would some of the villagers remain standing and face the fusillade? Return rifle and automatic weapons fire zipping past us quickly answered my questions. Those men beyond our perimeter were unmistakable in their dark green pajamas. They were a platoon-sized VC force that had hidden among the peasants and forced them to serve as a human shield and march on our district headquarters. When the villagers hit the ground, the VC lost their protection.

I was astonished that such professionals had been so easily unmasked, and they had no recourse but to run from the compound in disarray. The civilians lay prostrate, cowering, screaming, some wounded from the fire as Captain Duc's PFs streamed past them from the main gate firing in ferocious bursts. The PFs shrieked and howled as they ran down the hapless, outnumbered VC. Captain Duc's force was about sixty strong, and there were about thirty of the enemy. Within a few moments the firing ceased, and the silence seemed like a prelude as we awaited another attack. Route 1 was strewn with the bodies of VC, mostly young men, many not out of their teens. They lay contorted and twisted on the open ground.

Other PFs roughly pushed and shoved five captives toward the compound. Captain Duc shouted orders to the peasants, directing them away from the main gate. They made no attempt to retrieve the simple Tet baskets that lay in heaps just outside the compound. The contents of pickled pork and sweetened rice balls had spilled over the hardened dirt road surface.

I could not help but reflect on the pathos of the scene. The Tet baskets were a once-a-year extravagance for those poor peasants, simple gifts of affection for friends and relatives. In the fury of the war, they had been cast aside, their symbolism ignored. The terrified villagers also had been relegated to clumps on the dirty roadway, their finest clothes bloodied and torn. They were caught in between, and their only salvation would come when the war ended. They did not really care who won. I ordered Sergeant Denzine, our newly arrived medic, to assist the civilian wounded, one of whom was Captain Duc's mistress. She had suffered a superficial wound on the right arm. Captain Duc had ordered his men to fire over the heads of the peasants. As a result, none had been seriously hurt, but the VC captives had not fared as well. Several had severe head lacerations from beatings, and others suffered bullet wounds. One prisoner was noteworthy because he carried a satchel that indicated he may have been an officer. All were herded to the center of the compound and tied up beneath the flagpole.

I left Captain Duc the task of interrogating the prisoners and returned to our command bunker to make a report to my province advisor, but Captain Duc called me back a short time later. He stood with several of his officers around the prisoner who carried the satchel and who was tied to the compound's flagpole. Captain Duc jabbered in Vietnamese, and from the translation I knew we had captured a prize.

The man was an officer, a hard-core political cadre "from the north" who had led the attacking force. He could have been from North Vietnam or from the northern provinces of the South. Our prisoner talked freely. He said he was a former schoolteacher assigned to a VC unit in the mountains not far from our compound and that their task was to take the district headquarters. The morning of Tet, with the mist still clinging to the ground, we had no idea that the enemy was launching its greatest assault of the war across the width and breadth of Vietnam. We knew only that the VC had launched multiple attacks the night before throughout Ly Tin District and Quang Tin Province, but their effect seemed negligible.

Captain Duc handed me a letter written in Vietnamese. "Look, it say he sorry he have to kill me and to kill you," he said. Our prisoner looked on as Captain Duc explained the contents of his satchel, which included a People's Army of Vietnam flag that was to have flown over the compound. In his forties, the man was impressive looking, about five feet six inches tall, lean and muscular. Even with a deep cut on his forehead from the blow of a rifle butt, he remained steely-eyed and defiant.

Also included in the satchel were propaganda letters in Spanish from two Hispanic-Americans who were POWs in a VC prison camp. Each expressed concern for American involvement in the war and the effect it was having on the home front.

In retrospect, the VC plan is clear. Throughout December 1967 and January 1968, they built and honed their strength for the major assault on U.S. and South Vietnamese forces we now refer to as the Tet Offensive. The December 3 attack on Binh Son—a district headquarters a few miles south of Ly Tin—and the attack on our compound the night of January 2 were part of this plan. The multitude of attacks and skirmishes that occurred that January also fit into the scheme.

By the eve of Tet, the enemy believed we were softened by the repeated blows and so demoralized that the people were ready for a change of government. The VC's tactics Tet morning were simple: use the peasants as a shield and walk right into the district headquarters without a fight. They expected the PFs not to fire on their own people and to lay down their arms and greet their enemies warmly. That the VC remained standing when the villagers hit the ground indicates how much they believed their plan would work. For once, they had been duped by their own propaganda.

By mid-morning, Captain Duc had finished with his prisoner. The officer was too valuable to Captain Duc's career to be turned over to American forces. With his comrades, our prisoner was shipped off to Tam Ky for interrogation at the South Vietnamese provincial intelligence center, where he faced an uncertain fate. In the confusion of the hour with fighting erupting all over Vietnam, it is likely that no one there knew his value. He may have been regarded simply as another VC to be grilled and dispensed with.

It was only years later that I learned who this VC prisoner was. Robert Garwood, a marine held prisoner by the VC in the mountains near our Ly Tin district headquarters, refers to him in his book *Conversations with the Enemy* as Mr. Hum, who was a North Vietnamese cadre with the VC.[2] It was Mr. Hum who had carried the letters written by the two Hispanic-

Americans, Agostos Santos and Ortiz Rivera—one a marine, the other a
soldier—who wrote an open letter to all Hispanic servicemen in Southeast
Asia. Those letters were in Mr. Hum's satchel when he led the human
attack wave on Ly Tin district headquarters. I learned later that both Santos
and Rivera, who were prisoners in the same POW compound as Garwood,
were returned to American lines a few weeks before the Tet attack.[3] It was
a move calculated to undermine the morale and resolve of minority U.S.
troops. Garwood recalls the announcement of Mr. Hum's capture:

The Tet offensive was at its peak. Hum went to the American post with many
hundreds of Vietnamese. During the demonstration the puppet troops fired into the
demonstration to disperse it. Many were killed and wounded, many civilians. Hum
as one of the first to be sacrificed. He was shouting for the Americans to go home,
for them to lay down their weapons.[4]

When the prisoners left, I finally had time to catch my breath. It was
mid-morning, and the sun was nearing its zenith. The monsoon season was
ending, and the blistering, stultifying heat of summer would soon engulf
us. Even on these cooler monsoon days, the temperature rose into the eight-
ies.

Captain Duc's men were still cleaning up the battleground when I received a request from Lieutenant Colonel Hinson, commander of the 1st
Battalion, 46th Infantry, our hilltop neighbors a mile away, to accompany
him on a low-level reconnaissance mission around the district in his com-
mand-and-control helicopter.

It was becoming obvious that the attacks in Ly Tin were part of a nationwide offensive, and Colonel Hinson had to know if there were more
signs of VC activity in our area. His Huey landed at our helicopter pad,
and I climbed aboard.

As we lifted off, we could see black smoke drifting up from Chu Lai.
Beyond the Americal Division's base, the waters of the South China Sea
sparkled in the sunlight. We swung out low to the north, briefly following
Route 1.

To our right were the sandy islands of the bay that protected our compound from the open sea. We turned west toward the mountains, dipping
to less than 100 feet from the ground. The paddies shot by, and we exchanged glances with an occasional peasant at work in the fields.

We approached the spiny ridges where the mountains reached into the
coastal plain and turned south somewhere near the hamlet of Ky Sanh.
Colonel Hinson and I scanned the landscape, but there was no unusual
activity.

The Huey skimmed the fields and pulled up to hurdle a tree line just
beyond Ky Sanh. As we skipped over the trees, we saw a group of peasants
below us on a main dike that cut through the rice paddies. These were

some of the same villagers who had been forced toward the compound earlier that morning.

The chopper startled them, and they broke into a run. Suddenly, staccato bursts from the door gunner's M-60 machine gun blasted above the roar of the rotor blades. I turned to see the waist gunner jiggling against the recoil of the gun as it sent a stream of 7.62mm bullets into the group.

"Stop! Stop! Stop!" Colonel Hinson and I both yelled at the startled gunner as we scrambled to divert the aim of the weapon. The firing ceased, and I realized the gunner was a kid, a warrior still in adolescence for whom all Vietnamese were enemies.

He looked confused, unable to comprehend why he had been stopped from killing VC. Suddenly, I was aware of how Tet drew us all into the mayhem of Vietnam.[5]

The peasants lay sprawled on the dike, and Colonel Hinson ordered the pilot to hover to see if anyone had been hit. We saw the people gathering themselves up, and it appeared none was seriously hurt. We turned and continued our mission, now better illuminated, as well as complicated by the scope of the plan for the enemy's general offensive/general uprising.

NOTES

Parts of this chapter originally appeared as "The Day 'Big Trouble' Came to Tiny Ly Tin," *Army Magazine* (May 1988), coauthored with David P. Colley.

1. See Military Assistance Command, Vietnam Bulletin No. 8613, December 23, 1967.

2. Zalin Grant, *Survivors* (New York: W. W. Norton, 1985), pp. 80–85, 92.

3. Ibid.

4. Ibid.; Winston Groom and Duncan Spencer, *Conversation with the Enemy* (New York: G. P. Putnam's Sons, 1983), pp. 163–168, 206, 397.

5. *Editors' note:* Tobias Wolff, an advisor with an ARVN artillery battalion based outside of My Tho, offers a more cynical view of the place of the Vietnamese populace in the American battlefield response to Tet. See Tobias Wolff, *In Pharoah's Army: Memories of the Lost War* (New York: Knopf, 1995), p. 140.

12

The Battle of Khe Sanh, 1968

Peter Brush

INTRODUCTION

In late 1967, U.S. commander General William Westmoreland and People's Army of Vietnam (PAVN) commander General Vo Nguyen Giap deployed the forces under their commands to Khe Sanh. Giap's and Westmoreland's own tactical and strategic goals, combined with their perceptions of each other's intentions, led them into combat at this particular time and place.

The controversy surrounding this battle has lasted long after the silencing of the guns. Westmoreland was convinced that the Communists were attempting a repetition of their triumph over the French at Dien Bien Phu. Giap, on the other hand, claimed that Khe Sanh itself was not of importance, but only a diversion to draw U.S. forces away from the populated areas of South Vietnam. Both sides claimed victory at Khe Sanh, fueling a debate that continues today—was Khe Sanh a territorial imperative or a bait and switch?

BACKGROUND

It was Indochina's geography that made Khe Sanh important. The Ho Chi Minh Trail had been used as a communications link between North and South since the fighting began between the French and Viet Minh in the First Indochina War.[1] This series of trails and roads began in North Vietnam and entered Laos through various mountain passes. Several branches of the Trail penetrated South Vietnam while other branches continued into Cambodia. Khe Sanh was located where North Vietnam, South Vietnam, and Laos came together. For the Communists the region around

Khe Sanh was a major avenue for entry into northern South Vietnam. For the Americans a physical presence at Khe Sanh would allow observation of traffic on the Ho Chi Minh Trail.

It was in July 1962 that the Americans began to arrive at Khe Sanh, when a U.S. Army Special Forces detachment moved into an old French fort near the village of Khe Sanh. Also at this time, a Vietnamese engineer unit constructed the first airstrip at Khe Sanh. In 1962 and 1963, U.S. Marine Corps helicopter units were deployed around Khe Sanh to support operations by U.S. Special Forces and the Army of the Republic of Vietnam (ARVN). In April 1964, the marines sent a communications intelligence unit to the area to monitor Viet Cong and PAVN radio communications. General Westmoreland visited Khe Sanh for the first time during the period of these early intelligence-gathering operations.[2]

Westmoreland felt the "critical importance" of Khe Sanh was readily apparent. It would serve as a patrol base for the interdiction of enemy personnel and supplies coming down the Ho Chi Minh Trail from Laos into northern South Vietnam, a base for covert operations to harass the Communists along the Trail, an airstrip for aerial reconnaissance of the Trail, the western terminus for the defensive line along the Demilitarized Zone (DMZ) separating North and South Vietnam, and a jump-off point for invading Laos by land in order to cut the Ho Chi Minh Trail. According to the general, abandoning the U.S. military presence at Khe Sanh would allow the PAVN the ability to carry the fight into the populated coastal regions of northern South Vietnam.[3]

THE BUILDUP OF FORCES

In the spring of 1966, Giap began to deploy large numbers of PAVN forces within the DMZ, in Laos, and in the southern panhandle of North Vietnam. According to Giap, the purpose of these deployments was to frustrate U.S. pacification efforts by pulling the Americans away from the populated areas of South Vietnam.[4] By opening a new front away from central I Corps (the northernmost military region of South Vietnam) the Communists would have shorter supply lines and their movements would be harder for the Americans to detect, while the less accessible terrain would reduce the efficacy of the Americans' supporting arms.

The U.S. military command considered this buildup of enemy forces a precursor to a major attack across the DMZ.[5] The marines responded by moving units further north. During the remainder of 1966 and early 1967, fighting along the DMZ between the PAVN and marines increased in intensity. U.S. sources claimed the Communists lost 3,492 confirmed killed in action (KIA) while the marines lost 541 KIA.[6] According to the official U.S. Marine Corps history of the battle at Khe Sanh, these casualties were unacceptable for the PAVN. The PAVN response was to infiltrate South

Vietnam by an end run around the DMZ. The Khe Sanh area was the logical avenue of entry.[7]

In March 1967, only one company of marines was assigned to the Khe Sanh area. At this time the Americans did not have the helicopter assets, troop strength, or logistical bases in the region to adopt a mobile type of defense. Consequently, the troops at Khe Sanh stayed in relatively static positions with an emphasis on patrolling, aerial and artillery interdiction of enemy infiltration routes, and occasional reconnaissance-in-force operations to break up enemy infiltration attempts.

In April 1967, the PAVN stepped up offensive activity against the marine base at Khe Sanh. The overland supply route into the base along Route 9 was cut by Communist demolition teams. A PAVN regiment moved into positions around the base. Other PAVN units launched diversionary 1,200-round rocket, artillery, and mortar barrages at marine fire support bases and helicopter facilities in I Corps.[8] The main thrust was an attack designed to overrun the Khe Sanh combat base and capture the airfield. A successful secondary attack was launched against the nearby special forces camp at Lang Vei. The marines airlifted two battalions of infantry to Khe Sanh. Several days of bitter fighting allowed the marines to defeat the PAVN attack and end the first PAVN attempt to take Khe Sanh. With this immediate threat over, marine forces in the Khe Sanh area were reduced.

By mid-1967, the war-related hardships were increasing for the Communists, especially in the North. The U.S. bombing of the North, although unable to halt infiltration, was taking a severe toll. The United States still seemed convinced of its ability to achieve a military victory in the South. A Maoist-style rural struggle alone was not likely to defeat the Americans. There was concern in Hanoi that the United States was planning an invasion of North Vietnam. After much discussion the Communists decided that the time had come to implement a different strategy. This new strategy was designed to end the achievements of the U.S. pacification program, expand Communist control in the countryside, end any U.S. plans to invade the North, destroy U.S. faith in its ability to achieve a military victory, and nudge the Americans in the direction of negotiations. Moreover, this new strategy would bring the war, for the first time, to the cities of South Vietnam.

In October 1967, Giap ordered men and materiel sent down the Trail to be infiltrated across the border in the vicinity of Khe Sanh. PAVN units included the 304th Division, the first large regular formation of the People's Army to enter South Vietnam. The 304th had fought at Dien Bien Phu and came to Khe Sanh supported by attached artillery and antiaircraft units. The other major units in this siege force were the 325-C and 320th Divisions. The U.S. Central Intelligence Agency (CIA) concluded that the Communists had stockpiled enough supplies for a sixty-to-ninety-day engagement. Experts estimated that, all totaled, PAVN military forces at

Khe Sanh came to 22,000.[9] Supporting troops in nearby Laos and the central DMZ pushed the total forces facing the Americans to between 35,000 and 40,000.[10]

By the fall of 1967, U.S. strength at Khe Sanh was one marine infantry battalion reinforced with marine and army artillery and tanks. In December and January three more marine battalions and one ARVN ranger battalion were airlifted to Khe Sanh. By the time the U.S. buildup at the Khe Sanh combat base and surrounding fortified hill positions was complete on January 27, allied strength numbered 6,053—a reinforced regiment.

Control of the prominent terrain features to the north and northwest of the combat base was felt to be crucial to its defense. Approximately half of the marine forces were deployed outside the base perimeter. These positions were named for the height of the hills in meters: Hill 558, Hill 861, Hill 861 A or Alpha, Hills 881 North and South, and Hill 950. The base at Khe Sanh was constructed on a slight plateau, while the hill positions provided observation of enemy infiltration routes from the northwest and west. The hill positions were heavily fortified with infantry, light artillery, mortars, recoilless rifles, and tracked antitank weapons.[11]

In addition to the marines at Khe Sanh, Westmoreland sent his best army units north into I Corps matching the PAVN buildup. The 1st Cavalry Division and the 101st Airborne Division, plus other U.S. and ARVN units, were situated within striking distance of Khe Sanh. Clearly, Giap's attempts to draw U.S. forces away from the populated coastal areas were successful. In response to this Communist buildup in I Corps, the U.S. military command had deployed 50 percent of all its maneuver battalions in Vietnam to the region, realizing that by doing so it would be hard-pressed to meet all potential enemy threats directed at other targets in the South.[12] The United States was so convinced of the severity of the threat to Khe Sanh that it was willing to strip the rest of the country of adequate military reserves, curtail its ability to go on the offensive, and risk tactical reverses in other areas of South Vietnam.[13]

U.S. military leadership in Vietnam soon informed the marines at Khe Sanh that they were surrounded by thousands of North Vietnamese. They were instructed to quickly improve their positions to the greatest extent possible—to "dig in" in order to be prepared for a forthcoming ground attack.[14] By mid-January, evidence of a strong NVA presence around the combat base became overwhelming. On January 17, a U.S. reconnaissance patrol was ambushed by a PAVN force near one of the Marine hill positions around Khe Sanh. Near daybreak on January 20, Company I, 3rd Battalion, 26th Marines, under the command of Captain William H. Dabney, set out to find the ambush site of the reconnaissance patrol in order to recover classified communications information. Dabney's men initiated their march from their position on Hill 881 South, the westernmost U.S. position in South Vietnam. As they marched north, they ran into a heavily fortified enemy defensive line constructed on an east-west axis. Elements of an NVA battalion opened fire on the advancing marines with small arms, heavy machine guns, and grenade launchers. Heavy fighting continued for hours. Eventually, Colonel David Lownds, overall marine commander at Khe Sanh, fearing an enemy attack on the entire base, ordered the marines to break off the battle and return to their defensive positions on Hill 881 South.[15]

On January 21, the Communists began a hundred-round mortar and rocket attack against the base. Several helicopters were destroyed, a mess hall was flattened, several trucks were riddled with shrapnel, and the base commander's quarters were destroyed. At about 5:15 a.m., one or more NVA shells scored a direct hit on the main ammunition dump at Khe Sanh. This attack set off an explosion that resulted in the destruction of 16,000 artillery shells, a large supply of C.S. tear gas which spread over the entire base, and, about five hours later, a sizable quantity of C-4 plastic and other explosives. In fact, due to the incessant fire caused by the original explosions the ammunition supplies continued to set off smaller subsequent explosions or, as the marines described it, to "cook off" in the flames for the next forty-eight hours. This spectacular event soon became headline news throughout the United States and the Western world. It helped make the situation at Khe Sanh a cornerstone of most national evening newscasts over the next several weeks.[16]

To assure the efficient use of the remaining shells, the senior artillery officer, Major Roger Campbell, measured the enemy artillery craters in order to target the distance and direction of the enemy guns. The immediate crisis was overcome that afternoon, when C-124s and C-130s began aerial resupply efforts to make up for the lost ordnance. This resupply effort grew throughout the siege. Later, as the enemy began to effectively target the landing strip, resupply was carried out by helicopter drops. One indication of just how seriously the U.S. leaders took this battle came on January 23, when a cargo plane unloaded four large crates addressed to "Fifth Graves Registration Team, Khe Sanh." They were filled with 4,000 pounds of body bags.[17]

STRATEGY AND TACTICS

Was it a diversion or a serious attempt to seize the combat base? General Westmoreland was convinced it was no diversion. On the contrary, given the existence of the large buildup of PAVN forces in the vicinity of Khe Sanh and the DMZ, Westmoreland felt it would be much more logical for the Communists to stage diversionary attacks *elsewhere* in Vietnam "while concentrating on creating something like Dien Bien Phu at Khe Sanh and seizing the two northern provinces [of South Vietnam]."[18] Westmoreland's intelligence officer, General Philip Davidson, calls the notion that Giap viewed Khe Sánh as a strategic diversion to cover his attacks against the cities of South Vietnam during Tet a "myth . . . with no factual basis."[19]

No matter what the intentions of his enemy, Westmoreland was more than willing to shift his assets to Khe Sanh. His great frustration in waging war in Vietnam was the inability of U.S. forces to locate and close with large enemy units on the battlefield in order to destroy them with massive firepower. Indeed, Westmoreland felt the Viet Cong were "uncommonly adept at slithering away."[20] Westmoreland wanted the enemy to meet him on the battlefield at Khe Sanh; it was the perfect place for a decisive engagement. Khe Sanh was reinforced gradually by the U.S. military so as to not scare the enemy away. The area was considered to be uninhabited by civilians[21] and held few South Vietnamese government facilities, thereby minimizing coordination problems with the ARVN. Most important of all was the fact that the NVA seemed willing to fight at Khe Sanh. Westmoreland hoped that U.S. firepower would turn Khe Sanh into a killing ground for the North Vietnamese. The process by which this would be accomplished was described by the base target selection officer, Major Mirza Baig:

Our entire philosophy [is] to allow the enemy to surround us closely, to mass about us, to reveal his troop and logistic routes, to establish his dumps and assembly areas, and to prepare his siege works as energetically as he desires. The result [will be] an enormous quantity of targets . . . ideal for heavy bombers.[22]

For the U.S. military command, the marines at Khe Sanh were bait; chum liberally spread around the Khe Sanh tactical area to entice large military forces of North Vietnam from the depths of their sanctuaries to the exposed shallows of America's high-technology killing machine. Many marine commanders did not care for this role that had been assigned to them by their U.S. Army superiors. The marines thought Khe Sanh was too isolated and too hard to support. The assistant commander of the 3rd Marine Division summed up the feelings of the marines regarding the importance of the base by saying, "When you're at Khe Sanh, you're not really anywhere. You could lose it, and you really haven't lost a damn thing." Third Marine Division commander General Rathvon M. Thompkins felt that General Westmoreland was particularly sensitive about Khe Sanh, perhaps because the nearby special forces camp at Lang Vei had been overrun in 1967 (and would be overrun again by the PAVN during the fighting around Khe Sanh in 1968).[23]

When Hanoi began sending its forces to Khe Sanh the Communists were hoping to divert U.S. military assets away from the populated areas; it is not reasonable to think Giap would tie up an entire army corps with the mission of overrunning a single battalion of Americans. To the extent both sides sought to bait one another by their presence around Khe Sanh, both the U.S. military and Vietnamese Communists were successful. The tens of thousands troops facing one another at Khe Sanh represented the largest concentration of military forces on a single battlefield during the Second Indochina War.

There is evidence, however, to support the notion that the Communists planned on overrunning the base at Khe Sanh. On January 2, 1968, a sentry dog at a listening post near the combat base signaled the marines that there was activity nearby. A squad of marines was sent to investigate this sighting. Although no friendly patrols were reported to be in the area, the squad detected six men in Marine Corps uniforms. The squad leader challenged these men in English. When the challenge went unanswered, the marines opened fire. Five of the six trespassers were killed. The dead were North Vietnamese, and among them was a PAVN regimental commander, his operations officer, and a communications officer. For the PAVN commanders to conduct such a close personal reconnaissance indicated to the marines that their intentions were serious. The PAVN would have no need to get so close to the combat base if they were only engaged in a diversion.[24]

On January 20, marines guarding the eastern end of the airstrip at Khe Sanh saw a PAVN soldier entering the base carrying a white flag. The PAVN soldier surrendered to a marine fire team sent to investigate the sighting. This soldier turned out to be PAVN Senior Lieutenant La Thanh Tonc, commander of the PAVN 14th Antiaircraft Company of the 325-C Division. Tonc was full of information and was willing to share it with the marines. Counterintelligence experts were suspicious of Tonc's eagerness to talk and the quality of his information. The base commander, Colonel Lownds, however, felt there was nothing to lose and much to gain by regarding Tonc's information as accurate. Marine intelligence realized that deception and spreading disinformation were trademarks of the PAVN, but Tonc's revelations were supported by other intelligence information. If Tonc was legitimate it would be the biggest intelligence coup of the war. Tonc was too important to be ignored.

Lieutenant Tonc claimed he had surrendered because he was disgruntled over being passed over for promotion, tired of being told things by his superior officers that he knew not to be true, and demoralized by the casualties inflicted on his men by the Americans. According to Tonc, the PAVN attack on the base was planned to begin that very evening, commencing with an infantry assault on a nearby outpost, Hill 861 (all hills were designated according to their height in meters). When Hill 861 had been overrun, two PAVN regiments would attack the base from the northeast and from the south. PAVN infantry and mortar units would interdict helicopters sent to resupply the base, fire at the marine heavy weapon positions, and bombard the airstrip to close it to incoming aircraft. According to Tonc, the PAVN had tanks in reserve north of the DMZ which could support the attack. This campaign was to be the most important PAVN effort against the United States since the Americans intervened in South Vietnam. The purpose of the campaign was to gain bargaining leverage at the negotiating table by the conquest of the U.S. bases along the DMZ, resulting in the liberation of Quang Tri Province. The campaign was being conducted by General Giap personally.

In late 1967, Robert Brewer, the CIA officer for Quang Tri, received a Communist Party document from a North Vietnamese double agent. This document explicitly referred to an upcoming attack, in early 1968, on Khe Sanh and other bases in the northern provinces. This earlier intelligence report seemed to confirm Tonc's revelations.[25] Intelligence obtained from U.S. radio intercepts also substantiated the deserter's information. Tonc had predicted that the attacks would begin on January 20. The marines were ordered to a heightened state of readiness but nothing happened. Then a few minutes after midnight on the twenty-first, hundreds of enemy rockets, mortar rounds, and rocket-propelled grenades pounded Hill 861. Shortly thereafter 250 PAVN soldiers attacked the hill position, thereby validating the information provided by the deserter.

By the time of the attack on Hill 861, General Giap had successfully effected a diversion of U.S. military assets from the heavily populated coastal regions to northern I Corps. But the size of the Communist forces surrounding the Khe Sanh combat base suggests that a diversion was not all that he hoped to accomplish. The PAVN force include three infantry divisions, a fourth infantry division nearby in a support role, tanks, and two artillery regiments with antiaircraft capabilities. A diversion could have been achieved with less of a troop deployment than this. According to General Davidson, as of January 20, Giap "obviously intended to overrun Khe Sanh and its marine defenders."[26]

At Dien Bien Phu the Communists achieved victory by successfully attacking the French outposts that surrounded the base, effectively isolating it. At Khe Sanh, the Communists launched five battalion-sized attacks against surrounding outposts. These actions are consistent with siege warfare tactics, which call for the attacking force to seize the high ground and cut the lines of communication leading to a fortified position. But unlike the circumstances at Dien Bien Phu, the Communists were unable to capture the marine outposts ringing Khe Sanh. Only the special forces base at Lang Vei and Khe Sanh village were successfully assaulted.

The marines at Khe Sanh had air and artillery assets vastly superior to those of the French at Dien Bien Phu. The area around Khe Sanh had been liberally seeded with remote sensors to track the movements of the PAVN. U.S. firepower, alerted by these sensors and reconnaissance patrols, was able to break up formations of PAVN soldiers whenever they tried to mass for assaults on the base and the hill positions.

Giap faced a dilemma at Khe Sanh he did not encounter at Dien Bien Phu. Marine defenses around Khe Sanh were too strong to succumb to small and medium-sized PAVN ground attacks. A successful attack on Khe Sanh required the PAVN to mass their forces for an overwhelming assault. Yet, whenever the PAVN attempted to mass their forces, they provided rich targets for U.S. firepower and were decimated.

Perhaps the best example of this situation occurred at the end of February 1968. Sensors placed along Route 9 between the base and the Laotian border began sending large numbers of signals to monitors at Khe Sanh. By computing the length of the column of soldiers from sensor readouts, the commander at Khe Sanh became convinced that a PAVN regiment was attempting to close on the base. B-52 bombing runs and artillery attacks from within the base broke up the attempted attack. Only one company out of this PAVN regiment was able to reach the base, and this company was destroyed by the South Vietnamese ranger battalion positioned on the southeast corner of the base perimeter.[27]

General Davidson, Westmoreland's intelligence officer, feels that Giap's primary goal at Khe Sanh was to overrun the base. When this proved impossible, according to Davidson, Giap changed his plans, and gave up his attempt to turn Khe Sanh into another Dien Bien Phu. Cecil Currey, a retired U.S. Army colonel and professor of military history, says that Giap's primary intention was to stage a diversion, and that the notion of overrunning the base was secondary.[28] Both Davidson and Currey allow that the PAVN had dual motives at Khe Sanh. The difference between their interpretations seems to be one of emphasis.

One bit of evidence that Davidson offers in support of his position is the possible presence of General Giap himself in the vicinity of Khe Sanh. Radio signal intelligence detected the presence of a major PAVN headquarters in caves just north of the DMZ. Aerial reconnaissance indicated significant vehicular activity in this area. Numerous radio antennae were observed there, and PAVN prisoners of war reported that Giap himself was directing PAVN operations in the region. Davidson notes that at Dien Bien Phu, Giap set up headquarters nearby and directed operations from this command post. Further, an intelligence report indicates that Giap was not seen in Hanoi between September 2, 1967, and February 5, 1968. Davidson feels the "best guess" is that Giap was in this forward headquarters planning the battle for Khe Sanh.

Peter McDonald, on the other hand, in his biography of General Giap, states that Giap "was not there [near Khe Sanh]." McDonald notes that the PAVN did not have the helicopter assets that would allow a quick move to the front and that he could not have afforded to be away from the center of military control in Hanoi. McDonald does not otherwise account for Giap's absence from Hanoi during this period, and certainly the lack of PAVN helicopters does not preclude the possibility of Giap's presence in the vicinity of Khe Sanh.

Robert J. O'Neill believes it is most unlikely that Giap personally directed the battle at Khe Sanh. Hanoi was the only headquarters from which all the activities of the entire NVA could be controlled. Issues of reputation and status were at stake. Westmoreland was willing to leave tactical battlefield decisions in the hands of local marine commanders at Khe Sanh. Had the PAVN suffered a clear defeat at the hands of the United States, Giap would have sacrificed much of his reputation. In any event, the cave headquarters was bombed repeatedly by the U.S. Air Force, and while it remained in operation for several weeks, its tactical importance faded over time.[29]

No matter how we define the intentions of the PAVN regarding Khe Sanh, the fact is that they had diverted large amounts of U.S. military assets to its vicinity by the time the fighting began. Most of the Communist military forces sent into attack during the 1968 Tet Offensive were soldiers of the People's Liberation Armed Force (PLAF), the military arm of the National Liberation Front (NLF). Only in I Corps did the Communists commit large numbers of their regular army troops. This assignment of PAVN units reflects the special determination of the Communists to inflict severe and permanent military damage upon the South Vietnamese government in the northern provinces. If Khe Sanh was only meant to be a ruse by the Communists to divert U.S. forces, then why did the Communist continue their attacks on Khe Sanh after a diversion had been accomplished?

In addition to Khe Sanh, Hue was another place where the Communists committed large numbers of their regular army forces to battle during Tet 1968. On January 30, seven to ten battalions of PLAF and PAVN forces struck Hue city. Their goal was to capture this important Vietnamese cultural and political center, destroy the Saigon administration there, establish a revolutionary administration, and hold the city for as long as possible.[30]

In support of this goal, on about February 10, the Communists shifted some of their military forces from Khe Sanh to Hue. This deployment supports the notion that, at least by this stage of the fighting during Tet 1968, the Communists had important priorities for their Khe Sanh forces in addition to the capture of the marine base. After bitter fighting, the Communists were unable to hold Hue, and by February 25 the enemy forces there had either fled or been killed. Yet, during the night of February 29–March 1, the PAVN staged their largest massed attack upon the Khe Sanh combat base. This regimental-sized strike was broken up after sustaining overwhelming casualties at the hands of U.S. firepower. An attack of this magnitude, although not large enough to be effective, does not lend itself to the notion that the Communists only planned a diversion at Khe Sanh. Giap shifted five infantry battalions from Khe Sanh to Hue. Had he shifted more troops it could have had an important effect on the fighting around Hue. In effect, Giap left too few troops at Khe Sanh to overrun it, and shifted too few troops from Khe Sanh to Hue to affect the outcome of the fighting there.[31]

At Dien Bien Phu the Viet Minh constructed trenches to within a few meters of the French positions. On February 25, a U.S. aerial observer noted a PAVN trench running only twenty-five meters from the combat base perimeter. This represented an addition to an existing trench network and added 700 meters of trenching in a single night.[32] As the PAVN dug ever closer, the U.S. defenders tried a variety of means to neutralize the trenches, including napalm, one-ton bombs, and huge amounts of artillery fire. In earlier battles such as Ia Drang and Con Thien, the PAVN concluded that this tactic of "hugging the belts" of the Americans would make the United States reluctant to employ its massive firepower due to fear of causing casualties among its own forces. The U.S. response was to employ all manner of firepower against these close-proximity targets, including B-52 strikes. To be sure, the willingness of the Communists to construct positions at the very edge of the combat base is not consistent with the idea of only staging a diversion.

By early March, it appeared as if the North Vietnamese were giving up on Khe Sanh. On March 9, General Westmoreland reported to President Lyndon Johnson that enemy forces in the vicinity of Khe Sanh had fallen to between 6,000 and 8,000 men. On March 10, it was reported that the enemy had stopped repairing their trench system. The fighting was winding down. After succeeding in creating a diversion but failing to overrun the base at Khe Sanh, why would the Communists leave the battlefield at that particular time?

General Davidson feels that one reason the Communists withdrew their forces from the Khe Sanh area was the fear of nuclear weapons. Senior members of the U.S. military command had been comparing Khe Sanh to Dien Bien Phu. The chairman of the U.S. Joint Chiefs of Staff asked Westmoreland if there were targets in the vicinity of Khe Sanh that lent themselves to nuclear strikes and asked if contingency nuclear planning would be appropriate. Westmoreland replied that if the situation in the DMZ were to change dramatically he could "visualize that either tactical nuclear weapons or chemical agents should be active candidates for employment." Davidson notes that the issue of the use of nuclear weapons was leaked to the press, which published reports that Westmoreland had asked for permission to use nuclear weapons at Khe Sanh.[33]

Davidson speculates that Giap was aware of the nuclear weapons issue. Giap must have known that the United States had considered using nuclear weapons against Viet Minh forces besieging Dien Bien Phu. If the United States had been willing to consider the use of nuclear weapons in support of the French, there existed an even greater possibility that it would use atomic bombs to protect the marines at Khe Sanh. Davidson notes that the possibility of the use of nuclear weapons must have frightened the North Vietnamese Politburo and thoroughly alarmed the Soviets and the Chinese. Davidson's conclusion is that the North Vietnamese did not consider Khe

Sanh to be a goal of sufficient tactical importance to risk World War III. Davidson notes it may have been more than just coincidental that PAVN attacks against the marine outposts in the vicinity of Khe Sanh ceased at the same time that nuclear weapons were being considered for use in the area.

It seems that Davidson has overemphasized the importance of the nuclear weapons issue at Khe Sanh. If it is correct to assume that the North Vietnamese believed Khe Sanh was not worth the risk of a general nuclear war between the superpowers, then the same logic must hold for the United States. President Johnson was unwilling to mine North Vietnamese ports, strike at lines of communication near the Vietnam-China border, or bomb North Vietnamese civilian population centers for fear of risking a confrontation with the U.S.S.R. or China. Certainly the use of nuclear weapons in Vietnam would be viewed as a greater provocation by the Russians and Chinese than the other actions which President Johnson was unwilling to implement.[34]

Davidson feels that due to lack of sufficient information it is impossible to explain some of the reasoning behind North Vietnamese tactics at Khe Sanh. Surely, current evidence strongly suggests that on or about February 10 the Communists decided not to overrun Khe Sanh. Yet, on February 23 the base received 1,307 rounds of incoming rockets, artillery, and mortar rounds—a record amount of incoming fire for one day.[35] It seems to me that the best explanation for this heavy shelling incident is one of logistics. PAVN forces had gone to considerable efforts to stockpile these munitions in the Khe Sanh area. By February 23, the diversion had been accomplished and attempts to seize the base had proved unsuccessful. Rather than move this ammunition back into Laos under the constant threat of U.S. air strikes, the Communists chose to fire it at the marine positions.

The regimental-sized attack of February 29 is also inexplicable to Davidson. The attacking force was not sufficiently large to have any possibility of success and was launched after the North Vietnamese had been withdrawing from the region. Again, its purpose may have been to exploit media coverage of the battle; it occurred two days after CBS reporter Walter Cronkite prophesied the fall of Khe Sanh to the American public.[36]

Thomas L. Cubbage II, a former U.S. Army intelligence analyst during the Vietnam War, claims that the attack on Khe Sanh was an attempt to achieve a decisive victory in the war. According to Cubbage, Hanoi's Tet Offensive failed because the attack on Khe Sanh failed. Khe Sanh was meant to be another Dien Bien Phu and was unsuccessful because the Dien Bien Phu model was out of date. That is to say that the new technologies of warfare represented by overwhelming American firepower was something the Communists were unable to overcome. The capture of Khe Sanh was a major component of Hanoi's general offensive/general uprising. The attack was launched ten days before the attacks on the cities with the purpose of clearing the way for PAVN forces to move from the border areas to the coastal plain. Success at Khe Sanh would have allowed the PAVN to seal Hue's fate and put Danang in grave danger. According to Cubbage, Khe Sanh was not an attempt to bait the Americans. It was a serious attempt to create another Dien Bien Phu.

Cubbage says that Westmoreland knew about the intentions of the Communists due to good intelligence information. When the attack on Khe Sanh failed, Hanoi's whole Tet Offensive was weakened and eventually failed in a military sense. Cubbage feels that Khe Sanh was of such overwhelming strategic importance that its capture could have allowed Hanoi to achieve its military goals during the Tet Offensive and caused an earlier end to the U.S. involvement in Vietnam.[37]

In fact, a decisive victory, which Cubbage feels was the true goal of the PAVN at Khe Sanh, was possible; they could have forced the Americans out of Khe Sanh, but they never realized the means by which this could have been achieved.

Concerns over the ability of the United States to successfully defend Khe Sanh were manifest at the highest levels of government. President Johnson, his national security adviser, the adviser's military assistant, and the National Security Council staff representative for Vietnam were all kept abreast of the developing situation around Khe Sanh. The president summed up his feelings regarding Khe Sanh while the fighting was in progress: "I don't want any damn Dinbinphoo."[38] Both General Earle G. Wheeler, chairman of the Joint Chiefs of Staff, and General Westmoreland assured the president that preparations for the defense of Khe Sanh were adequate and that the base would be successfully supplied.[39] Indeed, support for the defense of Khe Sanh received priority over all other operations in Vietnam.[40]

The job of supplying the marine base at Khe Sanh fell to various Marine Corps and U.S. Air Force aviation units. This airlift would have been a massive operation even under ideal circumstances. The purely logistical problems were compounded by poor visibility that fell below minimum requirements for airfield operations 40 percent of the time. The PAVN added to the difficulty by directing a heavy volume of antiaircraft and artillery fire at incoming aircraft.[41]

The resupply process suffered a sharp setback on February 10 when PAVN gunners shot up a marine C-130, fully laden with fuel bladders, while it was attempting a landing at the Khe Sanh airstrip. As a result of this incident and fire damage sustained by other aircraft already on the ground, C-130 landings were temporarily suspended during February. At the beginning of March this suspension was made permanent. Consequently, during these periods, the marines were denied the use of the best heavy-lift aviation assets in their inventory. Most supplies thereafter were delivered by parachute. According to the official Marine Corps history of the battle of Khe Sanh, these parachute drops "were sufficient for bulk commodities such as rations and ammunition."[42] However, certain functions, such as provision of replacement troops, medical evacuations, and medical supplies, could only be performed by aircraft that made actual landings on the runway at Khe Sanh.

This official assessment of the success of U.S. supply capabilities regarding rations was overly optimistic. A hot meal was defined as heated C rations; the marines at Khe Sanh sometimes went weeks without hot meals. Rations were routinely limited to two meals per man per day. One marine reported that he went several days with only one C ration meal per day.[43] A company commander on Hill 861, located about two miles northwest of the combat base, reported that his men were forced to go for days without water.[44] Another reported that his water ration was one half-canteen cup of water per day, which had to suffice for drinking, shaving, and brushing teeth.[45]

Water is an extremely difficult commodity to deliver to a besieged garrison. It is heavy, it must be handled in special containers that cannot be used for the delivery of other liquids, and water containers are vulnerable to incoming artillery attacks. One helicopter crew attempting to deliver water to Hill 861 was rattled by PAVN fire, panicked, and released its cargo from a height of 200 feet. The parched marines watched the water containers burst apart in midair.[46]

Had the Communists realized the vulnerability of the marine water supply, they might well have been able to force the marines to abandon their combat base high above Khe Sanh. The marines occupied various hilltop positions surrounding Khe Sanh. These positions, initially supplied from the combat base itself, were later provisioned by helicopters flying from the 3rd Marine Division forward base at Dong Ha. Water for the combat base came from the small Rao Quan River, which flowed through hills to the north occupied by the PAVN.

Even though the combat base was not dependent on airlifted water, as the hill positions were, water was nevertheless often a scarce commodity. The water point itself was located about 150 meters outside the northern sector of the base perimeter. There was a small hill and tall grass that obscured visual contact with the water point. The water was lifted ninety feet over an 800-foot span by pumps. A dirt dam twenty-five meters wide caused the formation of a reservoir six feet deep. During the extensive rains of September and October 1967 the dam broke. U.S. Navy EO1 (Equipment Operator First Class) Rulon V. Rees led a detail to repair the dam in the fall of 1967 using old scrapped Marston matting from the airstrip. This detail blasted a crater in the riverbed about thirty feet in front of the dam to act as a reservoir in case the river level fell, and Marston matting was placed on the face of the dam.

No patrols went out to get the water. It was pumped inside the perimeter and went to a large black rubber water tower container. This reservoir was frequently punctured during the siege, causing temporary lack of water on the base.[47]

Had the PAVN realized how vulnerable the marines' water supply was, they could have interdicted it by diverting the Rao Quan River or contaminating it, thereby forcing the marines to attempt a breakout.[48] However, General Giap, who achieved victory at Dien Bien Phu in part due to his meticulous battlefield planning, seems not to have realized the vulnerability of the marines' water supply. Nor did the local PAVN commander. General Westmoreland did not become aware of the magnitude of the potential water problem until the base was surrounded by the North Vietnamese. By that time, a successful evacuation was not possible.[49]

The concept of an overland evacuation of a reinforced regiment, fighting its way through two or three PAVN divisions that held every tactical advantage, presented a problem of such magnitude that Westmoreland was reluctant to consider it. The Joint Chiefs refused to consider it.

General Tompkins, commander of the 3rd Marine Division, latter asserted that had the PAVN succeeded in interdicting the combat base's water supply, it would have been impossible to provision Khe Sanh with water in addition to its other resupply requirements.[50] However, at the time, in a letter to General Davidson, General Tompkins stated that water could have been added to the provisions already being supplied to support the base. By examining the supply requirements and the logistical capabilities of the Americans it is possible to determine which of these contradictory statements is correct.

The III Marine Amphibious Force (III MAF) headquarters established the official supply requirement for Khe Sanh at 235 tons per day. The Americans were hard-pressed to meet these requirements. The airstrip was completely closed on various occasions due to the weather or damage sustained from enemy fire. During the month of February alone, the combat base had a deficit of 1,037 tons of supplies actually delivered compared to scheduled deliveries. The air delivery problems were compounded when the use of the large C-130 cargo planes was curtailed due to hostile fire. Passenger requirements were met by the use of C-123 aircraft. The smaller capacity of the C-123s necessitated a fivefold increase in landings. More landings meant more targets. Maintenance personnel of one aircraft upon its return to Danang found 242 holes before they gave up counting. In the first month of the siege four major aircraft were lost to hostile fire. The most serious loss occurred on March 6, when a C-123 transport was attempting to land at Khe Sanh. Forty-eight U.S. military personnel were killed when the plane crashed after being hit by PAVN antiaircraft fire.[51]

Helicopters were widely used as resupply vehicles. Only helicopters could reach the hilltop positions, whose supply requirements were 32,000 tons per day. Helicopters were stationed at the combat base at the beginning of the fighting. These aircraft became so vulnerable to hostile fire that they had to be kept constantly in the air whether they had missions to perform or not. Indeed, at the height of the siege U.S. helicopters were being lost at a rate faster than they could be replaced. Thus, eventually losses became so great that this unit was deployed away from Khe Sanh. No fewer than thirty-three helicopters were destroyed or permanently disabled between the beginning of the siege and the end of March 1968.[52]

These losses were sustained without the implementation of an additional requirement for water delivery. According to the relevant U.S. Army field manual, the water supply requirement for drinking, personal hygiene, food preparation, laundry, and medical treatment is six pounds of water per man per day. These levels provide enough water to support continuous combat operations for extended periods.[53] The implementation of this requirement would have added 158 tons per day, an additional load of 67 percent over the supply requirement without water. Unlike ammunition and food rations, which could be palletized and delivered by parachute without the need for special containers, water was difficult to stockpile during the periods when resupply was possible, for use when landings were not permitted due to weather or hostile fire. The official optimism of U.S. commanders regarding resupply at Khe Sanh notwithstanding, the Americans would not have been able to provide the base with water under the existing tactical conditions.

By March the PAVN began withdrawing from the Khe Sanh area, and in April the marine regiment was replaced, allowing it to withdraw via the recently reopened Route 9. The primary goal of the American forces at Khe Sanh was to destroy large numbers of North Vietnamese soldiers. In this they were successful. Although the official body count of enemy soldiers killed at Khe Sanh was 1,602, the U.S. command placed the total number of North Vietnamese at between 10,000 and 15,000 killed in action. American deaths sustained in the siege itself, plus mobile operations in the Khe Sanh tactical area after the siege, totaled approximately 1,000 KIA.[54] In a war that focused on kill ratios and body counts as a measure of success, Khe Sanh was placed in the win column by the American military.

As with the Americans at Khe Sanh, the French garrisoned Dien Bien Phu as "bait" for the Vietnamese Communist forces. An American observer there reported that the French base could "withstand any kind of attack the Viet Minh are capable of launching."[55]

The commander of French forces in Indochina, General Henri Navarre, believed that French forces would carry the day due to their superiority in ground and air firepower. When the Viet Minh knocked out the airfield at Dien Bien Phu, resupply became impossible and the French became isolated and vulnerable. On May 7, 1954, after sustaining heavy losses, the French were forced to surrender. The very next day the Indochina phase of the

Geneva Conference began. France's loss at Dien Bien Phu led directly to its withdrawal from Indochina.[56]

Victory in combat, however defined, often hangs by a tenuous thread. Even with the claim of victory by the United States at Khe Sanh and during the Tet 1968 fighting in general, the psychological victory of the Vietnamese Communists during this period led to the beginning of the end for the United States in Vietnam. It was during the 1968 Tet Offensive that opposition in the United States to the war in Vietnam, in terms of regarding involvement as a mistake, first rose above 50 percent and exceeded the level of support. Approximately one-fourth of all the television film reports on the evening news programs in the United States during February and March 1968 were devoted to portraying the situation of the marines at Khe Sanh.[57] Had the North Vietnamese simply interdicted the water supply of the marines at the Khe Sanh combat base in 1968, thereby forcing the marines to evacuate and inflicting heavy casualties upon them in the process, the United States could have easily met a fate similar to that of the French.

In February 1969, General Giap was specifically asked if the fighting at Khe Sanh had been meant to achieve another Dien Bien Phu for the Communists. Giap replied that Khe Sanh had not been meant to be, nor could it have been, a replay of the earlier Communist victory. The evidence shows, however, that too many of the tactics employed by the Communists at Khe Sanh were inconsistent with this simplistic explanation.[58]

CONCLUSION

Neither the diversionary model alone nor the notion that Khe Sanh was only meant to be another Dien Bien Phu adequately explain the events that transpired there. It is necessary to ignore much evidence to make either of those explanations fit the facts.

The conclusion that the primary motive of the North Vietnamese was to overrun the base, and that a diversion was only secondary, is refuted by the fact that when the Communists began to deploy their forces to Khe Sanh there were insufficient U.S. forces there to make the effort of an assault worthwhile. If Giap's priority had been to capture the base, he would not have needed the 22,000 men he deployed to Khe Sanh in the fall of 1967. He could have overwhelmed the few hundred American defenders with only a fraction of that number of troops.

Giap, if he had access to sufficient intelligence information, could very well have concluded that the Americans would be likely to reinforce the base in response to a massive deployment of PAVN forces, pulling men from other areas in Vietnam to do so. What he may not have known is that there was a disagreement between the army and the marines regarding the value of sending large numbers of reinforcements to Khe Sanh. If Giap did have intelligence regarding this, he had no way of knowing what the outcome of the conflict between the two services would be. Had the marine position against sending reinforcements and advocating abandonment of the base prevailed, Khe Sanh would have been but lightly garrisoned or abandoned when Giap's units arrived, and his strategy would have been for naught. His army, instead of creating a diversion, would have diverted nothing, since the Americans would not have deployed troops to a base they had decided to abandon.

The best explanation is that Giap's primary motivation at Khe Sanh was to divert large numbers of U.S. forces away from the heavily populated coastal areas. In this he was successful. But the desire to achieve a victory over the marines there must have been a major consideration. Giap's forces stayed on the battlefield too long, fought too hard, and sustained too many casualties to justify the explanation that the creation of a diversion was the only concern. Having achieved his diversion, Giap had little to lose by seeking a victory for the North Vietnamese. While the fighting at Khe Sanh was still in progress, President Johnson remarked, "The eyes of the nation and the eyes of the entire world—the eyes of all of history itself—are on that little brave band of defenders who hold the pass at Khe Sanh."[59] Giap knew this, and an agonizing defeat for the United States at Khe Sanh could have forced history to repeat itself. Giap had successfully achieved his diversion and had nothing to lose by continuing the fight with the intent of overrunning the Khe Sanh combat base.

In April 1968, the marine regiment at Khe Sanh was relieved and its units were assigned elsewhere throughout I Corps. In June the U.S. command in Vietnam decided to abandon the base at Khe Sanh. The marine positions were bulldozed flat, the airstrip was removed, and the bunkers were destroyed. No physical presence remained due to fear that the Communists would take propaganda pictures of the combat base. In July the last marine departed Khe Sanh. Although both sides claimed victory, Khe Sanh provided neither clear victory nor definite defeat for either adversary. Both sides withdrew and Khe Sanh once again became merely unimportant.

No understanding of the significance of the battle at Khe Sanh is possible if the fighting there is considered in isolation. Khe Sanh was a part of the Tet Offensive, which itself was part of the yearlong Communist winter-spring offensive. For the Americans Khe Sanh was meant to be the best opportunity to implement the strategy of attrition, to destroy Communist military forces at a rate above that at which they could be replaced.

At Khe Sanh the United States achieved its most satisfying body counts and kill ratios of American deaths to enemy deaths. At the end of the campaign, the total enemy body count stood at 1,602. However, General Thompkins, upon hearing that only 117 individual and 39 crew-served weapons had been captured in the fighting around Khe Sanh, termed the official body count "false."[60]

Even so, Colonel Lownds, the marine commander at Khe Sanh, was convinced that the United States destroyed two entire North Vietnamese army divisions. Westmoreland's staff estimated that between 10,000 and 15,000 PAVN soldiers were lost (considering recent evidence, a dubious number).[61]

The official casualty figures for U.S. forces was placed at 205 KIA, 1,668 WIA (wounded in action), and 1 MIA (missing in action). These official figures are both erroneous and misleading, and reflect only U.S. casualties sustained at the combat base and hill positions. Ray Stubbe, a navy chaplain attached to the marine forces at Khe Sanh, put the total U.S. military personnel killed in the fighting around Khe Sanh at 476. This still does not account for allied troops deaths, which included 219 killed at Lang Vei, about 25 killed at Khe Sanh village, 125 killed in the relief of Khe Sanh, called Operation Pegasus, and 52 killed in plane crashes, ambushes, and so on. All totaled, the allied casualty toll for fighting at Khe Sanh, the relief operation, and operations immediately after the siege were approximately 1,000 KIAs and 4,500 WIAs.[62]

No matter what the number of enemy casualties, the marines and their allies delivered massive volumes of firepower against the Communist forces. The artillery battalion at the base camp alone fired 158,891 rounds in direct support of marine forces, thus living up to the Fire Support Coordination Center's motto—"Be Generous."[63] In addition, 7th Air Force fighter-bombers flew 9,691 sorties, dropping 14,223 tons of bombs and rockets. Marine aircraft added 7,078 sorties and 17,015 tons of ordnance, while navy aviators flew 5,337 sorties and dropped 7,491 of bombs. Moreover, air force B-52s flew 2,548 sorties and unleashed a staggering 59,542 tons of munitions around Khe Sanh. These B-52 ARC LIGHT raids delivered the equivalent of a 1.3-kiloton nuclear device every day of the siege. Putting PAVN force estimates at around 30,000, the United States expended over five tons of artillery and aerial munitions for every NVA soldier at Khe Sanh.[64]

But, in the larger scheme of things, these impressive ordnance tonnages and body counts, even if close to reality, made little difference. The Vietnamese Communists were willing to absorb losses of this magnitude in order to continue, and win, their struggle.

If the siege of Khe Sanh was meant to be only a Communist ruse then it was a successful one. Large amounts of U.S. military assets were diverted to this isolated area of South Vietnam. Nevertheless, in a strictly military sense, this diversion had little effect on the outcome of the fighting during Tet 1968. The goals of the Communists, as presented before the fighting began, remained largely elusive. The huge psychological victory of the Communists was largely unintentional and represented an unexpectedly positive consequence of the fighting. If Khe Sanh was meant to be another Dien Bien Phu, it was a strategic failure on the Communist side. All in all, Khe Sanh had little impact on the outcome of the Vietnam War. Seen in this context, and given the intentions of the participants at the beginning, Khe Sanh was an overall failure for both sides.

One final point must be made regarding the intentions of the Communist forces at Khe Sanh. Today, at the site of the former marine combat base, there is a masonry monument erected by the Vietnamese. The text on the monument explicitly refers to the fighting at Khe Sanh as another Dien Bien Phu. Thus, the Communists appear to regard the battle of Khe Sanh as the victory that enabled them to win the war in Indochina, or at least prefer to have it remembered that way.[65]

In 1994, the journalist Malcom W. Browne of the *New York Times* visited the former Khe Sanh combat base. Browne noted that there are seventy-two graveyards for Communist troops in Quang Tri Province alone. An official of the local People's Committee near Khe Sanh village looked across a vast field of grave markers and remarked, "We paid dearly for this land."[66] Of that there can be no doubt.

NOTES

1. The fighting in Vietnam continued from the beginning of Vietnam's war for independence from France in 1946 until after 1975, when Vietnam was unified by the Vietnamese Communists. The fighting between the Vietnamese and the French is referred to as the First Indochina War. The Vietnamese war with the Americans is termed the Second Indochina War, and the fighting between Vietnam and its neighbors after 1975 is known as the Third Indochina War.

2. For the early history of the U.S. involvement at Khe Sanh, see John Prados and Ray W. Stubbe, *Valley of Decision* (Boston: Houghton Mifflin, 1991), pp. 13–24 [hereafter *Valley*].

3. General William C. Westmoreland, *A Soldier Reports* (Garden City, N.Y.: 1976), p. 336 [hereafter *A Soldier*].

4. Giap made these remarks in a series of articles published in September 1967, in North Vietnam's armed forces newspaper, *Quang Doi Nhan Dan*, quoted in Edwin H. Simmons, "Marine Corps Operations in Vietnam, 1967," in *The Marines in Vietnam, 1954–1973* (Washington, D.C.: History and Museums Division, Headquarters, U.S. Marine Corps, 1985), p. 97.

5. General Willard Pearson, *The War in the Northern Provinces 1966–1968* (Washington, D.C.: Department of the Army, 1975), p. 6.

6. Captain Moyers S. Shore II, *The Battle for Khe Sanh* (Washington, D.C.: History and Museums Division, Headquarters, U.S. Marine Corps, 1969), p. 6 [hereafter *Battle*].

7. Ibid., pp. 5–6.

8. Ibid., p. 11.

9. Prados and Stubbe, *Valley*, pp. 270–271.

10. Peter Macdonald, *Giap: The Victor in Vietnam* (New York: W. W. Norton, 1993), p. 279 [hereafter *Giap*].

11. Robert Pisor, *The End of the Line: The Siege of Khe Sanh* (New York: Ballantine Books, 1982), p. 112 [hereafter *End of the Line*].

12. The number of maneuver battalions was a measure of U.S. tactical offensive capability in Vietnam. A maneuver battalion is a combat battalion that can be maneuvered, such as infantry, mechanized infantry, and armor. It is contrasted with support battalions such as artillery, engineering, and aviation units. See Westmoreland, *A Soldier,* p. 128 n, for this distinction.

13. New York Times, *The Pentagon Papers* (New York: Bantam Books, 1971), pp. 616–617.

14. Personal recollection of the author from late December 1967.

15. Shore, *Battle,* pp. 33–42.

16. Ibid., pp. 42–45; Prados and Stubbe, *Valley,* pp. 251–255.

17. *New York Times,* January 24, 1968, pp. 1, 3.

18. Westmoreland, *A Soldier,* p. 316.

19. Lieutenant General Philip B. Davidson, *Vietnam at War* (Novato, Calif.: Presidio Press, 1988), pp. 552–553 [hereafter *Vietnam at War*].

20. Westmoreland, *A Soldier,* p. 102.

21. Davidson, *Vietnam at War,* p. 553. This assertion effectively ignores the Bru tribesmen who lived in the area around Khe Sanh. In a pamphlet published on Memorial Day, 1985, by the Khe Sanh Veterans, Inc., the author, Chaplain Ray W. Stubbe, noted that there were 8,930 Bru Montagnards in the area according to a census taken in July 1967. "In addition, there were reports from many sources that many more migrated into the Khe Sanh area from just inside Laos when the conflict began." There were also 500 Laotians plus their dependents when the 33rd Laotian Elephant Battalion was overrun and took refuge in Lang Vei village. Only approximately 5,000 Montagnards made it safely to the Cam Lo refugee village. It is therefore a very conservative estimate that over 5,000 Bru Montagnards were killed during the siege. See also Pisor, *End of the Line,* pp. 235–236.

22. Pisor, *End of the Line,* p. 86.

23. Ibid., pp. 72, 78.

24. Don Oberdorfer, *Tet!* (New York: Avon Books, 1971), pp. 126–127 [hereafter *Tet!*].

25. The CIA officer, Robert Brewer, remained unconvinced as to the legitimacy of Tonc's information, apparently because the PAVN conducted some attacks in the Khe Sanh area that Tonc never mentioned. For details on Lieutenant Tonc, see Prados and Stubbe, *Valley,* pp. 231–233.

26. Davidson, *Vietnam at War,* p. 562.

27. Paul Dickson, *The Electronic Battlefield* (Bloomington: Indiana University Press, 1976), p. 74.

28. I am indebted to Professor Cecil B. Currey, professor of military history at the University of South Florida and chaplain (colonel), U.S. Army Reserve (Ret.), for this interpretation. Colonel Currey has interviewed and corresponded with Vietnamese Senior General Vo Nguyen Giap. According to Currey, Giap planned Khe Sanh primarily as a diversion but also thought the fighting there could have resulted in a second Dien Bien Phu. Personal communication from Colonel Currey to the author dated April 11, 1994.

29. Davidson, *Vietnam at War,* p. 563; McDonald, *Giap,* p. 282; Robert J. O'Neill, *General Giap* (North Melbourne, Australia: Cassell, 1969), pp. 195–196.

30. D. Gareth Porter, "The 1968 'Hue Massacre' " *Indochina Chronicle,* Vol. 3 (June 24, 1974), p. 8.

31. Davidson, *Vietnam at War*, pp. 567–569, describes this attack as "useless." The only explanation he can offer is that the attack was meant to cover the withdrawal of PAVN forces from the vicinity of Khe Sanh, and claims there was no sound tactical reason for it.

32. Prados and Stubbe, *Valley*, p. 397.

33. Davidson, *Vietnam at War*, pp. 564–565. For a more detailed discussion regarding the uses of tactical nuclear weapons at Khe Sanh, see Prados and Stubbe, *Valley*, pp. 291–293. Westmoreland's quote is from ibid., p. 291. See Pisor, *End of the Line*, pp. 261–262, for detail on the widespread discussion in the press of the use of nuclear weapons at Khe Sanh.

34. Leslie H. Gelb and Richard K. Betts, *The Irony of Vietnam: The System Worked* (Washington, D.C.: Brookings, 1979), pp. 264–265.

35. Next to the marine positions at the Khe Sanh combat base was FOB-3, a special forces position. A FOB-3 officer maintained that if the shells hitting their positions that day were included, the total for February 23 would be over 1,700. The figure of 1,307 is the official tally. See Prados and Stubbe, *Valley*, p. 399.

36. Davidson, *Vietnam at War*, p. 567. Cronkite is quoted in Oberdorfer, *Tet!*, pp. 268–269.

37. Thomas L. Cubbage II, review of *The Tet Offensive: Intelligence Failure in War*, in *Conflict Quarterly*, Vol. 13, No. 3 (Summer 1993), pp. 78–79.

38. *Time*, February 9, 1968, p. 16.

39. Prados and Stubbe, *Valley*, pp. 289–290.

40. Shore, *Battle*, p. 93.

41. Ibid., p. 74.

42. Ibid., p. 79.

43. Prados and Stubbe, *Valley*, p. 282.

44. Pisor, *End of the Line*, pp. 188, 199; and personal recollection of the author.

45. Prados and Stubbe, *Valley*, p. 306.

46. Shore, *Battle*, p. 199.

47. I am indebted to Ray W. Stubbe, Lutheran chaplain of the 1st Battalion, 26th Marines, at Khe Sanh, for this description of the water source. It was taken from Stubbe's diary written during the siege. Personal correspondence from Stubbe to the author dated March 21, 1994.

48. Westmoreland's intelligence chief, General Philip B. Davidson, Jr., U.S. Army (Ret.) notes that it was not benevolence on the part of the PAVN that kept them from poisoning the water supply. According to the Geneva Protocol of 1925, which the North Vietnamese ratified in 1957, the chemical pollution of a stream is permitted as long as the stream is only used by military personnel. The Rao Quan served no civilians and legally could have been poisoned. See Davidson, *Vietnam at War*, pp. 568–569.

49. Davidson, *Vietnam at War*, p. 570.

50. Prados and Stubbe, *Valley*, p. 364; Pisor, *End of the Line*, p. 202. Pisor's quotation from General Tompkins is taken from an official Marine Corps Oral History collection published in 1973. General Davidson notes that Tompkins felt at the time he wrote to Davidson and at the time of the siege that the base could have been provisioned with water by airlift. These contradictory claims remain inexplicable to this writer. See Davidson, *Vietnam at War*, p. 569.

51. Prados and Stubbe, *Valley*, pp. 373, 374, 375, 390.

52. Ibid., pp. 381, 382, 391.

53. FM 101-10-1-1/2, *Staff Officers' Field Manual: Organizational, Technical, and Logistical Data Planning Factors,* Vol. 2, (Washington, D.C.: Headquarters, Department of the Army, 1987), pp. 2–8, 2–9.

54. Pisor, *End of the Line,* p. 237; Prados and Stubbe, *Valley,* pp. 451, 454.

55. Report of Special U.S. Mission to Indochina, February 5, 1954, Eisenhower Papers, "Cleanup" File, Box 16, quoted in George C. Herring, *America's Longest War: The United States and Vietnam, 1950–1975* (New York: Alfred A. Knopf, 1972), p. 28.

56. Bernard Fall, *Hell in a Very Small Place* (Philadelphia: Lippincott, 1967), p. 50.

57. Leslie H. Gelb and Richard K. Betts, *The Irony of Vietnam: The System Worked* (Washington, D.C.: Brookings, 1979), p. 160; Oberdorfer, *Tet!,* p. 258.

58. Oriana Fallaci, *Interview with History* (New York: Liveright, 1976), pp. 85–86.

59. Quoted in Pisor, *End of the Line,* p. 207.

60. Ibid., p. 237.

61. Ibid., pp. 233, 237.

62. Prados and Stubbe, *Valley,* pp. 453–454.

63. Shore, *Battle,* p. 107.

64. Prados and Stubbe, *Valley,* p. 297.

65. I visited the site of the Khe Sanh combat base in 1993. The English translation of the Vietnamese text on the monument reads as follows:

LIBERATED BASE MONUMENT THE AREA OF TACON PONT [*sic*] BASE BUILT BY U.S. AND SAI GON PUPPET. BUILT 1967. AIR FIELD AND WELL CONSTRUCTED DEFENSE SYSTEM. CO LUONG [town] DONG HA [county] QUANG TRI [province]. U.S. AND ARMY PUPPETS USED TO MONITOR THE MOVEMENT AND TRIED TO STOP ASSISTANCE FROM THE NORTH INTO THE BATTLE OF INDO CHINA (3 COUNTRIES). AFTER 170 DAYS AND NIGHTS OF ATTACK BY THE SURROUNDING LIBERATION ARMY, TACON (KHE SANH) WAS COMPLETELY LIBERATED. THE LIBERATION ARMY DESTROYED THE DEFENSE SYSTEM FOR THE BATTLE OF INDO CHINA. 112,000 U.S. AND PUPPET TROOPS KILLED AND CAPTURED. 197 AIRPLANES SHOT DOWN. MUCH WAR MATERIEL WAS CAPTURED AND DESTROYED. KHE SANH ALSO ANOTHER DIEN BIEN PHU FOR THE U.S.

66. Malcolm W. Browne, "Battlefields of Khe Sanh: Still One Casualty a Day," *New York Times,* May 13, 1994, pp. A1, A6.

13

President Johnson and the Decision to Curtail Rolling Thunder

Mark Jacobsen

Within two months of Tet, President Johnson ended the bombing of North Vietnam north of the twentieth parallel. His decision neither ended Rolling Thunder (the bombing of North Vietnam) nor reduced the weight of the air war in Southeast Asia. But, combined with his public decision not to run for reelection and his private decision not to send reinforcements to General Westmoreland, the decision on the bombing marked a watershed.

To some extent the well-known story of how Johnson decided against reinforcing Westmoreland and the decision to stop bombing North Vietnam above the twentieth parallel are one and the same. At the strategic and operational levels, however, the two decisions differed. The choice not to send reinforcements was conditioned by lack of American resources, military and financial. The separate but related choice to stop the bombing north of the twentieth parallel represented less of a departure in policy, because LBJ had already publicly offered to stop bombing North Vietnam. The previous September, President Johnson had declared in a speech at San Antonio that

The United States is willing to stop all aerial and naval bombardment of North Vietnam when this will lead promptly to productive discussions. We, of course, assume that while discussions proceed North Vietnam will not take advantage of the bombing cessation or limitation.[1]

Having by this time chosen to mount the go-for-broke Tet Offensive, North Vietnam did not respond. As Tet wound down in March 1968, the president found himself, however, in a political box from which a curtailment of Rolling Thunder offered the simplest escape. This chapter describes the multifaceted quandary that Johnson faced.

It's important to bear in mind the extent to which Rolling Thunder had always been understood and directed from Washington as primarily a tool to pressure North Vietnam into ending its support of the Viet Cong. Actual direction of Rolling Thunder from 1965 onward was governed primarily by negative objectives. President Johnson had sought to balance the pressure objective of Rolling Thunder with the imperative of avoiding both Chinese intervention and international complications, particularly from the Soviet Union. At the other end of the spectrum, he had managed the air war to defuse criticism from political conservatives, whose attacks Johnson (remembering the Korean War) discerned as his greatest domestic peril. Throughout the war, LBJ had feared a military backlash, something on the order of the Truman-MacArthur clash. Johnson squared this political circle by resisting appeals from the military to strike politically sensitive targets while simultaneously allocating ever increasing numbers of sorties to the air war. He accomplished this delicate mission by steadily assigning these additional sorties to armed reconnaissance while in a graduated fashion increasing the number of permitted targets and the area in which targets could be hit and armed reconnaissance flown. As early as 1966, 98 percent of all sorties flown against North Vietnam and Laos were armed reconnaissance. In this fashion, he sought to blunt hawkish complaints that he was not making full use of American airpower.

Even before Tet, Rolling Thunder had failed to attain anything close to the desired affect. Despite increasing intensity, its program of steadily increasing pressures had failed to persuade North Vietnam even to approach the negotiating table. During the summer, despite strikes at power plants in Hanoi and Haiphong, the administration had still come under terrific heat from conservative supporters of the war for the limited nature of the air war. These complaints, culminating in the hearings before Senator John Stennis' Preparedness Subcommittee (which then Senator Johnson had used during the Korean War to embarrass the Truman administration), had induced President Johnson to authorize strikes against more targets hitherto off limits, notably the MiG base at Phuc Yen north of Hanoi.

There is no need here to rehearse the events of Tet, only to remember its political context. To simplify what might seem a confusing narrative, I want to categorize the three concepts that structured the response of President Johnson and his advisors to Tet. Initially, from the onset of Tet to mid-February 1968, they thought in terms of aerial retaliation, hitting hitherto off-limits targets in the prohibited zones girdling Haiphong, Hanoi, and the Chinese border. Secondly, after mid-February, Johnson and his advisors recognized that although the immediate Communist offensive had been stopped, the enemy retained the ability to fight a sustained ground campaign in the South that might readily destroy the South Vietnamese

Army. Because the cupboard was bare of potential American ground re-inforcements, they returned to airpower as the only available theater reserve to stave off what they saw as looming disaster. They now evaluated Rolling Thunder and related "escalation" measures for their potential to cripple the ability of North Vietnam to maintain the war at the present level of intensity. Finally, from mid-March onward, recognizing the difficulty of smashing a sustained Tet with ground forces, the administration began to look at diverting the assets employed by Rolling Thunder to defeat the feared immediate threat of a renewal of the Tet Offensive in the South.

A reading of the day-by-day deliberations of the president and his senior advisors contained in the recently released Tom Johnson meeting notes suggests first that the final decision was the product of disparate consid-erations and fully reflected the president's well-known penchant for achiev-ing consensus. Secondly, President Johnson throttled back Rolling Thunder not against military advice but because the senior military men disagreed over the proper role of airpower and the merits of Rolling Thunder in particular.

THE FIRST REACTIONS TO TET: RETALIATION

The attack on the U.S. Embassy in Saigon immediately reminded Presi-dent Johnson of the attack on Pleiku in February 1965, the sort of challenge that could not go unanswered. He quickly met General Westmoreland's requests for more troops and despatched 10,500 previously authorized air-borne troops and marines. Whether to loosen the limits on Rolling Thun-der—what I refer to as the retaliation option—proved harder to decide. Initially, the spectacular Communist offensive did little to alter well-established postures.

On February 6 the president and his regular Tuesday lunch group met for their first sustained discussion of the events of the past week. Secretary McNamara presented the Joint Chiefs' recommendations that the prohib-ited zones be reduced from the current five miles to three miles around Hanoi and a mile and a half around Haiphong. These measures would have greatly expanded the miles of roads, canals, and railroads available for armed reconnaissance, that is, the chance for roving American aircraft to strike transportation targets of opportunity. Fixed targets within the shrunken prohibited zones would still require specific approval. Despite Tet, the civilians close to the president were not swayed. Secretary Rusk opposed this loosening, warning that "this action also opens up the pos-sibility of large civilian casualties and leads to extensive devastation of the area." Secretary McNamara agreed, "cautioning that to do so would lead to increased aircraft losses and civilian destruction."[2] So President Johnson did nothing.

Five days later, on February 9, the president and his key advisors met with the Joint Chiefs of Staff, one of the few times in the entire conflict that the Chiefs met directly with the president, to consider Westmoreland's request for the 82nd Airborne Division. General Wheeler warned the president against sending the troops without first reconstituting strategic reserves in the United States. If the 82nd Airborne were sent to Vietnam, Johnson would have to federalize a National Guard division to deal with the expected urban disorders that had become a summertime staple in northern cities.[3] The difficulty with calling up such reserve elements was the need to go to Congress for authorization and funding, which in turn raised the certainty of debate and possible frustration by filibuster. For practical purposes, any option that required going to Congress was out of the question. Westmoreland did not get the 82nd.

FIGHTING A SUSTAINED CONFLICT

But if troops could not safely be sent to deal with the emergency, what could be done? From its inception in 1965, President Johnson and his advisors had always divorced Rolling Thunder from the ground war in the South. To them, the ground war was an indigenous insurrection in the South assisted from without. The air war against the North was something else, an attempt to persuade North Vietnam to withdraw its forces from South Vietnam and stop assisting the Viet Cong. The anomalous division of command responsibilities between Admiral U. S. Grant Sharp, CINC-PAC in Honolulu, who ran Rolling Thunder, and General William Westmoreland, head of the quaintly named Military Assistance Command in Saigon, testified to this understanding.

The air war and the ground war were less complementary than antithetical. Rolling Thunder had begun in 1965 as an alternative to the introduction of U.S. ground forces, and appreciable numbers of American soldiers had entered the South only when Rolling Thunder was seen to have "failed" to persuade by midsummer. In mid-February 1968, President Johnson and his advisors reconsidered their earlier opposition to shrinking the prohibited zones. With the 82nd Airborne mortgaged to the inner cities, airpower represented the only available reserve.

Meeting with President Johnson on February 13, the chairman of the JCS, General Earle Wheeler, forcefully emphasized that American aircraft would be going after trucks and watercraft that were presently safely parked along city streets or harbor areas. They were genuine military targets, never more than at present. Wheeler did not deny that enemy civilians would die, but he reminded the group that North Vietnam had both an excellent early warning system and extensive civil defense programs, which were most highly developed for the benefit of cadres and key workers concentrated in the two major cities.

Clark Clifford, not yet sworn in as McNamara's replacement, sided with

Wheeler. With masterful understatement, he observed of the North Vietnamese that "their action over the past two weeks shows a dramatic answer
to the San Antonio Formula and to the request for talks." This was no
dove speaking. Unlike Rusk and McNamara, Clifford spoke for a more
intense air war, even as he questioned the desirability of sending the ground
reinforcements.[4] Secretary Rusk still hesitated, at length agreeing equivo-
cally that fourteen critical but as yet unstruck targets within the prohibited
zones of Hanoi and Haiphong should be hit. But he did not want to shrink
the existing prohibited zones. Hearing this, Wheeler vented the frustration
of years:

I am fed up to the teeth with the activities of the North Vietnamese and the Viet
Cong. We apply rigid restrictions to ourselves and try to operate in a humanitarian
manner with concern for civilians at all times. They apply a double standard. Look
at what they did in South Vietnam last week. In addition, they place their munitions
inside of populated areas because they think they are safe there. In fact, they place
their SAMs in civilian buildings to fire at our aircraft.[5]

Hearing this and balancing all, the president compromised once again.
He reduced the five-mile limit around Hanoi but not Haiphong. He approved strikes at the fourteen individual targets within the prohibited zones.
He agreed that once these targets were hit, the issue of unlimited armed
reconnaissance within the formerly prohibited area would be discussed yet
again.[6]

In another week, they had this discussion. At a Tuesday lunch on February 20, Johnson and his advisors reconsidered permitting armed reconnaissance within the prohibited areas as well as attacking additional
sensitive targets. With the Tet Offensive nearly a month old, Johnson and
his advisors now expected renewed attacks on South Vietnamese cities that
might buckle the ARVN. Accordingly, they thought increasingly in terms
of bombing that would impair the ability of North Vietnam to sustain its
offensive in the South. Given the weather and the shortness of the days,
even the idea of making instrument attacks, "systems runs," on targets
came up. Clifford's support for these measures sufficed to bring Rusk on
board, a major departure given that visual identification had always been
required for Rolling Thunder. More importantly, Rusk was prepared to
consider the possibility of further reducing the prohibited zones around the
cities.[7] President Johnson, however, contented himself with listening, not
deciding one way or the other.

General Wheeler returned from a visit to Saigon on February 28 with
Westmoreland's request for 207,000 additional troops, the figure that
would be necessary to reconstitute the nation's strategic reserve. In reaction,
President Johnson, always concerned to achieve a consensus, asked Clifford
that day to chair an interagency review of Westmoreland's request.[8] Its

tasking soon grew to include a review of the entire war, including Rolling Thunder.[9] Secretary Clifford scrupulously solicited opinions from all the relevant decision makers. General Wheeler, speaking for the JCS and for Admiral Sharp, endorsed keeping the Hanoi prohibited zone at a three-NM (nautical mile) radius and shrinking that around Haiphong to 1.5 NM. Of Hanoi, Wheeler said, "Rather than an area for urban living, the city has become an armed camp and a large logistics storage base."[10]

From Honolulu, Sharp appealed once more for greater latitude in conducting the air war and for blockading or mining the entrance to Haiphong, "the single most important and damaging offensive action we could take."[11] The problem with mining Haiphong was that the experts were badly divided over its legality, possible consequences, and effectiveness. At best, Sharp admitted, mining the approaches to Haiphong would begin to affect the North Vietnamese war machine within six months. A year later, the North Vietnamese Army would be badly degraded—a long time to wait. The real issue over which Washington lost sleep was the possible reaction of China and the Soviet Union. The intelligence community thought actual military intervention from either China or the Soviet unlikely but feared renewed pressure on Berlin or Korea as distinct possibilities. The seizure of the *Pueblo* in January represented what form that pressure might take.[12] The difficulty with Sharp and Wheeler's recommendations was that they amounted to "more of the same" with no special promise of imminent success. Yet the Johnson administration needed urgently to attain results both visible and prompt.

The strongest pressure against expanded bombing or dispatching fresh reinforcements to Westmoreland came from within Clifford's own Defense Department, notably from Deputy Secretary of Defense Paul Nitze and the Pentagon's "little State Department"—the office of the assistant secretary of defense for international security affairs (ISA), held in early 1968 by Paul Warnke. Ably supported by Nitze, ISA fought hard and ultimately successfully against General Westmoreland's request and against Rolling Thunder. Among the most telling arguments that these in-house doves advanced were domestic. ISA warned that the financial costs of these reinforcements would probably require new taxes or wage and price controls. The administration would then have no choice but to enter into a Faustian bargain with political conservatives:

Many Senators will demand, as the price of their support, that we eliminate all restrictions on our bombing of the North and mine Haiphong Harbor. This action could run grave risks of greater Chinese and Soviet involvement in the war without affecting enemy capability to support current or increased force levels in the South.[13]

As ISA saw things, the Tet Offensive proved that both Rolling Thunder and Steel Tiger had failed to halt the infiltration of men and supplies into

South Vietnam. Indeed, in its view "bombing in Route Packages 6A and 6B [that is, the Red River Delta] is therefore primarily a political tool," not an effective military strategy. Mining the approaches to Haiphong would simply lead to more supplies being imported via China, something that

would tend to increase Chinese leverage in Hanoi and would force the Soviets and Chinese to work out cooperative arrangements for their new and enlarged transit . . . it would force them to take a wider range of common positions that would certainly not be favorable to our basic interests.[14]

These subtleties were submerged throughout the post-Tet period by the urgent and ultimately pivotal debate within the administration about West-moreland's request for troops, which catalyzed the thinking of a number of senior administration officials, notably Clifford. As noted, Clifford was no dove and indeed shared a faith in the ability of airpower to achieve results. Yet this most keenly political of all Johnson's advisors experienced a Damascene conversion during these days, as he recognized the uselessness of telling the country that a victory had been won while pleading for many more troops.

At a meeting of the president's senior foreign policy advisors on March 4, Clifford delivered the results of the special assessment team. Critical of "that same road of 'more troops, more guns, more planes, more ships,' " he advocated a version of the "enclave strategy," whereby populous areas would be held but movement into the country curtailed. Clifford's recommendations were startling coming from one who had staunchly and even enthusiastically advocated military solutions to the war. In March 1968 his views were even more effective for representing not only his considered judgment but that of Deputy Secretary Paul Nitze, Director of Central Intelligence Richard Helms, and Dean Rusk, with whom Clifford had prepared the paper. Nitze bluntly told the president to initiate negotiations as soon as possible, no later than May or June: "We must make up our own minds when we want to cease the bombing and see what happens." Rusk agreed, proposing cannily that "we could stop the bombing during the rainy period in the North." Rusk, too, thought that the administration should engage in some public diplomacy, more for the benefit of world opinion than for practical results. The likelihood of talks, he admitted, was "quite bleak." Hearing Rusk and Nitze counsel a bombing halt, President Johnson directed his advisors to "Really 'get on your horses' on that."[15]

And so they did. A day later, the president met again with his senior foreign policy advisors. Rusk read a brief statement about a temporary bombing pause during the prevailing bad weather that would make the cessation of bombing contingent upon Communist military activity in the South. As Rusk explained the proposed halt, "My guess is that it would last about three days. It would not hold up if they attacked Khe Sanh or the cities. By the time the bad weather had ended, if there is no response by Hanoi, we could resume it [the bombing]."[16]

On March 12 Democratic primary voters in New Hampshire dealt a surprising blow to the president's reelection hopes. Maverick senator Eugene McCarthy (D-Minn.), running as an opponent of the war, won 42 percent of the primary vote but twenty of twenty-four convention delegates. The press interpreted the result as a rebuff to President Johnson and as a solid vote against the war. On the very day of the voting, Senator Robert Kennedy (D-N.Y.) met privately with Clifford and demanded that the president appoint a high-level panel of outsiders to assess the Vietnam War and deliver a speech confessing his errors. Johnson declined, and Kennedy announced his candidacy on March 16.[17]

On March 19 UN Ambassador Arthur Goldberg and veteran diplomat Chester Bowles proposed that the administration reiterate the San Antonio Formula, both to ascertain the attitude of North Vietnam and to clarify in the minds of Americans what the war was being fought for. Rusk by now was ready to halt the bombing of Vietnam if Hanoi responded, publicly or privately. Clifford, once more the champion of Rolling Thunder, opposed this idea and proposed instead another meeting of the senior nongovernmental advisors. The president agreed to have the "Wise Men" pay another visit.[18]

OPTIONS FOR DEFEATING THE SUSTAINED TET

The immediate military situation was the greatest obstacle to any dramatic gesture. The peril of the marines at Khe Sanh held the public and the administration in suspense. What was even more apparent to the president, who had spent virtually his entire political life on Capitol Hill, was the congressional problem. By this time, Johnson knew that anything requiring fresh congressional authorization, whether an expanded Gulf of Tonkin Resolution, a declaration of war, new taxes, or even the reserve call-up, faced intense congressional criticism, perhaps even a filibuster in the Senate. Accordingly, the president and his advisors turned increasingly to the prospects for negotiations.[19]

The difficulty with curtailing the bombing as Goldberg, Rusk, and Bowles proposed was that the administration was simultaneously preparing to announce a limited call-up of reserves. Congressional barons such as Senators Stennis and Russell had made it plain that they would not support sending additional troops to Vietnam unless the president extended the bombing to Haiphong. The political box in which the president found himself was that the measures necessary to deal with the emergency in South Vietnam would increase his political perils. If he took the opposite tack and halted Rolling Thunder, he would lose nothing. On the twentieth, those consummate hawks, Clifford and Supreme Court Justice Abe Fortas, dismissed Hanoi's demand that the United States take the first step and halt the bombing. To Fortas, the formula amounted to a "one horse–one rabbit deal."[20] Although rejecting a total halt, Clifford suggested that the United States stop bombing above the twentieth parallel. In return, the enemy would be asked only to stop artillery and rocket attacks in the DMZ, that is, in the vicinity of Khe Sanh. This was an old idea, but it was one whose time had come. By this time Johnson too was convinced that bombing in the vicinity of Haiphong and Hanoi was a loser. "It brings fury and violence from abroad," he acknowledged, but he also worried about another "Panmunjom," the negotiations that dragged on for months while some of the most intensive fighting of the Korean War continued.[21]

Much earlier, Johnson had accepted the need to deliver a presidential address on the war, but he remained uncertain whether to use it to rally the nation or to announce a readiness to seek peace. On March 20 critical briefing material from the State Department incorporating Rusk's reservations about Rolling Thunder reached the White House. It was discussed that day and on March 22.[22]

The State Department and the administration had always hoped that the U.S.S.R. would use its good offices to induce North Vietnam to open negotiations. Here arose the opportunity for doing that. Making what proved to be a critical distinction, National Security Adviser Walt Rostow pointed out that the Soviets distinguished between bombing Hanoi and Haiphong, for example, and bombing in the vicinity of the battlefield. Rusk agreed, noting that "Moscow cares more about what is happening in North Vietnam than what is happening in the South."

This perception in effect offered an opening by which the beleaguered president could continue to employ American airpower and support American troops in the field and, more problematically, get North Vietnam to consent to negotiations. Rusk urged that the president reiterate the San Antonio Formula, viewing it as a long shot for peace but a better prospect of unifying the nation. Goldberg jumped on this idea, emphasizing as Rusk had earlier that a bombing halt need not be permanent and urging that Rolling Thunder sorties be reallocated to "more effective" uses in the South and doubled around Khe Sanh.[23]

One key factor in these decisions was the attitude of the U.S. military, which was by no means ignored. Although he had little time for Admiral Sharp, Johnson awarded the photogenic Westmoreland the courtesies of a theater commander as if he were Douglas MacArthur. Westmoreland had long sought greater control over aerial assets and preached the need to concentrate bombing on interdiction in Laos and southern North Vietnam and on close air support in-country.

Convinced by late 1967 that North Vietnam was about to stage a massive attack in the northern reaches of the I Corps, he had tried to gain control of additional airpower even before Tet erupted. Sharp had thwarted him; Tet revived this dispute. Westmoreland immediately tried to concentrate Rolling Thunder's aircraft on territory south of Vinh. At Khe Sanh, he remained convinced, the great battle of the war was about to begin in earnest. He had some reason to think that interdiction might now succeed where it had not earlier.[24]

By early 1968 the air force and navy at last had an adequate supply of the Mk 86 destructor, a delayed-action aerial mine of which much was expected. Previously destructors, which were sown broadcast on communications chokepoints, crossroads, rivers, harbors, and canals alike, had been so scarce that their full impact had scarcely been felt. No longer![25] Here lay an opening for the administration. By shifting the air war to southern North Vietnam and to Laos, it could not only relieve Khe Sanh, but placate the best-known military commander of the war, and proffer a diplomatic opening that might not be accepted but would certainly rally the nation. Best, it could make this offer without permanently sacrificing any of the air assets in the theater and without foreclosing future options to resume Rolling Thunder.

The inescapable issue, however, remained whether South Vietnam would survive another month or not. From Saigon came alarming news that North Vietnam had increased its forces in the South and actually outnumbered American and ARVN troops in the vital I Corps military area. Moreover, the enemy could reinforce with an additional two divisions in as few as thirty days, bringing the possibility of catastrophe that much nearer. Westmoreland's deputy, General Creighton Abrams, confirmed that the North Vietnamese appeared to be shifting their strategy so as to maintain a year-round offensive in the South, a sort of continuing Tet. This estimate was a remarkably prescient view of the strategy that North Vietnam would pursue in 1968, and one can see the appeal of shifting air power from Rolling Thunder to close support and battlefield interdiction.[26]

Exactly when LBJ decided to end bombing and open peace negotiations cannot be pinpointed. Dean Rusk was probably as close to correct as anyone when he reminisced in 1990 that the president had reached his decision sometime between March 26 and 31.[27] About the best surviving direct indication of what was on Johnson's mind is his anguished declaration to Wheeler and Abrams on March 26:

Our fiscal situation is abominable. We have a deficit running over $20 billion. We are not getting the tax bill. The deficit could be over 30 [billion]. . . . Unless we get a tax bill, it will be unthinkable.

They say to get $10 billion in taxes we must get $10 billion in reductions of appropriations. We have to take one half from non-Vietnam defense expenditures. That will cause hell with [Sen. Richard] Russell. If we don't do that we will have hell. What happens when you cut poverty, housing and education?

This is complicated by the fact it is an election year. I don't give a damn about the election. . . . There has been a panic in the last three weeks. . . . The leaks to the *New York Times* hurt us. The country is demoralized. You must know about it. It's thought you can't have communications. A worker writes a paper for the Clifford group, and it's all over Georgetown. . . . I will have overwhelming disapproval in the polls and elections. I will go down the drain. I don't want the whole alliance and military pulled in with it. . . . I wouldn't be surprised if they repealed the Tonkin Gulf Resolution. Senator Russell wants us to go in and take out Haiphong. Senator McCarthy and Senator Kennedy and the left wing have informers in the departments. The *Times* and the *Post* are against us. Most of the press is against us. How can we get this job done? We need more money in an election year, more taxes in an election year, more troops in an election year, and more cuts in an election year. . . .

We have no support for the war. This is caused by the 206,000 troop request, leaks, Ted Kennedy and Bobby Kennedy. . . . The Stennis hearings hurt us. The civilians in both departments [State and Defense] hurt us. I started in 1966 trying to get a surtax. I've made no progress on taxes. I've got a deficit of $30 billion.[28]

On Sunday, March 31, President Johnson delivered his long-awaited televised address to the nation on Vietnam. Originally to have been an assessment of the war, his speech announced that the United States would in an unspecified manner limit the bombing in order to facilitate negotiations. His words were simple but vague:

Tonight, I have ordered our aircraft and our naval units to make no attacks on North Vietnam, except in the area north of the demilitarized zone where the continuing enemy buildup directly threatens allied forward positions and where the movements of their troops and supplies are closely related to that threat. The area in which we are stopping our attacks includes almost 90 percent of North Vietnam's population, and most of its territory. Thus there will be no attacks around the principal populated areas, or in the food-producing areas of North Vietnam.[29]

Fond of the media and the public, he included in his delivered remarks material absent from the prepared text released a few hours earlier, the announcement that he would not run for reelection but devote the remainder of his presidency to a search for peace.

Not surprisingly, President Johnson made his decision to curtail Rolling Thunder without consulting Admiral Sharp. General Wheeler alerted Sharp that at 21:00, March 31 (Washington time), all combat air operations north of the twentieth parallel, roughly Thanh Hoa, would be canceled. Wheeler explained that the reasons for the cutback were primarily political—to reverse the strength of the antiwar movement and to counter foreign criticism in the face of additional troop movements to Vietnam:

Since the Tet offensive support of the American public and the Congress for the war in Southeast Asia has decreased at an accelerating rate. . . . If this trend continues unchecked, public support of our objectives in Southeast Asia will be too frail to sustain the effort.[30]

To blunt the inevitable accusations that he was "escalating" the war, Wheeler said, President Johnson would launch yet another peace initiative; hence the need for a curtailment, at least temporarily, of Rolling Thunder. Because the weather over northern North Vietnam would remain poor for the next thirty days or so, April represented the optimum period for such an initiative. The Chiefs knew these matters, Wheeler said, and they wanted all military commanders to fall in behind the president and to accept the need to curtail the bombing. Moreover, Wheeler loyally pointed out, they should not mention the president's decisions, only the authority of the Joint Chiefs. "Every effort should be made to discourage military personnel from expressing criticism to news media representatives," cautioned the general, displaying the qualities that commended him to two successive presidents.[31]

Whatever his nominal position as CINCPAC, Sharp was not the military person who mattered. General Westmoreland in Saigon was, and, as might be expected, he welcomed the decision to suspend bombing above the twentieth parallel, since it freed air assets for in-country uses as well as for what he liked to call the extended battle areas.[32]

What the President actually sought to accomplish by curtailing Rolling Thunder can only be inferred. Such testimony as that just quoted has to be treated skeptically. Johnson believed they would inevitably read into his words what they wanted to hear and agree that he was the man to implement those wishes. What Wheeler told Sharp represented what the president wanted the military to think—that he was on their side and was doing the most for the American fighting man that difficult circumstances permitted. To be sure, Johnson feared that the military might rebel against his management of the war, and Wheeler's words to Sharp reflected the politician's concern to protect that flank. As for his international audience, Johnson's carefully ambiguous language left him as much flexibility as possible.

It seems that Johnson accepted the interpretation of Rusk that bombing had to be scaled back in the interest of stabilizing public support and dealing with a threatening situation that was otherwise impossible to address. Remember that he could not go to Congress for additional troops or funding; he had only the means that were already at hand. Reorienting air assets already in the theater addressed the looming catastrophe that Westmoreland forecast. Getting talks started was secondary to demonstrating American bona fides. The olive branch extended that Sunday in March was less than that offered the previous September in San Antonio.

The San Antonio Formula offered a total cessation of bombing in return for a nebulous promise to accept restraints on reinforcing and supplying troops whose existence North Vietnam never acknowledged. The key element in the decision to curtail Rolling Thunder south of the twentieth parallel went unnoticed—the reorientation of air assets to Laos, South Vietnam, and the southernmost provinces of North Vietnam, the logistic funnels through which North Vietnam supplied its forces. In this way and this alone the North Vietnamese offensive could be struck directly and halted without risking defeat and the turmoil involved the call-up of reservists.

CONCLUSION

What stands out in the record of these discussions is the way in which all these considerations were weighed simultaneously and with apparent equality of attention in the presidential computer. On the one hand, President Johnson wanted to defuse the liberal opposition to the war; on the other hand, he sought to retain military support. Unable simultaneously to secure the support of such paladins of the Senate as Richard Russell, who had made their support of a reserve call-up contingent on a wholehearted attack on Haiphong, Johnson did what circumstances permitted.

President Johnson curtailed Rolling Thunder because doing so offered the best chances of defusing an explosive political situation at home, one that General Westmoreland's request for 200,000 more troops threatened to detonate. Johnson had never thought of the air war as part of a strategic offensive directed against the nation with whom the United States was at war; rather, Rolling Thunder remained a tool of coercive diplomacy.

But its reorientation south of the twentieth parallel was neither an afterthought nor a trick played upon a war-weary population. The redirection of the air war to battlefield interdiction addressed the military peril that Westmoreland feared and did so with negligible political costs. Because the reorientation of the air war obviated the need for a reserve call-up or otherwise having to go cap in hand to Congress in an election year, the president curtailed Rolling Thunder, confident that he could restore it if necessary.

In reality, he had taken a step from which there was no return. This decision was not the first time in the war that he had misjudged his adversary and its patrons, the American people, and the dynamics of the military and political setting. He acted as he did because he was preeminently a political tactician, thinking one or at most two moves ahead. He did not expect peace to result, only that Khe Sanh would now not fall and the ARVN would survive to fight another day. Because of the failure of its Tet Offensive, the North Vietnamese accepted the bid to negotiate while they regrouped and reorganized their rearward areas. Their need to regroup coincided, of course, with the Johnson administration's desperate need to do the same.

NOTES

1. For specifics on the San Antonio Formula see Thomas G. Paterson, J. Garry Clifford, and Kenneth J. Hagan, *American Foreign Relations: A History since 1900*, 2d edition (Lexington, Mass.: D. C. Heath, 1983), pp. 562–563; George W. Ball, *The Disciple of Power* (Boston: Little, Brown, 1968), p. 321; Clark M. Clifford, "A Viet Nam Reappraisal," *Foreign Affairs*, Vol. 47, No. 4 (July 1969), p. 608.

2. "Notes of the President's Tuesday Luncheon Mtg," February 6, 1968, Diary Backup Files, Box 89, LBJ Library.

3. Tom Johnson meeting notes, January 30, 1968, in which these options were discussed. By February 9 Westmoreland had requested both the 82nd Airborne and the 69th Marine Division "to prevent the ARVN from falling apart" (Wheeler's words) and to constitute an in-country strategic reserve to deal with further unexpected enemy thrusts. A day later, Johnson told his advisors, "I am afraid to move the 82nd because of the possibility of civil disturbances here in the US." February 10 mtg. notes, LBJ Library.

4. Tom Johnson meeting notes, February 13, 1968, LBJ Library.

5. Ibid.

6. Ibid. Clark Clifford's extensively researched memoirs, *Counsel to the President* (New York: Random House, 1991), omit any references to his advice or even to this meeting, p. 476 [hereafter *Counsel to the President*].

7. Tom Johnson meeting notes, February 20, 1968, LBJ Library.

8. Clifford, *Counsel to the President*, pp. 483–485, 492–526, which replaces his near contemporary account, "A Viet Nam Reappraisal," *Foreign Affairs*, Vol. 47, No. 4 (July 1969), pp. 601–622.

9. Draft presidential memo, March 4, 1968, Clark Clifford Papers, Box 3, LBJ Library.

10. Sharp Oral History, No. 10, June 6, 1970, pp. 590–592, summarizing message of March 3, 1968.

11. Ibid.

12. These expressions of opinion derive from a memo by Colonel Robert Ginsburgh, U.S. Air Force, for Walt Rostow, March 1, 1968, "Mining North Vietnamese Ports," NSF/CF/VN, Box 127, LBJ Library.

13. ISA "Alternative Strategies in South Vietnam," draft memo to Secretary Clifford, March 1, 1968, Clark Clifford Papers, Box 3, LBJ Library.

14. "The Campaign against North Vietnam: A Different View," TAB F-2 to draft ISA memo for Clifford, "Alternative Strategies in South Vietnam," March 1, 1968, Clark Clifford Papers, Box 3, LBJ Library.

15. Tom Johnson meeting notes, March 4, 1968, LBJ Library.

16. Tom Johnson meeting notes, March 6, 1968, LBJ Library.

17. Arthur Schlesinger, *Robert Kennedy and His Time* (New York: Ballantine, 1978), pp. 888–891, for this amazing episode.

18. Tom Johnson meeting notes, March 19, 1968, LBJ Library.

19. See Rusk remarks at Tuesday luncheon, March 19, 1968, Box 2, Tom Johnson meeting notes, LBJ Library.

20. Clifford's famous *Foreign Affairs* article previously cited and his more recent

memoirs misrepresent the opinions that he actually expressed at the time and minimize the far more influential change of heart experienced by Dean Rusk.

21. Tom Johnson meeting notes, March 20, 1968, LBJ Library.

22. Herbert Y. Schandler, *The Unmaking of a President* (Princeton, N.J.: Princeton University Press, 1977), p. 250 [hereafter *The Unmaking of a President*].

23. Tom Johnson meeting notes, March 20, 1968, LBJ Library.

24. Westmoreland to Wheeler/Sharp, 300400Z January 1968, Westmoreland Papers, U.S. Army Center of Military History, Washington, D.C. [hereafter WCW Papers, CMH]. Westmoreland's memoirs, *A Soldier Reports* (Garden City, N.Y.: Doubleday, 1976), pp. 335–349, articulately defends his conduct of this battle but also reveals the importance that this firebase had acquired.

25. CINCPAC to CJCS, 090735Z January 1968, WCW Papers, CMH.

26. See Wheeler and Abrams' remarks at a meeting with President Johnson and his foreign policy advisors, March 26, 1968, Tom Johnson Notes, Box 3, LBJ Library.

27. See, for example, Dean Rusk, *As I Saw It* (New York: W. W. Norton, 1991), p. 480; Schandler, *The Unmaking of a President,* pp. 270–271.

28. Tom Johnson meeting notes, March 26, 1968, LBJ Library.

29. See *The Public Papers of the Presidents: Lyndon B. Johnson, 1968* (Washington, D.C.: U.S. Government Printing Office, 1970), p. 470.

30. Wheeler to Sharp, March 31, 1968, WCW Papers, CMH.

31. Wheeler to Sharp/component commanders, 3102332Z March 1968, WCW Papers, CMH.

32. Westmoreland to Sharp 040633Z April 1968, WCW Papers, CMH.

14

The Myth of Tet: American Failure and the Politics of War

Robert Buzzanco

In concluding his CBS news special, "Report from Vietnam," on February 27, 1968, America's most respected newsman urged the United States to disengage from the Vietnam War, "not as victors but as an honorable people who lived up to their pledge to defend democracy, and did the best they could."[1] Thus Walter Cronkite shocked the country with his appraisal of the enemy's Tet Offensive—a nationwide but loosely coordinated series of attacks on political and military targets in South Vietnam launched by the combined forces of the Viet Cong (VC) and the northern People's Army of Vietnam (PAVN). Cronkite's stark evaluation was a turning point in America's reaction to the Tet attacks, just as Tet marked a turning point in the U.S. experience in Vietnam. "If I've lost Cronkite," President Lyndon Johnson lamented, "I've lost middle America." Needless to say, he had lost the war as well. After early 1968 it was evident that the United States would not soon or successfully conclude its involvement in Indochina.[2]

Over the past decade the Tet Offensive has become a central consideration in the historiography of Vietnam. Indeed, as influential conservative revisionists see it, Tet is a metaphor for the entire war. The United States was militarily successful during Tet, various political, military, and academic figures argue, but had its best efforts undermined at home by the media, the peace movement, and craven politicians who had forced American soldiers to fight with "one hand tied behind their back."[3] In reality, then, the United States achieved a decisive military victory but suffered an equally conclusive political and psychological defeat.[4] Even scholarly critics of the war have generally accepted that view, essentially agreeing that, as Loren Baritz put it, "Tet was, as the military believed, a great American victory." Others—including Chalmers Johnson, Robert Asprey, Andrew

Krepinevich, Neil Sheehan, and Gabriel Kolko—do conclude that Tet was an American failure, but they do not question whether the military believed its own rhetoric about the offensive as a decisive victory. To these analysts the U.S. generals had conducted the war ineffectively, but had also sincerely believed their own claims of success.[5]

Accordingly, the range of interpretations regarding Tet is not as diverse as it may seem. Both conservative revisionists and critics of the war focus on the military aspects of Tet, but in that process fail to adequately address the domestic politics of war. Thus they neglect many of the assessments made by U.S. military leaders at the outset of the offensive. Simply put, they overlook the critical fact that officers in the Military Assistance Command, Vietnam (MACV) and the Joint Chiefs of Staff (JCS) understood immediately that Tet had posed intense, perhaps intractable, difficulties for the United States. As Clark Clifford, secretary of defense during the Tet crisis, observed, "Despite their retrospective claims to the contrary, at the time of the initial attacks the reaction of some of our most senior military leaders approached panic."[6]

Indeed the U.S. military recognized its dilemma in Vietnam at once. Despite public assertions of success, the military candidly reported that conditions in the South had deteriorated, that the Republic of Vietnam's (RVN) government and military lacked the means necessary to recover effectively, and that the Democratic Republic of Vietnam (DRV) in the North was replacing its losses and remained a viable and effective threat. In addition to noting such problems, military leaders also understood that civilian officials—who had rejected substantively escalating the war for some time before Tet—had been unnerved if not shocked by the enemy offensive. Yet in late February Westmoreland and JCS Chair Earle Wheeler requested 206,000 additional troops and the activation of 280,000 reservists.

Rather than change course after Tet, the military had thus sent notice that it would continue to rely on its now discredited war of attrition. That approach, however, reflected the armed forces' political rather than military appraisal of the war to that point. The MACV and JCS had recognized the enemy's capacity to match American reinforcements, thus seriously limiting the value of any additional troop deployments, and were also aware that the president and especially his defense secretary, Robert McNamara, were adamantly opposed to escalating the war and calling up reserves.[7] Under those circumstances it hardly seems likely that Westmoreland and Wheeler could have expected the White House to approve such an immense reinforcement request.

But given the nature of civil-military relations over the decade preceding Tet, the political maneuvering over the reinforcement request had a certain logic. Since the New Look budget battles in the 1950s and civil-military acrimony after the Bay of Pigs disaster in 1961, American service and political leaders had been increasingly distrustful of each other, a condition exacerbated by the intervention into and strategy employed in Vietnam.[8] By February 1968 then, it was clear to U.S. policy makers in both Saigon and Washington that they would not "win" in Vietnam. Thus, American military leaders requested additional troops in such vast numbers in order to more forcefully shift the burden for the conduct of the war onto the president. Long aware of the parlous nature of the war, and angry and frustrated by their inability to defeat the enemy and by Johnson's vacillating and indecisive approach to Vietnam, Generals William C. Westmoreland, the MACV commander, and Earle Wheeler, the JCS chair, forced the president into the dilemma of either authorizing the deployment of 206,000 more troops and activating the reserves, which would cause inestimable public hostility, or of rejecting the request, which would provide the armed forces with an alibi for future problems. Thus the revisionist critique of Vietnam that would find so many adherents in the decade after the war was developed long before the war ended.

In the few months before the Tet Offensive, American military appraisals of the situation in Vietnam had been optimistic. In public appearances and private cables in November 1967, Westmoreland contended that military trends were favorable and that American troop withdrawals might begin within two years. Despite problems, the MACV commander could see "some light at the end of the tunnel." Less than two months later, however, the MACV began to anticipate large-scale enemy action, and in late January the PAVN massed perhaps 40,000 troops for an attack on U.S. outposts at Khe Sanh, in the northwest RVN near the Laotian border, just below the seventeenth parallel.[9]

By late spring, it would become clear that Khe Sanh had been a DRV ruse to draw U.S. troops from urban centers in anticipation of the Tet attacks. Nonetheless, on January 20 Westmoreland warned of the enemy's "threatening posture" in the North and also anticipated further enemy initiatives, warning of a "country-wide show of strength just prior to Tet." Wheeler similarly warned that the MACV "is about to have the most vicious battle of the Vietnam War." And during a press briefing just days before the Tet attacks began, General Fred Weyand, one of Westmoreland's deputies, admitted that "there is no question about it, the South Vietnamese Army is outgunned by the Vietcong."[10]

The light at the end of the tunnel, critics joked, was probably a train headed toward Westmoreland, and on the night of January 29–30 it thundered through the RVN. Taking advantage of a Tet New Year cease-fire, roughly 60,000 PAVN and VC forces attacked virtually every military and political center of importance, even invading the U.S. Embassy grounds. Initially Westmoreland, still focusing on the war in the northern provinces, argued that the attacks were a Communist diversion to move military emphasis from I Corps and Khe Sanh in particular, but he also claimed that the U.S. forces had the situation "well in hand," while President Johnson interpreted the attacks as a "complete failure" for the DRV.[11]

General Weyand, however, pointed out that the enemy had successfully concentrated on "remunerative" political and psychological objectives in its attacks. Wheeler likewise admitted that the Communist presence was expanding because "in a city like Saigon people can infiltrate easily. . . . This is about as tough to stop as it is to protect against an individual mugging in Washington, D.C." General Edward Lansdale, special assistant to Ambassador Ellsworth Bunker in Saigon, also lamented that Tet had practically "destroyed all faith in the effectiveness" of the government of the RVN, brought Vietnamese morale "dangerously low," and made southern villagers even more "vulnerable to further VC exploitation." Still worse, any possible American countermeasures appeared to Lansdale to be "rather shopworn and inadequate."[12]

General John Chaisson, director of the MACV Combat Operations Center, elaborated on such problems. "We have been faced with a real battle," he admitted at a February 3 briefing in Saigon; "there is no sense in ducking it; there is no sense in hiding it." Because of the offensive's coordination, intensity, and audacity, Chaisson had to give the Communists "credit for having engineered and planned a very successful offensive in its initial phases." Moreover, the DRV and VC had withheld their main force and PAVN units in many areas; Westmoreland pointed out that the enemy "continues to maintain a strong capability to re-initiate attacks country-wide at the time and place of his choosing." Although Chaisson then concluded that the Communists' sizable casualties might eventually constitute a "great loss," his analysis had revealed the depth and nature of the MACV's dilemma as a result of the offensive.[13]

At the outset of Tet, then, military officials inside Vietnam recognized that the situation there was perilous. This was also true of the JCS in Washington, which conceded that "the enemy has shown a major capability for waging war in the South." But on February 3 the brass requested an intensified bombing campaign against Hanoi, even though the scope of the Tet attacks had demonstrated the ineffectiveness of airpower in preventing or containing enemy initiatives. Accordingly, the military had already developed what the *Pentagon Papers* authors termed the *non sequitur* approach to the situation in the South: despite admitting that grave problems existed, the armed forces asked for bold but unsound responses that placed the burden for a decision firmly on the shoulders of civilian officials in Washington.[14]

As Washington debated the bombing request and the full dimensions of Tet began to emerge, military officials remained worried. "From a realistic point of view," Westmoreland reported to General Wheeler, "we must accept the fact that the enemy has dealt the GVN [Government of Vietnam] a severe blow. He has brought the war to the towns and cities and has inflicted damage and casualties on the population. . . . Distribution of the necessities has been interrupted . . . and the economy has been disrupted. . . . The people have felt directly the impact of the war." As a result, the RVN faced a "tremendous challenge" to restore stability and aid those who had suffered. But Westmoreland's report ended on an upbeat note. Because enemy losses were sizable and the VC had not gained political control in the South, he contended, the offensive had been a military failure.[15]

Westmoreland then contradicted himself, making the crucial recognition that the enemy's objectives were finally clear and "they were primarily psychological and political." The Communists, he observed, sought to destroy southern faith in the government of the RVN, intimidate the population, and cause significant desertions among the Army of the RVN (the ARVN). The DRV's military objectives, Westmoreland admitted, were secondary to its political goals, and included diverting and dispersing U.S. forces throughout the South. The enemy, moreover, posed major threats at many areas, including Saigon, Khe Sanh, the Demilitarized Zone, and Hue, and more attacks were likely. Thus at the same time that Westmoreland claimed military success, he conceded that the Communists were engaged in psychological and political warfare. Throughout the next two months, his and other officers' reports would further reveal that the enemy criteria for success—undermining the southern government and military, prompting popular discontent, and destabilizing American policy—had indeed been accomplished throughout the RVN.[16]

Such military concern was further evident when Westmoreland and the JCS reported on 9 February that the DRV had added between 16,000 and 25,000 troops in the Khe Sanh area and continued to pose a threat of "major proportions." The enemy, Wheeler predicted, "is going to take his time and move when he has things under control as he would like them." To that end PAVN infiltration had risen from 78 to 105 battalions, and the ratio of U.S. and ARVN forces to Communist troops, which had been 1.7 to 1, was now at 1.4 to 1. The Communists were also applying heavy pressure in Hue and Danang, had cut off the Ai Van pass, and threatened Highway 1—the major transportation route in South Vietnam. In Quang Tri and Thua Thien, in northernmost I Corps, the controlling factor in America's performance would be logistics, which Westmoreland admitted were "now marginal at best" even though he had redirected the 101st Airborne Division and 1st Air Cavalry Division to the north. But further to the south, the MACV claimed, the enemy posed no serious threat. The ally, however, did.[17]

Extensive damage to lines of communication and populated areas, heavy casualties—about 9,100 between January 29 and February 10—and significant desertion rates had riddled the ARVN. Accordingly, Westmoreland urged RVN president Nguyen Van Thieu to begin drafting eighteen- and nineteen-year-old southerners to increase the armed forces by at least 65,000 troops, the number depleted in the initial Tet attacks. "Realistically," the MACV commander lamented, "we must assume that it will take them [ARVN] at least six months to regain the military posture of several weeks ago." Consequently, Westmoreland, for the first time after Tet, asked for additional forces. Wheeler had encouraged the MACV commander to seek reinforcements, which he admitted he could not guarantee. "Our capabilities are limited," the JCS chair explained, with only the 82d Airborne Division and half of a marine division available for deployment to Vietnam. Nonetheless, as Wheeler saw it, "The critical phase of the war is upon us," and the MACV should not "refrain in asking for what you believe is required under the circumstances." The JCS chair's timing in raising the reinforcement issue was appropriate, for Westmoreland had thinned out III Corps by transferring forces to the north after a PAVN strike at Lang Vei days earlier. That diversion had troubled the MACV because it needed those forces to fight the enemy's main force units and support pacification, but the commander did not see it as an unacceptable risk.[18]

It was "needless to say," however, that Westmoreland would welcome reinforcements to offset casualties and desertions, to react to the DRV's replacement of southern forces—which was conditioning the MACV's own plans—and to put friendly forces in a better position to contain Communist attacks in the north and take the offensive if given an opportunity. Again Westmoreland finished an otherwise frank evaluation of the military situation in South Vietnam with a *non sequitur:* high hopes that additional forces would facilitate greater U.S. success.[19] Washington was not so enthusiastic. Having turned down the JCS's bombing request three days earlier, on February 9 the Department of Defense directed the Chiefs to furnish plans to provide for the emergency reinforcement of the MACV. The resulting memoranda between Westmoreland and Wheeler demonstrated that the military understood that its position in Vietnam was untenable.

Although the MACV publicly claimed that only pockets of resistance remained, Wheeler told the president that the JCS "feel that we have taken several hard knocks. The situation can get worse."[20] In fact, at a February 12 meeting, White House officials found that Westmoreland's reports had raised as many questions and concerns as they had answered. The MACV reports from Vietnam had made the president and his advisors anxious, and they had interpreted Westmoreland's messages and requests for reinforcements as indications of the ARVN's weaknesses and evidence that the troubled logistics and transport systems in the north had made deployment of additional forces imperative simply to maintain the American position.[21] Such candid reports continued to unnerve Johnson, who wondered "what has happened to change the situation between then [initial optimism] and now." Maxwell Taylor, the president's military advisor, also "found it hard to believe" that the bleak reports reaching Washington were "written by the same man [Westmoreland]" as the earlier optimistic cables. Against that backdrop Washington began to discuss the reinforcements issue. The president and Defense Secretary Robert McNamara reiterated already strong reservations over additional deployments because of the impact of Tet and the spiraling financial burdens of the war. General Taylor, however, believed that the situation was urgent, interpreting Westmoreland's cables as proof that "the offensive in the north is against him."[22]

Westmoreland told the White House that defeat was not imminent. Nonetheless, he admitted that he could not regain the initiative without additional forces, and he warned that "a setback is fully possible" if he was not reinforced, while it was "likely that we will lose ground in other areas" if the MACV had to continue diverting forces to I CTZ. But Westmoreland still maintained that the enemy's strong position at Khe Sanh and the DMZ, not the VC in the cities, was the most serious threat, and if it was not contained the U.S. position in the northern RVN would be in jeopardy. The MACV commander also expected another Communist offensive in the north, which he pledged to contain either with "*reinforcements, which I desperately need*" or at the risk of diverting even greater numbers of forces from other areas. Thus far, Westmoreland added, Vietnam had been a limited war with limited objectives and resources, but, as a result of Tet, "we are now in a new ballgame where we face a determined, highly disciplined enemy, fully mobilized to achieve a quick victory."[23]

Based on such communication with Westmoreland, the JCS developed its analysis for McNamara. As of February 11, the Chiefs noted, the PAVN and VC had attacked thirty-four provincial towns, sixty-four district towns, and all of the autonomous cities. Despite heavy losses, the enemy had yet to commit the vast proportion of its northern forces, while the PAVN had already replaced much of its losses and equaled U.S. troop levels in I Corps. Westmoreland and his deputy Creighton Abrams were, moreover, concerned that the ARVN was relying on American firepower to avoid combat and that widespread looting was alienating the population. The ARVN, additionally, had suffered its worst desertion rates prior to the 1975 breakdown of the RVN. Its average battalion was at 50 percent strength, its average ranger battalion was at 43 percent strength, and five of nine airborne battalions were not combat effective, according to MACV standards.[24]

Even when using questionable criteria such as enemy losses or inability to capture control of government as measures of military success, the MACV and JCS appraisals pointed out increasing problems. As a result, the Chiefs had strong reservations about reinforcing the MACV. Admiral Sharp had urged the White House to meet Westmoreland's request, arguing that additional forces could exploit enemy weaknesses. If Communist strength had been underestimated, Sharp added, "we will need them even more." Nonetheless the JCS warned that transferring forces to Vietnam would drain the strategic reserve and exacerbate shortages of skilled personnel and essential equipment. Thus, for the first time the Chiefs rejected a MACV request for additional support. "At long last," the *Pentagon Papers* authors explained, "the resources were beginning to be drawn too thin, the assets became unavailable, the support base too small."[25]

The JCS thus rejected Westmoreland's plea for more troops principally to pressure the president to activate reserves in the United States, or face responsibility for continued deterioration. But McNamara on February 13 directed an emergency force of 10,500 troops, including the remainder of the 82d Airborne—the only readily deployable division among continental U.S. forces—to be deployed to Vietnam to reconstitute the MACV reserve and to "put out the fire." President Johnson hoped that the additions would reinforce stretched lines and guard against another series of enemy attacks, but clearly the defense secretary and president were wary of increasing their commitment in Vietnam by that point. Westmoreland, however, remained alert to the VC threat in the cities, continued to expect a major DRV blow at Khe Sanh, and accordingly sought at least six additional combat battalions. At the same time MACV officials and General Lansdale continued to warn of future enemy action and point out problems associated with the ARVN. Thus the president remained anxious about the U.S. position in Vietnam and dispatched Wheeler to Saigon on February 23 to review the situation.[26]

Wheeler visited Westmoreland from February 23 to 25 and filed his report with the president on February 27. The chair's appraisals contrasted sharply with public optimism about the war. As Westmoreland publicly continued to claim success—concluding that he did "not believe Hanoi can hold up under a long war"—Wheeler told reporters that he saw "no early end to this war," and cautioned that Americans "must expect hard fighting to continue." Privately, Wheeler was more pessimistic.[27]

Wheeler, a skilled veteran of Pentagon politics, was losing confidence in the MACV commander and, as Clark Clifford put it, "presented an even grimmer assessment of the Tet offensive than we had heard from Westmoreland and Bunker."[28] "There is no doubt that the enemy launched a major, powerful nationwide assault," Wheeler observed. "This offensive has by no means run its course. In fact, we must accept the possibility that he has already deployed additional elements of his home army." The JCS chair also admitted that American commanders in Vietnam agreed that the margin of success or survival had been "very small indeed" during the first weeks of Tet attacks. The enemy—with combat-available forces deployed in large numbers throughout the RVN—had "the will and capability to continue" and its "determination appears to be unshaken." Although the Communists' future plans were not clear, he warned, "the scope and severity of his attacks and the extent of his reinforcements are presenting us with serious and immediate problems." Several PAVN divisions remained untouched, and troops and supplies continued to move southward to supplement the 200,000 enemy forces available for hostilities. The MACV, however, still faced major logistics problems due to enemy harassment and interdiction, and the massive redeployment of U.S. forces to the north. Westmoreland in fact had deployed half of all maneuver battalions to I Corps while stripping the rest of the RVN of adequate reserves.[29]

Worse, Wheeler, though surprisingly pleased with the ARVN's performance, nonetheless questioned their stamina to continue, pointing out that the army was on the defensive and had lost about one-quarter of its pre-Tet strength. Similarly, the government of the RVN had survived Tet, but with diminished effectiveness. President Thieu and his vice president, Nguyen Cao Ky, faced "enormous" problems with civilian casualties, morale, and a flood of over 500,000 additional refugees—all part of the huge task of reconstruction which would require vast amounts of money and time. The offensive, moreover, had undermined the American pacification program, considered a keystone in the U.S. effort since the early 1960s. Counterinsurgency programs, Wheeler admitted, had been "brought to a halt. . . . To a large extent, the VC now control the countryside." He added that the guerrillas, via recruiting and infiltration, were rebuilding their infrastructure and its overall recovery was "likely to be rapid." Clearly, then, the military had developed its analyses and policy recommendations in February 1968 from candid, at times desolate, views of the effects of Tet. Later claims of success aside, in February Wheeler at best found the situation "fraught with opportunities as well as dangers" and conceded that only the timely reaction of U.S. forces had prevented Communist control in a dozen or so places. "In short," Wheeler had to admit, "it was a very near thing."[30] Army Chief of Staff Harold K. Johnson did not resort to such euphemism. "We suffered a loss," he cabled to Westmoreland, "there can be no doubt about it."[31]

Having been concerned up to Wheeler's visit with the shorter-term results of Tet, the military understood clearly throughout February 1968 that the enemy offensive had created more intense problems for its forces in Vietnam. Subsequently, Tet entered its "second phase," and the MACV and JCS began to discuss longer-term policy in the wake of the enemy's attacks. Yet in doing so service leaders continued to acknowledge problems in the RVN but rejected developing new approaches to the war. Instead they insisted that the MACV simply continue its war of attrition, but with a huge increase in American soldiers—206,000 troops and the activation of 280,000 reservists. With such a proposal, which "simply astonished Washington" and "affect[ed] the course of the war and American politics forever," in Clark Clifford's words, and which the White House would not view favorably, the brass virtually conceded that substantive success would not be forthcoming, but left it to the president to accept responsibility for subsequent military failures in Indochina.[32] Wheeler's reports and request caused a political hurricane in Washington in February 1968, and since then they have had central places in considerations of Tet. While scholars correctly point to Wheeler's candid assessments as proof of American problems in Vietnam, they tend to see the subsequent reinforcement request as a military response to the crisis: having failed to stem the enemy's advances with 525,000 forces, the military sought a 40 percent increase in troop strength to either stave off defeat or take the offensive, and also to replenish the strategic reserve at home.[33] It seems likely, however, that there was an essentially political character to the proposal for additional troops. By February and March 1968 military and civilian leaders understood that the political environment in Washington had made reinforcement—especially in such vast numbers—virtually impossible.[34]

Wheeler recognized the pervading gloom in the White House, admitting that "Tet had a tremendous effect on the American public . . . on leaders of Congress . . . on President Johnson." General Dave Richard Palmer pointed out that the JCS chair had asked for such reinforcement a year earlier and was thus, in effect, recycling an old request. "The ground had already been fought over," Palmer observed; "the sides were already chosen." Indeed, throughout the previous year military and civilian officials had been debating the reinforcement issue, with Washington always reluctant to escalate the war in any dramatic fashion. The JCS and MACV understood this and in May 1967—over a half year before the Tet Offensive—they expected the Pentagon to "avoid the explosive congressional debate and U.S. reserve call-up implicit in the Westmoreland troop request." Similarly, in February 1968, while Wheeler was in Vietnam, General Bruce Palmer, another MACV officer, informed Westmoreland that General Dwight Beach, the army's Pacific commander, had been aware of the new reinforcement request and "had commented that it would shock them [Washington officials]."[35]

Clearly, then, any major reinforcement was unlikely in February and March 1968. As Westmoreland himself admitted, he and Wheeler "both knew the grave political and economic implications of a major call-up of reserves." But Westmoreland also suspected that even Wheeler was "imbued with the aura of crisis" in Washington and thus had dismissed the MACV's sanguine briefings. "In any event," the MACV commander added, the JCS chair "saw no possibility at the moment of selling reinforcements" unless he adopted an alarmist tone to exploit the sense of crisis. "Having read the newspapers," Westmoreland wondered, "who among them [civilian leaders] would even believe there had been success?" Wheeler's approach to the issue notwithstanding, Westmoreland suspected that "the request may have been doomed from the first in any event" due to long-standing political pressure to de-escalate.[36]

Political leaders had also made it clear that substantive reinforcements would not be forthcoming. Even before Tet, the PAVN strike at Khe Sanh had alarmed Johnson. Meeting with his advisors, the president charged that "all of you have counseled, advised, consulted and then—as usual—placed the monkey on my back again . . . I do not like what I am smelling from those cables from Vietnam."[37] During his first post-Tet press conference the president asserted that he had already added the men that Westmoreland thought were necessary. "We have something under 500,000," Johnson told reporters. "Our objective is 525,000. Most of the combat battalions already have been supplied. There is not anything in any of the developments that would justify the press in leaving the impression that any great new overall moves are going to be made that would involve substantial movements in that direction." By the following week, with more advisors expressing their concern about Tet and the war in general, it was clear to the president that the military could exploit White House division over Vietnam. "I don't want them [military leaders] to ask for something," Johnson worried aloud, "not get it, and have all the blame placed on me."[38]

Similarly, Secretary of State Dean Rusk was arguing that then current levels of U.S. and RVN troops were adequate to achieve American objectives, and he thus recommended against any increase. Moreover, congressional hawks began to waver, thereby complicating the political nature of the reinforcement request. As Stanley Karnow has observed, hard-line senators such as John Stennis and Henry Jackson who had "consistently underwritten the military establishment now began to see the hopelessness of the struggle." McNamara, moreover, was pointing out the costs of escalation. The Wheeler-Westmoreland request would require an increase in uniformed strength of 400,000 men, which, the defense secretary estimated, would require additional expenditures of at least $10 billion in fiscal year 1969, with an automatic addition of $5 billion for fiscal year 1970. McNamara further questioned the military's motives in asking for the additional 206,00 men, which, as he saw it, was "neither enough to do the job, nor an indication that our role must change."[39]

Thus, by mid-February, as Clark Clifford has pointed out, "the President did not wish to receive a formal request from the military for reinforcements, for fear that if it leaked he would be under great pressure to respond immediately." More importantly, Clifford added that the military was conscious of the situation and so "a delicate minuet took place to create the fiction that no request was being made." Similarly, Philip Habib, a State Department specialist in East Asian affairs, reported that there was "serious disagreement in American circles in Saigon over the 205,000 request." White House aide John P. Roche elaborated that "Johnson hadn't under any circumstances considered 206,000 men. Wheeler figured this Tet offensive was going to be his handle for getting the shopping list okayed." Along those lines, Ambassador Bunker, in late February, had warned Westmoreland about asking for those troops, explaining that such reinforcement was now "politically impossible" even if the president had wanted to, which was also more unlikely than ever.[40] To say the least, the military's candid, bleak outlooks throughout the first month of Tet followed by the huge reinforcement request had created an atmosphere of crisis in the White House.

Even worse, economic problems were becoming more acutely dangerous in February and March 1968. As American troops and materiel began to pour into Vietnam during the Kennedy administration and thereafter, inflation steadily increased, the U.S. balance of payments deficit almost tripled between 1964 and 1968, when it rose to over $9 billion, and America's gold reserves declined precipitously.[41] In January the president, alarmed by such financial conditions, proposed a tax surcharge to finance the war. Congress, no doubt annoyed by Johnson's repeated attempts to shift the burden for economic sacrifice onto it, stalled, thereby creating even greater anxiety among European bankers. Even before Tet, Gardner Ackley, head of the Council of Economic Advisers, was warning of a "possible spiraling world depression" if the dollar and gold issues were not resolved, while Allan Sproul, past head of the New York Federal Reserve Bank, lamented that the Vietnam War was "at the core" of America's "domestic and international political, social, and economic difficulties." In late February, another $118 million in bullion left the United States in just two days and "the specter of 1929 haunted [Lyndon Johnson] daily."[42]

By mid-March European banks had withdrawn another $1 billion in gold; on March 14 the U.S. Treasury lost $372 million in bullion, and, fearing the possible loss of another billion the next day, closed the gold market. Administration officials then called an emergency meeting in Washington with European central bankers, who rejected an American request to give up their right to claim gold for dollars from the U.S. Treasury. The Europeans essentially told the president that they would restrain their gold purchases only if he put the defense of the dollar above all other economic considerations, including Vietnam. Given the confluence of military and economic calamities that had struck Washington in early 1968, the administration had to acknowledge that further troop increases threatened not only the U.S. economy, but America's position in the world political economy as well. Tet, it is not an exaggeration to suggest, marked the end of America's postwar hegemony.[43]

Accordingly, Johnson, already floored by the dollar-gold crisis and further alarmed by the Wheeler report and similar evaluations from the Central Intelligence Agency (CIA) and Pentagon civilians, directed incoming Secretary of State Clark Clifford to begin an "A to Z Reassessment" of the war. Johnson charged the Clifford group with reviewing current and alternative courses of action, with two questions central to its study: Should the United States stay the course in Vietnam? And could the MACV succeed even with 206,000 additional forces? Both the CIA and the Pentagon sent back pessimistic analyses, warning that additional deployments would further Americanize the war and prompt DRV escalation in kind. General Taylor urged the White House to consider the political effects of future policy. "In the end," the president's military advisor cautioned, "military and political actions should be blended together in an integrated package."[44]

The JCS instead concentrated on military solutions, urging a wholly unrestrained air war against the North. Westmoreland and Wheeler, moreover, were appalled by the charge, made by Pentagon civilian officials, that the military sought reinforcements as "another payment on an open-ended commitment." Instead, the MACV argued that it needed the forces to ensure "the security of the GVN in Saigon and in the provincial capitals." In Washington, however, military officials seemed more introspective regarding the impact of Tet. Even the hawkish Joint Staff of the JCS challenged the MACV's assessment and goals. Not only would Westmoreland need another 200,000 forces, but would also have to regain the military initiative, cause heavy enemy losses, train the ARVN, and escalate the air war. Without such improvements and reinforcement the DRV would retain the military initiative and "allied forces can expect increasingly grave threats to their security with high casualty rates." Despite a continued, hopeful reliance on the strategy of attrition and airpower, the Joint Staff had provided a desolate view of the war.[45]

The late February–early March reports in Vietnam and the debate over reinforcements provided the clearest demonstration to that point of the armed forces' *non sequitur* approach to policy. The military's candid, usually pessimistic reports and analyses might have led to a new American outlook on the war. But the brass advocated more of the same. By insisting on huge reinforcements and attacking temperate views of the situation, the military rejected opportunities to seek a quicker and less violent solution to Vietnam, but more clearly thrust onto the White House the burden for an ultimate decision regarding America's future in the war.

While the heated debate over reinforcements continued, the situation in Vietnam remained explosive as well. From late February to mid-March the enemy continued its politico-military pressure throughout the RVN, causing significant damage and casualties. In II Corps, Lieutenant Colonel John Paul Vann (Ret.), a deputy in the Civil Operations and Revolutionary Development Support (CORDS) program, pointed out that native resentment against U.S. and ARVN troops who had damaged homes and villages had risen. "Unless stopped," he warned, "the destruction is going to exceed our capability for recovery and battles we win may add up to losing the war." Similarly, Lansdale warned the Embassy that the ARVN command, which included several "notoriously corrupt" officers, was undermining U.S. efforts to recover the pre-Tet military position.[46]

Vann also complained that MACV officers had duped Westmoreland with optimistic briefings. During a visit to II Corps to "kick ass and energize offensive operations," the MACV commander had been preempted by army briefers who stressed the impressive Tet body counts as measures of success. These officers, however, had ignored government and military inaction in the South and did not mention that the VC was "being given more freedom to intimidate the rural population than ever before in the past two-and-a-half years." Vann, in fact, pitied Westmoreland because "even his best subordinates . . . continually screen him from the realities of the situation in Vietnam. As an honorable man he has no choice but to accept what they say and to report it to all his superiors." Thus the MACV—whether duping its commander as Vann judged, or openly aware of its problems as the Wheeler reports indicated—understood the severity and extent of its dilemma in March 1968.[47]

In fact, the MACV itself was in organizational disarray as the army, marines, and air force, already involved in a long-simmering feud over strategy, heightened their interservice conflict. Under the pressures of Tet many army officers complained about the marines' conduct of the war in I Corps, and thus Westmoreland reorganized the MACV by replacing marine commanding general Robert Cushman with army general William Rosson. General Victor Krulak, the marines' Pacific Fleet commander, blasted such developments. After a *Los Angeles Times* article detailed the army-marine rift, Krulak, though excoriating the paper in a letter to its publisher and in cables to the MACV commander, privately charged that "the attack—one of several—was launched by the army, of course." If possible, Krulak added, he would publish a rejoinder titled "The Army Is at It Again."[48]

Marine aviation commander General Norman Anderson similarly complained that the "immense" logistical problems caused by the influx of new units after Tet had become "almost too great to comprehend." Yet, Anderson charged, "in spite of our pleas to slow down the introduction of troops, the four stars in Saigon merely wave their hands and release dispatches directing the units to move. I think much of it is by design, with the ultimate aim of embarrassing" the marines in I Corps. Some of the marines' "biggest battles," he added, were "with the other Services rather than the VC and NVA [North Vietnamese Army]." Indeed, infighting over operation control of tactical aircraft was so intense that air force commanders "would rather see Americans die than give in one iota of the Air Force's party line."[49]

Amid such division and uncertainty, the Clifford group forwarded its recommendations to the White House on March 4. The new defense secretary had been particularly alarmed by the Wheeler report and thus urged Johnson to meet the first increment of Westmoreland's request with a 22,000-troop deployment, but he otherwise rejected the MACV proposals. Citing instability in the government and ARVN, the Clifford group found "no reason to believe" that 206,000 more troops—"or double or triple that quantity"—could rout the Communists from South Vietnam. If granted, reinforcement requests might then continue "with no end in sight." The new secretary then called for the MACV to consider new strategies. Wheeler balked, principally because he resented Pentagon civilians developing strategic guidance for field commanders, and because the 22,000 reinforcements, though useful, were insufficient. The MACV needed assistance urgently, Wheeler asserted, particularly because Westmoreland had reported "no change in his appraisal of the situation" since the chair's visit two weeks earlier.[50]

In early March 1968 the United States was surely at the crossroads in Vietnam. Following a month of candid, bleak assessments, Wheeler and Westmoreland unleashed their bombshell request on Washington. But if, as the MACV boasted, it had decisively eliminated the enemy during Tet, Westmoreland would hardly have needed 206,000 more troops to complete the rout. Even if the MACV sincerely believed that more forces would turn the tide, it certainly understood that they would not be forthcoming. Indeed, given the brass's pessimistic evaluations and the president's attendant anxiety, it is not likely that the military was surprised that Tet seemed to be an American defeat. Although the *New York Times* front-page story of March 10 shocked Americans with its stark portrayal of the U.S. position in Vietnam, it in large measure reflected the military's own appraisals of the war from the previous six weeks.[51]

Obviously the continuing public outcry over Tet did little to assuage the White House. The president, who on March 13 had agreed to send 30,000 more forces to Vietnam with two reserve call-ups to sustain the deployments, then called on the "Wise Men"—former government and military officials—to help decide the reinforcement issue. General Matthew Ridgway, Douglas MacArthur's replacement during the Korean War and an outspoken critic of the Vietnam War, was one of the Wise Men, and he urged that the United States equip and train the ARVN for two additional years and then hand over responsibility for the war and begin troop withdrawals. With a few exceptions, Ridgway and the other Wise Men urged the president to de-escalate. At the same time, General David Shoup, marine commandant in the early 1960s and outspoken critic of Vietnam, gave the White House another political setback as he told the Senate Committee on Foreign Relations that "it would take a rather great stretch of the imagination" to believe that Tet was an American victory. The general also scored the reinforcement request, pointing out that the United States might need 800,000 troops just to protect the cities attacked during the offensive. When asked how many forces might be required to actually repel the enemy, Shoup lamented, "I think you can just pull any figure you wanted out of the hat and that would not be enough."[52]

Simultaneously, Johnson met with Wheeler and Creighton Abrams, who had just been designated the new MACV commander, replacing Westmoreland, who had been "fired upstairs" to become army chief. Days earlier Abrams had sought to "divorce myself from somewhat more optimistic reports coming out of Saigon" and he recognized "a tough fight ahead against a skilful [sic] and determined enemy." Wheeler reported that the MACV did not fear general defeat, but pointed out that continued DRV infiltration—possibly 60,000 Communist troops had moved southward—and lack of adequate reserves "could give the enemy a tactical victory." The ARVN remained "frozen" in a defensive posture, while the enemy had established a "stranglehold" around numerous cities, especially near Saigon and Hue. Khe Sanh, Wheeler also conceded, had suited the DRV's purposes by diverting U.S. forces to the north as Communist troops moved south- and eastward.[53]

Upon receiving such appraisals Johnson interpreted the reinforcement request as a defensive reaction to continued Communist success rather than as a means to defeat the enemy, and he lamented that *everybody is recommending surrender.*" Clearly the president was feeling the political heat from Tet. In a sometimes rambling soliloquy to Wheeler, Abrams, and Rusk, he expressed alarm at the economic and political repercussions of the war. "Our fiscal situation is abominable," Johnson pointed out, with rising deficits and interest rates and devaluation of the dollar making a new tax bill necessary. The military's request for more troops and reserves, at a cost of $15 billion, "would hurt the dollar and gold." Such economic considerations, the president admitted, were "complicated by the fact it is an election year" and "we have no support for the war." Johnson then complained that the media and "Senator Kennedy and the left wing" were undermining the war. As a result, "I will have overwhelming disapproval in the polls and elections. I will go down the drain. I don't want the whole alliance and the military pulled in with it."[54]

Westmoreland's March 28 report was equally depressing. The enemy, in its post-Tet strategy, was targeting the people of the RVN; its "main objective is to destroy, or greatly weaken, the GVN." Accordingly, the VC was continuing to isolate the cities, put the ARVN on the defensive, agitate against the government, and proselytize among villagers. The Communists also maintained the politico-military initiative. The enemy, Westmoreland reported, "has no predesignated point for his main effort, no timetable, only a constant opportunism which will take advantage of vacuums [sic] in rural and border areas, weakness in city defenses, or any other favorable circumstances that provides [sic] an opening in the tactical situation." And, the MACV commander conceded, the enemy retained the capability to exploit circumstances. It had between 100 and 110 combat-effective battalions in the South and was replacing its losses with infiltration and by taking advantage of the absence of U.S. and ARVN forces to recruit in the countryside. "In view of past performances and capabilities," Westmoreland noted, "the enemy could bring two division equivalents into the RVN over the next two or three months."[55]

Given such considerations, it was an obviously dismayed president who addressed the nation on March 31. Johnson again claimed that Tet had been a U.S. success, and he announced a token increase of 13,500 troops to be deployed to Vietnam. But he also ordered a partial bombing halt as an incentive for peace talks, and he stunned the country by withdrawing from the 1968 presidential campaign. So, precisely two months after the initial enemy attacks, Lyndon Johnson had become the latest and best-known casualty of the Tet Offensive.[56]

Westmoreland, however, continued to smile through the storm, optimistically claiming in early April that the enemy had suffered a "colossal military defeat" and that the United States had "never been in a better position in South Vietnam." Yet he also informed Wheeler that the enemy had infiltrated between 35,000 and 40,000 troops into the South, and feared that such figures were "increasing almost daily. . . . The final total may be significantly higher." Such admissions, in fact, continued for the next two months as Communist replacement of Tet losses, human and materiel infiltration, and recruiting persisted.[57]

Even into late summer military leaders continued to lament the impact of Tet. Westmoreland and Sharp reported that pacification had suffered a "substantial setback" as Vietnamese forces withdrew from the countryside to defend urban centers. General Abrams added that counterinsurgency had ground to a "virtual halt," and that Tet attacks had devastated local Vietnamese units charged with village protection (so-called RF/PF units—Regional Forces and Popular Forces). Due to continued VC infiltration, only provincial capitals and district towns were "marginally safe," and the "situation was subject to further deterioration." Abrams also scored the inchoate political atmosphere in the RVN, conceding that perhaps the "most serious—and telling—flaw in the GVN/Allied effort has been the conspicuous shortage of good Vietnamese leadership (both civilian and military) at all levels of command."[58]

Only months after Westmoreland had forecast America's bright prospects in Vietnam, the Communist Tet Offensive had torpedoed U.S. efforts and shocked a hopeful nation. Yet in early 1968 and thereafter supporters of the war claimed that Tet was in fact a decisive American victory undermined at home by antiwar forces. Such claims, however, are disingenuous at best, for American military leaders themselves had consistently recognized that the enemy offensive was laying bare the contradictions inherent in the U.S. war in Indochina. Despite committing billions of dollars and 500,000 men, and inflicting huge casualties and massive hardship, the United States could neither contain the enemy nor protect its allies. Communist attacks had continued throughout 1968, and the DRV retained the capacity to match American escalation of the war. If, as Westmoreland and others contend, such conditions constituted a decisive military victory, then America had been waging war through the looking glass.

On a more salient level, the military also recognized that Tet had been a devastating political failure for the United States. Accusations of being "stabbed in the back" notwithstanding, the military realized that political factors in Vietnam, far more than in Washington, had doomed the American effort. Westmoreland and others had recognized the DRV's conception of political warfare, understood the enemy's psychological goals, and lamented the RVN's instability. The military also understood that the already volatile domestic situation seemed ready to boil over. Media and public perceptions of Tet—as military leaders charged at the outset of the offensive and repeatedly since—had made any attempt to escalate the war politically risky. When considered in light of the president's, defense secretary's, and key political leaders' misgivings about, and opposition to, an increased commitment, reinforcement became politically impossible. Yet after the shock of Tet Westmoreland and Wheeler chose to continue their war of attrition and asked for 206,000 more troops and 280,000 reserves. Why was American military thought so apparently barren in early 1968?

It seems that the military implicitly expected and understood the ramifications of its behavior. Operating from the unspoken assumption that the war had descended to its nadir and that reinforcements would not be forthcoming, the military made its immense request for troops in order to defer its share of responsibility for the American failure in Vietnam onto the White House.[59] Although recognizing the American dilemma in Vietnam, Westmoreland and Wheeler discounted advice to change strategy and instead proposed a massive escalation of the war, which necessarily would have made the president accountable for the failed conduct of Vietnam policy. Bewildered by the enemy's initiative and under increasing fire at home, the military asked for more of the same and forced Johnson to choose between the reinforcement and its attendant consequences, or staying the course and bearing responsibility for the continued stasis. More than simply conniving for troops, military leaders sought to immunize themselves from greater culpability for the U.S. failure in Indochina and in the process forced the president into an intractable political dilemma. By rejecting the military's request to escalate, Johnson provided the services with an alibi for future failures, as the emergence of postwar revisionism on the war attests.

For over two decades the specter of Tet helped define and limit America's international behavior. To General Matthew Ridgway, the post-Tet deescalation had indicated that Americans had "learned our lesson." But, he asked, "Have we thought out how we can prevent another such catastrophe in the long run, when memories begin to fade?" At the end of the 1991 Persian Gulf War George Bush answered, proclaiming that "by God, we've kicked the 'Vietnam syndrome' once and for all."[60] Clearly, control over the historical memory of Vietnam had become a foreign policy strategy as well, for, as George Orwell had warned, those who define the past can control the present and thus the future. To George Bush and many others, America had failed because its warriors had been undermined at home, not vanquished in Vietnam. Such interpretations, however much political currency they create, do not constitute good history. The legacy of Vietnam is so much more complex than the revisionists would have Americans believe. From a study of Tet one can learn valuable lessons about not only tactics and strategy, but the nature of civil-military relations, the effect of public opinion on military affairs, and the politics of war as well. Recognizing and analyzing the myth of Tet may only be a small step toward learning such lessons. It must be taken, however, for Walter Cronkite and Earle Wheeler, among others, understood on February 27 that the United States faced a harsh and perilous future in Vietnam. But, from similar premises, they offered divergent solutions—negotiated withdrawal and escalation. Perhaps that is one of the greater tragedies of the Vietnam War.

NOTES

1. Cronkite in Don Oberdorfer, *Tet!* (New York: Doubleday, 1984), pp. 250–251, and in Peter Braestrup, *Big Story* (New Haven, Conn.: Yale University Press, 1983), p. 493.

2. Cronkite quote in Philip B. Davidson, *Vietnam at War: The History, 1946–1975* (New York: Oxford University Press, 1991), p. 486; On the impact of Cronkite's broadcast from Vietnam, see Oberdorfer, *Tet!* and Braestrup, *Big Story;* Kathleen Turner, *Lyndon Johnson's Dual War: Vietnam and the Press* (Chicago: University of Chicago Press, 1985); Herbert Schandler, *Lyndon Johnson and Vietnam: The Unmaking of a President* (Princeton, N.J.: Princeton University Press, 1977).
Military leaders themselves immediately recognized that Tet marked a definite turning point in the war. The chair of the Joint Chiefs of Staff, General Earle Wheeler, told the president that it was "the consensus of responsible commanders" that 1968 would be a pivotal year. The war might continue but would not return to pre-Tet conditions. Wheeler to Johnson, February 27, 1968, "Report of the Chairman, J.C.S., on Situation in Vietnam and MACV Requirements," in Neil Sheehan et al., eds., *The Pentagon Papers,* New York Times edition (New York: Quadrangle, 1971), pp. 615–621. Similarly General Edward Lansdale, special assistant at the U.S. Embassy in Saigon, asserted that 1968 would be a "year of intensity," a "change point" in history, as a result of the Tet Offensive. Lansdale to Members, U.S. Mission Council, March 21, 1968, "Viet-Nam 1968," Lansdale Papers, Box 58, Folder 1511, Hoover Institution on War, Peace, and Revolution, Stanford University, Palo Alto, California. Later, General Bruce Palmer, a MACV deputy in Vietnam, forthrightly added that Tet "ended any hope of a U.S. imposed solution to the war." See *The 25-Year War: America's Military Role in Vietnam* (New York: Simon and Schuster, 1985), p. 103.

3. On conservative revisionism of Vietnam, see Robert Divine, "Vietnam Re-

considered," *Diplomatic History* 12 (Winter 1988), pp. 79–94; Thomas Paterson, "Historical Memory and Illusive Victories: Vietnam and Central America," *Diplomatic History* 12 (Winter 1988), pp. 1–18; Bob Buzzanco, "The American Military's Rationale against the Vietnam War," *Political Science Quarterly* 101, 4 (Winter 1986), pp. 559–576; Walter LaFeber, "The Last War, the Next War, and the New Revisionists," *Democracy* 1 (1981), pp. 93–103. Indeed, the legacy of Vietnam continues to condition military affairs. Just before unleashing U.S. airpower against Saddam Hussein, George Bush told a national audience that "no hands are going to be tied behind backs." Quoted in *Washington Post,* January 17, 1991.

4. For interpretations of Tet as a military victory but psychological/political defeat, see, among others, William Westmoreland, *A Soldier Reports* (New York: Doubleday, 1980); Lyndon Johnson, *The Vantage Point: Perspectives of the Presidency* (New York: Holt, Rinehart and Winston, 1971); Maxwell Taylor, *Swords and Plowshares* (New York: W. W. Norton, 1971); U. S. G. Sharp, *Strategy for Defeat: Vietnam in Retrospect* (San Rafael, Calif.: Presidio Press, 1978); Dave Richard Palmer, *Summons of the Trumpet: U.S.-Vietnam in Perspective* (San Rafael, Calif.: Presidio Press, 1978); Oberdorfer, *Tet!*; Braestrup, *Big Story.*

5. Frances FitzGerald, *Fire in the Lake: The Vietnamese and the Americans in Vietnam* (New York: Random House, 1972); Sandra Taylor, "Vietnam: America's Nightmare, Lyndon's War," *Reviews in American History* 18 (March 1990), pp. 130–136; George Herring, *America's Longest War: The United States and Vietnam, 1950–1975* (New York: Alfred A. Knopf, 1986); Loren Baritz, *Backfire* (New York: Morrow, 1985), p. 180. Chalmers Johnson, *Autopsy on People's War* (Berkeley: University of California Press, 1973); Robert B. Asprey, *War in the Shadows: The Guerrilla in History,* Vol. 2 (Garden City, N.Y.: Doubleday, 1975); Andrew Krepinevich, *The Army and Vietnam* (Baltimore: Johns Hopkins University Press, 1986); Neil Sheehan, *A Bright Shining Lie: John Paul Vann and America in Vietnam* (New York: Random House, 1988); Gabriel Kolko, *Anatomy of a War: Vietnam, the United States, and the Modern Historical Experience* (New York: Pantheon, 1985); David Hunt, "Remembering the Tet Offensive," in Marvin Gettleman et al., eds., *Vietnam and America: A Documented History* (New York: Grove, 1985), pp. 355–372.

6. Clark Clifford with Richard Holbrooke, "Annals of Government (The Vietnam Years—Part II)," *The New Yorker* (May 13, 1991), p. 52.

7. The military was undoubtedly aware of White House reluctance, and often outright opposition, to escalate the war for over one year before the Tet offensive! Throughout 1967, the president and other high-ranking officials made it clear to the MACV and JCS that the military's requests for massive reinforcement would not be met, although additional forces would be deployed to Vietnam. Indeed, the military's requests for 100,000 or more reinforcements repeatedly caused the White House to review and analyze the situation in Vietnam in order to find ways to remain committed to the RVN without escalating the war. By late 1967, official Washington seemed about to crack, with Defense Secretary Robert McNamara's strong reservations about the war gaining force and even Secretary of State Dean Rusk beginning to question the American commitment. See *The Pentagon Papers: The Defense Department History of United States Decisionmaking in Vietnam,*

Senator Gravel edition, Vol. 4 (Boston: Beacon Press, 1971) pp. 427–538, 678–680 [hereafter cited as *PP-Gravel* with appropriate volume and page numbers].

8. On civil-military relations during the New Look controversy see Stephen Ambrose, *Eisenhower: The President* (New York: Simon and Schuster, 1984). On the Bay of Pigs see Taylor, *Swords and Plowshares,* pp. 187–189. On civil-military relations in general during the Vietnam War see Mark Perry, *Four Stars* (Boston: Houghton Mifflin, 1989); Robert Buzzanco, "Division, Dilemma, Dissent: Military Recognition of the Peril of War in Viet Nam," in *Informed Dissent: Three Generals and the Viet Nam War, Essays by Robert Buzzanco and Asad Ismi* (Chevy Chase, Md.: Vietnam Generation, 1992), pp. 9–37.

9. Substance of General Westmoreland's Opening Remarks to the JCS, November 17, 1967, Vietnam Country File, National Security File, General Military Activity, Boxes 68–69, Lyndon B. Johnson Library, Austin, Texas [hereafter cited as Vietnam CF, NSF, GMA, LBJL]; Westmoreland to Abrams, November 26, 1967, in *Vietnam: A Documentary History—Westmoreland v. CBS,* Clearwater Publishing Company, Microform, Joint Exhibit [JX] 285, microfiche card 637 [hereafter cited as *Westmoreland v. CBS* with appropriate document numbers]; Westmoreland to Wheeler and Sharp, January 15, 1968, *Westmoreland v. CBS,* JX 400, card 699.

Khe Sanh was in the northernmost military zone, just below the DMZ. The MACV separated the RVN into four military zones in all, moving north to south, with I Corps Tactical Zone (CTZ) furthest north, II Corps including Danang and the Central Highlands, III Corps encompassing Saigon, and IV Corps surrounding the Mekong Delta area in southernmost Vietnam.

10. Westmoreland to Wheeler, January 20, 1968, subject: Tet Ceasefire, *Westmoreland v. CBS,* JX 402, card 709; see also Westmoreland to Sharp, January 21, 1968, JX 402, card 699 and Westmoreland assessment of situation, January 22, 1968, JX 981, card 816; Notes of the President's Luncheon Meeting, January 25, 1968, Tom Johnson's Meeting Notes, Box 2, folder: January 25, 1968, LBJL; Weyand in *New York Times,* January 29, 1968 [hereafter cited as *NYT*].

11. Westmoreland to Wheeler and Sharp, January 30, 1968, Vietnam Country File, NSF, GMA, Boxes 68–69, LBJL: Westmoreland phone report to Walt Rostow, *Declassified Documents Reference System,* 79, 367C [hereafter cited as *DDRS* with appropriate document number]; Notes of the President's Foreign Affairs Luncheon, January 30, 1968, Tom Johnson's Notes, Box 2, folder: January 30, 1968–1 p.m., LBJL; Wheeler to JCS, January 31, 1968, Vietnam CF, NSF, GMA, Boxes 68–69, LBJL; transcript of President Johnson's press conference in *NYT,* February 2, 1968.

12. Weyand in *NYT,* January 31–February 1, 1968; Wheeler to JCS, January 31, 1968, Vietnam CF, NSF, GMA, Boxes 68–69; Lansdale to Bunker, February 2, 1968, subject: GVN Actions, Lansdale Papers, Box 57, folder 1510; for maps of Tet attacks, see Oberdorfer, *Tet!,* pp. 123, 135, 199.

13. Chaisson press briefing, February 3, 1968, in Record Group 319, Papers of William Childs Westmoreland, folder 9, Washington National Records Center, Suitland, Maryland [hereafter cited as Westmoreland papers with appropriate filing designations]; Msg., COMUSMACV 29/68 to VMAC, February 4, 1968, Westmoreland papers, folder 389: COMUSMACV Outgoing Message File.

14. *PP-Gravel,* Vol. 4, pp. 234–236.

15. Westmoreland to Wheeler, February 4, 1968, in National Security Council History, *The War in Vietnam,* "March 31st Speech," Box 47, volume 2, LBJL [also

in University Publications of America microform edition; hereafter cited as NSC History—*The War in Vietnam*. Citations will be from Box 47 of the LBJ Library or reel 6 of the UPA microfilm edition].

See also Westmoreland to Wheeler, February 4, 1968, Declassified and Sanitized Documents from Unprocessed Files [DSDUF], Vietnam, Box 4, folder: Vietnam, Box 69, 2C (4), GMA, LBJL; NSC History—*The War in Vietnam*.

16. Westmoreland cable, February 8, 1968, *DDRS*, 85, 001576.

17. Notes of President's Meeting with the JCS, February 9, 1968, Tom Johnson's Notes, Box 3, folder: February 9, 1968—11:02 a.m., LBJL, and in *Westmoreland v. CBS*, JX 1608, card 872. See also Westmoreland to Wheeler and Sharp, February 9, 1968, in NSC History—*The War in Vietnam*, and in *DDRS*, 79, 368B; Westmoreland to Wheeler, February 12, 1968, DSDUF, Vietnam, Box 70, 2C(5), GMA, LBJL.

18. Westmoreland to Wheeler, in previous note; *Pentagon Papers: NYT* Edition, pp. 593–596; Msg., COMUSMACV 30/68 to VMAC, February 4, 1968, Westmoreland papers, folder 389: COMUSMACV Outgoing Message File.

19. See sources cited in previous note.

20. Notes of President's Meeting with Senior Foreign Policy Advisors, February 9, 1968, *DDRS*, 85, 000747; Notes of President's Meeting with JCS, February 9, 1968, Tom Johnson's Notes, Box 2, folder: February 9, 1968—11:02 a.m., LBJL; Report on RVNAF strength, February 1968, *DDRS*, 79, 369C; briefing on VC/PAVN threat, February 11, 1968, *Westmoreland v. CBS*, JX 759, card 775; Westmoreland cable for Sharp, February 11, 1968, Papers of Clark Clifford, Box 4, folder: 2nd set [Memos on Vietnam: February 1968], LBJ Library; Notes of President's Meeting with Senior Foreign Policy Advisors, February 11, 1968, Clifford Papers, same as above.

21. Wheeler Memo to the President, February 12, 1968, Clifford Papers, same as previous note; Wheeler to Westmoreland, February 12, 1968, NSC History—*The War in Vietnam*, and in *Westmoreland v. CBS*, JX 664, card 758; *PP-Gravel*, Vol. 4, p. 539.

22. Westmoreland to Sharp, February 11, 1968, Papers of Clark Clifford, Box 4, folder: 2nd set [Memos on Vietnam: February 1968], LBJL; Notes of President's Meeting with Senior Foreign Policy Advisors, February 11, 1968, Clifford Papers, same as above; Taylor to Johnson, February 12, 1968, Vietnam Country File, National Security File, Box 108, folder: 8 I, 1/67–12/68 [2 of 2], LBJL; Report on RVNAF strength, February 1968, *DDRS*, 79, 369C; Briefing on VC/PAVN threat, February 11, 1968, *Westmoreland v. CBS*, JX 759, card 775.

23. Emphasis in original. Westmoreland added that the United States had yet to open Highway 1 from Danang and Highway 9 to Khe Sanh, two tasks which were "not unreasonable" if reinforcements were provided. But, the MACV commander explained, even the redeployment of the 101st Airborne Division from III CTZ to the north "will put me in no better than a marginal posture to cope with the situation at hand." Expecting the enemy to "go for broke" in the Quang Tri–Thua Thien area, Westmoreland was confident that he could contain a Communist offensive. He warned Wheeler, however, that he would have to maintain the U.S. position in other CTZs, which was already a difficult task and was being exacerbated by lack of troops. Westmoreland to Wheeler and Sharp, February 12, 1968, Papers of Clark Clifford, Box 2, folder: the White House [Vietnamese War], Memos

on Vietnam: February–August 1968, LBJL; NSC History—*The War in Vietnam; DDRS, 79*, 369A.

In relating Westmoreland's report to the president, Wheeler told Johnson that, without reinforcements in I Corps, the MACV would have to take "unacceptably risky" courses such as diverting huge numbers of forces from elsewhere in the RVN. The JCS chair moreover noted that it would be mandatory to open and keep open transportation in the north, and "that will cost troops." Wheeler memo for Johnson, February 12, 1968, NSC History—*The War in Vietnam; PP-Gravel*, Vol. 4, p. 359–540.

24. *PP-Gravel*, Vol. 4, pp. 539–540; Msg., Abrams PHB 154 to Westmoreland, February 23, 1968, Westmoreland Papers, folder 377a: COMUSMACV Message File: Though the enemy may have lost, through kill or capture, over 30,000 men, it had nonetheless committed only about 20 percent of its northern forces, with those employed mainly as gap fillers where VC forces were not adequate to launch a full-scale offensive. The PAVN, which had added about twenty-five battalions in three months, might thus begin another round of attacks. Report of JCS (February 12, 1968) in *Westmoreland v. CBS*, JX 453, card 715; see also Clarke, *Advice and Support*, pp. 327–329; Kolko, *Anatomy of a War*, pp. 259–260.

25. *PP-Gravel*, Vol. 4, pp. 539–540; Sharp to Wheeler, February 12, 1968, NSC History—*The War in Vietnam*.

26. *PP-Gravel*, Vol. 4, pp. 238, 542–546; *NYT*, February 14, 1968; Rostow to Johnson, *re* General Johnson's report on conversation with Westmoreland, February 22, 1968, Papers of Clark Clifford, Box 2, folder: Mr. Clark Clifford, LBJ Library, and *DDRS*, 82, 001264; Lansdale to Bunker and Westmoreland, February 23, 1968, subject: IV Corps, Lansdale Papers, Box 57, folder 1510.

With regard to Khe Sanh, the president gave what appeared to be a rather backhanded vote of confidence to the MACV strategy when he asserted that "if General Westmoreland wishes to defend Khe Sanh he will be supported; if he wishes to avoid a major engagement in a fixed position which does not utilize the peculiar mobility of U.S. forces, he will also be supported." In Department of Defense Report, February 15, 1968, *DDRS*, 85, 000052.

Besides U.S. problems at Khe Sanh, the week of February 10–17 marked the worst U.S. casualty rates in the war, with 543 Americans killed and 2,547 wounded.

27. Wheeler and Westmoreland in *NYT*, February 26, 1968; see transcript of Wheeler telephone conversation in Rostow to Johnson, February 25, 1968, *DDRS*, 84, 002989.

28. Clifford, "The Vietnam Years," p. 58.

29. Wheeler's February reports concerning his trip to Saigon can be found in several sources, including Lyndon Johnson, *The Vantage Point*, pp. 390–393; Papers of Clark Clifford, Box 2, folder: Memos on Vietnam: February–March 1968, LBJL; *DDRS*, 79, 382B and 383A; NSC History—*The War in Vietnam, PP-Gravel*, Vol. 4, p. 546ff., *Pentagon Papers: NYT* edition, pp. 615–621; Notes of President's Meeting to Discuss General Wheeler's Trip to Vietnam, February 28, 1968, Tom Johnson's Notes, Box 2, folder: February 28, 1968—8:35 a.m., LBJL.

30. See sources cited in previous note; for criticism of the ARVN see Msg., Abrams PHB 154 to Westmoreland, February 23, 1968, Westmoreland Papers, folder 377a: COMUSMACV Message File; on the impact of the refugee problem, see Sheehan, *Bright Shining Lie*, p. 712; John Paul Vann and Lansdale also stressed

the damage done to the pacification effort during Tet. See Vann to ACS, CORDS, n.d., subject: DIOCC-Ops-ICEX [Elimination of the VCI], and Vann to Komer, March 5, 1968, subject: Attack on the Infrastructure, John Paul Vann Papers, folder: 1968, Military History Institute, Carlisle Barracks, Pennsylvania [hereafter cited as Vann Papers with appropriate filing designation]; Lansdale to Bunker, March 27, May 7, May 12, 1968, Lansdale Papers, Box 58, folders: 1511 and 1513; for an excellent overview of pacification see Douglas Blaufarb, *The Counter-Insurgency Era* (New York: Free Press, 1977).

31. Johnson WDC 3166 to Westmoreland and Abrams, March 1, 1968, Westmoreland Papers, folder 380: Eyes Only Message File, WNRC.

32. Clifford, "The Vietnam Years," p. 58.

33. For interpretations of the reinforcement request, see, among others, Herring, *America's Longest War,* p. 194; Guenter Lewy, *America in Vietnam* (New York: Oxford University Press, 1978), pp. 127–129; Andrew Krepinevich, *The Army and Vietnam,* p. 241; Schandler, *Lyndon Johnson and Vietnam,* pp. 115–116; Kolko, *Anatomy of a War,* p. 315; Clarke, *Advice and Support,* pp. 291–337, *passim*.

Walt Rostow dismisses Wheeler's February reports, virtually out of hand. Wheeler was ill, Johnson's national security adviser asserted, and the reports from his visit to Vietnam were the only instance in which such pessimism was raised. Of course Wheeler's reports prior to his visit and into March show that Rostow was wrong; on this issue, like most others dealing with Vietnam, he still refuses to confront reality. Personal interview, June 27, 1988, Austin, Texas.

34. For background on the politics of military-civilian relations and its impact on policy making for Vietnam, see Bob Buzzanco, "Division, Dilemma, Dissent," and Perry, *Four Stars.* For specific examples see, among others, Jack Valenti to Lyndon Johnson, November 14, 1964, Confidential File, C.O. 312 Vietnam, Box 12, folder: CO 312, Vietnam, 1964–1965, LBJL; Summary Notes of 552nd NSC Meeting, June 11, 1965, by Bromley Smith, NSF, NSC Meetings File, Box 1, folder: v. 3, tab 34, LBJL; Sharp to Westmoreland quoted in NMCC to White House, June 13, 1965, NSC History—*The War in Vietnam,* reel 3; Westmoreland in George Herring, "Cold Blood: LBJ's Conduct of Limited War in Vietnam," paper presented at the Military History Symposium, Colorado Springs, Colo., 8–9; Wheeler CJCS 1810-67 to Westmoreland, March 9, 1967, *Westmoreland v. CBS,* DA/WNRC Files, Box 2, folder: Suspense; Notes on Discussion with the President, April 27, 1967, Papers of Paul Warnke—McNaughton Files, Box 2, folder: McNTN Drafts 1967 [2], LBJL.

35. Wheeler in Merle Miller, *Lyndon: An Oral Biography* (New York: Ballantine Books, 1980), p. 611; Palmer, *Summons of the Trumpet,* p. 261; on 1967 civilian opposition to reinforcement, see note 7 above; Msg., Wheeler JCS 3891 to Sharp and Westmoreland, May 25, 1967, Westmoreland Papers, folder 364: COMUS-MACV Message File; Record of COMUSMACV Fonecon with General Palmer, 0850, February 25, 1968, sub.: Discussion, Westmoreland Papers, folder 450: Fonecons, February 1968. See also the sources cited in note 34.

36. Westmoreland added, disingenuously it would seem, that he and Wheeler "had developed our plans primarily from the military viewpoints, and we anticipated that other, nonmilitary considerations would be brought to bear on our proposals during an intensive period of calm and rational deliberation." Westmoreland paper, "The Origins of the Post-Tet 1968 Plans for Additional Forces in the Re-

public of Vietnam," April 1970, Westmoreland Papers, folder 493 [1 of 2]: #37 History Files, January 1–June 30, 1970; Westmoreland, *A Soldier Reports*, p. 469. Ironically, both Westmoreland and Gabriel Kolko believe that Wheeler was trying to exploit the circumstances of Tet with his alarmist reports in order to get reinforcements and a reserve call-up. In Kolko's case, however, he argues that Wheeler was "conniving" for more troops principally to meet U.S. needs elsewhere; see *Anatomy of a War*, p. 315.

37. Notes of the President's Meeting with the NSC, January 24, 1968, Tom Johnson's Meeting Notes, Box 2, folder: January 24, 1968—1 p.m., LBJL.

38. Johnson in *NYT*, February 2, 1968; Notes of the President's Meeting with Senior Foreign Affairs Advisory Council, February 10, 1968, Tom Johnson's Meeting Notes, Box 2, folder: February 10, 1968—3:17 p.m., LBJL.

39. Dean Rusk with Richard Rusk, *As I Saw It*, edited by Daniel S. Papp (New York: W. W. Norton, 1990), p. 478; Stanley Karnow, *Vietnam: A History* (New York: Viking, 1983), p. 557; Clifford, "The Vietnam Years," p. 70; McNamara in Notes of Meeting, February 27, 1968, Vietnam CF, NSF, Box 127, folder: March 19, 1970 part I.

40. Clifford and Habib in Clifford, "The Vietnam Years," pp. 54, 60; Roche in Miller, *Lyndon*, p. 611; Bunker in Sheehan, *Bright Shining Lie*, p. 720; see also *PP-Gravel*, Vol. 4, pp. 239–243, 549–553.

41. On the economic consequences of Vietnam, see, among others, Kolko, *Anatomy of a War*, pp. 283–290; Anthony S. Campagna, *The Economic Consequences of the Vietnam War* (Westport, Conn.: Praeger, 1991), pp. 19–40.

42. Doris Kearns, *Lyndon Johnson and the American Dream* (New York: Harper & Row, 1976), p. 347.

43. Kolko, *Anatomy of a War*, pp. 312–315; Campagna, *Economic Consequences of the Vietnam War*, pp. 40–42.

44. Clark Clifford, "A Vietnam Reappraisal: The Personal History of One Man's View and How It Evolved," *Foreign Affairs* Vol. 47, No. 4 (1969), pp. 601–622; *PP-Gravel*, Vol. 4, pp. 240–250, 550–555; on importance of Taylor's views see pages 247, 553.

45. *PP-Gravel*, Vol. 4, pp. 553–572; Joint Staff report at pp. 571–572.

46. On enemy military success, see *NYT*, February 29–March 10, 1968; John Paul Vann to Weyand, February 29, 1968, Vann Papers, MHI; Lansdale to Bunker, March 2, 1968, subject: ARVN Generals, Lansdale Papers, Box 58, folder 1511.

47. Vann to LeRoy Wehrle, March 7, 1968, Vann Papers, folder: 1968, MHI.

48. Krulak to "Bill," March 1968 (enclosures include cables to and from Westmoreland, *Los Angeles Times* article, and Krulak's letter to publisher), Victor Krulak Papers, Box 2, Marine Corps Historical Center. For background on army-marine rift, see, Krulak to Don Neff, October 25, 1967, Krulak Papers, Box 1; Keith McCutcheon to Colonel M. R. Yunck, February 7, 1966, Keith McCutcheon Papers, Box 15, Marine Corps Historical Center; Buzzanco, "Division, Dilemma, Dissent"; Kolko, *Anatomy of a War*, p. 181; James Donovan, *Militarism U.S.A.* (New York: Scribner's, 1970), pp. 161–62.

49. Anderson to McCutcheon, February 19, 1968, McCutcheon Papers, Box 20. Similarly, marine general Homer Hutchinson concluded that his complaints concerning aviation control were an "empty exercise" because the marine leadership offered little support. To Hutchinson's "utter amazement," Marine Commandant

Leonard Chapman "folded completely" when discussing with Admiral John
McCain, the CINCPAC, the return of fixed-wing assets to the marines. Chapman's
"cave in," Hutchinson suspected, resulted from continued threats from Westmoreland and the army to "relieve or alter in a major way" marine control in I Corps.
Hutchinson to McCutcheon, July or August 1968, McCutcheon Papers, Box 20.

50. *PP-Gravel,* Vol. 4, pp. 575–585; Draft Memos of Clifford Group, Papers of
Clark Clifford, Box 2, folder: Draft Memo for the President—Alternative Strategies
in Vietnam, March 1 and 4, 1968, LBJL; Notes of President's Meeting with Senior
Foreign Policy Advisors, March 4, 1968, Tom Johnson's Notes, Box 2, folder:
March 4, 1968—5:33 p.m., LBJL.

51. For the president's views on the reinforcement debate, see *The Vantage
Point,* especially pp. 365–438; *NYT,* March 10, 1968; on public perception of Tet
as an American failure see Clarke, *Advice and Support,* p. 291; on impact of *New
York Times* story, see Westmoreland, *A Soldier Reports,* p. 471, and Clifford, "The
Vietnam Years," p. 70.

52. For accounts of the Wise Men meetings see Johnson, *The Vantage Point,* pp.
409–422; *PP-Gravel,* Vol. 4, pp. 592–593; Oberdorfer, *Tet!,* pp. 308–315; Schandler, *Lyndon Johnson and Vietnam,* pp. 256–265.
Ridgway's suggestions during the Wise Men meetings formed the genesis of a
1971 article in which he lamented that America was continuing along the same
paths in Vietnam after the shock of Tet, and he renewed calls for U.S. withdrawal.
"Indochina: Disengaging," *Foreign Affairs,* Vol. 49, No. 4 (1971), pp. 583–592.
Shoup in U.S. Congress, Senate, Committee on Foreign Relations, *Present Situation
in Vietnam,* 90th Cong., 2nd. session, 1968, pp. 7–27; Shoup's associate, marine
colonel James Donovan—past editor of the *Armed Forces Journal*—likewise complained to the commandant that the "current news reports of the administration's
lame attempts to white-wash the successes of the recent V.C. offensives is sicken-
ing." Donovan to Shoup, February 19, 1968, David Monroe Shoup Papers, Box
26, Donovan Envelope, Hoover Institution on War, Peace, and Revolution, Palo
Alto, California.

53. Msg., Abrams MAC 03966 to Wheeler, Westmoreland, Sharp, March 22,
1968, Westmoreland Papers, folder 380: Eyes Only Message File; Notes of the
President's Meeting with Generals Wheeler and Abrams, March 26, 1968, Tom
Johnson's Meeting Notes, Box 2, folder: March 26, 1968—10:30 a.m., Meeting
with Wheeler and Abrams, LBJL and in *Westmoreland v. CBS,* JX 1611A, card
873; see memo of NSC meeting, March 27, 1968, *DDRS,* 82, 001267; Notes of
President's Meeting with Foreign Policy Advisors, March 26, 1968, Tom Johnson's
Meeting Notes, Box 2, folder: March 26, 1968—1:15 p.m., Foreign Policy Advisors
Luncheon; on enemy capability ca. late March 1968 see Msg., Peers NHT 0305 to
Westmoreland, March 6, 1968, Westmoreland Papers, folder 380: Eyes Only Mes-
sage File.

54. Emphasis in original. Briefing by DePuy and Carver, March 27, 1968, Tom
Johnson's Meeting Notes, Box 2, folder: March 27, 1968—CIA-DOD Briefing
LBJL; Notes of President's Meeting with Wheeler and Abrams, March 26, 1968,
Tom Johnson's Meeting Notes, Box 2, folder: March 26, 1968—10:30 a.m., Meet-
ing with Wheeler and Abrams, LBJL.

55. Westmoreland to Wheeler and Sharp, March 28, 1968, Papers of Clark Clifford, Box 3, folder: Southeast Asia: Cables, LBJL, and in *DDRS,* 85, 000054. On

enemy infiltration capabilities see Msg., Westmoreland MAC 04324 to Sharp, March 30, 1968, Westmoreland Papers, folder 382: COMUSMACV Message File.

56. On Johnson's March 31 decision, see *The Vantage Point,* pp. 425–438.

57. Westmoreland in *NYT,* April 7, 1968; Notes of President's Meeting with Westmoreland, April 6, 1968, Tom Johnson's Notes, Box 3, folder: April 6, 1968— 1:30 p.m., LBJL.

For the next two months Westmoreland, Wheeler, and others would report that Communist infiltration into the South was continuing, and that the enemy retained the capacity to effectively wage war. The military's public claims of decisive success simply do not stand up to the close scrutiny of such documents. See, for instance, Westmoreland to Wheeler, April 16, 1968, *DDRS,* 85, 001578; Honolulu Meeting with Foreign Policy Advisors, April 16, 1968, Tom Johnson's Notes, Box 3, folder: April 16, 1968—10:25 a.m., LBJL; MACV estimate, May 11, in *DDRS,* 86, 000669; Notes of Tuesday Luncheon Meeting with Foreign Policy Advisors, May 21 and 28, 1968, Tom Johnson's Notes, Box 3, LBJL; Department of Defense report, June 11, 1968, *DDRS,* 85, 000923.

58. U.S.G. Sharp and William Westmoreland, *Report on the War in Vietnam (As of 30 June 1968)* [Washington, D.C.: Government Printing Office, 1968], p. 170; COMUSMACV [Abrams] to CINCPAC, August 6, 1968, subject: Pacification in South Vietnam during January–June 1968, in Vann Papers, MHI, folder: 1968. On the impact of Tet on pacification efforts see also Msg., COMUSMACV 08814 to CINCPAC, March 29, 1968, Westmoreland Papers, folder 390: COMUSMACV Outgoing Message File.

General Lansdale had also long warned that the byzantine politics of the RVN might doom the U.S. effort. See Lansdale to Bunker, May 7, 1967, subject: Thieu and Ky, Lansdale Papers, Box 58, folder: 1527, and Lansdale to Bunker, June 14, 1968, Lansdale Papers, folder: 1514.

59. For other interpretations of the failure of U.S. military policy and the meaning of the reinforcement request, see George Herring, "The War in Vietnam," in Robert Divine, ed., *Exploring the Johnson Years* (Austin: University of Texas Press, 1981), pp. 27–62; Schandler, *Lyndon Johnson and Vietnam;* and Townsend Hoopes, *The Limits of Intervention* (New York: David McKay, 1969).

60. Ridgway's comments on the Asprey paper, December 1, 1972, Matthew Ridgway Papers, MHI, Box 34B; Bush in *Washington Post,* March 2, 1991.

Selected Bibliography

The following is a composite of the major works and sources used by the various authors in their individual chapters.

PRIMARY SOURCES

The vast majority of documents are still found at their original sources. Among these sources are the Departments of State and Defense. Other government records were gleaned from the U.S. Senate and House of Representatives, including the Committees on Foreign Affairs, Armed Services, and the various subcommittees. In addition, the immense numbers of military records have been derived from such agencies as the Departments of the Army, Navy, and Air Force as well as from the Joint Chiefs of Staff. Other sources for documents included the National Archives in Washington, D.C.; the Eisenhower and Johnson presidential libraries; army archival holdings at Carlisle Barracks, Pennsylvania, and the Center for Military History (CMH) in Washington, D.C.; and air force archival holdings at the Air Force Historical Research Agency at Maxwell Air Force Base, Alabama. Among the items used by the authors were situation reports; after-action reports; site team reports; mission reports from various military units; background reports; command-service- and secretary-level briefings; letters of various kinds; telephone transcripts; meeting minutes of various kinds; statements before Congress and other government agencies; public speeches; press releases from official agencies; transcripts of congressional testimony; author interviews with key figures—of note are Cecil Currey's numerous personal interviews and correspondence with Senior General Vo Nguyen Giap; citations from various war monuments in Vietnam and the United States; and microfilm copies of significant document collections.

Among the specific papers and holdings examined were Tom Johnson Meeting notes; Tom Johnson Notes; National Security Council History; Papers of Clark Clifford; Lyndon Baines Johnson Presidential and Personal Papers—including the

Vietnam Country File, National Security File, General Military File, Diary Backup File, and so on, Declassified Documents Reference System (DDRS) Files, MACV Combined Documents Exploitation Center (CDEC) Files, Captured Documents/Cables Files, and several Oral History Interviews at the Lyndon Baines Johnson Presidential Library, Austin, Texas; Eisenhower Presidential Papers at the Dwight David Eisenhower Presidential Library, Abilene, Kansas; Edward Lansdale Papers and David Monroe Papers at the Hoover Institution on War, Peace, and Revolution, Stanford University, Stanford, California; the Papers of General William Childs Westmoreland, including the COMUSMACV Message Files at the Washington National Records Center, Suitland, Maryland; the John Paul Vann Papers at the Military History Institute, Carlisle Barracks, Pennsylvania; the Douglas Pike Papers at the Indochina Archives, University of California, Berkeley, California; the Victor Krulak Papers and Keith McCutcheon Papers at the USMC Historical Center, Washington, D.C.; and depositions, letters, documents, transcripts, and so on from the *Westmoreland v. CBS* trial located in the Westmoreland Papers and at the LBJ Library.

GOVERNMENT PUBLICATIONS

The following items are published reports by government agencies or institutions/ individuals contracted by the government to publish reports and analyses for the U.S. government. This also includes published (internal or otherwise) interviews with key leaders. Also included are official histories, white papers, state publications, and publications from foreign governments.

Central Intelligence Agency. Saigon Station Reports Numbers 65, 66, 67, December 3–9, 1967.

Congress, U.S., House of Representatives, Select Committee on Intelligence. *Hearings: U.S. Intelligence Agencies and Activities: The Performance of the Intelligence Community.* 94th Congress, First Session, 1972. Washington, D.C.: Government Printing Office, 1975.

Congress, U.S., Senate, Committee on Foreign Relations. *Present Situation in Vietnam.* 90th Congress, Second Session, 1968. Washington, D.C.: Government Printing Office, 1971.

Defense Intelligence Agency. DD Form 1396 [September 1, 1962]. Report Number 6 832 0761 69, "Biographical Sketch of Vo Nguyen Giap," 1969.

FM 101-10-1-1/2. *Staff Officers' Field Manual Organizational, Technical, and Logistical Data Planning Factors.* 2 Volumes. Washington, D.C.: HQ USA, 1987.

Military Assistance Command, Vietnam Bulletin No. 8613. December 23, 1967.

Mission, U.S. to Vietnam. "The Decisive Hour: Two Directives for Tet." *Vietnam Documents and Research Notes.* Numbers 28 and 29, April 1968.

SECONDARY SOURCES

Magazines and Journals

The following are the journals and magazines used by the authors in writing their chapters. For specific titles and publication information see the notes at the end of each chapter.

Indochina Chronicle, Conflict Quarterly, Diplomatic History, Democracy, Political Science Quarterly, Reviews in American History, Viet Nam Generation, The New Yorker, Foreign Affairs, Time, Newsweek, U.S. News and World Report, Peking Review, Proceedings of the Indiana Academy of the Social Sciences, China News Analysis, Indochina Newsletter, Tap Chi Lich Su Quan Doi [Journal of Military History], *Tap Chi Lich Su Quan Su* [Journal of Military Affairs], *Lich Su Quan Su* [Military Affairs], *Intelligence and National Security, The Journal of American–East Asian Relations, Studies in Comparative Communism,* and *Army Magazine.*

Newspapers, Media Reports, and Press Releases

The following are the newspapers and other media materials used by the various authors in writing their chapters. For complete information on the specific articles cited by the authors, see the notes at the end of each chapter.

Quang Doi Nhan Dan, Washington Post, Vietnam Courier, New York Times, Washington Times, Hoc Tap, Nhan Dan, Los Angeles Times, Muncie Star, Muncie Evening Press, Ball State News, Chicago Tribune, Renmin Ribao [People's Daily], *Le Figaro, Than Chung, Chang Dao, L'Aurore,* Reuters News Agency reports, Associated Press news reports, New China News Agency, Vietnam News Agency, Foreign Broadcast Information Service, and Liberation Radio report transcripts.

Books

The following are selected book-length works (including dissertations) from the notes of the various authors. They are books directly or indirectly dealing with the Vietnam War, the Tet Offensive, the military and its history, and/or America's presence in Southeast Asia. For other sources, see the notes following each chapter.

Ambrose, Stephen. *Eisenhower: The President.* New York: Simon and Schuster, 1984.
Asprey, Robert B. *War in the Shadows: The Guerrilla in History.* 2 volumes. Garden City, N.Y.: Doubleday, 1975.

Baggs, Andrew, "Bombing, Bargaining, and Limited War: North Viet Nam, 1965–1968." Ph.D. dissertation, University of North Carolina, 1972.

Ball, George, *The Disciple of Power*. Boston: Little, Brown, 1968.

Bao Cao Dien Bien 21 Nam Khang Chien Chong My Va Nhung Bai Hoc ve Toan Dan Danh Giac cua Long An [Reports on Developments in the 21 Years of Resistance against the Americans and the Lessons of the Entire Population Fighting the Enemy in Long An]. Long An, Vietnam: Ban Tong Ket Chien Tranh Tinh Long An [Committee on Assessment of the War in Long An Province], no date.

Baritz, Loren, *Backfire: A History of How American Culture Led Us into Vietnam and Made Us Fight the Way We Did*. New York: Ballantine, 1986.

Berger, Carl, ed. *The United States Air Force in Southeast Asia, 1961–1973: An Illustrated Account*. Washington, D.C.: Office of Air Force History, 1984.

Bergerud, Eric. *The Dynamics of Defeat: The Vietnam War in Hau Nghia Province*. Boulder, Colo.: Westview Press, 1991.

Berman, Larry. *Planning a Tragedy: The Americanization of the War in Vietnam*. New York: W. W. Norton, 1982.

———. *Lyndon Johnson's War: The Road to Stalemate in Vietnam*. New York: W. W. Norton, 1989. Paperback, 1991.

Betts, Richard K., and Leslie H. Gelb. *The Irony of Vietnam: The System Worked*. Washington, D.C.: Brookings Institute, 1979.

Blaufarb, Douglas. *The Counter-Insurgency Era*. New York: Free Press, 1977.

Bo Chi Huy Quan Su Tinh Ben Tre [The Military Command of Ben Tre Province]. *Cuoc Khang Chien Chong My Cuu Cuoc Cua Nhan Dan Ben Tre* [Resistance against the Americans for National Salvation of the Population of Ben Tre]. Ben Tre, Vietnam: no publisher, 1985.

Bowers, Ray L. *The United States Air Force in Southeast Asia: Tactical Airlift*. Washington, D.C.: Office of Air Force History, 1983.

Bowman, John S., ed. *The Vietnam War: An Almanac*. New York: World Almanac Publications, 1985.

Braestrup, Peter. *Big Story!* 2 volumes. New Haven, Conn.: Yale University Press, 1983.

———, ed. *Vietnam as History*. Washington, D.C.: University Press of America, 1984.

Buzzanco, Robert. *Masters of War: Military Dissent and Politics in the Vietnam Era*. New York: Cambridge University Press, 1996.

Brodie, Bernard. "The Tet Offensive." In Christopher Dowling and Noble Frankland, eds., *Decisive Battles of the Twentieth Century*. London: Oxford University Press, 1976.

Cable, Larry. *Unholy Grail: The US and the Wars in Vietnam, 1965–1968*. New York, London: Routledge, 1991.

Campagna, Anthony S. *The Economic Consequences of the Vietnam War*. Westport, Conn.: Praeger, 1991.

Chanoff, David, and Bui Diem. *In the Jaws of History*. Boston: Houghton Mifflin, 1987.

Chanoff, David, and Van Toai Doan. *Portrait of the Enemy*. New York: Random House, 1986.

Chu Tich Ho Chi Minh Voi Cong Tac Ngoai Giao [President Ho Chi Minh and His Diplomatic Works]. Hanoi: Nha Xuat Ban Su That, 1990.

Clarke, Jeffrey J. *Advice and Support: The Final Years, 1965–1973,* (U.S. Army in Vietnam Series). Center for Military History: U.S. Government Publishing Office, 1988.

Clifford, Clark M. *Counsel to the President.* New York: Random House, 1991.

Clodfelter, Lt. Col. Mark. *The Limits of Air Power: The American Bombing of North Vietnam.* New York: Free Press, 1989.

Craghill, Francis H. III and Robert C. Zelnick. "Ballots or Bullets: What the 1967 Elections Could Mean." In *Vietnam: Matter for the Agenda.* San Francisco: Center for the Studies of Democratic Institutions, 1968.

Crile, George, et al. *CBS Reports:* "The Uncounted Enemy: A Vietnam Deception." Television broadcast, January 23, 1982.

Cubbage, Thomas L. III. "Intelligence and the Tet Offensive: The South Vietnamese View of the Threat." In Elizabeth Jane Errington and B.J.C. McKercher, eds., *The Vietnam War as History.* Westport, Conn.: Praeger, 1990.

Currey, Cecil B. *Edward Lansdale: The Unquiet American.* New York: Houghton Mifflin, 1988.

Davidson, Lt. Gen. Philip B. *Vietnam at War: The History, 1946–1975.* Novato, Calif.: Presidio Press, 1988.

Davidson, Philip B. *Vietnam at War: The History, 1946–1975.* New York: Oxford University Press, 1991.

Dickson, Paul. *The Electronic Battlefield.* Bloomington: Indiana University Press, 1976.

Dinh, Van [pseud. for Vo Nguyen Giap], and Qua Ninh [pseud. for Truong Chinh]. *The Peasant Question, 1936–1938.* Hanoi: no publisher, 1938.

Donavan, James. *Militarism U.S.A.* New York: Scribner's 1970.

Duan, Le. *On Some Present International Problems.* 2d edition. Hanoi: Foreign Languages Publishing House, 1964.

———. *Thu Vao Nam* [Letters to the South]. Hanoi: Nha Xuat Ban Su That, 1986.

Duiker, William J. *The Communist Road to Power in Vietnam.* Boulder, Colo.: Westview Press, 1981.

———. *Historical Dictionary of Vietnam.* Metuchen, N.J.: Scarecrow Press, 1989.

Falk, Richard, *Appropriating Tet.* Princeton, N.J.: World Order Studies Program, Occasional Paper No. 17, Center for International Studies, Woodrow Wilson School for Public and International Affairs: Princeton University Press, 1988.

Fall, Bernard. *Hell in a Very Small Place.* Philadelphia: Lippincott, 1967.

Fallaci, Oriana. *Interview with History.* New York: Livernight, 1976.

FitzGerald, Frances. *Fire in the Lake: The Vietnamese and the Americans in Vietnam.* New York: Random House, 1972.

Floyd, David. *Mao against Khruschev: A Short History of the Sino-Soviet Conflict.* New York: Praeger, 1963.

Garver, John W. *Foreign Relations of the People's Republic of China.* Englewood Cliffs, N.J.: Prentice Hall, 1993.

Giap, Senior General Vo Nguyen. *"Big Victory, Great Task!"* New York: Praeger, 1968.

Giap, Vo Nguyen. *Addresses: Third National Congress of the Viet-Nam Worker's Party.* 3 volumes. Hanoi: Foreign Languages Publishing House, 1960.

————. *People's War, People's Army*. Hanoi: Foreign Languages Publishing House, 1961.

Gittinger, Ted, ed. *The Johnson Years: A Vietnam Roundtable*. Austin: Lyndon Baines Johnson Library, University of Texas Press, 1993.

Grant, Zalin. *Survivors*. New York: W. W. Norton, 1985.

Groom, Winston, and Duncan Spencer. *Conversation with the Enemy*. New York: G. P. Putnam's Sons, 1983.

Gurtov, Melvin. *Hanoi on War and Peace*. Santa Monica, Calif.: Rand Corporation, 1967.

Hallin, Daniel. *The Uncensored War: The Media and Vietnam*. New York: Oxford University Press, 1986.

Herring, George C. *America's Longest War*. New York: John Wiley & Sons, 1979.

————. "The War in Vietnam." In Robert Divine, ed., *Exploring the Johnson Years*. Austin: University of Texas Press, 1981.

————. *The Secret Diplomacy of the Vietnam War: The Negotiating Volumes of the Pentagon Papers*. Austin: University of Texas Press, 1983.

————. *America's Longest War: The United States and Vietnam, 1950–1975*. 2d edition. New York: Alfred A. Knopf, 1986.

————. "Cold Blood: LBJ's Conduct of Limited War in Vietnam." Harmon Memorial Lecture. U.S. Air Force Academy, Colorado, 1990.

————. *LBJ and Vietnam: A Different Kind of War*. Austin: University of Texas Press, 1994.

Hoan, Hoang Van. *A Drop in the Ocean*. Beijing: Foreign Language Press, 1988.

Hoan, Tran. "Xung Quanh Ham Chi Huy" [Around the Command Tunnel]. In *Hue Nhung Ngay Noi Day* [Hue during the Days of Uprising]. Hue: Sach Giao Khoa, 1979.

Hoopes, Townsend. *The Limits of Intervention*. New York: David McKay, 1969.

Hunt, David. "Remembering the Tet Offensive." In Marvin E. Gettleman, et al., eds., *Vietnam and America: A Documented History*. New York: Grove Press, 1985.

Johnson, Chalmers. *Autopsy on People's War*. Berkeley: University of California Press, 1973.

Johnson, Lyndon. *The Vantage Point: Perspectives of the Presidency, 1963–1969*. New York: Holt, Rinehart, and Winston, 1971.

Jones, Bruce E. *War without Windows*. New York: Vanguard, 1987.

Karnow, Stanley. *Vietnam: A History*. New York: Viking, 1983.

Kearns, Doris. *Lyndon Johnson and the American Dream*. New York: Harper and Row, 1976.

Kinnard, Douglas. *The War Managers*. Hanover, N.H.: University Press of New England, 1977.

Kissinger, Henry. *The White House Years*. Boston: Little, Brown, 1979.

Kolko, Gabriel. *Anatomy of a War: Vietnam, the United States, and the Modern Historical Experience*. New York: Pantheon, 1985.

Kraslow, David, and Stuart Loory. *The Secret Search for Peace in Vietnam*. New York: Random House, 1968.

Krepinevich, Andrew. *The Army and Vietnam*. Baltimore: Johns Hopkins University Press, 1986.

Latimer, Thomas. "Hanoi's Leaders and Their South Vietnamese Policies, 1954–1968." Ph.D. dissertation, Georgetown University, 1972.

Lewy, Guenter. *America in Vietnam*. New York: Oxford University Press, 1978.

Lich Su Dang Bo Dang Cong San Viet Nam Tinh Ben Tre, 1930–1985 [History of the Communist Party Provincial Committee of Ben Tre, 1930–1985]. Ben Tre, Vietnam: Ben Nghien Cuu Lich Su Dang Ben Tre [Party Historical Research Committee of Ben Tre], 1985.

Loc, Lt. Gen. Vinh. *Why Plei Me?* Pleiku, Republic of Vietnam: Echo Press, 1966.

Loi, Luu Van, and Nguyen Anh Vu. *Tieo Xuc Bi Mat Viet Nam-Hoa Kv Truoc Hoi Nghi Pa-ri* [Secret Negotiations between Vietnam and the United States before the Paris Meetings]. Hanoi: Vien Quan He Quoc Te, 1990.

Long, Ngo Vinh. *The Tet Offensive and Its Aftermath*. Ithaca, N.Y.: Cornell University Press, 1991.

Lung, Hoang Ngoc. *Indochina Monograph: The General Offensives of 1968–1969*. Washington, D.C.: Office of Chief of Military History, Government Printing Office, 1976.

Luttwak, Edward. *Strategy: The Logic of War and Peace*. Cambridge, Mass.: Belknap Press, 1987.

Mao Zedong. *The Selected Works of Mao Tse-tung*. 5 volumes. Beijing: Foreign Language Press, 1967, 1972.

Mau Than Saigon [The Tet Offensive in Saigon]. Ho Chi Minh City: Nha Xuat Ban Van Nghe, 1988.

Macdonald, Peter. *Giap: The Victor in Vietnam*. New York: W. W. Norton, 1993.

McGarvey, Patrick J., ed. *Visions of Victory: Selected Vietnamese Communist Military Writings, 1964–1968*. Stanford, Calif.: Stanford University Press, 1969.

Moore, Lt. Gen. Harold G. and Joseph L. Galloway. *We Were Soldiers Once Brave and Young: Ia Drang—The Battle That Changed the War in Vietnam*. New York: Random House, 1992.

Moss, George Donnelson. *Vietnam: An American Ordeal*. Englewood Cliffs, N.J.: Prentice-Hall, 1990.

Mrozek, Donald J. *Air Power and the Ground War in Vietnam*. Washington, D.C.: Pergamon-Brassey's, 1989.

"North Vietnamese Instructions on Tet Celebrations." *BBC Summaries of World Broadcasts*, January 24, 1968.

Oberdorfer, Don. *Tet!* New York: Avon Books, 1971.

———. *Tet!* Garden City, N.Y.: Doubleday, 1973.

———. *Tet!* 2d edition. New York: Doubleday, 1984.

———. *Tet!* Reprint edition. New York: Da Capo Press, 1984.

Olson, James J., and Randy Roberts. *Where the Domino Fell: America and Vietnam, 1945–50*. New York: St. Martin's Press, 1991.

O'Neill, Robert J. *General Giap*. North Melbourne, Australia: Cassell Press, 1969.

Palmer, Dave Richard. *Summons of the Trumpet: U.S.-Vietnam in Perspective*. San Rafael, Calif.: Presidio Press, 1978.

Palmer, General Bruce. *The 25-Year War: America's Military Role in Vietnam*. New York: Simon and Schuster, 1985.

Paterson, Thomas G., et al. *American Foreign Relations: A History since 1900*. 2d edition. Lexington, Mass.: D.C. Heath, 1983.

Pearson, General Willard. *The War in the Northern Provinces, 1966–1968*. Washington, D.C.: Department of the Army, 1975.

Peng Dehuai. *Peng Dehuai Zishu* [Peng Dehuai Remembers]. Beijing: Renmin Chubanshe, 1981.

The Pentagon Papers: The Defense Department History of the United States Decisionmaking on Vietnam. Senator Gravel edition. 5 volumes. Boston: Beacon Press, 1971.

The Pentagon Papers. New York Times edition. New York: Bantam Books, 1971.

Perry, Mark. *Four Stars*. Boston: Houghton Mifflin, 1989.

Pike, Douglas. *Viet Cong: The Organization and Techniques of the National Liberation Front of South Vietnam*. Cambridge, Mass.: MIT Press, 1966, 1968.

———. *PAVN: People's Army of North Vietnam*. Novato, Calif.: Presidio Press, 1986.

Pisor, Robert. *The End of the Line: The Siege of Khe Sanh*. New York: Ballantine Books, 1982.

Pohle, Victoria. *The Viet Cong in Saigon: Tactics and Objectives during the Tet Offensive*. Santa Monica, Calif.: Rand Corporation, 1969.

Prados, John, and Ray W. Stubbe. *Valley of Decision*. Boston: Houghton Mifflin, 1991.

The Public Papers of the Presidents: Lyndon B. Johnson, 1968. Washington, D.C.: Government Printing Office, 1970.

Radvanyi, Janos. *Delusions and Reality: Gambits, Hoaxes, and Diplomatic One-Upmanship in Viet Nam*. South Bend, Ind.: Gateway Editions, 1978.

Refutation of the New Leaders of the CPSU on "United Action". Beijing: Foreign Language Press, 1965.

Rostow, Walt W. *The Diffusion of Power: An Essay in Recent History*. New York: Macmillan, 1972.

Rusk, Dean, with Richard Rusk, edited by Daniel S. Papp. *As I Saw It*. New York: W. W. Norton, 1990.

Schandler, Herbert Y. *The Unmaking of the President: Lyndon Johnson and Vietnam*. Princeton, N.J.: Princeton University Press, 1977.

Schlesinger, Arthur. *Robert Kennedy and His Times*. New York: Ballantine, 1978.

Sharp, Admiral Ulysses Simpson Grant. *Strategy for Defeat: Vietnam in Retrospect*. San Rafael, Calif.: Presidio Press, 1978.

———. *Strategy for Defeat: Vietnam in Retrospect*. Novato, Calif.: Presidio Press, 1986.

Sheehan, Neil. *A Bright Shining Lie: John Paul Vann and America in Vietnam*. New York: Random House, 1988.

Sheehan, Neil, et al., eds. *The Pentagon Papers—New York Times Edition*. New York: Quadrangle Books, 1971.

Shore, Captain Moyers S. II. *The Battle of Khe Sanh*. Washington, D.C.: History and Museums Division, HQ USMC, 1969.

Simmons, Edwin H. "Marine Corps Operations in Vietnam, 1967." In *The Marines in Vietnam, 1954–1973*. Washington, D.C.: History and Museum Division, HQ USMC, 1985.

Smith, R. B. *An International History of the Vietnam War: The Kennedy Strategy*. New York: St. Martin's Press, 1985.

Summers, Harry. *On Strategy: A Critical Analysis of the Vietnam War.* Novato, Calif.: Presidio Press, 1982.

Suo Shihui. "Bai Tuan Dazhan Ying Shongfen Kending" [The Hundred Regiments Offensive Should Be Substantially Upheld]. In Zhu Chenya, ed., *Zhonggong Dangshi Yanjiu Lunwenxuan* [Selection of Research Essays on CCP History]. Changsha: Hunan Renmin Chubanshe, 1984.

Taber, Robert. *The War of the Flea: A Study of Guerrilla Warfare, Theory and Practice.* New York: Citadel Press, 1965.

Taylor, General Maxwell. *Swords and Plowshares.* New York: W. W. Norton, 1971.

Thanh, Nguyen Chi. *Who Will Win in South Viet Nam?* Beijing: Foreign Languages Press, 1963.

Thayer, Carlyle A. *War by Other Means: National Liberation and Revolution in Viet-Nam, 1954–1960.* Sydney, Australia: Allen & Unwin, 1989.

Thies, Wallace. *When Governments Collide: Coercion and Diplomacy in the Vietnam Conflict, 1964–1968.* Berkeley: University of California Press, 1980.

Thompson, Kenneth, ed. *The Johnson Presidency.* Lanham, Md.: University Press of America, 1987.

Tilford, Earl H., Jr. *Setup: What the Air Force Did in Vietnam and Why.* Maxwell Air Force Base, Alabama: Air University Press, 1991.

———. *Crosswinds: The Air Force's Setup in Vietnam.* College Station: Texas A&M University Press, 1992.

Tin, Bui. *Memoirs.* Volume 1, *Hoa Xuyen Tuyet* [Snowdrop]. [No city], Calif.: Nhan Quyen Editeur, 1991.

———. *Memoirs.* Volume 2, *Mat That* [The Real Face]. Irvine, Calif.: Saigon Press, 1993.

Tra, Tran Van. *Ket Thuc Cuoc Chien Tranh 30 Nam* [History of the Bulwark B2-Theatre: Concluding the 30-Year War]. Volume 5. Ho Chi Minh City: Van Nghe, 1982.

———. *History of the Bulwark B2-Theatre.* English version in 5 Volumes. Ho Chi Minh City: Van Nghe, 1982.

———. "Tet: The 1968 General Offensive and General Uprising." In Luu Doan Huynh and Jayne S. Werner, eds., *The Vietnam War: Vietnamese and American Perspectives.* London: M. E. Sharpe, 1993.

Trinh, Lam Le. "Vo Nguyen Giap: Victory without Triumph." In *Vietnam's People.* Huntington Beach, Calif.: Saigon Press, 1993.

The Truth about Vietnam-China Relations over the Last Thirty Years. Hanoi: Ministry of Foreign Affairs, Socialist Republic of Vietnam, 1979.

Turley, William S. *The Second Indochina War: A Short Political and Military History, 1954–1975.* Boulder, Colo.: Westview Press, 1986.

Turner, Kathleen. *Lyndon Johnson's Dual War: Vietnam and the Press.* Chicago: University of Chicago Press, 1985.

Westmoreland, General William C. *A Soldier Reports.* Garden City, N.Y.: Doubleday, 1976.

———. *A Soldier Reports.* New York: Doubleday, 1980.

Willenson, Kim, ed. *The Bad War: An Oral History of the Vietnam War.* New York: New American Library, 1987.

Wirtz, James J. *The Tet Offensive: Intelligence Failure in War*. Ithaca, N.Y.: Cornell University Press, 1991.

Wolff, Tobias. *In Pharoah's Army: Memories of the Lost War*. N.Y.: Knopf, 1995.

Young, Marilyn B. *The Vietnam Wars, 1945–1990*. New York: HarperCollins, 1991.

Zagoria, Donald. *Vietnam Triangle: Moscow, Peking, and Hanoi*. New York: Pegasus, 1967.

Index

Tao Dan public garden, 103–104
Task Force Oregon, 177
Tay Ninh Province, 146
Taylor, Henry, 138
Taylor, Maxwell: as ambassador, 38, 39–40, 236; as general, 237, 243
Tet Mau Than (Vietnamese New Year), 21–23, 25–26, 29–30, 32, 34, 35, 42, 44n, 46, 48, 50, 68, 83, 91, 94, 96, 98, 102, 114, 125–127, 132–133, 134n, 135–138, 143, 148, 149, 151–153, 157–159, 161–162, 164n, 178, 182, 184, 186–187, 196, 215–216, 221, 224, 231–232, 234, 236, 238–249, 249n, 255n; holiday baskets, 186; New Year's celebration of 1968, 100
Tet Offensive of 1968 (general offensive/general uprising—*tong cong kich/tong khoi nghia* TCK/TKN), 27, 29, 31, 41, 43, 46–47, 49–50, 63–64, 69, 76, 83–85, 89, 92–93, 100–101, 104–105, 107–108, 112, 119, 125–131, 135–136, 140, 144–146, 148, 152–153, 160, 167–169, 181, 189, 200, 202, 203, 207–209, 215, 217, 219–220, 225, 227, 231, 233, 237, 247, 250n; New Year's cease-fire, 233; Urban Offensives, 174, 177, 179
The Tet Offensive: Intelligence Failure in War, 95, 135
Thai troops, 29, 36
Thai Van Kiem, 84, 86n
Thanh Hoa, 225
Third Indochina War, 210n
Third World, 96
Thompkins, General Rathvon M., 196, 208
Thu Duc District, 106
Thua Thien Province, 54, 75, 156, 235, 252n
Tran Bach Dang, 91, 98, 102–103, 106–107
Tran Chi Chu, 77
Tran Do, General, 84, 101, 102, 107
Tran Hoan, 99
Tran Ngoc Tam, General, 157

Tran Quy Cap Street, 161
Tran Van Quang, Lt. General, 100, 101, 103
Tran Van Tra, General, 4, 63, 84, 85, 91, 99, 106, 129
Tran Vu, 93
Treasury, U.S. Department of, 242
Tri Thien Military Command/Regional Committee, 100
Truman, President Harry S, 216
Truman Administration, 216
Truman-MacArthur clash, 216
Truong Chinh (Long March), 65–66, 75–78, 80. *See also* Dang Xuan Khu
Twentieth parallel, 215, 223, 226–227
Tu Than, General, 114
Tuyet Thi Vanh, 68, 69

"The Uncounted Enemy: A Vietnam Deception," 145
Union of Soviet Socialist Republics (U.S.S.R./Soviet Union), 51–53, 55, 56, 57–59, 65, 67, 75, 78, 80, 83, 86n, 87n, 139, 201–202, 216, 220–221, 223; nuclear umbrella, 51
United Nations (UN), 57, 80, 140; Security Council, 57
United Press International (UPI) News Service, 19
United States, 18, 22, 34, 37–39, 41, 44n, 63, 65–68, 79–82, 84–85, 89–90, 93–97, 99, 101–102, 104, 107, 109–111, 114, 119, 120n, 129–130, 132–133, 134n, 137, 139, 144, 146–147, 150–152, 154–155, 162, 169–173, 175–176, 178–179, 187, 191, 193–195, 198, 200–201, 203–204, 207–208, 215, 223, 225, 227, 228n, 231–232; aid, 119; aircraft, 28; Bachelor's Officers Quarters (Saigon), 21; bases, 81, 198; commitment to SVN, 133; decision makers, 176; declaration of war, 81; economic aid, 131; economy, 242; foreign policy/policy makers, 31, 135, 139, 169, 171, 233; government, 25, 170; government officials, 108; history, xiii, intelligence, 11–

About the Authors and Editors

LARRY BERMAN is Professor and Chair of the Department of Political Science at the University of California, Davis. Among his many articles, books, and presentations two of his most famous are *Planning a Tragedy: The Americanization of the War in Vietnam* (1982) and *Lyndon Johnson's War: The Road to Stalemate in Vietnam* (1989). He is currently working on a history of the war in Vietnam after 1973.

ROBERT BRIGHAM is Assistant Professor at Vassar College in Poughkeepsie, New York. He earned his Ph.D. from the University of Kentucky, where he worked with George C. Herring. He has conducted a significant amount of research on the Vietnam War in Hanoi and Saigon (Ho Chi Minh City) and has received generous funding from the Society for Historians of American Foreign Relations, the National Endowment for the Humanities, the Social Sciences Committee of Viet Nam, the University of Kentucky, and Vassar College. He is the author of several essays on the war and Vietnamese archives and is currently working on a book about the National Front for the Liberation of South Vietnam.

PETER BRUSH is contributing editor of the *Viet Nam Generation,* a journal of recent history and contemporary issues. He has taught history and political science at Clinton Community College and Empire State College in Plattsburgh, New York. He has authored several articles on the military history of the Vietnam War. In 1968 he served in a heavy mortar battery at Khe Sanh combat base in Vietnam.

AMBASSADOR BUI DIEM, Ph.D., former Ambassador of South Vietnam to the United States, is presently a Senior Director of the Pacific Basin Research Institute. He was previously Associate Director of the Indochina Institute at George Mason University in Fairfax, Virginia. He has also served as President of the National Congress of Vietnamese (NCVA) in America. He is the coauthor of *In the Jaws of History* (1987), recognized as one of the most important and illuminating books written about the U.S. experience in Vietnam. He is presently writing another book that analyzes negotiations between the United States and the Democratic Republic of Vietnam between 1965 and 1975.

ROBERT BUZZANCO is Assistant Professor of Diplomatic History and Strategic Studies at the University of Houston. His work on military criticism of the Vietnam War and civil-military relations has been published in *Political Science Quarterly, Diplomatic History,* and *Viet Nam Generation.* He is also the author of *Masters of War: Military Dissent and Politics in the Vietnam Era* (1996), from which the selection in this volume was partly derived. He is currently working on a study of the Tet Offensive and the gold crisis of early 1968.

LARRY CABLE is Associate Professor of History at the University of North Carolina, Wilmington. He served seventeen years with the military and civilian components of the national security community, including a variety of unconventional warfare assignments in Southeast Asia, before receiving his Ph.D in History from the University of Houston in 1984. He is the author of *Conflict of Myths: The Development of US Counterinsurgency Doctrine and the Vietnam War* (1986), *Unholy Grail: The US and the Wars in Vietnam, 1965–1968* (1991) and *Self Inflicted Wound: The US, Indochina and Global Policy, 1940–1975* (1996), as well as articles and papers on the Vietnam War, intelligence and low intensity conflict. In addition, he is Adjunct Professor of History at the USAF Special Operations School, where he received the 1995 General James Doolittle Award as educator of the year, and regularly lectures at the JFK Special Warfare Center and School, the Marine Corps Amphibious Warfare School, Marine Corps Command and Staff College, the Marine Corps War College, and other Service schools.

DAVID V. CONNOLLY was one of the founders of the William Joiner Center for the Study of Peace and War at the University of Massachusetts at Boston. He served with honor and was seriously wounded in combat as an infantryman assigned to the 11th Armored Cavalry Regiment (1968–1969). He takes pride in having been and continuing to be a Vietnam Veteran Against the War. Several of his poems and prose pieces were included in an anthology edited by Vivian Vie Balfour, *The Perimeter of*

Light: Short Fiction and Other Writings About the Vietnam War (1992).
His first poetry collection, *Lost in America* (1994) is fast becoming a staple
of courses on the Vietnam War and era.

CECIL CURREY is Professor of History at the University of South Florida
at Tampa and an Army Reserve chaplain with the rank of colonel. He
received his Ph.D. from the University of Kansas. He is author of nine
books, including *Edward Lansdale: The Unquiet American* (1988) and *Self-
Destruction: The Disintegration and Decay of the United States Army during the Vietnam Era* (1981), which he wrote under the pseudonym
"Cincinnatus." His exhaustive biography of Senior General Vo Nguyen
Giap, a project which has taken him to Vietnam three times in the last
three years, is in its production stage and is expected out next year.

ANTHONY EDMONDS is Professor of History at Ball State University,
where he teaches a course on the United States and the Vietnam War. The
author of a biography of Joe Louis and a resource guide for teaching the
Vietnam War, he has published articles and book reviews in *Viet Nam
Generation, Choice,* the *Journal of Popular Culture, Peace and Change,*
and the *American Historical Review,* among others. He is completing a
history of Ball State and is under contract with Greenwood Press to write
a book on the Vietnam War in its series Reference Guides to Historic
Events of the Twentieth Century.

JOHN GARVER is a specialist in Chinese foreign policy and Asian international relations and teaches international relations in the School of International Affairs at the Georgia Institute of Technology. He has authored
many articles and three books on Chinese foreign relations. The latter include *Chinese-Soviet Relations, 1937–1945: The Diplomacy of Chinese
Nationalism* (1988), and *The Foreign Relations of the People's Republic
of China* (1993). He is currently working on studies of the geopolitics of
Sino-Indian relations and dynamics of the U.S.-Nationalist alliance.

MARC JASON GILBERT is Professor of History at North Georgia State
University. He received his Ph.D. in History from UCLA in 1978. He has
written widely on Vietnam, its place in world history, and on the impact
of the Second Indochina War on the United States. He has lectured on the
Second Indochina War and Southeast Asian affairs for a variety of academic and government institutions, including the USAF Special Operations
School and the Army War College. He is the editor and chief contributing
author of *The Vietnam War: Teaching Approaches and Resources* (1991).
He is also the editor of a forthcoming study of the Vietnam War on American high school and college campuses and an analysis of the oral history
record of Vietnamese veterans of the Battle of Dien Bien Phu. He is cur-

rently completing *Lost Warriors,* a film documenting the plight of homeless veterans of the Second Indochina War.

WILLIAM HEAD is Chief Center Historian, Warner Robins ALC, Robins Air Force Base, Georgia. He received his Ph.D. in U.S. diplomatic history from Florida State University, 1980. His most recent publications include "Air Power in the Persian Gulf: An Initial Search for the Right Lessons," *The Air Force Journal of Logistics* (Winter 1992) [Outstanding Article for 1992]; coeditor, *Looking Back on the Vietnam War: A 1990s Perspective of Decisions, Combat, and Legacies* (1993); and *Every Inch a Soldier: General Augustine Warner Robins and the Development of American Air Power* (1995).

MARK JACOBSEN is Associate Professor of Military History at the United States Marine Corps Command and Staff College, Quantico, Virginia. He received his Ph.D. from the University of California, Irvine, where he studied under the late A. J. Marder. He helped complete Marder's final volume on the Royal Navy in the twentieth century: *Old Friends, New Enemies: The Royal Navy and the Imperial Japanese Navy, 1936–1945,* Vol. 2 (Oxford, 1990). Prior to teaching at the Command and Staff College, Dr. Jacobsen worked at the Naval Historical Center, Washington, D.C., for which he continues to work on the official history of the navy's part in Operation Rolling Thunder. The views expressed in his article are not those of the United States Marine Corps, the Navy Department, or any element of the Department of Defense. Neither have they been altered by official review.

NGO VINH LONG is Professor of History at the University of Maine. Among his many works are *Before the Revolution: The Vietnamese Peasants under the French* (1973 and 1991) and *Vietnamese Women in Society and Revolution* (1974). He is also coeditor of *Coming to Terms: Indochina, the United States, and the War* (1991).

ROBERT NOURSE served as a district advisor in Ly Tin District, Quang Tin Province, I Corps, in Vietnam during the Tet Offensive. He has taught a course at both Lafayette College and Muhlenberg College about the United States and the Vietnam experience. He is working on a book which is titled *Vietnam War, Lost in the Hamlets.*

JOHN PRADOS is a freelance historian working in the Washington, D.C., area. Among his many books is his famous coauthored work with Khe Sanh's marine chaplin Ray Stubbe entitled *Valley of Decision* (1991). His most recent work is about intelligence operations and functions in Vietnam and is entitled *Hidden History of the Vietnam War* (1995).